SIE EXAM

+

SERIES 7 STUDY GUIDE
(2-BOOKS-IN-1)

SIE Exam Prep Study Guide

Series 7 Exam Prep Study Guide

Introduction: Author's Background and Target Audience

Author's Background in Securities Licensing Exam Prep and Financial Services Training

With over a decade of dedicated service in financial education, the author has established a distinguished career in guiding aspirants through their securities licensing examinations. Renowned for a pragmatic and insightful teaching style, the author specializes in the Securities Industry Essentials (SIE) exam. This specialization is rooted in a profound understanding of the regulatory landscapes and a keen insight into the examination processes. Over the years, the author has crafted tailored preparation strategies that demystify complex concepts and align closely with evolving market standards. Through a blend of rigorous practice tests, real-world scenarios, and concise explanations, the author has empowered a multitude of candidates to achieve their licensing objectives with confidence.

Target Audience: Those Studying for and Needing to Pass the SIE Exam

This book is crafted for anyone embarking on the journey to pass the Securities Industry Essentials (SIE) exam. It is an indispensable tool for recent college graduates eager to enter the financial services field, career changers aiming to pivot into finance, and seasoned professionals seeking to reaffirm their knowledge base in a dynamic industry. The guide is meticulously designed to meet the needs of a diverse readership, ensuring clarity and accessibility regardless of one's background in finance. For those poised at the threshold of their financial careers or those looking to deepen their industry acumen, this book serves as a beacon, guiding readers through the essentials of securities and financial principles. It is your first step towards a flourishing career in the securities industry, providing the foundational knowledge necessary to navigate further professional certifications and real-world financial challenges.

Explanation of the SIE Exam: Focus, Format, Scoring, and Policies

The Securities Industry Essentials (SIE) Exam serves as the gateway for those aspiring to enter the securities industry. Designed to assess a candidate's foundational knowledge, the SIE exam covers the essential aspects of the securities business, including the types of products and their associated risks, market structure, and the roles of various regulatory agencies. Additionally, it evaluates the candidate's understanding of trading processes, customer account management, and the ethical considerations inherent in the industry.

Administered as a computer-based test, the SIE consists of 75 multiple-choice questions along with 10 additional unscored questions that are used for experimental purposes. These experimental questions are randomly interspersed throughout the exam and do not count towards the final score. Candidates are allotted 1 hour and 45 minutes to complete the test, which broadly covers four key areas: Knowledge of Capital Markets, Understanding Products and Their Risks, Understanding Trading, Customer Accounts, and Prohibited Activities, and an Overview of the Regulatory Framework.

Scoring for the SIE exam is straightforward. Each candidate's performance is scaled between 0 and 100, with 70 as the passing mark. This scoring reflects only the answers from the 75 scored questions. Upon completion, candidates receive immediate pass/fail feedback. If unsuccessful, a candidate receives a breakdown of their performance across different sections, aiding in targeted study for future attempts.

Candidates must register for the exam through FINRA's website, where they can also schedule their test at a Prometric testing center. On the day of the exam, valid government-issued identification with a photograph and signature is required to verify identity. For those needing to retake the exam, a waiting period of 30 days applies after the first attempt. Following three consecutive failures, a longer waiting period of 180 days is enforced before the exam can be attempted again.

Preparation for the SIE exam can be bolstered by utilizing the various resources provided by FINRA, including a detailed exam outline and sample questions. These materials are designed to help candidates familiarize themselves with the format of the exam and to identify areas requiring further study.

Understanding the structure and requirements of the SIE exam is crucial for effective preparation and success. This exam not only tests your knowledge but also prepares you for further qualifications in the securities industry, laying a solid foundation for a career in this field.

Keys to Success on the SIE Exam: Study Plan, Focused Practice, and Positive Mindset

Study Plan Template

A well-structured study plan is essential for success in the SIE exam. Begin with an initial assessment to gauge your knowledge level and identify areas needing focus. Over the next several weeks, dedicate time to learning the exam content in depth, using a variety of resources such as textbooks, online courses, and webinars. As the exam approaches, shift your focus to applying what you've learned through practice questions and simulated exams. Review all topics thoroughly in the final weeks, with a lighter load in the last days to avoid burnout.

Focused Practice

Focused practice is key to mastering the SIE exam content. This means not just passively reading or watching videos but actively engaging with the material. Techniques like active recall, where you try to remember key facts without looking at your notes, and practicing under timed conditions can be especially effective. It's important to concentrate on your weak spots by revisiting challenging concepts until they become familiar.

Positive Mindset

Maintaining a positive mindset is crucial as you prepare for the SIE exam. Visualize yourself succeeding and regularly remind yourself of your capability to pass the exam. Incorporate stress-reducing activities into your study routine, such as meditation, exercise, or any relaxation technique that works for you. Keeping a balanced routine with sufficient rest, nutritious meals, and breaks will also help maintain your mental and physical health during this intense preparation period.

Chapter one Introduction to Financial Markets

Welcome to the fascinating world of financial markets, the pivotal arenas where capital and investment opportunities meet. Financial markets play a critical role in the global economy by facilitating the efficient allocation of resources. Through these markets, money flows from those who have excess funds—savers, to those who need funds to grow—borrowers, whether they're governments, businesses, or individuals.

Imagine the financial markets as the bloodstream of the economy; just as blood distributes essential nutrients to different parts of the body, financial markets channel funds to areas where they are most needed. This process is vital for economic growth, enabling new businesses to start, existing companies to expand, and governments to deliver public services.

For candidates preparing for the Securities Industry Essentials (SIE) exam, understanding the different types of financial markets is not just a requirement—it's a necessity. These markets include:

- **Primary Markets**: Where new securities are issued and sold for the first time, providing companies, municipalities, and other entities with fresh capital.

- **Secondary Markets**: Where existing securities are traded among investors, ensuring liquidity and enabling price discovery.

- **Auction Markets**: Where buyers and sellers come together to trade securities based on competitive bidding.

- **Dealer Markets**: Where dealers buy and sell securities from their own inventories, acting as intermediaries between buyers and sellers.

Mastering the distinctions and functions of these markets equips you with the knowledge to make informed decisions and understand market movements, both of which are crucial for any securities professional. As Warren Buffet wisely advised, "Risk comes from not knowing what you are doing." Therefore, a thorough comprehension of financial markets reduces risk and enhances your ability to operate effectively within the industry.

As we dive deeper into each market type, remember that the goal is not only to prepare you for the SIE exam but also to lay a strong foundation for a successful career in securities. Each segment of these markets offers unique opportunities and challenges, understanding which can significantly impact both your exam performance and your professional growth.

Primary Market

The primary market plays a pivotal role in the financial ecosystem, acting as the birthplace for securities. This market is where securities are created and sold for the first time, through processes such as initial public offerings (IPOs), private placements, or government bonds issuance. Essentially, the primary market facilitates the conversion of capital from investors into liquid funds that corporations, governments, and other entities can use to fund operations, invest in development projects, or expand their businesses.

Definition and Purpose

At its core, the primary market's function is to aid in capital formation. This is the process through which companies and governments raise funds to invest in long-term assets and projects. When a company decides to go public, for instance, it issues shares in the primary market. Investors purchasing these shares are effectively providing the company with the capital it needs to grow. Similarly, when a government issues bonds in the primary market, it is seeking funds for public projects like infrastructure, education, or healthcare.

The issuance of securities in the primary market can be visualized as planting a seed. Just as a seed needs soil, water, and sunlight to grow, a business requires capital to expand and thrive. Investors who buy securities during an IPO or another form of issuance are providing the necessary resources for growth, akin to gardeners nurturing a plant. This relationship benefits both parties: the issuers obtain essential funds, while investors get the opportunity to be part of potentially profitable enterprises from the ground up.

Importance in the Financial System

The primary market is crucial for a healthy economy as it provides a direct channel for raising capital. Without this market, companies and governments would struggle to find the necessary funding for innovation, expansion, and service delivery. Moreover, the primary market supports employment by funding businesses at the grassroots level, leading to job creation and economic development.

For SIE exam candidates, understanding the primary market is essential not just for passing the exam but also for future careers in finance. Knowing how securities are issued, the reasons behind them, and their potential impact allows for better investment decisions and a deeper understanding of market dynamics.

As we delve into the specifics of how securities are traded and the various players involved in the primary market, remember the words of Benjamin Franklin: "An investment in knowledge pays the best interest." By comprehending the fundamental processes of the primary market, you are investing in a foundation that will support your career in the securities industry for years to come

Process of Issuing Securities

In the primary market, the process of issuing securities is a critical mechanism through which companies and governments secure the necessary funds to fuel growth and undertake new projects. This process can take various forms, most notably through initial public offerings (IPOs) and private placements. Understanding these mechanisms is essential for any aspiring finance professional.

Initial Public Offerings (IPOs)

An Initial Public Offering (IPO) is a pivotal moment for a company, marking its transition from private to public status and allowing it to raise capital by selling shares to the public for the first time. The IPO process begins with the selection of underwriters, typically financial institutions, which help set the share price based on anticipated demand and the company's valuation. The company then prepares a detailed prospectus, a document that includes comprehensive financial and operational information, which is reviewed and approved by regulatory bodies such as the SEC.

Following the approval, the company and its underwriters promote the IPO through a roadshow where they present the company's value to potential institutional investors. This feedback helps in setting the final share price. The IPO culminates in the shares launched on a stock exchange, where they become available for purchase by investors, providing the company with the capital it needs to grow.

Private Placements

In contrast to IPOs, private placements involve selling securities directly to a select group of sophisticated investors, such as venture capitals, private equity firms, and large banks, rather than the general public. This method is less regulated than IPOs, allowing for a quicker and more confidential process. Companies opt for private placements to maintain control while still accessing the necessary capital. The investors in private placements often bring in not just funds, but also strategic benefits such as industry expertise and valuable connections.

Participants: the roles of underwriters, investment banks, and initial investors.

In the primary market, particularly during an IPO, three key groups play crucial roles: underwriters, investment banks, and initial investors. Each group has distinct responsibilities that ensure the successful issuance of securities.

Underwriters

Underwriters are typically investment banks that the issuing company hires to manage the IPO process. Their primary role is to facilitate the transition of a company from private to public and ensure that the securities offered meet market demand at an optimal price. Underwriters assess the value of the company and its shares, a process that involves detailed financial analysis and market research. They determine the initial offering price of the stocks based on this assessment, taking into account the current market conditions and the prospective growth of the company.

Once the price is set, underwriters also take on the risk associated with the IPO by buying the shares from the issuer before selling them to the public and institutional investors. This process, known as underwriting, is fundamental because it guarantees the issuer will receive the funds they need, regardless of whether the shares sell to the end investors.

Investment Banks

Investment banks play a multifaceted role in the issuance of securities. While they often act as underwriters, their responsibilities extend beyond pricing and risk management. They provide strategic advice to the issuing company on the timing of the market launch, the best structure for the securities, and the marketing strategy that should be employed during the roadshow phase.

Investment banks also act as intermediaries between the issuing company and regulatory authorities, ensuring that all legal requirements are met and that the issuance complies with securities laws. This includes preparing and filing the necessary documents, such as the prospectus, with the Securities and Exchange Commission (SEC) or other regulatory bodies.

Initial Investors

Initial investors in an IPO, often referred to as cornerstone or anchor investors, are usually large institutions or wealthy individuals who commit to purchasing a significant portion of the shares at the offered price before the shares are publicly available. Their involvement is crucial as it signifies confidence in the company's value and prospects, which can attract further interest from other investors during the IPO.

The commitment from these initial investors can stabilize the demand and pricing of the shares during the IPO process. Their early support often plays a pivotal role in the success of the IPO, as it helps to mitigate the risk of under-subscription, where the demand for the shares is less than expected.

Example: metaphorical explanation for the primary market process.

Imagine the process of a company issuing securities in the primary market as its grand debut in a theater play. The company preparing for an initial public offering (IPO) or private placement is like a theater group getting ready for the opening night of a highly anticipated performance.

The Theater Production: Staging an IPO

In this theatrical debut, the company is the playwright who has crafted a compelling story—its business plan. The investment banks act as the directors, responsible for interpreting the play (the business plan) and deciding how best to present it to the audience to ensure a successful run. They fine-tune every detail, from the setting of the initial share price to the timing of the market entry, much like a director chooses set designs and scene timing to captivate the audience.

The Underwriters: The Stage Crew

The underwriters are akin to the stage crew and the producers who back the play financially. They take the script, believe in its potential, and put up the initial capital needed to bring the production to life. They guarantee that the play will go on, purchasing all the tickets (shares) upfront and taking on the risk of filling the theater (the market). Their role is crucial because their endorsement serves as a signal to the broader audience that the play is worth watching.

The Initial Investors: The Critics and VIP Guests

Initial investors in the IPO are like the revered critics and VIP guests at the premiere. Their early investment is like early reviews; if they are positive, they can significantly sway public opinion and build anticipation. Their commitment to buying tickets (shares) early on helps to generate buzz and confidence in the play's success, encouraging more attendees (investors) to secure their seats for future performances.

Opening Night: The Public Launch

The launch of the IPO is the play's opening night, when the curtain rises and the general public gets to see the production for the first time. The success of this night depends not only on the play itself but also on how well the directors (investment banks) and the stage crew (underwriters) have prepared and marketed the performance. If the audience (market investors) is pleased, the applause (investment) will be resounding, and the run of the play (trading of the shares) will be successful and potentially profitable for all involved.

Secondary Market

The secondary market is an essential component of the financial ecosystem, where securities such as stocks, bonds, and other financial instruments are traded among investors after their initial issuance in the primary market. This market operates continuously, enabling the buying and selling of securities, which is crucial for maintaining the flow of capital and providing the liquidity necessary to keep the financial system robust and efficient.

Definition and Purpose

At its core, the secondary market's primary role is to provide liquidity—the ease with which assets can be quickly bought or sold in the market without causing significant changes in their price. This liquidity is vital as it instills confidence among investors, knowing they can readily liquidate their holdings or acquire new ones with minimal impact on price levels. As Warren Buffett once insightfully noted, "Risk comes from not knowing what you're doing." The secondary market mitigates this risk by providing a platform for active trading, which helps in better understanding and managing market dynamics.

Importance of Liquidity

Liquidity benefits the financial markets and the economy in several key ways:

1. **Investor Confidence**: It enhances investor confidence and market participation, leading to more accurate price discovery and generally more stable markets. Confidence is key, as echoed by John Bogle, who believed that "If you have trouble imagining a 20% loss in the stock market, you shouldn't be in stocks."

2. **Risk Management**: It allows for effective risk management by enabling investors to adjust their portfolios quickly in response to personal financial changes or shifts in market conditions. This flexibility is crucial for navigating through market ups and downs.

3. **Economic Indicators**: High transaction volumes and stable prices in the secondary market often reflect broader economic confidence, while volatility might indicate economic distress or investor uncertainty.

4. **Capital Allocation**: Efficient trading in the secondary market helps in the optimal allocation of capital. Investors redirect resources towards businesses and projects that demonstrate potential for growth and profitability, as reflected in their market valuations.

5. **Support for the Primary Market**: An active secondary market ensures that securities initially sold in the primary market have a venue for subsequent trading. This interplay between the primary and secondary markets encourages more frequent issuances of new securities, knowing they will later be supported by active trading.

Trading Venues

After securities are initially offered in the primary market, they enter the secondary market, where they are traded among various participants. This continuous exchange of securities is facilitated through several types of trading venues, each with its unique characteristics and functions. These venues are crucial for providing liquidity and ensuring that securities can be bought and sold efficiently.

Stock Exchanges

One of the most well-known trading venues is the stock exchange. Examples include the New York Stock Exchange (NYSE) and the NASDAQ. These exchanges provide a structured and regulated environment where members can buy and sell securities. The exchanges ensure fair trading practices and transparency by displaying prices and managing the order flow. Securities listed on these exchanges are perceived as more credible due to the stringent listing requirements, which include regular financial reporting and adherence to other regulatory standards.

Electronic Trading Platforms

With technological advancements, electronic trading platforms have become central to modern finance, offering rapid execution of trades and access to global markets from virtually anywhere. **NASDAQ**, a pioneer in electronic exchanges, facilitates all trading via a network of computers without the need for traditional trading floors. Similarly, platforms like **Interactive Brokers** and **E*Trade** provide sophisticated tools that cater to both individual and institutional traders, allowing for a wide range of trading activities including stocks, options, and futures with enhanced speed and lower costs.

Over-the-Counter (OTC) Markets

In the OTC markets, trades occur outside of formal exchanges via a dealer network, making it possible to trade securities that are not listed on conventional exchanges. **OTC Markets Group**, for example, operates platforms like OTCQX and OTCQB, which host companies that do not meet the criteria of larger exchanges but still wish to offer securities to the public. These markets are known for their flexibility in trading terms and the diversity of traded products, although they often carry higher risks and offer less transparency compared to traditional exchanges.

Dark Pools

Dark pools offer a venue for trading large blocks of securities discreetly without immediate price impact. Major financial institutions operate these private exchanges, which are crucial for institutional investors looking to execute large transactions. Platforms like **Liquidnet** and **Sigma X** provide these services, maintaining confidentiality and minimizing market slippage by allowing transactions to occur away from the public eye.

Crossing Networks

Crossing networks function similarly to dark pools, facilitating the execution of trades at specific, predetermined times — often matching the closing price of stocks on major exchanges. These networks are designed to handle large volumes of trades by matching buy and sell orders at discrete times, which helps in reducing market impact. **POSIT** and **CBX (Continuous Block Crossing)** are examples of such platforms that help institutional investors trade substantial amounts without significantly affecting the market.

Each of these trading venues plays a vital role in the secondary market by catering to different types of securities, trading strategies, and investor needs.

Participants in the Trading Venues

In the secondary market, a diverse array of participants engage in the buying and selling of securities. Understanding the roles and functions of these participants is crucial for anyone entering the financial markets. Each type of participant contributes to the liquidity and efficiency of the market.

Investors

Investors are the cornerstone of the financial markets. They include individuals and institutions such as mutual funds, pension funds, and insurance companies that buy securities to meet various financial goals. Individual investors may be looking for capital appreciation, dividends, or interest payments, while institutional investors manage large pools of money and have a significant impact on the markets due to the large volumes they trade. Investors rely on the information available in the market to make informed decisions about buying and selling securities.

Brokers

Brokers act as intermediaries between buyers and sellers of securities. Individuals and institutions typically use brokers to access trading venues and execute transactions. Brokers do not trade on their own account but rather facilitate transactions for clients. They earn commissions for their services and are regulated to ensure they adhere to fair trading practices. Brokers are vital for individual investors who do not have direct access to the markets.

Dealers

Dealers are market participants who trade securities on their own account and are an essential part of the over-the-counter (OTC) markets. Unlike brokers, dealers actually own the securities they sell and buy securities they wish to sell later. They make profits by buying at lower prices and selling at higher prices, maintaining liquidity in the market through their continuous trade activity. Dealers also set bid and ask prices for securities and are known as market makers in certain contexts.

Market Makers

Market makers are a specific type of dealer who commit to buying and selling certain securities at publicly quoted prices. They ensure that there is always a buyer and seller for the securities they cover, which enhances market liquidity and helps smooth out price volatility. Market makers hold an inventory of stocks to facilitate trading and are particularly active on electronic trading platforms like NASDAQ, where they help match buy and sell orders.

These participants together create a dynamic and interconnected marketplace where securities are continuously traded. Investors provide the capital, brokers facilitate access, dealers ensure liquidity, and market makers stabilize prices through their trading activities. Each plays a distinct role that supports the overall health and efficiency of the financial markets,

Secondary Market as a Resale Shop

To better understand the function and dynamics of the secondary market, imagine it as a resale shop where items are bought and sold after their initial purchase. This analogy can help clarify the continuous cycle of trading that characterizes the secondary market.

Resale Shop Dynamics

In a resale shop, goods are not sold by the original producers but by previous owners who wish to sell items they no longer need. Similarly, the secondary market deals not with the issuance of new securities but with trading securities that are already owned. These securities have been initially sold in the primary market and are now being bought and sold among various investors.

Just as items in a resale shop can vary widely from vintage clothing to used books, the securities traded in the secondary market encompass a broad range of financial instruments, including stocks, bonds, and derivatives. The price of items in a resale shop often depends on their condition, demand, and rarity—similar factors influence the prices of securities in the secondary market, such as the financial health of the company, market conditions, and investor sentiment.

Role of Participants

The participants in a resale shop include the buyers looking for good deals, the sellers hoping to declutter or make some money, and the shop owner who facilitates these transactions. In the secondary market, investors (buyers and sellers), brokers (who help facilitate transactions), and market makers (who ensure liquidity by ready to buy or sell) play similar roles. The shop owner's role is akin to that of stock exchanges and trading platforms that provide the venue and infrastructure for trading activities.

Benefits of Trading

Shopping at a resale shop offers benefits like affordability, finding unique items, and the flexibility to buy and sell as needs change. Similarly, the secondary market provides crucial benefits such as liquidity—allowing investors to quickly buy or sell securities as their investment goals or market conditions change. It also enables price discovery, where the current value of securities is continuously updated based on supply and demand dynamics.

Impact on the Economy

Just as resale shops can give items a second life and make them accessible to more people, the secondary market plays a vital role in the financial ecosystem by enabling the free flow of capital and information across the economy. This activity helps to stabilize the financial system, facilitate economic growth, and provide investors with opportunities to manage their investments actively.

Auction Market: Mechanics of Trading

An auction market operates much like a traditional auction house where items are sold to the highest bidder, a concept directly applicable to financial markets like the New York Stock Exchange (NYSE). In this type of market, securities are traded based on real-time bids from buyers and asks from sellers. Prices are determined at the point where these bids and asks meet, establishing the execution or trade price for the security.

Bidding Process

Imagine the trading floor as an art auction. Each trading day begins with an opening bid, akin to an auctioneer calling for the starting price of a piece. Buyers state how much they are willing to pay (bid), and sellers indicate the lowest price they are willing to accept (ask). This dynamic interaction continues until a bid matches an ask, similar to an auctioneer's hammer falling when the highest bid is reached without further contest.

In scenarios where the market lacks immediate matches between buyers and sellers, market makers or specialists step in. These participants are crucial in maintaining liquidity and order in the markets. Market makers buy or sell from their own inventories to fill gaps, ensuring that trades can be executed even when direct matches between public bids and asks are not immediately available. Specialists, particularly on exchanges like the NYSE, oversee the flow of orders for specific stocks, stepping in to buy or sell as necessary to prevent excessive volatility and to ensure an orderly market.

Transparency and Fairness

The auction market's hallmark is its transparency, allowing all market participants to see real-time data on bids and asks. This visibility ensures that everyone has access to the same information and that the prices of securities reflect true market conditions, based on visible supply and demand. This transparency is essential for maintaining fairness, as it prevents price manipulation and ensures that the market operates efficiently and equitably.

This explanation integrates the core dynamics of auction markets and how they resemble traditional auctions, emphasizing the role of market makers and the importance of transparency in price formation. This approach not only educates about the basic operations but also underscores the fairness and regulatory aspects that maintain market integrity.

Key Features of Auction Markets: Transparency and Price Determination

Auction markets are pivotal in financial trading, primarily because they exemplify the principles of transparency and market-determined price setting. These features are fundamental to the integrity and efficiency of financial markets.

Transparency

Transparency in auction markets means that all market participants have equal access to crucial information regarding trading activities. This includes real-time visibility of all bid and ask prices, the volume of trades, and the identity of market participants (although the latter may be anonymized in some systems). Transparency ensures that every player, from individual investors to large institutions, operates on a level playing field.

The benefits of such transparency are manifold:

- **Confidence in Fairness**:

  Investors are more likely to participate actively in a market where they can see that prices are not being manipulated and that the trading process is open to scrutiny.

- **Improved Decision Making**:

  With clear, real-time information, traders can make more informed decisions, reacting swiftly to changes in market conditions.

- **Regulatory Compliance**:

  Transparent markets help regulatory bodies monitor trading activities more effectively, ensuring compliance with financial regulations and preventing fraudulent activities.

Market-Determined Price Setting

In auction markets, prices are determined through a process of bidding, where buyers submit bids, and sellers place asks until a match is found. This method is the epitome of market-determined pricing, directly reflecting the current supply and demand for securities. The final trade price, or the price at which a security is bought or sold, is established when the highest bid meets the lowest ask.

This pricing mechanism has several advantages:

- **Efficient Price Discovery**:

  The dynamic interplay of bids and asks facilitates the discovery of the most efficient price for securities at any given time.

- **Reflective of Real Market Sentiments**:

  Prices in an auction market are an immediate reflection of what the market collectively thinks security is worth, incorporating all available information and sentiments.

- **Adaptability**:

  This system is highly adaptable, quickly adjusting prices in response to changes in market conditions or in response to news affecting the securities or their underlying assets.

Role of Market Makers and Specialists

Although auction markets are primarily driven by the collective actions of buyers and sellers, market makers and specialists play a critical role in ensuring that the market operates smoothly and maintains liquidity. Market makers provide necessary buying and selling capacities when there are temporary shortages of buyers or sellers. Specialists, particularly in markets like the NYSE, are responsible for overseeing the trading of specific securities, ensuring that there is a fair and orderly market in those stocks.

Major Auction Markets

Auction markets are vital to the global financial system, facilitating transparent and efficient trading of securities. Prominent among these are exchanges like the New York Stock Exchange (NYSE) and NASDAQ, each playing a unique role in the economic landscape.

The NYSE, based in New York City, stands as one of the world's largest and most well-known stock exchanges. It operates with a hybrid model that combines electronic trading systems and traditional floor trading. The NYSE is recognized for its opening and closing bell ceremonies, iconic moments that signal the start and end of the trading day. As a hub for some of the largest companies globally, the NYSE is seen as a barometer of economic health. It employs designated market makers to ensure liquidity and stable pricing, adhering to stringent regulatory standards that companies must meet to be listed.

In contrast, NASDAQ is known for being the world's first electronic exchange, eliminating the trading floor entirely. It features a network of market makers who ensure that buying and selling orders have the best possible prices. Favored by technology and biotech companies, NASDAQ hosts major names like Apple, Google, and Amazon. Its fully electronic operation allows for rapid trading and has positioned it as a leader in market technology and innovation.

Across the Atlantic, the London Stock Exchange (LSE) merges deep historical roots with modern trading. Established in 1698, the LSE is one of the oldest stock exchanges and operates SETS (Stock Exchange Electronic Trading Service), an electronic order book that matches buy and sell orders without a traditional trading floor. The LSE's broad international appeal draws a diverse range of companies from across Europe, Africa, and the Middle East, making it a pivotal market in the global financial landscape.

These exchanges underscore the dynamic nature of financial trading where traditional practices meet innovative technologies. Each market adapts to its regulatory environment and market demands, providing tailored trading mechanisms that ensure liquidity and price stability. Whether through the bustling floor of the NYSE or the electronic precision of NASDAQ, these markets facilitate essential capital flows that drive economic growth and reflect the evolving nature of global finance.

Auction Market Analogy: Art Auctions and Securities Trading

To understand how securities are traded in auction markets like the New York Stock Exchange, consider the workings of an art auction. At an art auction, a piece of artwork is presented, and potential buyers place their bids. Each buyer decides the maximum amount they are willing to pay based on their valuation of the art. The auctioneer calls out the rising prices until no higher bids are offered. The highest bid wins, and the artwork is sold to that bidder.

Similarities in Trading Mechanisms

Starting the Bidding:

Just as an art auction begins with an opening bid, the trading day on a stock exchange starts with an opening price. This price represents the first transaction of the day, which sets the tone for subsequent trading.

Dynamic Bidding Process:

In an art auction, bidders react to each other's offers, adjusting their bids to secure the artwork. Similarly, in the stock market, traders adjust their buy or sell orders based on other market participants' actions. Buyers raise their bids to ensure a purchase, while sellers adjust their asks to make a sale, each reacting in real-time to market movements.

Winning the Bid:

 At the close of an art auction, the highest bidder acquires the artwork. In financial markets, a trade occurs when a buy order matches a sell order at the same price. The 'highest' bid that meets the 'lowest' ask results in a transaction, similar to the final hammer strike in an art auction sealing the deal.

Price Determination:

 The final price at an art auction reflects the highest value a buyer is willing to pay for the artwork, considered its market value at that moment. In stock exchanges, the last traded price of a stock, which results from the latest matched bid and ask, similarly represents the current market valuation of that security. This price is continuously updated as new bids and asks are placed.

Market Sentiment:

Just as the atmosphere and sentiment can drive prices up or down at an art auction, sentiment in the financial markets can cause significant fluctuations in stock prices. Positive news might spur bidding wars on stocks, driving prices up, while negative news can lead to lower bids and falling prices.

This analogy helps illustrate the dynamic and responsive nature of auction markets, where the interaction of bids and asks determines the prices of securities, much like how bidders determine the final price of artwork at an auction. Understanding this process is crucial for anyone involved in trading or investing, as it highlights the fundamental mechanics of price discovery in financial markets.

Dealer Market: Mechanics of Trading

In a dealer market, unlike auction markets where trading occurs through a centralized process, transactions are decentralized and occur through dealers who buy and sell securities from their accounts. This type of market structure is instrumental in facilitating the trade of stocks, bonds, and other securities, particularly when immediate counterparties are not available.

Role of Dealers

Dealers in a dealer market act as market makers. They hold inventories of securities and are ready to buy from sellers and sell to buyers at any time. This continuous availability ensures that investors can execute trades quickly and at known prices, contributing significantly to market liquidity.

Setting Prices in Dealer Markets

1. Bid and Ask Prices

In dealer markets, dealers facilitate the trading of securities by setting two key prices: the bid price and the ask price. The **bid price** is what the dealer is willing to pay to purchase securities from sellers, and the **ask price** (sometimes referred to as the offer price) is what the dealer will accept to sell securities to buyers. The difference between these two prices is known as the **"spread,"** which represents the potential profit for the dealer on the transactions.

- **Example**: Consider a scenario where a dealer is dealing with shares of Company XYZ. If the dealer sets a bid price at $50 per share and an ask price at $50.30 per share, the spread is

$0.30. This spread compensates the dealer for the risk of holding the stock and the service of providing liquidity.

2. Price Determination Factors

Dealers determine their bid and ask prices based on a variety of factors:

- **Market Conditions**: General market trends can influence how prices are set, with bullish conditions possibly leading to higher ask prices due to increased buying interest.

- **Security Characteristics**: The inherent volatility and liquidity of the security also play a critical role. More volatile securities might have wider spreads to compensate for the higher risk.

- **Supply and Demand Dynamics**: Prices are adjusted according to the current supply and demand for the security. A high demand with limited supply can drive up ask prices, while an oversupply might lower them.

- **Inventory Levels**: Dealers adjust prices based on their inventory levels to manage their holdings effectively.

- **Example**: If a dealer has an excess inventory of Company XYZ shares due to recent selling pressure, they might lower the ask price to $50.20 to encourage buyers, narrowing the spread to incentivize purchases. Conversely, if the dealer's inventory is low and there's high demand, they might increase the ask price to $50.40 to maximize profits.

3. Responsiveness to Market Changes

Dealers must remain agile, continually adjusting their bid and ask prices in response to market changes. This includes reactions to economic news, company performance updates, and broader financial market shifts.

- **Example**: Suppose Company XYZ announces better-than-expected earnings before the market opens. Anticipating increased buying interest, a dealer might increase both bid and ask prices from $50 and $50.30 to $51 and $51.30, respectively, to reflect the new market valuation and anticipated demand.

Importance of Dealer Markets

Dealer markets are particularly important for the trading of securities that are not highly liquid or widely traded. In such markets, dealers provide much-needed liquidity by ensuring that there is always a buyer or a seller for these securities, which might otherwise be difficult to trade quickly on an exchange without significant price concessions. Furthermore, by providing liquidity and setting prices, dealers help stabilize market fluctuations and ensure a smoother trading process for less active stocks.

Market Makers and Bid-Ask Spread in Dealer Markets

In dealer markets, the seamless operation and liquidity are largely attributed to the crucial roles of market makers and the mechanics of the bid-ask spread. These components are fundamental to ensuring efficient trading and stable pricing of securities.

Market Makers: Ensuring Liquidity and Stability

Market makers are dealers who actively buy and sell securities on their own accounts, committing to both provide liquidity and help stabilize market prices. By continuously offering to buy (bid) and sell (ask) securities, they ensure that investors can execute trades quickly, even in the absence of a direct buyer or seller match. This readiness to trade reduces transaction delays and helps prevent large price swings, thus maintaining a more stable trading environment.

Market makers set the prices at which they are willing to buy and sell, which influences the market pricing of securities. These prices reflect a combination of current market conditions, anticipated future changes, and the market makers' own inventory levels and risk tolerance. Their role is especially critical during periods of high volatility or economic news, where they help absorb shocks by adjusting their bid and ask prices to reflect new information.

Bid-Ask Spread: Indicating Liquidity and Cost

The bid-ask spread is a fundamental concept in trading and investment, representing the difference between the highest price a buyer is willing to pay for an asset (the bid price) and the lowest price a seller is willing to accept (the ask price). This spread is crucial for understanding market liquidity and the costs associated with trading.

Functions of the Bid-Ask Spread:

- **Provides Liquidity**: The bid-ask spread compensates market makers and dealers for providing liquidity, making it easier for traders to buy and sell securities without causing significant price movements.

- **Indicates Market Liquidity**: A narrower spread typically indicates a highly liquid market, where securities can be bought or sold quickly at prices close to market value. Conversely, a wider spread suggests less liquidity.

- **Influences Trading Costs**: For traders, the spread represents a transaction cost. To profit, an investor must overcome the spread, as they buy at the higher ask price and sell at the lower bid price.

Real-World Example:

Consider a day in the stock market where shares of Company XYZ are being actively traded. On this day, the bid price for XYZ's stock might be $50.00, and the ask price might be $50.20. This $0.20 spread indicates several things:

- **Liquidity**: The relatively small spread suggests XYZ is a liquid stock, often traded throughout the day, which allows traders to execute orders quickly at prices close to the market rate.

- **Transaction Costs**: An investor looking to buy and then immediately sell XYZ's stock would incur a $0.20 per share loss in the absence of price movement, illustrating the direct cost imposed by the spread.

Further, suppose an economic event suddenly increases uncertainty about XYZ's future profitability. Traders might lower their bid prices or raise ask prices to account for the added risk, causing the spread to widen to $0.50. This change signals decreased liquidity and higher transaction costs, reflecting traders' hesitance amid new economic uncertainties.

Major Platforms in Dealer Markets

Dealer markets, characterized by their network of dealers who buy and sell securities from their own accounts, play a pivotal role in today's financial ecosystems. These markets facilitate transactions across various securities by ensuring liquidity and immediate trade execution, which are critical in fast-moving financial environments. Among the platforms where dealer markets are prominently featured, NASDAQ stands out as a leading example.

NASDAQ: A Premier Electronic Dealer Market

NASDAQ, short for the National Association of Securities Dealers Automated Quotations, is one of the largest and most well-known electronic dealer markets globally. Unlike traditional stock exchanges that operate via a physical trading floor, NASDAQ utilizes a network of computers that execute trades across a vast electronic network, making it a prime example of a dealer market.

- **Operational Model**: NASDAQ's model involves multiple market makers for each stock, each of whom posts bids and asks through an electronic system. This structure promotes competition among dealers, leading to narrow bid-ask spreads and high liquidity, which are advantageous for traders.

- **Innovation and Technology**: NASDAQ is renowned for its technological innovation, which has been crucial in its evolution from a mere quotation system to a fully operational trading platform. The use of advanced trading technologies ensures efficient market operations and facilitates rapid execution of trades.

- **Listing Dominance**: NASDAQ is preferred by many high-tech, biotech, and growth companies looking to benefit from its modern trading environment and international visibility. Companies like Apple, Amazon, and Google are among the heavyweights that are traded on NASDAQ, underlining its importance in global financial markets.

Other Notable Dealer Markets

While NASDAQ is one of the most prominent examples, other platforms around the world also operate as dealer markets:

- **OTC Markets Group**: Operates a network of dealer markets where over-the-counter securities are traded. These markets tend to list smaller, often more speculative companies that do not meet the criteria to be listed on larger exchanges like NASDAQ or NYSE.

- **Toronto Stock Exchange's TSX Venture Exchange**: This Canadian exchange features a dealer market for smaller or early-stage companies, with a system similar to NASDAQ, focusing on growth companies.

These platforms exemplify how dealer markets function, providing liquidity and enabling efficient trading through a network of dealers. Each platform caters to specific segments of the market, offering tailored services that meet the needs of various investors and companies. Understanding the dynamics and offerings of these platforms is essential for participants in the financial markets, especially for those involved in trading or investing in sectors that demand rapid transaction capabilities.

Dealer Markets: The Car Dealership Analogy

To understand how dealer markets function in the financial world, consider the operations of a car dealership. Just as a car dealer buys and sells vehicles from their own inventory, influencing the prices based on various factors, dealers in financial markets operate in a similar manner with securities.

Buying and Selling from Inventory

A car dealership purchases vehicles either from manufacturers or through trades and then sells these vehicles to consumers. The dealer must manage an inventory of cars, deciding when to buy new models and when to sell existing ones based on demand, market conditions, and inventory levels. Similarly, financial market dealers buy securities to hold in their inventory and sell them to investors. The decisions about when to buy or sell securities from their inventory are influenced by market demand, price fluctuations, and the dealer's assessment of market trends.

Influencing Prices

In a car dealership, the price of vehicles can be adjusted based on various factors including the popularity of a model, the introduction of new models, and market competition. Dealers may offer discounts to clear out older models or raise prices on popular models that are in high demand. In dealer markets, financial dealers set the buying (bid) and selling (ask) prices for securities they handle. The spread between these prices (bid-ask spread) represents the dealer's potential profit margin. Just like car dealers, securities dealers adjust their prices to manage their inventory effectively while aiming to maximize their profits.

Market Conditions and Pricing Strategy

Car dealers must adapt to changing market conditions, such as economic downturns or shifts in consumer preferences, which can drastically affect vehicle pricing and sales strategies. Financial dealers similarly adjust their bid and ask prices based on economic indicators, company performance, and overall market sentiment. This flexibility helps them manage risks associated with holding inventory while still catering to investor demand.

Role in Facilitating Transactions

Just as a car dealership facilitates vehicle purchases for customers, providing a necessary service for those looking to buy or sell cars, dealers in financial markets facilitate transactions for securities. They ensure that investors can always find a counterparty to trade with, thereby providing liquidity and smoother market operations. This role is crucial, especially for less liquid securities that might otherwise be difficult to trade.

This analogy helps demystify the operations of dealer markets by comparing them to a familiar everyday business, enhancing understanding of how these markets provide liquidity and influence pricing in the financial world

Comparison of Market Types: Auction Markets vs. Dealer Markets

Understanding the differences and similarities between auction markets and dealer markets is crucial for anyone involved in trading or investing. These two fundamental market structures facilitate transactions and set prices in distinct ways, each catering to specific needs within the financial ecosystem.

Auction Markets

In auction markets, such as the New York Stock Exchange (NYSE), transactions are facilitated through a centralized process where buyers and sellers submit their bids and asks. This method is similar to a traditional auction:

- **Price Determination**:

  Prices in auction markets are determined by the highest bid (the maximum price a buyer is willing to pay) and the lowest ask (the minimum price a seller is willing to accept). The actual transaction occurs at a price where these two meet, known as the market-clearing price.

- **Transparency**:

  Auction markets are highly transparent, as all bid and ask prices are visible to all market participants, which helps in maintaining fairness and allows for informed decision-making.

- **Participation**:

  Both individual and institutional investors can directly participate, contributing to a dynamic and competitive bidding environment that reflects the true market sentiment.

Dealer Markets

Dealer markets, exemplified by NASDAQ, operate through a network of dealers who buy and sell securities from their own inventories. This structure resembles how a car dealership operates:

- **Price Determination**:

  Dealers set their own bid and ask prices based on their assessments of market conditions and their inventory levels. The spread between these prices (the bid-ask spread) represents the dealer's potential profit on transactions.

- **Transparency**:

  While prices are readily available, the reasons behind a dealer's specific bid and ask prices may not be as transparent as in auction markets. Dealers have discretion over their pricing, which might not always directly reflect broader market sentiment.

- **Participation**:

  Investors typically do not interact directly with each other but must go through dealers to execute trades, making dealers crucial intermediaries that ensure liquidity and market continuity.

Similarities

Despite their differences, both market types share some fundamental characteristics:

- **Liquidity Provision**:

Both market types strive to provide liquidity, which is vital for the healthy functioning of financial markets. Liquidity ensures that securities can be bought and sold with minimal impact on their prices.

- **Regulation**:

  Both auction and dealer markets are regulated by financial authorities to ensure fair trading practices and protect investor interests. This regulatory oversight helps maintain trust in the financial markets.

- **Market Efficiency**:

  Both types contribute to the overall efficiency of the market by facilitating the discovery of prices and enabling the transfer of securities. They allow the aggregation of different market participants' views on the value of securities, which is reflected in the security prices.

feature	Auction Market	Dealer Market
Price Determination	Prices determined through bidding; the transaction occurs at the price where the highest bid meets the lowest ask.	Dealers set bid and ask prices based on their assessments; the spread between these prices indicates potential profit.
Transparency	High transparency; all bid and ask prices and volumes are visible to all market participants.	Lower transparency compared to auction markets; dealer's pricing decisions may not be fully visible.
Participation	Direct participation by both individual and institutional investors, influencing price formation.	Participants interact through dealers, who act as intermediaries; direct participant interaction is limited.
Liquidity Provision	Facilitated by the open bidding process, which can attract a large number of participants.	Provided by dealers who are ready to buy or sell to ensure continuous market operations.
Market Efficiency	Highly efficient in reflecting real-time supply and demand through visible bids and asks.	Efficiency achieved through dealers who manage inventory and respond to market demands, though less transparent.
Regulation	Stringently regulated with requirements for fair disclosure and trading practices.	Also regulated, but the focus is on ensuring dealers operate fairly and transparently within their roles.

Advantages and Disadvantages of Auction and Dealer Markets

Investors navigating the financial markets must weigh the benefits and potential drawbacks of different market structures—particularly auction markets and dealer markets. Each type offers unique features that can significantly impact investment strategies and outcomes.

Auction Markets

Auction markets, such as the New York Stock Exchange, are known for their transparency. All bids and asks are visible to participants, promoting an informed trading environment. This transparency aids in efficient price discovery, ensuring that the prices of securities reflect true market demand and supply. Moreover, investors in auction markets can directly participate in price setting, which can be empowering and strategically advantageous.

However, these markets can also be volatile, with prices fluctuating rapidly in response to new information or market sentiment. This volatility requires investors to be vigilant and responsive, which can be challenging for those who cannot continuously monitor the market. Additionally, the complexity of trading mechanisms and strategies in auction markets might be daunting for novice investors.

Dealer Markets

In dealer markets, like NASDAQ, dealers ensure liquidity by being ready to buy or sell securities at any time, which is crucial for trading less liquid securities. This setup is beneficial for managing large transactions without significantly impacting the market price, providing a smoother trading experience for large volume traders. The process is generally simpler for retail investors, as it does not necessitate a deep understanding of complex trading strategies.

However, dealer markets often lack the level of transparency seen in auction markets. The prices in dealer markets are set by dealers based on their inventory and market position, which might not always align with the broader market conditions. This can sometimes lead to less favorable prices for investors. The reliance on dealer integrity adds a layer of counterparty risk, and the typically wider bid-ask spreads in dealer markets translate to higher transaction costs for traders.

Both auction and dealer markets offer distinct advantages and pose unique challenges. The choice between these markets should consider an investor's need for transparency, comfort with market volatility, trading frequency, and the size of transactions. Understanding these differences helps investors align their trading practices with their financial goals and risk profiles, enabling more informed and strategic decision-making in complex financial environments.

Practical Implications for SIE Candidates: Understanding Market Dynamics

For those preparing to take the Securities Industry Essentials (SIE) exam, a deep understanding of market dynamics across different market types is not just about passing the test—it's about laying the groundwork for making informed investment decisions in their future careers.

Understanding Market Dynamics

Market dynamics, including how prices are set and how transactions are facilitated in auction and dealer markets, are fundamental concepts that SIE candidates need to grasp. This knowledge goes beyond theoretical understanding; it equips future securities professionals with the tools to analyze and interpret market movements effectively.

1. **Informed Decision Making**: Knowing how auction and dealer markets operate helps candidates appreciate the factors that influence stock prices and liquidity. For instance, understanding that dealer markets may have wider bid-ask spreads can influence a professional's strategy regarding entry and exit points for trading certain securities.

2. **Strategic Trading**: Grasping the nuances of how orders are executed in these markets allows future traders and brokers to devise strategies that minimize costs and maximize returns. For example, a deeper understanding of auction market mechanisms can help in timing trades more effectively to take advantage of price volatility.

3. **Risk Assessment**: Comprehensive knowledge of market structures aids in assessing and managing risk. Recognizing the inherent risks in less transparent dealer markets or the potential for rapid price changes in highly liquid auction markets allows emerging professionals to better manage their clients' portfolios and their own.

4. **Client Communication**: As future securities professionals, SIE candidates will need to explain market conditions and investment strategies to clients. A solid understanding of market dynamics ensures that they can provide clear, accurate advice based on current market realities.

5. **Regulatory Compliance**: Understanding the regulatory environment for different market types ensures that SIE candidates can navigate compliance issues effectively. Knowledge of trading regulations, which can differ significantly between markets, is critical for maintaining ethical standards and legal compliance in professional practices.

Exam Tips: Key Aspects of Financial Markets Emphasized in the SIE Exam

The Securities Industry Essentials (SIE) Exam tests foundational knowledge that is crucial for beginning a career in the securities industry. Understanding what aspects of financial markets are emphasized can help candidates focus their study efforts effectively. Here are several key areas likely to be highlighted in the SIE exam, along with tips on how to approach these topics:

Market Types and Structures

- **Focus**: Understand the differences between auction markets and dealer markets, including how trades are executed and how prices are determined in each type. Knowing the roles of market makers and specialists in these markets is also essential.

- **Tip**: Create comparison charts that outline the characteristics of each market type, such as transparency, price determination, and participant roles. This visual aid can help clarify distinctions and similarities.

Market Participants

- **Focus**: Familiarize yourself with the various participants in the financial markets, including brokers, dealers, investment advisors, and retail investors. Knowing the role each plays in the ecosystem is crucial.

- **Tip**: Use real-world examples or case studies to see how these participants interact within different market environments. This approach can help solidify theoretical knowledge through practical scenarios.

Regulatory Agencies and Their Functions

- **Focus**: The exam will cover the roles and responsibilities of major regulatory bodies like the Securities and Exchange Commission (SEC), Financial Industry Regulatory Authority (FINRA), and the Municipal Securities Rulemaking Board (MSRB).

- **Tip**: Study the specific regulations that these agencies enforce and understand how they impact market operations. Flashcards can be an effective tool for memorizing the functions of each regulatory body.

Securities Products and Their Risks

- **Focus**: A thorough understanding of various securities products (stocks, bonds, mutual funds, options) and the risks associated with each is expected.

- **Tip**: Break down each product type into its core components—what it is, how it works, and what risks it carries. Diagrams illustrating how these securities function within the larger market can be particularly helpful.

Trading, Settlement, and Anti-Fraud Provisions

- **Focus**: Knowledge of the trading process, including order types, settlement cycles, and ethical practices, is key. Anti-fraud provisions and practices to prevent money laundering are also crucial areas.

- **Tip**: Practice with scenarios or hypothetical transactions to better understand how trades are processed from initiation to settlement. Review case studies that involve compliance failures to better understand what practices to avoid.

For SIE candidates, mastering the details of how different markets operate is about more than just academic achievement; it's about preparing for real-world challenges in the financial sector.

Roles of investment banks, brokers, and exchanges

The Significance of Investment Banks, Brokers, and Exchanges in Financial Markets

Investment banks, brokers, and exchanges are pivotal institutions within the financial markets. Each plays a unique role that supports the ecosystem's infrastructure, ensuring the efficient flow of capital and providing services essential for economic growth and stability.

Investment Banks

Investment banks are key players in capital markets, primarily serving corporations, governments, and other large institutions. They facilitate the process of capital formation, crucial for economic development, by underwriting new debt and equity securities for all types of projects. Investment banks also offer strategic advisory services for mergers, acquisitions, and other significant financial transactions. In addition to these roles, they provide guidance on managing financial risks and help companies navigate complex financial landscapes.

Brokers

Brokers act as intermediaries between buyers and sellers in the financial markets, facilitating transactions for a variety of securities including stocks, bonds, and derivatives. Their primary role is to ensure that their clients, whether individual investors or large institutions, can execute trades efficiently and at the best possible prices. Brokers provide valuable market intelligence and investment advice, helping clients make informed decisions. They also ensure compliance with regulatory standards, protecting the interests of their clients and maintaining the integrity of the markets.

Exchanges

Exchanges provide the physical and electronic marketplaces where securities are traded. They are the backbone of the trading environment, offering a transparent, regulated platform for market participants to buy and sell securities. Exchanges help in the price discovery process, reflecting the supply and demand for securities in their pricing. By ensuring sufficient liquidity and enforcing trading rules, exchanges contribute to the orderly functioning of market operations and bolster investor confidence.

Contribution to Market Operations and Financial Services

Together, these entities enhance the operational capacity and service quality of financial markets:

- **Capital Accessibility**: Investment banks mobilize large amounts of capital, making it accessible for enterprises and governments, which is critical for economic growth and infrastructure development.

- **Liquidity and Market Access**: Brokers and exchanges facilitate market access and liquidity, ensuring that capital can freely move to where it is most needed and that investors can enter and exit positions with ease.

- **Regulatory Compliance and Market Stability**: Through rigorous adherence to financial regulations, these institutions help maintain market stability and protect investor interests, which is crucial for sustaining confidence in the financial markets.

Each of these roles is integral to the financial markets, contributing not only to the operations within the markets but also to the broader economic context by enhancing transparency, efficiency, and stability.

Multifaceted Roles of Investment Banks in Financial Markets

Investment banks are integral to the functioning of the financial markets, serving as critical conduits for capital formation, risk management, and strategic advisory. Their expertise and services support a wide array of client needs, from corporate finance to personal investment strategies.

Capital Formation and Underwriting Services

Investment banks are pivotal in helping companies and governments raise funds needed for expansion and development. They do this through underwriting services, where they guarantee the sale of new stock and bond issues. This involves purchasing securities directly from the issuer and selling them to investors, assuming the risk of the sale. The process is vital during initial public offerings (IPOs) and secondary offerings, where investment banks manage everything from setting the price of securities to navigating regulatory landscapes.

Strategic Advisory Services

Beyond capital raising, investment banks offer advisory services that play a crucial role in major corporate decisions. They provide expert guidance on mergers and acquisitions (M&A), helping companies identify potential acquisition targets or merger partners, valuing those opportunities, and negotiating terms that enhance shareholder value. Additionally, they offer restructuring and reorganization advice to companies needing to alter their financial or operational structures, often critical for overcoming financial challenges and improving profitability.

Risk Management

In the realm of risk management, investment banks develop sophisticated financial products that allow their clients to hedge against a wide range of risks. This includes derivatives such as options, futures, and swaps, which are used to manage exposure to fluctuations in interest rates, currency values, and commodity prices. By offering these instruments, investment banks help clients stabilize their financial operations against market volatilities.

Research and Analysis

Investment banks also contribute to the financial markets through comprehensive research and analysis. Their teams of analysts produce detailed market research reports and investment advice, informing clients about current market trends, economic conditions, and investment opportunities. This research underpins much of the investment advice provided to clients, ensuring that decisions are based on solid, well-researched information.

Through these roles, investment banks not only facilitate the efficient flow of capital across the economy but also support their clients in navigating complex market conditions and making informed financial decisions. Their services ensure that both companies and investors can optimize their strategies in alignment with broader economic trends and individual financial goals.

Roles of Brokers in Financial Markets

Brokers are pivotal figures in the financial markets, serving as the essential link between investors and the investment opportunities that markets offer. Their roles span from trade execution to providing expert financial advice, all underpinned by a commitment to regulatory compliance.

Trade Execution and Intermediary Functions

At the core of a broker's duties is the execution of trades—buying and selling securities on behalf of their clients. This function is critical because the timing and efficiency of trade execution can significantly affect investment outcomes. As intermediaries, brokers manage the logistical aspects of these transactions, which includes everything from the initial order placement to the final settlement. This role extends to maintaining detailed records and managing the administrative tasks associated with trading, ensuring that each transaction seamlessly aligns with client instructions and market regulations.

Client Services

Beyond executing trades, brokers provide a spectrum of services designed to enhance the investment experience and outcomes for their clients. They offer tailored investment advice, helping clients to navigate complex market conditions and align investment strategies with their financial goals. This involves a deep understanding of each client's risk tolerance, financial status, and long-term objectives.

Additionally, brokers manage investment portfolios on behalf of their clients, actively making decisions to buy or sell assets in a way that aims to maximize returns and minimize risks. This portfolio management service is particularly beneficial for investors who may not have the expertise or time to manage their investments directly.

Brokers also ensure that their clients have access to both domestic and international markets, broadening the scope of investment opportunities available to them. This access is crucial for building a diversified investment portfolio.

Market Information and Compliance

A key advantage of working with a broker is their ability to provide up-to-date market information. This includes insights into market trends, potential investment opportunities, and detailed analyses of economic conditions. Such information is vital for making informed investment decisions.

Furthermore, regulatory compliance is a fundamental responsibility for brokers. They are required to ensure that all transactions conform to legal and regulatory standards, which protects both the client and the integrity of the markets. This includes adopting ethical trading practices and safeguarding client interests by maintaining confidentiality and transparency.

Roles of Exchanges in Financial Markets

Exchanges play a central role in the global financial landscape, acting as the backbone for market operations. These platforms are essential for maintaining the order and efficiency of securities trading, providing key services that facilitate the smooth functioning of financial markets.

Marketplace Provision

Exchanges provide a structured and regulated environment for the trading of securities. This platform allows various market participants, including individual investors, financial institutions, and corporations, to buy and sell securities in an organized manner. By offering a centralized venue for trading, exchanges help standardize prices and ensure that the trading process is fair, transparent, and efficient. The regulation of these platforms ensures that trading adheres to legal and ethical standards, protecting investors from fraud and manipulation.

Price Discovery

One of the fundamental roles of exchanges is to facilitate price discovery. This process involves determining the price of securities based on the dynamics of supply and demand. As buyers and sellers interact within the exchange, their collective actions and reactions to market developments help establish the fair value of securities. Price discovery is crucial as it reflects the financial health and market sentiment toward a company or asset, guiding investors' decisions on buying, holding, or selling stocks.

Liquidity Provision

Exchanges are instrumental in providing liquidity to the market. Liquidity refers to the ease with which securities can be bought or sold in the market without causing a significant movement in the price. High liquidity is essential for enabling investors to enter and exit positions easily and with minimal cost. Exchanges facilitate this by pooling a large number of buy and sell orders, which helps to ensure that there is always enough volume for transactions to occur promptly and at stable prices.

Market Oversight

Another critical role of exchanges is market oversight. Exchanges monitor trading activities to ensure compliance with financial regulations and to prevent fraudulent and manipulative practices. This oversight function includes scrutinizing transactions for irregular patterns that might indicate insider trading, market manipulation, or other unethical activities. By enforcing trading rules and maintaining surveillance, exchanges uphold the integrity of the financial markets, fostering investor confidence and ensuring that the markets operate smoothly and transparently.

Exchanges are indispensable to the financial markets, providing the infrastructure and services necessary for effective trading. Their roles in marketplace provision, price discovery, liquidity provision, and market oversight ensure that financial markets remain robust, fair, and efficient.

Understanding these functions is essential for anyone engaged in trading, investing, or managing financial operations.

Interaction Between Entities: Investment Banks, Brokers, and Exchanges

The financial ecosystem is a complex network where various entities such as investment banks, brokers, and exchanges interact and collaborate to facilitate the smooth functioning of markets. Each entity plays a distinct but interconnected role that enhances market efficiency and investor access.

Collaboration and Interaction

1. Investment Banks and Exchanges

Investment banks and exchanges interact primarily during the issuance and trading of securities. For instance, when an investment bank manages an initial public offering (IPO), it coordinates with exchanges to list the new shares. This interaction ensures that once the shares are issued, they can be traded on a regulated and structured marketplace. Investment banks may also work with exchanges to develop new financial products that meet specific investor needs or fill market gaps, such as the creation of new derivative products.

2. Investment Banks and Brokers

Investment banks often rely on brokers to distribute the securities they underwrite to a broader audience. After an investment bank structures a deal and sets the initial price for the securities, brokers help in the actual sale of these securities to end investors, utilizing their networks and client relationships. Furthermore, investment banks provide brokers with research and analysis that can be passed on to the retail or institutional investor, thus aiding brokers in servicing their clients better.

3. Brokers and Exchanges

Brokers serve as the direct link between individual investors and the exchanges. They execute trades on behalf of their clients on these platforms, ensuring that investors can buy and sell securities efficiently. Exchanges provide the technology and regulatory framework within which brokers can operate safely and transparently. In return, brokers facilitate liquidity and trading volume on the exchanges, which is crucial for the overall health of the financial markets.

4. Regulatory Compliance and Information Sharing

All these entities are regulated under financial laws and guidelines, which ensures that they operate under a common set of rules and standards. Investment banks, brokers, and exchanges share important market information and adhere to regulatory requirements that help maintain market integrity and protect investor interests. This compliance is monitored by financial regulatory bodies, and adherence helps in preventing financial fraud and enhancing the stability of the financial markets.

Benefits of Collaboration

The collaboration between these entities helps in enhancing market liquidity, ensuring efficient price discovery, and providing investors with diverse financial products and services. This interaction also supports innovation in financial markets through the introduction of new securities and investment vehicles that can meet evolving investor needs.

The intricate interactions and collaborations between investment banks, brokers, and exchanges are fundamental to the functionality and robustness of the global financial markets. By understanding these relationships, individuals working within the financial sector can better appreciate their role and potential impact within this ecosystem.

Cooperative Initiatives and Systems Enhancing Market Efficiency and Transparency

In the financial ecosystem, cooperation among investment banks, brokers, and exchanges is vital for maintaining efficient and transparent markets. Several initiatives and systems illustrate how these entities collaborate to improve the functionality and integrity of the financial markets.

1. Electronic Trading Platforms

One of the most significant cooperative efforts is the development and utilization of electronic trading platforms. These platforms, supported by exchanges and used by brokers and investment banks, facilitate the instant execution of trades and provide all market participants with real-time price data. This immediate access to trading information increases market transparency and allows for more efficient price discovery.

2. Central Clearing Parties (CCPs)

Investment banks, brokers, and exchanges support the implementation of central clearing parties, which are entities that act as intermediaries between buyers and sellers in the derivatives market. CCPs help manage counterparty risk by ensuring that both sides of a transaction fulfill their obligations. This system enhances market stability and transparency, reducing the risk of default and increasing confidence in financial markets.

3. Post-Trade Reporting Tools

Post-trade reporting tools are systems used to report and disseminate information about securities transactions after trades are executed. These tools are crucial for regulatory compliance and market transparency. By ensuring that details of transactions are promptly reported to the market and regulatory bodies, these systems help maintain a fair and orderly market environment.

4. Automated Compliance Systems

Automated compliance systems are collaborative initiatives where technology developed by exchanges is used by brokers and investment banks to ensure compliance with trading rules and regulations. These systems monitor transactions in real-time to detect potential violations such as insider trading or market manipulation. By automating compliance checks, these systems enhance the integrity of financial markets and protect investor interests.

5. Market Data Sharing Agreements

Exchanges, brokers, and investment banks often enter into agreements to share market data among themselves. This shared data includes detailed analytics on trading activities, market trends, and liquidity patterns. By having access to a broader dataset, each entity can better understand market dynamics and make more informed decisions, thereby contributing to overall market efficiency.

6. Joint Educational and Training Initiatives

These entities also collaborate on educational and training programs that aim to raise the industry standards. By providing joint training sessions on new regulations, technologies, or financial products, investment banks, brokers, and exchanges ensure that their staff and clients are well-informed and equipped to participate effectively in the financial markets.

These examples of cooperative initiatives and systems not only illustrate the commitment of financial market entities to enhancing efficiency and transparency but also highlight how collaboration is essential in adapting to the evolving needs of the global financial ecosystem.

Exam Tips: Focus Areas on Investment Banks, Brokers, and Exchanges for the SIE Exam

The Securities Industry Essentials (SIE) exam is designed to assess a foundational understanding of the securities industry, including the roles and functions of investment banks, brokers, and exchanges. Knowing what to focus on within these areas can significantly aid candidates in their exam preparation.

Investment Banks

- **Underwriting and Capital Markets**: Understand the processes of underwriting securities, including the roles of investment banks in IPOs and the mechanisms behind bond offerings. Expect questions on how investment banks price securities and manage offerings.

- **Advisory Services**: Be familiar with the services provided by investment banks in mergers and acquisitions (M&A), including advising on deal structure and valuation. Know the basics of how investment banks assist companies in restructuring and strategic financial planning.

- **Risk Management**: Learn how investment banks use various financial instruments to manage risk, including derivatives like futures, options, and swaps.

Brokers

- **Role and Responsibilities**: Know the primary functions of brokers in the financial markets, including executing trades and providing investment advice. Understand the types of accounts managed by brokers and the significance of each.

- **Regulatory Compliance**: Focus on the compliance and regulatory obligations of brokers, including ethical standards, reporting requirements, and the rules governing their interactions with clients.

- **Client Interaction and Support**: Be aware of how brokers facilitate client access to markets and the types of information and support they provide to investors.

Exchanges

- **Market Operations**: Understand the structure and function of exchanges, including how they facilitate trading through order types, market making, and electronic trading systems.

- **Price Discovery**: Grasp the concept of price discovery in exchanges, how supply and demand dynamics influence prices, and the role of liquidity in this process.

- **Regulatory Oversight and Market Surveillance**: Study how exchanges monitor trading activities and enforce market rules to prevent fraudulent and manipulative practices.

Exam Preparation Tips

1. **Practice Questions**: Focus on practice questions that cover the operations of investment banks, brokers, and exchanges. This will help you become familiar with the types of questions that are likely to appear on the exam.

2. **Summary Charts**: Create summary charts that compare and contrast the roles of these entities in the financial markets. This can help in visualizing their interconnections and understanding their unique functions.

3. **Real-World Applications**: Try to relate theoretical knowledge to real-world scenarios. Understanding practical applications can enhance your ability to recall information during the exam.

4. **Regulatory Focus**: Given the regulatory emphasis of the SIE exam, pay particular attention to any laws, regulations, and ethical considerations associated with investment banks, brokers, and exchanges.

By focusing on these areas, candidates can prepare more effectively for the SIE exam, ensuring a comprehensive understanding of the critical roles played by investment banks, brokers, and exchanges in the financial markets.

Importance of Regulatory Bodies in Financial Markets

Regulatory bodies play a crucial role in maintaining the integrity and stability of financial markets. These entities, which include organizations like the Securities and Exchange Commission (SEC), Financial Industry Regulatory Authority (FINRA), and Municipal Securities Rulemaking Board (MSRB), among others, are essential in establishing a framework that supports safe, fair, and efficient market operations. Their activities help protect investors, maintain order in the marketplace, and foster environments conducive to economic growth.

Protecting Investors

One of the primary roles of regulatory bodies is to protect investors from fraud, manipulation, and unethical practices that can lead to financial loss. These entities enforce rules and regulations that require transparency from issuers and market participants, ensuring that all material information is disclosed and that no deceptive practices are used. By holding participants to high ethical and operational standards, regulators help safeguard the investments made by individuals and institutions, enhancing investor confidence and participation in the markets.

- **Examples**: The SEC enforces stringent disclosure requirements for publicly traded companies, while FINRA oversees the behavior of brokerage firms and their agents to prevent misdealing with clients' funds and investments.

Maintaining Fair, Orderly, and Efficient Markets

Regulatory bodies are tasked with ensuring that financial markets operate in a fair, orderly, and efficient manner. This includes overseeing the mechanisms of trading, the dissemination of price information, and the execution of transactions.

- **Market Fairness**: By enforcing trading rules, regulators help prevent abusive trading practices and conflicts of interest, ensuring that no single participant can unfairly influence market prices.

- **Order and Efficiency**: Regulators monitor market activities to detect and deter disruptions that could lead to disorderly trading. This oversight helps prevent severe market volatility and ensures that markets react to changes in fundamentals rather than speculative or manipulative influences.

- **Example Initiatives**: The MSRB regulates bond trading to ensure fairness and transparency within the municipal bond market, while the SEC's oversight of securities exchanges guarantees that trading systems operate efficiently and reliably.

Facilitating Capital Formation

Regulatory bodies also play a significant role in facilitating capital formation, a critical process for economic development and growth. By ensuring that the securities markets operate smoothly and transparently, regulators help businesses access the capital they need to grow and expand.

- **Regulation of Offerings**: Regulators oversee the process by which companies issue new securities to ensure that the offerings are conducted in a manner that protects investors and meets legal standards. This oversight helps maintain investor trust in the market, which is crucial for companies looking to raise funds through public offerings.

- **Promoting Innovation**: Regulatory bodies also work to adapt and evolve market regulations to accommodate new financial technologies and investment products, thus supporting innovation within the financial markets.

regulatory bodies are indispensable to the proper functioning of financial markets. They ensure that markets operate smoothly, that investors are protected, and that companies can raise the funds they need to fuel growth and innovation. Through these efforts, regulators not only maintain the integrity and stability of financial markets but also contribute to the broader economic health.

Securities and Exchange Commission (SEC): Roles and Responsibilities

The Securities and Exchange Commission (SEC) is a crucial regulatory body in the United States, tasked with overseeing and regulating the securities markets to protect investors, maintain fair, orderly, and efficient markets, and facilitate capital formation. Established in the wake of the Great Depression, the SEC's mandate is to restore investor confidence in the transparency and integrity of the financial markets.

Primary Functions of the SEC

1. Overseeing Securities Transactions

- The SEC monitors and regulates the sale and transfer of securities to ensure that all transactions adhere to the laws designed to protect investors and the market. This oversight extends to all aspects of securities transactions, from the initial public offerings (IPOs) to secondary market trading. The SEC's oversight ensures that securities transactions are conducted in a manner that is fair to all participants.

2. Enforcing Securities Laws

- One of the most critical roles of the SEC is the enforcement of federal securities laws. The SEC actively investigates and prosecutes cases of market manipulation, fraud, insider trading, and other violations of securities law. This enforcement is essential to maintaining the integrity of the financial markets and protecting investors from unethical practices and financial harm.

3. Regulating Stock and Options Exchanges

- The SEC regulates major securities exchanges, such as the New York Stock Exchange (NYSE) and NASDAQ, ensuring that these marketplaces operate in a transparent and fair manner. This regulation includes overseeing the practices of the exchanges, the conduct of listed companies, and the actions of brokers and dealers.

Major Functions of the SEC

1. Enforcement of Securities Laws

- The SEC's enforcement division works to identify and prosecute violations of securities laws. They have the authority to bring civil suits against individuals and companies that break these laws, and they work closely with law enforcement agencies to tackle serious securities fraud and misconduct.

2. Oversight of Public Company Reporting

- The SEC requires public companies to disclose meaningful financial and other information to the public. This ensures that a company's investors, both potential and current, are provided with a transparent view of the company's operations and financial condition. The SEC reviews the documents filed by companies, such as annual and quarterly reports, to monitor their compliance with the law.

3. Regulation of Investment Management Firms

- Investment advisers, funds, and other investment management entities come under the SEC's regulatory purview. The SEC ensures that these firms comply with the legal standards intended to protect investors. This includes overseeing the practices and promoting the disclosure of mutual funds, hedge funds, and investment advisers.

Through its comprehensive regulatory and enforcement framework, the SEC plays a pivotal role in ensuring the stability and integrity of the U.S. financial markets. By enforcing rules, regulating entities, and overseeing transactions, the SEC helps create a safer and more transparent trading environment for all market participants.

Understanding the Financial Industry Regulatory Authority (FINRA)

The Financial Industry Regulatory Authority (FINRA) is a non-governmental organization vital to the regulation of brokerage firms and securities agents in the United States. Operating under the oversight of the Securities and Exchange Commission (SEC), FINRA ensures that the nation's brokerage firms operate ethically and comply with regulatory requirements, playing a crucial role in maintaining market integrity and protecting investors.

Role and Functionality of FINRA

FINRA regulates both the firms and professionals selling securities in the U.S. and oversees the operation of the U.S. brokerage firms and their branches. This includes monitoring trading activities in equities, corporate bonds, securities futures, and options. By ensuring that the securities industry operates fairly and honestly, FINRA helps safeguard the market against fraud and abuse, thereby enhancing investor protection.

One of FINRA's primary responsibilities is licensing brokers and other securities agents. It administers qualification exams to ensure that industry professionals meet adequate standards of expertise and ethical behavior. Once these agents are active, FINRA continues to enforce rules regarding their conduct to ensure they deal fairly with the public. This includes enforcing standards for transparent and honest communication about investment products and their risks, and fair pricing practices.

Dispute Resolution and Regulatory Exams

In addition to its regulatory functions, FINRA plays a key role in resolving disputes that arise between investors and brokers or between brokerage firms themselves. It operates the largest securities dispute resolution forum in the United States, facilitating arbitration and mediation to settle disagreements in a manner that is equitable, efficient, and less burdensome than traditional litigation.

Moreover, FINRA conducts comprehensive regulatory examinations of brokerage firms to ensure compliance with financial regulations. These exams are crucial for early identification of compliance issues and potential risks that could harm investors or the integrity of the market. By addressing these issues proactively, FINRA helps maintain a stable and reliable market environment.

Impact on the Securities Industry

Through its rigorous enforcement of regulations, effective dispute resolution mechanisms, and ongoing oversight and examinations, FINRA helps ensure that the securities industry remains a fair and trustworthy market for investors and maintains its critical role in the overall financial system of the United States.

Municipal Securities Rulemaking Board (MSRB): Ensuring Integrity in the Municipal Securities Market

The Municipal Securities Rulemaking Board (MSRB) is a regulatory body that plays a critical role in the United States financial markets by overseeing the municipal securities sector. This includes bonds issued by cities, towns, and states to fund public projects such as schools, highways, and infrastructure development.

Role and Responsibilities

The MSRB is charged with protecting investors, municipal entities, and the public interest by promoting a fair and efficient municipal securities market. It achieves this by regulating securities firms, banks, and municipal advisors that engage in municipal bond transactions. The MSRB's authority is derived from the Securities Exchange Act of 1934, and it operates under the oversight of the Securities and Exchange Commission (SEC).

One of the MSRB's primary roles is to establish rules that safeguard the practices of selling and advising on municipal securities. By setting standards for fair dealing and ethical conduct, the MSRB ensures that financial professionals in the municipal bond market act in the best interests of state and local governments, and taxpayers who rely on municipal bonds to fund essential public projects.

Regulatory Focus

1. Rule-making

The MSRB engages in comprehensive rule-making to address evolving market practices and potential risks in the municipal securities market. These rules cover a wide range of activities, including trading, pricing, transparency, underwriting, and the fiduciary responsibilities of municipal advisors.

The MSRB's rules are designed to prevent fraudulent and manipulative acts and practices, promoting a fair and equitable market.

2. Market Transparency Initiatives

One of the MSRB's significant contributions to the municipal market is its focus on enhancing market transparency. The MSRB operates the Electronic Municipal Market Access (EMMA) website, a comprehensive public online database that provides free access to municipal securities data and documents. This includes real-time trade price reporting and disclosures related to municipal bond issues, which helps investors make informed decisions.

3. Investor Protection Policies

Protecting investors is at the heart of the MSRB's mission. The board creates policies that ensure investors have access to essential information and are treated fairly in transactions. This includes rules regarding disclosure of bond information, conflicts of interest, and the conduct of brokers and advisors in the municipal securities market.

State Regulators in the U.S. Securities Market

State regulators play a crucial role in overseeing securities transactions within their jurisdictions. These entities, often referred to as State Securities Regulators, are primarily responsible for enforcing state securities laws, also known as "Blue Sky" laws, which are designed to protect investors from fraud.

Role and Responsibilities

State regulators oversee a broad range of activities related to securities within their states, ensuring that all participants comply with both state and federal securities laws. Their responsibilities include:

- **Regulatory Oversight**: State regulators monitor the activities of brokers, dealers, investment advisers, and other financial professionals operating within their jurisdiction. This oversight is crucial for maintaining the integrity of the securities market at the state level and for protecting local investors.

- **Coordination with Federal Regulators**: State regulators work closely with federal agencies, such as the Securities and Exchange Commission (SEC) and the Financial Industry Regulatory Authority (FINRA), to ensure that securities practices comply with nationwide standards. This coordination helps create a cohesive regulatory environment across state and federal levels, facilitating effective oversight of cross-state operations.

Areas of Influence

1. Licensing

State regulators are responsible for the licensing of brokerage firms, investment advisors, and their representatives operating within their states. This process involves reviewing applications to ensure that candidates meet all the necessary qualifications and adhere to ethical standards. Licensing is a critical function as it helps ensure that only qualified and reliable professionals are permitted to offer investment advice and services.

2. Compliance Inspections

Regular inspections of registered firms are conducted to ensure ongoing compliance with securities laws and regulations. These inspections help identify issues such as poor record-keeping, inadequate supervisory practices, or other compliance failures that could pose risks to investors. By addressing these issues proactively, state regulators help maintain high standards of practice within the financial services industry.

3. Enforcement of State Securities Laws

State regulators have the authority to enforce state securities laws through investigations and legal actions against entities and individuals who violate these laws. Enforcement actions can include fines, restitution orders, and the suspension or revocation of licenses. These measures are essential for deterring misconduct and protecting the public from fraudulent investment schemes and unethical practices.

Self-Regulatory Organizations (SROs) in Financial Markets

Self-Regulatory Organizations (SROs) are non-governmental organizations that have the authority to create and enforce industry regulations for their members. SROs play a critical role in the oversight of the financial markets, supplementing governmental regulation by applying their specialized knowledge and resources to regulate specific aspects of the industry effectively.

Definition and Examples

SROs are private organizations that regulate their members through the adoption of rules designed to ensure fair and ethical business practices. Unlike government agencies, which are funded and run by the government, SROs operate independently, although they must comply with broader government regulations and are subject to government oversight.

Examples of SROs include:

- **Financial Industry Regulatory Authority (FINRA)**: Perhaps the most well-known SRO, FINRA oversees U.S. brokerage firms and exchange markets, ensuring that the securities industry operates fairly and honestly.

- **National Futures Association (NFA)**: This organization regulates the futures market, including derivatives and swaps, focusing on the protection of investors and the integrity of the markets.

- **Major Stock Exchanges**: Many stock exchanges, such as the New York Stock Exchange (NYSE) and NASDAQ, function as SROs, regulating their own operations and the activities of their members.

- **Industry Councils**: These include organizations like the Municipal Securities Rulemaking Board (MSRB), which regulates municipal securities dealers, and other councils that focus on specific sectors of the financial markets.

Regulatory Functions

1. Rule-making

SROs have the authority to develop and implement rules that govern the conduct of their members. These rules are designed to protect investors from fraud, ensure market transparency, and enhance the integrity of the financial markets. For example, FINRA develops rules that brokers and dealers must follow, covering everything from trading practices to how they manage confidential client information.

2. Enforcement

SROs enforce compliance with their regulations through monitoring, examinations, and disciplinary actions. They have the power to impose penalties, including fines, suspensions, and the expulsion of members who violate the rules. This enforcement mechanism is vital for maintaining investor confidence in the integrity of the markets.

3. Dispute Resolution

Many SROs provide mechanisms for resolving disputes between their members and between their members and the public. This service includes arbitration and mediation services, which help resolve conflicts efficiently without the need for court litigation, thus saving time and resources for all parties involved.

4. Market Surveillance

SROs conduct surveillance of trading activities to detect and prevent manipulative and fraudulent trading practices. They use sophisticated technology to monitor trades and ensure that the markets function smoothly and transparently.

Interaction Among Regulators in Financial Markets

Regulatory bodies in the financial markets often collaborate to ensure that the markets operate smoothly, transparently, and fairly. This cooperation is crucial for bridging regulatory gaps, enhancing market surveillance, and maintaining high standards across different segments of the market.

Cooperative Efforts

Regulators such as the Securities and Exchange Commission (SEC), Financial Industry Regulatory Authority (FINRA), Municipal Securities Rulemaking Board (MSRB), and various state regulators, along with Self-Regulatory Organizations (SROs), work together in a number of ways:

- **Shared Information and Data**: Regulatory bodies frequently share information and data to monitor market activities more effectively and prevent fraud. This collaboration helps in identifying irregularities that might indicate manipulative practices or potential threats to market integrity.

- **Joint Rulemaking**: Often, regulators collaborate on rulemaking to ensure consistency in regulations that affect multiple areas of the financial markets. This helps in creating a uniform regulatory environment that applies to all market participants, regardless of which regulator oversees them.

- **Coordinated Examinations and Audits**: Regulators sometimes conduct joint examinations of financial entities to streamline the process and reduce the regulatory burden on market participants. This coordination ensures thorough oversight while minimizing duplication of efforts.

Example Initiatives

Several initiatives illustrate how these regulatory bodies work together to enhance regulatory standards and improve market surveillance:

- **Consolidated Audit Trail (CAT)**: Initiated by the SEC and involving multiple SROs, including FINRA and the exchanges, the CAT is designed to track orders throughout their life cycle and identify the market participants handling them. This comprehensive database enhances the ability of regulators to monitor and analyze market activity, aiding in the detection and investigation of market misconduct.

- **Cross-Market Surveillance Group**: Comprising various SROs and led by FINRA, this group focuses on identifying and investigating fraudulent activities that span multiple markets and jurisdictions. By pooling resources and sharing expertise, the group enhances the detection of complex fraud schemes that might otherwise evade single-market surveillance.

- **Intermarket Surveillance Group (ISG)**: An international group of exchanges and regulators, including both U.S. and international entities, the ISG promotes and enhances cooperative efforts to prevent market manipulation and fraud. The group facilitates the exchange of information related to market surveillance and regulatory practices, improving the global oversight of securities markets.

- **Protocol for Broker Recruiting**: This is a joint initiative by multiple regulatory bodies designed to regulate how brokers move between firms and how they handle client lists during transitions. The protocol helps protect client privacy and prevents disputes between firms over client poaching.

Recap of Regulatory Roles

Regulatory bodies such as the Securities and Exchange Commission (SEC), Financial Industry Regulatory Authority (FINRA), Municipal Securities Rulemaking Board (MSRB), and various state regulators play pivotal roles in maintaining the integrity and stability of the financial markets. Here's a brief recap of their roles:

- **SEC**: Overseeing and regulating all participants and processes in the securities industry, including exchanges, brokers, and public companies. The SEC ensures transparency, fights illegal activities, and protects investors from fraudulent practices.

- **FINRA**: As a self-regulatory organization, FINRA specifically focuses on governing the conduct of brokerage firms and their agents, ensuring they operate in an honest and fair manner.

- **MSRB**: Specializing in the municipal securities market, the MSRB ensures that the market for state and local government bonds is secure, fair, and transparent.

- **State Regulators**: These entities enforce state securities laws and regulations, providing local oversight of securities transactions and professional practices within their jurisdictions.

Importance of Regulatory Bodies

Regulatory bodies are crucial for fostering a secure investment environment. They implement and enforce rules that maintain market integrity and protect investor funds. By ensuring that financial markets operate under strict guidelines and transparent processes, these organizations build investor trust, which is essential for the healthy functioning of the financial system.

Their role in investor protection also includes educating the public on investment risks and rights, which further helps to make the markets more accessible and safer for retail and institutional investors alike.

Emphasis in the SIE Exam

In the Securities Industry Essentials (SIE) exam, candidates are likely to encounter topics that emphasize the importance of regulatory knowledge:

- **Understanding Regulatory Frameworks**: Candidates need to understand the scope of each regulatory body's authority and the specific regulations they enforce.

- **Compliance Obligations**: Knowledge of compliance requirements for financial firms and professionals, which ensures that those entering the industry are aware of the legal and ethical standards they must adhere to.

- **Investor Protection Measures**: The exam covers how regulatory actions protect investors, which is crucial for anyone looking to work in the securities industry.

These insights into the roles and importance of regulatory bodies not only prepare candidates for the SIE exam but also provide a foundational understanding essential for a successful career in finance. Understanding these principles ensures that future securities professionals appreciate the significance of regulatory compliance and investor protection in their daily operations.

Understanding Capital Markets and Their Participants

Capital markets are essential financial sectors where savings and investments are transferred between those who have capital and those who need it. These markets, encompassing venues for trading securities such as stocks and bonds, are crucial for the smooth functioning of a modern economy.

Role in the Economy

Capital markets perform several vital functions. They allocate resources efficiently, allowing capital to flow to its most productive uses which enhances economic growth and development. Through the mechanism of price discovery, capital markets determine the value of securities, reflecting the collective judgment of all market participants about the future prospects of public companies and other entities. They manage financial risks by enabling the trading of diverse financial instruments, offering opportunities for risk diversification.

Capital markets also provide liquidity, making it easier for investors to convert securities into cash quickly and with minimal loss in value. This liquidity is essential for encouraging investment and fostering economic activity. Furthermore, these markets aggregate and coordinate information from various sources, which is reflected in securities prices and guides investment and consumption decisions.

Importance of Market Participants

The efficiency and stability of capital markets rely heavily on the roles played by various participants:

- **Investors**, including both individuals and institutions, supply the capital that fuels economic activities. Their investment choices directly affect sectors and industries.

- **Issuers** such as companies and governments raise funds for expansion and development projects by selling securities.

- **Intermediaries**, including brokers, dealers, and investment banks, facilitate market transactions, offer advisory services, and ensure liquidity and price stability.

- **Regulators** ensure that the markets operate transparently and fairly, maintaining investor confidence and protecting their interests.

- **Supportive Entities** like market makers, rating agencies, and clearinghouses provide the necessary infrastructure to ensure the market functions smoothly and remains stable.

Understanding the functions of these participants is critical. It helps stakeholders navigate the financial landscape effectively, fosters informed investment decisions, and deepens comprehension of how regulatory frameworks and market dynamics influence economic outcomes. This knowledge is especially crucial for investors looking to optimize their investment strategies and for entities aiming to leverage these markets for fundraising.

Chapter 2: Introduction - Products and Their Risks

Understanding Investment Products

Investment products form the backbone of financial markets, offering numerous opportunities for wealth creation and income generation. Each type of investment, from stocks to bonds to alternative assets, serves a unique role in a portfolio, catering to different investor needs, time horizons, and risk tolerances. For candidates preparing for the SIE exam, a deep understanding of these products is not just about passing a test; it's about laying a foundational knowledge that will aid in making informed investment decisions throughout a financial career.

The Dual Relevance of Knowledge

The complexity and variety of investment products mean that they each carry inherent risks which can vary greatly in nature and magnitude. Recognizing these risks and knowing how to navigate them is crucial. This knowledge is equally important for exam success and real-world financial planning. By mastering the details of these products, candidates can better prepare themselves not only to achieve a passing score on the SIE exam but also to excel in practical financial decision-making scenarios.

Importance for the SIE Exam

The Securities Industry Essentials (SIE) Exam tests an aspiring professional's knowledge of basic securities industry information including the structure and function of the markets, regulatory agencies and their functions, and the underlying securities products. Understanding the risks associated with these products is a significant part of the exam, emphasizing not only the ability to recognize different investment vehicles but also to understand the inherent risks they pose. In practice, the ability to assess and manage investment risks directly influences the success of financial strategies. Professionals who can effectively identify the risks associated with different investment products can offer better advice, anticipate market changes more effectively, and develop more robust investment strategies that optimize returns while managing exposure to loss.

The Role of Stocks in Capital Markets

What are Stocks?

Stocks, also known as equities, represent ownership shares in a company. When investors buy stocks, they essentially purchase a part of the company's assets and earnings. Stocks play a crucial role in capital markets as they allow companies to raise capital by selling shares to investors. This capital is typically used for expansion, research, and other activities that contribute to the company's growth, which in turn can lead to economic growth at a broader scale. Imagine stocks as small pieces of a company's future potential that are bought and sold in vibrant marketplaces, much like items in a bustling bazaar.

Common Stocks: The Backbone of Equity Investments

Common stocks are the most prevalent type of stock that investors encounter. Holding common stocks provides shareholders with the right to vote at shareholder meetings and to receive dividends, although dividends are not guaranteed and can vary based on the company's profitability.

Features of Common Stocks

- **Voting Rights**: Each share typically grants the shareholder one vote, empowering them to vote on important company decisions, including the election of the board of directors. This is akin to having a vote in the election of a city's council members, where each vote influences the city's future.

- **Dividends**: Common stocks may provide dividends, which are a share of the company's profits distributed to shareholders. The distribution and amount of dividends can fluctuate and are not guaranteed. Dividends are like fruits that grow on a tree you partly own; the healthier the tree (company), the more fruits (dividends) it might bear.

- **Capital Appreciation**: Besides dividends, stockholders often benefit from capital appreciation, which occurs when the stock's market price rises above the price initially paid. This is similar to buying a piece of art; its value may increase over time as it becomes more desirable.

- **Liquidity**: Common stocks are generally liquid, meaning they can be quickly and easily sold in the public market. This liquidity is like being able to sell your car at a fair market price relatively quickly when you decide you no longer need it.

The Significance of Common Stocks in an Investment Portfolio

Common stocks are a fundamental component of many investment portfolios because they offer the potential for high returns. However, they also come with higher risks compared to bonds or other fixed-income investments. This risk arises from market volatility and the uncertainty of returns, particularly in the short term. Over the long term, however, equities have historically provided substantial returns to investors who can withstand market ups and downs, making them an essential part of a balanced investment strategy.

By investing in common stocks, investors essentially bet on a company's future, taking part in its potential success or failure. This dynamic makes common stocks an exciting, though risky, investment that can teach valuable lessons about both the company's strategic direction and broader market trends. Understanding these aspects is crucial for anyone preparing for the SIE exam and for practical financial planning.

Risks Associated with Common Stocks

Market Volatility

Market volatility refers to the fluctuations in stock prices that occur in stock markets. This can be imagined as a sea with its ever-changing tides. Just as calm seas can suddenly turn stormy, stock prices can swing widely in a short period due to various factors, including economic indicators, changes in market sentiment, and global events. Volatility is a double-edged sword; it presents opportunities for high returns when prices swing favorably, but it also poses significant risk as prices could plummet.

For example, during the financial crisis of 2008, the stock market experienced extreme volatility, with the S&P 500 index losing about 38% of its value over the year. Investors who understand this risk know that stock investing requires a stomach for this kind of roller coaster ride, much like a surfer needs to understand and respect the powerful waves they ride.

Company Performance

The performance of the company whose stocks an investor holds is another critical risk factor. This can be compared to a hot air balloon ride; the quality of the balloon and the expertise of the operator (company management) critically influence whether the ride (investment) will soar high or take a disappointing turn. Stocks in a company are directly impacted by how well the company is managed and how effectively it can capitalize on opportunities and navigate challenges.

For instance, a company that fails to innovate or keep up with its competitors may see its profits decline, which in turn can lead to a fall in its stock price. Conversely, a company that launches a successful new product or enters a new market may see its stock price rise. An example of this is Apple Inc., which saw significant increases in its stock price following the successful launch of innovative products like the iPhone and iPad, which reshaped the tech landscape.

Interplay of Market Volatility and Company Performance

It's essential to recognize that these risks are often interrelated. Market volatility can exacerbate the effects of poor company performance, and vice versa. Investors need to be adept at reading these interconnected signals to navigate the stock markets effectively. This understanding is crucial not only for passing the SIE exam but also for making informed investment decisions in real-world scenarios.

Understanding these risks and learning to manage them through diversified investments and a clear, long-term investment strategy can help mitigate the impact and leverage opportunities that arise from market volatility and company performance.

Preferred Stocks: Understanding the Hybrid Features

What are Preferred Stocks?

Preferred stocks are often described as a hybrid between bonds and common stocks, combining elements of both. Think of them as a "VIP pass" within the corporate finance world; they provide some privileges that common stocks do not, primarily in how dividends are handled.

Features of Preferred Stocks

Dividend Prioritization

One of the key features of preferred stocks is dividend prioritization. Holders of preferred stocks are entitled to receive dividends before common stockholders in the event of a payout. This can be likened to having a "first dibs" ticket at a concert, where you get priority access to the seats or experiences before the general ticket holders. This feature makes preferred stocks particularly attractive during economic downturns or in situations where a company's cash flow becomes constrained, as it provides a layer of security concerning dividend payments.

Lack of Voting Rights

Unlike common stockholders, preferred shareholders typically do not have voting rights. This can be compared to being a season ticket holder for a sports team but not having a say in the team's management or strategic decisions. The trade-off here is stability versus control; while preferred stockholders enjoy more stable returns, they have little influence over corporate governance.

Convertibility

Some preferred stocks come with an option to convert into a specified number of common shares, usually at the discretion of the shareholder. This feature is similar to holding a ticket to an event that can be upgraded to a VIP pass under certain conditions. It offers the potential for capital appreciation while providing income stability.

Callable Feature

Preferred stocks are often callable, meaning the issuing company can buy them back at a predetermined price after a certain date. This is akin to a lease with a buy-back clause; the company leases capital from investors with the option to terminate the lease (repurchase the shares) under predefined conditions. This feature is beneficial for the issuing company as it allows them to reduce dividend expenses when it is financially advantageous to do so.

The Role of Preferred Stocks in an Investment Portfolio

Preferred stocks occupy a niche position in investment portfolios, offering a blend of risk and return that attracts conservative investors seeking higher yields than bonds but lower risk than common stocks. Their unique features, particularly the prioritization of dividends and lack of voting rights, make them an important tool for investors looking for income with relatively lower volatility.

Understanding the nuanced features of preferred stocks is crucial for any financial professional and is particularly emphasized in securities examinations like the SIE. Recognizing the role and functionality of preferred stocks helps in crafting diversified investment strategies and understanding corporate financial structures.

Risks of Preferred Stocks

Fixed Dividends: Double-Edged Sword

Preferred stocks typically offer fixed dividends, which means the dividend amount does not change regardless of the company's profitability. While this feature provides a predictable income stream, akin to a fixed salary in a job, it also limits the potential for income growth that might be available through common stocks, which can offer rising dividends in line with increasing profits. The fixed dividend of preferred stocks can be seen as a double-edged sword—providing stability but capping potential upside.

For instance, in a booming market where companies are seeing significant profit growth, preferred shareholders will not benefit from increased dividends beyond their fixed rate. This situation is similar to being on a fixed contract salary in a rapidly growing industry; you watch others ride the wave of success while your income remains constant, regardless of the surrounding economic prosperity.

Callable Features: Company's Option, Investor's Risk

The callable feature of preferred stocks allows the issuing company to repurchase the stock from shareholders at predetermined times and prices. This feature is generally favorable to the company but poses a risk to investors. Imagine planning a long, scenic road trip (representing the long-term holding of a high-yield stock), only to find out part-way that you must return the rental car (the stock being called back by the company) because the rental agency (the issuing company) needs it back sooner than expected.

This can be particularly disruptive if the call happens during favorable market conditions, where the preferred stock is paying higher dividends than what could be obtained elsewhere. When the stocks are called, investors are forced to reinvest their capital, potentially at lower yields. The call feature is similar to a landlord who has the right to terminate a lease under certain conditions; just as a tenant might have to leave a desirable living situation, an investor might have to exit an investment prematurely and under less favorable conditions.

Strategic Considerations

Investors must weigh these risks when considering preferred stocks. Fixed dividends provide predictable returns but lack upside potential, while the callable nature of these stocks can lead to reinvestment risk. Understanding these risks is essential for anyone preparing for the SIE exam and for investors aiming to build a balanced, informed portfolio.

Corporate Bonds

Overview: Corporate Bonds as Investment Vehicles

Corporate bonds are essentially loans that investors make to companies. In exchange for borrowing the money, the company agrees to pay back the principal amount on a predetermined maturity date, along with interest payments at specified intervals, typically semi-annually. This is akin to giving a loan to a neighbor for starting a business, where in return, they agree to pay you regular interest until the full amount is repaid by a certain date.

The Role of Corporate Bonds in the Market

Corporate bonds serve as critical tools for companies looking to raise capital without diluting ownership through issuing additional stock. Imagine a company wants to expand its operations, buy new equipment, or refinance existing debts; issuing bonds allows it to secure the necessary funds while keeping control firmly in the hands of current shareholders. For investors, corporate bonds offer a relatively safe investment compared to stocks because they provide regular income through interest payments and are generally prioritized over stocks in case of bankruptcy.

Investing in Corporate Bonds

When investors purchase a corporate bond, they are buying a piece of the company's debt. This debt is categorized by different levels of risk depending on the creditworthiness of the issuing company. Credit rating agencies assign ratings to these bonds, reflecting the company's ability to repay its debts. High-rated bonds (like AAA) are deemed safer but typically offer lower interest rates, much like a well-secured loan with lower interest due to the reduced risk. Conversely, lower-rated bonds, known as high-yield or "junk" bonds, offer higher returns but come with an increased risk of default.

Benefits and Drawbacks

One of the main attractions of corporate bonds is their potential to provide steady, predictable returns. They are less volatile than stocks, making them an appealing choice for conservative investors or those nearing retirement who prioritize income over growth. However, they are not without risks—economic downturns or poor management decisions can affect a company's ability to make interest payments or to repay the bond at maturity. This is similar to lending money to a friend whose financial stability is uncertain; while the promised interest sounds appealing, there's always the risk they might not manage their finances well enough to pay you back.

By understanding corporate bonds as investment vehicles, potential investors can make informed decisions that align with their financial goals and risk tolerance. This knowledge is not only crucial for the SIE exam but also for practical investment strategies in real-life scenarios

Coupon Rates: The Pulse of a Bond's Value

Understanding Coupon Rates

The coupon rate of a bond is the annual interest rate paid on the bond's face value by the bond's issuer. It is called a "coupon" because historically, bonds had physical coupons attached that bondholders would clip and redeem to receive their interest payments. In today's electronic age, the process is automated, but the principle remains the same. Think of the coupon rate as the steady heartbeat of the bond, providing a rhythmic cash flow to investors that is predictable and reliable.

Impact on Bond Pricing

The coupon rate directly influences the price of a bond in the secondary market. Bonds are typically issued at par value (often $1,000), but their market price can fluctuate based on changes in interest rates in the economy. If interest rates rise above the bond's coupon rate, the bond's price will usually fall below its face value, selling at a discount. Conversely, if interest rates fall below the bond's coupon rate, the bond's price will rise, selling at a premium.

This dynamic can be compared to a seesaw, where the bond's price and the prevailing interest rates are on opposite ends. When interest rates go up, the bond's price goes down, and when interest rates drop, the bond's price goes up. This inverse relationship is a fundamental principle of bond investing.

Coupon Rates and Yield

The yield of a bond refers to the return an investor can expect to receive by holding the bond until maturity, and it can vary from the coupon rate based on the bond's price. For instance, if you buy a bond at a discount (below par value), your yield will be higher than the coupon rate because you paid less for the bond but still receive the full coupon payments. Conversely, if you purchase a bond at a premium, your yield will be lower because you paid more for the bond relative to its coupon payments.

Using a simple example, imagine you buy a bond with a $1,000 face value and a 5% coupon rate for $900. You'll still receive $50 annually (5% of $1,000), but since you only paid $900, your yield is approximately 5.56%. This higher yield reflects the discount at which you purchased the bond.

Strategic Implications

Understanding how coupon rates affect bond pricing and yield is crucial for investors who need to manage the income generation and risk of their portfolios effectively. Just as a gardener must understand the amount of water each plant needs, investors must understand how changes in interest rates affect the bond values and yields to nurture and protect their investment portfolios.

Grasping the concept of coupon rates and their impact on bond pricing and yield is not only key for those preparing for the SIE exam but also for anyone involved in bond investing, providing a solid foundation for making informed financial decisions.

Maturity Terms: Timing the Investment Horizon

Understanding Maturity Terms

The maturity term of a bond is the time period at the end of which the bond will expire, and the principal amount (the initial loan amount) is repaid to the bondholder. Maturity terms can range from a few months to several decades, and they are a critical factor in bond investment decisions. Like planning a journey, where short trips offer quick returns home while longer expeditions promise extended experiences but require more commitment, short-term and long-term bonds cater to different investor needs and risk profiles.

Short-Term Bonds

Short-term bonds are typically those with maturities of less than five years. These bonds are akin to a sprint in the world of athletics; they are over quickly, meaning they return the principal to investors sooner, which reduces the exposure to risks like interest rate changes over the long run. This can be particularly appealing during periods of volatility or when interest rates are expected to rise, as the shorter duration limits the potential for bond values to decrease. Investors might prefer short-term bonds when they seek less risk and need liquidity or when they anticipate needing access to their invested capital in the near future.

Long-Term Bonds

On the other hand, long-term bonds, with maturities often exceeding ten years, are more like a marathon. They require a long-term commitment and are generally associated with higher yields to compensate for the greater risk of interest rate fluctuations over time. The longer duration allows more time for interest to compound on reinvested coupon payments, potentially increasing the total returns. However, these bonds are more susceptible to price volatility due to changes in interest rates; if rates rise, the bond's fixed interest payments become less attractive relative to newer issues that might offer higher rates.

Investment Implications

Choosing between short-term and long-term bonds involves balancing yield against risk. Long-term bonds often suit investors looking for higher yields and who are comfortable with the risk of price fluctuations. In contrast, short-term bonds are preferable for those prioritizing stability and quick return of capital. The decision is similar to choosing between planting annuals, which bloom quickly and last for a season, and perennials, which take longer to establish but provide beauty for many years. Investors need to consider their financial goals, risk tolerance, and time horizon when selecting the maturity term of the bonds in their portfolios.

Strategic Considerations

knowing the implications of bond maturities is essential for effective portfolio management. Just as a gardener chooses plants that will thrive in the available growing season, investors must select bond maturities that align with their investment horizon and income needs. This knowledge is crucial for anyone preparing for the SIE exam and for investors aiming to construct a diversified and resilient investment portfolio.

This detailed exploration of maturity terms sheds light on how they influence investment strategies, providing a foundational understanding that is vital for both exam preparation and real-world investing.

Credit Risk: Evaluating the Stability of Your Investment

Understanding Credit Risk

Credit risk in the context of corporate bonds refers to the potential for a bond issuer to default on their financial obligations to bondholders, which includes failing to make scheduled interest payments or not repaying the principal at maturity. Imagine lending money to a friend; the certainty that you'll be repaid depends greatly on your friend's financial stability and reliability. Similarly, the safety of investing in corporate bonds hinges on the issuer's financial health and stability.

The Role of Credit Ratings

Credit ratings, assigned by rating agencies such as Moody's, Standard & Poor's, and Fitch, serve as a gauge of the issuer's creditworthiness. These ratings are akin to a report card that evaluates a student's performance and likelihood of success in future courses based on past achievement. In bond investing, higher ratings (AAA to AA) suggest a low risk of default, indicating that the bond issuer is in robust financial health and has a strong ability to meet its debt obligations. Conversely, lower ratings (BBB and below) indicate higher credit risk, suggesting financial instability or challenging economic conditions for the issuer.

Impact of Credit Ratings on Bond Prices

The credit rating of a bond directly influences its price and yield. Bonds with high credit ratings are seen as safer investments, and thus they typically offer lower yields compared to bonds with lower credit ratings, which must offer higher yields to attract investors. This relationship is similar to insurance premiums; safer cars cost less to insure, just as safer bonds cost less in terms of yield.

For example, consider two companies—Company A has an AAA rating while Company B has a BB rating. Investors will demand a higher yield from Company B to compensate for the greater risk of default. This demand affects bond prices in the secondary market: if investors perceive increased risk, they will be less willing to pay a high price for bonds, which drives down the bond's price.

Credit Risk and Investment Strategy

 managing credit risk is crucial for bond investors. It requires a careful analysis of the issuer's financial statements, market position, and economic environment, as well as ongoing monitoring of any factors that might affect the issuer's ability to meet its obligations. For investors, this risk assessment is not unlike a mechanic's evaluation of a car; just as the mechanic predicts future problems based on current conditions, investors must assess potential risks based on current and projected financial health of the bond issuer.

Credit risk adds a layer of complexity to bond investing but also presents opportunities for higher returns. Investors willing to take on higher credit risks might achieve greater yields, but this requires a tolerance for potential volatility and an understanding of market dynamics.

Government Bonds

Overview: The Spectrum of Government Bonds

Government bonds are essentially loans provided by investors to governmental entities. Just like lending money to a trusted family member with the assurance they will repay you, government bonds are considered low-risk because they are backed by the government's ability to tax its citizens or print money. However, not all government bonds are created equal; they vary by the level of government issuing them, their purposes, and their repayment terms.

Types of Government Bonds

Treasuries

Issued by the federal government, Treasury bonds are seen as one of the safest investment options available because they are backed by the "full faith and credit" of the U.S. government. This category includes:

- **Treasury Bills (T-Bills)**: Short-term securities that mature in one year or less. They do not pay periodic interest but are sold at a discount to face value. The return to investors is the difference between the purchase price and the amount paid at maturity.

- **Treasury Notes (T-Notes)**: Medium-term securities that mature between two and ten years. T-Notes pay semi-annual interest at a fixed rate and are highly popular for their balance of yield and security.

- **Treasury Bonds (T-Bonds)**: Long-term securities with terms typically extending 20 to 30 years. Like T-Notes, they pay semi-annual interest and are used by the government to fund longer-term financial needs.

Municipal Bonds

Issued by states, cities, counties, and other local government entities, municipal bonds or "munis" are primarily used to fund public projects like roads, schools, and infrastructure. Munis come in two primary forms:

- **General Obligation Bonds**: These are backed by the full faith and credit of the issuing municipality and are supported by the issuer's taxing power. Investing in general obligation bonds is like lending money to a well-established business with a steady income—relatively safe with a reliable return.

- **Revenue Bonds**: Unlike general obligation bonds, revenue bonds are supported by the revenue from the specific project they are issued to fund, such as a toll bridge or a public utility. This makes them more like investing in a start-up business that relies on the success of its sole product for income.

Investment Considerations

Choosing between these types of government bonds involves assessing risk tolerance, investment timeline, and tax considerations. Treasuries offer unparalleled security and are excellent for conservative investors, while municipal bonds offer tax advantages that may appeal to those in higher tax brackets looking to reduce taxable income.

Understanding the different types of government bonds and their unique characteristics is essential for any financial professional and particularly for those preparing for the SIE exam. It equips candidates with the knowledge to navigate the complexities of the bond market

Treasuries: The Bedrock of Financial Security

Features of Treasuries

Treasuries, issued by the U.S. Department of the Treasury, are government securities that represent a loan by the investor to the federal government. These instruments include Treasury bills (T-bills), Treasury notes (T-notes), and Treasury bonds (T-bonds), each differing primarily in their term lengths:

- **Treasury Bills**: Short-term instruments that mature in one year or less. They are sold at a discount and do not pay periodic interest, rather the profit is made at maturity when they are redeemed for their full face value.

- **Treasury Notes**: Medium-term securities that have maturities ranging from two to ten years. T-notes pay investors a fixed interest rate every six months, making them attractive for those seeking steady income.

- **Treasury Bonds**: Long-term securities, with maturities extending up to 30 years. Like T-notes, T-bonds offer semi-annual interest payments at a fixed rate.

The structured variety of Treasuries makes them a versatile tool for different investment strategies, akin to having different types of tools in a toolkit—each one designed for a specific task, from quick repairs (T-bills) to long-term projects (T-bonds).

Safety of Treasuries

Treasuries are widely regarded as one of the safest investments available. This is because they are backed by the "full faith and credit" of the U.S. government, which has the power to tax its citizens and print currency—measures that virtually guarantee the government's ability to meet its debt obligations. Investing in Treasuries is like placing your money in a vault within a fortified castle; the security is unparalleled because the backing authority is the most powerful entity in the land.

Liquidity of Treasuries

One of the most compelling features of Treasuries is their high liquidity. Treasuries are among the most heavily traded securities in the world, meaning they can be easily bought or sold in the open market at prevailing market prices. This liquidity is similar to water in a municipal supply system—always available when you need it, and easily accessible. For investors, this means that Treasuries can be quickly converted into cash, providing flexibility to adjust portfolios or respond to changes in the financial landscape without significant price concessions.

Strategic Role in Investment Portfolios

The combination of safety, predictable income, and liquidity makes Treasuries a cornerstone of conservative investment strategies, particularly suitable for risk-averse investors or those nearing retirement. They are also used extensively for diversifying investment portfolios and hedging against market volatility. Just as a balanced diet combines various food types to maintain health, a balanced portfolio incorporates secure assets like Treasuries to manage and mitigate risk.

the unique characteristics of Treasuries is crucial for financial professionals, especially those preparing for the SIE exam. It equips them with the knowledge to recommend and manage these instruments effectively, ensuring clients can achieve their financial goals with an appropriate level of risk.

Municipal Bonds: Investing in Community Growth

Tax Benefits of Municipal Bonds

Municipal bonds, often called "munis," offer significant tax advantages that are a key attraction for investors. The interest income earned from most municipal bonds is exempt from federal income tax, and if the bonds are issued within the state where the investor resides, they may also be exempt from state and local taxes. This triple tax exemption is akin to a tax shield, protecting portions of an investor's income from taxes much like an umbrella shields you from rain. For investors in higher tax brackets, this can translate to a substantially higher effective yield compared to taxable bonds with similar risk profiles.

Use of Proceeds

The funds raised through municipal bonds are typically used for public projects that enhance the community and local infrastructure—such as schools, highways, hospitals, and water treatment facilities. Investing in municipal bonds can be likened to investing in the future of one's community. The money you lend to the local government not only earns you interest but also plays a part in building and maintaining the civic infrastructure that benefits everyone in the area. It's a way to see your investment dollars at work locally, improving streets, schools, and utilities, contributing to the overall quality of life.

Credit Risks of Municipal Bonds

While municipal bonds are generally considered safe, they are not without risk. Credit risk in munis depends on the financial health of the issuing authority. General obligation bonds, which are backed by the full faith and credit of the issuer (and supported by the issuer's taxing power), typically carry lower credit risk. Revenue bonds, however, are secured by specific revenue sources, which could be less predictable. This setup is somewhat like a business relying solely on the revenue from a new product line—any disruption in the expected revenue (such as lower demand or regulatory changes) can impact the ability to meet financial obligations.

The credit risk of municipal bonds can vary widely from one issuer to another, making thorough analysis crucial. Economic downturns, budget shortfalls, and changes in tax policies can all adversely affect an issuer's creditworthiness. Investors must assess not just the bond's initial rating but also keep an eye on any changes in the issuer's financial conditions. It's like monitoring the health of a family member; ongoing observation can catch potential problems early before they become more serious.

The Strategic Value of Municipal Bonds

Municipal bonds hold strategic value for many portfolios, offering a balance of risk and reward that is enhanced by tax benefits. Their role in funding essential public services also adds a layer of social return, making them appealing to socially conscious investors. Like planting a tree in your yard that provides shade and beauty while also increasing property values, investing in municipal bonds can yield personal financial benefits while enhancing the community.

Understanding the nuances of municipal bonds is essential for anyone preparing for the SIE exam and for investors aiming to build a diverse and resilient portfolio. This knowledge helps in making informed decisions that align financial goals with personal values and community welfare.

Packaged Products

Overview: The Convenience of Packaged Investment Products

Packaged investment products, like mutual funds, exchange-traded funds (ETFs), unit investment trusts (UITs), and real estate investment trusts (REITs), bundle various assets to offer investors convenient and diversified investment opportunities. These products can be likened to a meal kit delivery service that provides all the ingredients you need to make a meal. Just as a meal kit allows you to create a dish with various ingredients that have been pre-selected and measured, packaged products provide a mix of investments that are professionally managed and tailored to meet specific investment objectives, risk tolerance, and time horizons.

Purpose of Packaged Investment Products

Diversification

One of the primary advantages of packaged products is diversification. By pooling money from many investors, these funds can invest in a wider array of assets than most individuals could afford or manage on their own. This diversification reduces the risk of loss by spreading investments across different assets, sectors, or geographical areas. Think of it as not putting all your eggs in one basket. Instead, you have several baskets, each holding eggs of different sizes and colors, protecting your overall investment from significant impact if one basket were to fall.

Professional Management

Packaged products are typically managed by experienced investment professionals who make decisions about buying and selling assets within the fund. This management style is akin to hiring a skilled chef to prepare your meals; just as the chef uses their expertise to ensure each dish is balanced and delicious, fund managers use their knowledge and experience to try to achieve the best possible performance for the fund, adjusting the ingredients (investments) according to market conditions and investment strategy.

Accessibility

Another significant benefit of packaged products is accessibility. They allow individual investors to participate in a range of markets and asset classes that might otherwise be out of reach due to cost or complexity. For example, a small investor may not be able to buy individual stocks of all the biggest global companies, but through an international equity fund, they can invest in a diversified portfolio that includes these companies. It's similar to joining a community-supported agriculture (CSA) program, where your single subscription gives you access to a variety of produce from across many farms.

Liquidity

Most packaged products offer daily liquidity, meaning investors can buy or sell shares of the fund at the end of each trading day at the net asset value (NAV) of the shares. This liquidity is akin to being able to order or cancel a meal kit subscription on any given day, providing flexibility to adjust your investment as your financial needs or market conditions change.

The Role of Packaged Products in Investment Portfolios

Understanding the structure and benefits of packaged investment products is crucial for anyone involved in investment management, especially those studying for the SIE exam. These products provide a straightforward way to achieve diversified, professionally managed investment exposure, making them a fundamental option in many investment strategies.

This comprehensive overview not only helps candidates prepare for questions related to investment products on the SIE exam but also aids in developing practical knowledge for managing personal or client investment portfolios effectively.

Mutual Funds: Collaborative Investment Powerhouses

How Mutual Funds Work

Mutual funds operate on a simple yet powerful concept: pooling resources. Imagine a group of farmers coming together to purchase a piece of farming equipment that no single farmer could afford alone. Similarly, a mutual fund collects money from many investors and uses these collective funds to buy a diversified portfolio of stocks, bonds, or other securities. Each investor in a mutual fund owns shares, which represent a part of the holdings of the fund.

The management of a mutual fund is handled by professional investment managers, who decide which securities to buy and sell in alignment with the fund's objectives. The ability of these managers to make informed decisions based on thorough market analysis is akin to a seasoned chef who knows exactly which ingredients will work together to create a sought-after dish.

Diversification Benefits

Diversification is one of the key advantages of investing in mutual funds. By owning a wide array of securities, mutual funds mitigate the risk that a single security's poor performance might adversely affect the overall portfolio. This strategy is similar to planting a variety of crops in different seasons; if one crop fails due to unforeseen conditions, others will likely thrive, ensuring the farmer's livelihood is not compromised by any single failure.

Mutual funds can include hundreds—or even thousands—of different securities, making them far more diversified than most individuals could achieve on their own. This extensive diversification reduces the investment risk and smooths out returns. For an investor, participating in a mutual fund is like joining a large, varied investment club where the collective power and wisdom of the group help safeguard and potentially grow your money.

Strategic Importance in Investment Portfolios

Investing in mutual funds is particularly appealing for individual investors who seek exposure to a broad spectrum of assets but may lack the time or expertise to manage such investments on their own. Mutual funds offer a convenient way to gain significant diversification and professional management, making them a cornerstone of many personal investment strategies.

how mutual funds function and the benefits they offer is crucial for anyone preparing for the SIE exam and for investors looking to build a robust, diversified portfolio. These funds not only provide access to a wide range of asset classes and sectors but also entrust investment decisions to experts, potentially enhancing the chances of achieving strong financial returns. This knowledge helps demystify one of the most common investment vehicles, enabling aspiring professionals and personal investors to make informed decisions.

Understanding the Risks of Mutual Funds

Management Fees

One of the primary risks involved with mutual funds is the cost of management fees. These fees are paid to the fund managers for their expertise in managing the fund's portfolio. Management fees can vary widely and can significantly impact the overall returns of an investment over time. Think of these fees like a service charge at a restaurant; just as service charges are the price you pay for the convenience and expertise of the staff, management fees are the cost of having professionals manage your investments. However, if these fees are too high relative to the returns the fund is generating, it can eat into your savings, much like how excessive service charges can make a meal not worth its price.

Market Risk

Market risk refers to the potential losses that could be incurred due to movements in the market. No investment is immune to market fluctuations, and mutual funds, which hold a variety of stocks, bonds, or other assets, are also subject to this risk. The analogy here could be sailing on a vast ocean; just as sudden storms or changing currents can challenge even the most experienced sailors, market shifts can impact mutual fund investments, regardless of the diversity or quality of the assets within the fund. This risk is inherent and unavoidable, reflecting the reality that investment values can fluctuate day-to-day due to factors outside anyone's control.

Underperformance

Another significant risk with mutual funds is underperformance, which occurs when a fund does not achieve returns commensurate with those of its benchmark or similar funds. This can happen due to poor management decisions, unfavorable asset allocation, or other strategic missteps. Imagine a coach of a sports team who fails to utilize his players effectively, resulting in the team underperforming despite having talented individuals. Similarly, a mutual fund can falter if its managers do not make wise investment choices or fail to adapt to changing market conditions.

The Impact of These Risks on Investment Decisions

Understanding these risks is crucial for anyone investing in mutual funds. While mutual funds offer numerous benefits, such as diversification and professional management, they are not without their downsides. Investors need to be aware of the fees they are paying and how these fees impact their net returns. They must also recognize that no investment is free from market risk and that the potential for underperformance is an ongoing challenge.

It's important for investors to conduct thorough due diligence and regularly review the performance and fee structure of the mutual funds they are considering. This vigilance is akin to a gardener who not only plants seeds but also consistently tends to his garden, checking for signs of disease or poor growth, to ensure a healthy and productive crop.

By exploring these risks in detail, candidates preparing for the SIE exam, as well as individual investors, can better navigate the complexities of mutual fund investments and make informed choices that align with their financial goals and risk tolerance.

Exchange-Traded Funds (ETFs): Harnessing Market Dynamics

Overview of ETFs

Exchange-Traded Funds (ETFs) are innovative financial instruments that combine the features of mutual funds and stocks. Like mutual funds, ETFs hold a diversified portfolio of assets such as stocks, bonds, or commodities. However, they trade on stock exchanges similar to individual stocks. This unique structure allows ETFs to offer the best of both worlds: the diversification of mutual funds with the liquidity and accessibility of stocks.

Key Features of ETFs

Trading on Stock Exchanges

One of the defining features of ETFs is their ability to be bought and sold on stock exchanges throughout the trading day. This is akin to shopping in a retail store where you can buy and sell products at any time during business hours, as opposed to a mutual fund, which is more like making a catalog order where transactions are only processed at the end of the business day. This feature provides ETF investors with flexibility and control over their investment timing, allowing them to respond quickly to changes in market conditions.

Tracking Indexes

Most ETFs are designed to track the performance of a specific index, such as the S&P 500, NASDAQ, or other benchmarks. This means that an ETF aims to mirror the asset composition and performance of its target index. Think of an ETF as a photographic snapshot of a garden; just as the snapshot aims to capture the garden's appearance at a particular moment, an ETF aims to reflect the makeup and performance of its index at any given time. This feature makes ETFs a popular choice for passive investment strategies, as they provide a simple way to gain exposure to a broad segment of the market without the need to select individual stocks or assets.

Strategic Benefits of ETFs

The combination of these features makes ETFs an attractive investment option. They offer transparency, as the holdings are disclosed daily, and they often come with lower expense ratios compared to mutual funds due to their passive management nature. Furthermore, the ability to trade ETFs throughout the day provides liquidity and price transparency, which can be crucial during volatile market periods.

the features of ETFs is essential to understand for anyone preparing for the SIE exam and for investors looking to enhance their portfolios. By leveraging the trading flexibility and index-tracking capabilities of ETFs, investors can effectively manage their market exposure and align their investments with their broader financial strategies.

Understanding the Risks of ETFs

Liquidity Risks

While one of the key advantages of ETFs is their liquidity, meaning they can be bought and sold like stocks on an exchange, this liquidity is not guaranteed. The liquidity of an ETF depends on the trading volume of its shares and the liquidity of the underlying assets it holds. In situations where the underlying assets are illiquid—such as in the case of certain bonds or exotic assets—the ETF shares themselves might become hard to trade without significant price concessions.

Think of it like trying to sell a specialty item, like a rare antique, in a local market. If there's low demand for such unique items, you might find it difficult to find a buyer willing to pay a fair price quickly. Similarly, an ETF focusing on a niche market or holding less liquid assets might see wider bid-ask spreads or experience significant price impact on trades, especially in volatile market conditions.

Tracking Error

Tracking error is another significant risk associated with ETFs. This error refers to the discrepancy between the performance of the ETF and the performance of the index it is supposed to replicate. Although ETFs aim to mirror the performance of an index, various factors can cause them to deviate from this target. These factors include transaction costs, management fees, and the timing of dividend reinvestments.

Using the metaphor of a mirror in a funhouse, which is intended to reflect your image as you pass by, imagine if the mirror is slightly warped or smudged. Even though its purpose is to show a clear reflection, slight imperfections can distort the image. Similarly, while an ETF aims to reflect its index accurately, imperfections in execution, changes in the ETF's composition, or timing issues can lead to a tracking error, distorting the "reflection" of the index's actual performance.

Navigating ETF Risks

Investors interested in ETFs must consider these risks when incorporating them into their portfolios. Understanding that liquidity can vary and that tracking error can affect performance is crucial for developing a balanced and informed investment strategy. Just as a driver might choose a different route based on traffic reports to avoid delays, investors might choose or avoid certain ETFs based on their liquidity profiles and historical tracking errors.

These insights are not only vital for those studying for the SIE exam but also for any investor looking to leverage ETFs effectively within their investment strategy. Recognizing the potential pitfalls and knowing how to mitigate them can help investors maintain a resilient and adaptable investment portfolio.

Unit Investment Trusts (UITs): Structured Investment Vehicles

Understanding the Structure of UITs

Unit Investment Trusts (UITs) are a type of investment company that offers investors shares, known as units, in a fixed portfolio of securities. Unlike mutual funds, which are dynamically managed with no predetermined end date, UITs have a fixed term and a static investment portfolio. You can think of UITs as a curated art exhibition that is set up for a specific period and does not change its displays until the exhibition ends. Each piece of art (security) is selected to fit the theme of the exhibition (investment objective) and remains until the exhibition closes (the UIT matures).

Key Characteristics of UITs

- **Fixed Portfolio**: Once the UIT is created, its portfolio does not change. Securities are selected based on the trust's objectives and are held until the UIT matures. This is like buying a set menu meal at a restaurant; you know exactly what dishes you will get, and they remain the same each time that menu is ordered.

- **Termination Date**: UITs have a predetermined termination date, at which point the trust is liquidated and proceeds are paid out to the unit holders. This is similar to a limited-run theater show, which runs for a set number of performances before the final curtain call.

- **Lack of Active Management**: Unlike mutual funds, which are actively managed by portfolio managers who buy and sell securities to achieve the best possible return, UITs are not actively managed. The initial investment strategy is maintained without any changes influenced by market conditions. This can be likened to a time capsule, where items are placed inside once and not altered until it is opened at a future date.

How UITs Differ from Mutual Funds

- **Management Style**: The most significant difference lies in management style. While mutual funds are actively managed, allowing fund managers to adjust the holdings in response to market changes, UITs do not permit any changes to the portfolio once it is set. This offers a more predictable investment outcome but less flexibility compared to mutual funds.

- **Investment Strategy**: Mutual funds aim to outperform their benchmarks and can adapt their strategies to changing market conditions. UITs, however, stick to a predetermined strategy, which can be appealing for investors looking for stability and predictability.

- **Costs**: Typically, UITs have lower management fees than mutual funds, mainly because they do not incur costs associated with active management. This can be advantageous for cost-conscious investors.

The Role of UITs in Investment Portfolios

UITs provide a unique investment option for those seeking a predictable return profile and limited investment duration. They are particularly suitable for investors who prefer a hands-off approach but still want exposure to a diversified portfolio. Just like a collector might buy a complete set of themed stamps in a presentation pack, knowing exactly what they are getting and for how long they intend to keep it, investors in UITs appreciate the certainty and structure that these investments bring.

knwoing the structure and distinctions of UITs compared to mutual funds is crucial for financial professionals and investors preparing for the SIE exam. This knowledge helps in making informed decisions about incorporating UITs into diversified investment strategies, balancing predictability with performance potential.

Risks of Unit Investment Trusts (UITs)

Fixed Portfolio: The Double-Edged Sword

The fixed portfolio of a UIT, while providing stability and predictability, also poses a significant risk. Since the securities in a UIT cannot be changed during the life of the trust, the investment is vulnerable to shifts in market conditions that could negatively impact the performance of the assets within it. Think of a UIT as a pre-planned garden where you plant a variety of flowers at the beginning of the season and are not allowed to replace them, regardless of how the weather changes. If unexpected conditions arise, such as a drought, you cannot replace wilting plants with more resilient ones, potentially leading to a less flourishing garden.

This inflexibility can be particularly disadvantageous during volatile or declining markets where the ability to adjust the portfolio in response to economic shifts can protect against losses. Investors in UITs, therefore, accept the risk that their fixed basket of securities may underperform if market conditions turn unfavorable after their investment is locked in.

Limited Duration: Timing Constraints

The defined termination date of a UIT is another risk factor. While it allows investors to plan for a specific investment period, it also means that the assets are liquidated regardless of whether it is an optimal time to sell. This can be compared to having to sell a house at a predetermined future date, regardless of current market conditions. If the real estate market is down when this date arrives, you may end up selling at a loss.

This timing constraint can impact investment returns, especially if the UIT's termination coincides with a low in the market cycle, forcing liquidation at unfavorable prices. Furthermore, the need to reinvest proceeds at termination can pose an additional challenge, as suitable new investments may not be readily available at the same risk and return levels as the UIT.

Strategic Considerations

While the predictability of a fixed portfolio and a set duration can align well with certain financial goals and investment horizons, these same features can also restrict flexibility and adaptability to changing market environments.

Investors should weigh these risks against their investment objectives and consider how a UIT fits within their broader financial strategy. For instance, a UIT might be appropriate for achieving short-term goals where the investor values stability over flexibility, or as part of a larger diversified portfolio where other investments provide the adaptability that UITs lack.

By delving into the risks of fixed portfolios and limited durations, this section helps candidates for the SIE exam and investors understand the nuanced trade-offs involved in choosing UITs as investment vehicles. This knowledge is crucial for making informed decisions that balance predictability with the potential for adjusting to market dynamics.

Real Estate Investment Trusts (REITs): Investing in Property Through a Corporate Structure

Overview of REITs

Real Estate Investment Trusts (REITs) are companies that own, operate, or finance income-generating real estate across a range of property sectors. Think of a REIT as a large shopping mall owner, except instead of just malls, a REIT might own apartment complexes, office buildings, hospitals, hotels, or even timberlands. Investing in a REIT allows individuals to buy shares in commercial real estate portfolios, much like purchasing stocks in other industries. This provides investors an opportunity to earn a share of the income produced through real estate ownership without actually having to buy, manage, or finance any properties themselves.

The Structure of REITs

REITs are structured to provide a straightforward way for investors to gain exposure to real estate markets while receiving dividends. Legally, REITs must distribute at least 90% of their taxable income to shareholders in the form of dividends, making them a popular choice for income-seeking investors.

Income Generation

The primary appeal of REITs lies in their ability to generate a steady stream of income. This income is derived from the rent payments collected on the real estate properties they own, which is similar to receiving rent from a tenant in a house you own. However, instead of dealing with the headaches of being a landlord—like midnight calls about a broken water heater—you own a portion of a large portfolio of properties managed by professionals.

Diversification Benefits

REITs also offer diversification benefits. Since they often own a variety of property types across many geographic areas, investing in REITs can help reduce the unsystematic risk associated with owning individual properties. For example, if you only owned an apartment complex in one city, your income could be severely impacted if that city experienced a downturn. REITs spread this risk across many types of properties and locations, akin to spreading your bets across different numbers and colors at a roulette table.

The Role of REITs in Investment Portfolios

REITs are a valuable component of a diversified investment portfolio. They offer exposure to real estate, which is typically counter-cyclical to stocks and bonds, providing potential protective diversification during market downturns. The tangible nature of real estate investment, coupled with the liquidity of being able to buy and sell shares of REITs on major stock exchanges, makes them uniquely attractive.

how REITs function as companies that invest in real estate is essential for anyone involved in financial markets to know, especially those preparing for the SIE exam. It allows investors to access real estate markets without the complexities and capital requirements of direct property ownership, offering a blend of income potential and liquidity not typically available with traditional real estate investments.

Risks of Real Estate Investment Trusts (REITs)

Market Risk

Market risk refers to the potential volatility in the income and value of REITs due to changes in economic conditions. Like a boat on the ocean, REITs can be affected by economic tides and storms. Factors such as interest rate fluctuations, economic recessions, or changes in real estate market conditions can impact the overall performance of real estate investments. For instance, an increase in interest rates often raises borrowing costs, which can reduce the profitability of REITs and lower their share prices. Similarly, during economic downturns, decreased demand for real estate can lead to lower occupancy rates and rental incomes, directly impacting the returns from REITs.

Property-Specific Risks

Property-specific risks are those risks directly related to the properties owned by the REIT. Each property in a REIT's portfolio can be affected by a range of local factors such as changes in market demand, increased competition, or issues related to property management.

Location and Economic Dependency

The performance of real estate is highly dependent on its location. Properties in economically vibrant areas are likely to experience high demand and value appreciation, whereas properties in declining regions might suffer from low occupancy and decreasing values. This is akin to the business prospects of a restaurant: a restaurant in a bustling, upscale neighborhood is likely to perform better than one in a declining part of town.

Physical Condition and Management Effectiveness

The physical condition of the properties and the effectiveness of their management also play crucial roles in their success. A poorly maintained property or one managed by an inefficient team can lead to higher maintenance costs, difficulties in attracting and retaining tenants, and ultimately, reduced income. This scenario is similar to owning a vintage car; without proper maintenance and skilled handling, its performance and value can deteriorate over time, turning a potentially lucrative investment into a financial burden.

Navigating REIT Risks

Investors in REITs must be aware of these risks and consider them when making investment decisions. Monitoring economic trends, diversifying investments across different types of properties and geographic areas, and choosing REITs with strong management teams are all strategies that can help mitigate these risks. It's much like a sailor needing to understand the sea conditions and having the right crew and strategies to navigate through storms.

Options: The Flexibility of Financial Instruments

Introduction to Options

Options are financial derivatives that give buyers the right, but not the obligation, to buy or sell an underlying asset at a specified price before a certain date. This type of financial instrument can be likened to a ticket to a concert. Just as you might buy a ticket that allows you the option to attend a concert on a specific date at a predetermined price, buying an option gives you similar rights with respect to financial assets.

Basics of Options Trading

Options trading revolves primarily around two types of contracts: calls and puts. Each type of option serves a different purpose and offers different opportunities and risks.

Call Options

A call option gives the holder the right to buy an asset at a fixed price (known as the strike price) within a specific time period. This can be compared to a reservation at a popular restaurant; you secure the right to have a table at a future date but are not obligated to dine there. If the restaurant becomes extremely popular and reservations become hard to get (akin to the asset's price rising above the strike price), your reservation has added value. You can either use it to dine at the restaurant or sell it to someone else for a profit.

Put Options

Conversely, a put option gives the holder the right to sell an asset at a predetermined price within a specific time frame. This is similar to having an insurance policy on a valuable item. You pay a premium to have the option to sell the item at a set price, regardless of its current market value. If the market value drops significantly below the agreed-upon price (the strike price), you can exercise your option to sell at the higher price, thus limiting your financial loss.

Strategic Uses of Call and Put Options

Options are used for various strategic purposes including:

- **Speculation**: Traders use options to speculate on the future direction of asset prices. Speculators might buy call options if they expect prices to rise, or put options if they anticipate a decline.

- **Hedging**: Options can also be used to hedge or reduce risk in an investment portfolio. For instance, an investor worried about potential declines in stock values might buy put options to cover those positions.

Learning the Dynamics of Options Trading

the mechanics and potential uses of options is crucial for those preparing for the SIE exam and investors interested in sophisticated trading strategies. Options offer unique advantages, such as leveraging a position for a relatively low upfront cost (the premium), but they also carry risks, particularly the potential for rapid losses and the complexity of predicting market movements accurately.

Grasping the basics of options trading, including calls and puts, equips candidates and investors with the knowledge to navigate these instruments effectively, enhancing their ability to manage risks and capitalize on market opportunities.

Risks of Options Trading

Complexity

Options are among the more complex financial instruments available to investors. The intricacies of options trading involve understanding various factors such as strike prices, the intrinsic and extrinsic value of options, and their sensitivity to changes in the underlying asset's price, volatility, and time decay. This complexity can be likened to playing a strategic board game like chess. Just as chess requires an understanding of different pieces, moves, and strategies to win, options trading requires a deep understanding of numerous variables to be executed profitably. Missteps in strategy or miscalculations can lead to significant losses, just as a wrong move in chess can lead to a quick checkmate by the opponent.

Leverage

Options provide significant leverage, allowing traders to control a large amount of the underlying asset with a relatively small investment (the cost of the option's premium). While leverage can magnify profits, it also increases the potential for substantial losses, much more than the initial premium paid. This leverage effect can be compared to using a lever to lift a heavy object—the lever allows you to move a much heavier load than you could manage on your own, but if not handled properly, it can snap back, resulting in damage or injury. In financial terms, while you might invest a small amount on the option premium, a small move in the wrong direction can lead to a complete loss of this investment, and potentially more if not properly managed.

Expiration Timing

Another key risk in options trading is the expiration timing. All options have an expiration date, after which they become worthless if not exercised or sold. This aspect of options is similar to buying perishable goods; just as milk has a sell-by date after which it is no longer good to consume, options have an expiration date after which they no longer hold value. This creates a time pressure on the investor to make the right decision about when to exercise or sell the option. Poor timing can lead to options expiring worthless, resulting in a total loss of the premium paid.

Navigating the Risks

Understanding and managing the risks associated with options is crucial for traders. Educating oneself about the intricacies of options, respecting the leverage they involve, and keeping a vigilant eye on expiration dates are vital steps in mitigating these risks. Just as a pilot must understand the complexities of flying an aircraft, manage its powerful engines properly, and time the flight accurately, so must an options trader navigate the complexities, leverage, and timing issues inherent in options trading.

This detailed exploration of the risks in options trading is essential for those preparing for the SIE exam and investors interested in diversifying their trading strategies. By fully understanding these risks, traders can more effectively manage their portfolios and potentially harness the benefits of options to achieve their investment objectives.

Alternative Investments: Diversifying Beyond Traditional Markets

Understanding Alternative Investments

Alternative investments include a range of assets that fall outside the conventional investment categories of stocks, bonds, and cash. These investments often require more complex management strategies and carry different risk profiles compared to traditional investments. Investing in alternative assets can be likened to exploring exotic cuisines from around the world—while they offer a unique experience and can enhance your dining pleasure, they also require a more adventurous palate and a deeper understanding of the ingredients involved.

Examples of Alternative Investments

Hedge Funds

Hedge funds are private investment partnerships that use a range of strategies to achieve high returns, including long and short positions, leverage, derivatives, and arbitrage. Think of hedge funds as an elite sports team, where the manager acts as the coach, using sophisticated strategies and plays to win in competitive and diverse conditions. Hedge funds aim to achieve positive returns regardless of market direction, seeking to mitigate risk while capitalizing on market inefficiencies. However, they are typically only accessible to accredited investors due to their complex strategies and higher risk levels.

Commodities

Investing in commodities involves buying and selling physical substances like oil, gold, or agricultural products. This type of investment can be compared to trading in rare collectibles—values can fluctuate widely based on market conditions and scarcity. Commodities are often used as a hedge against inflation because their prices typically rise when the cost of living increases. However, they can be highly volatile and influenced by unpredictable factors like weather, political instability, or technological changes that affect supply and demand.

Private Equity

Private equity consists of capital investment made into companies that are not publicly traded on a stock exchange. Investing in private equity is like funding a local playwright to produce a play that could either become a hit, providing substantial returns, or fail to attract attention. Private equity investors often play an active role in managing the companies in which they invest, similar to a producer in a play. This form of investment typically requires long-term commitments and involves high degrees of risk and illiquidity, as exiting the investment usually depends on a future sale or public offering of the company.

The Role of Alternative Investments in Portfolios

Alternative investments can provide diversification benefits to a portfolio because their returns often have low correlations with those of traditional asset classes. This diversification can be akin to adding a safety net to a trapeze act, providing protection against falls (market downturns) by spreading risk across different types of performances (investments). However, due to their complex nature and higher risk profiles, alternative investments require thorough due diligence and an understanding of the unique risks involved.

Risks of Alternative Investments

Higher Complexity

Alternative investments are inherently more complex than traditional investment vehicles like stocks and bonds. This complexity stems from the sophisticated strategies employed, such as the use of leverage, derivatives, and non-traditional asset classes, as well as the unique structures of investments like hedge funds and private equity. Understanding these investments can be likened to mastering a foreign language; just as fluency requires a deep understanding of grammar, vocabulary, and cultural nuances, successful investment in alternatives demands a comprehensive knowledge of their mechanisms, strategies, and market contexts. This complexity can lead to difficulties in accurately assessing risk and potential returns.

Less Regulation

Alternative investments typically operate under less regulatory oversight than traditional investments, which are subject to strict reporting requirements and governance standards. This lesser degree of regulation can be compared to wild west territories, where fewer rules and the potential for lawlessness can increase the risks for settlers. For investors, this means there may be less transparency and fewer protections in place, increasing the potential for fraud or mismanagement. Investors must rely more heavily on the diligence and integrity of fund managers, which can sometimes lead to significant financial consequences if misplaced.

Potentially Higher Returns But Increased Risk

The allure of alternative investments often lies in their potential for higher returns, which can significantly outpace those of the traditional markets. However, these potentially higher returns come with increased risks. This relationship can be thought of as akin to high-stakes gambling; just as the promise of a large payout can tempt a gambler to bet large sums of money, the potential for substantial financial gains can attract investors to these high-risk alternatives. However, just as in gambling, the potential for high rewards is matched by the possibility of substantial losses, especially if market conditions turn unfavorable or if the investment strategies do not perform as expected.

Managing the Risks

Navigating the risks associated with alternative investments requires a sophisticated approach to risk management, similar to a tightrope walker using a balance pole. Investors need to carefully balance their desire for higher returns with the ability to bear higher risks. This involves conducting thorough due diligence, understanding the specific risks associated with each type of investment, and appropriately diversifying their investment portfolios to spread risk. Investors must also maintain a keen awareness of market conditions and regulatory changes that might impact their investments.

Understanding the complex risks associated with alternative investments is crucial for anyone studying for the SIE exam and for investors looking to diversify their portfolios into these high-risk, high-reward assets. By recognizing the intricacies and challenges posed by these investments, candidates and investors can better prepare themselves for the volatile yet potentially lucrative world of alternative investments.

Conclusion: Navigating Investment Products and Their Risks

Recap of Investment Products and Associated Risks

This chapter has provided an exploration into various investment products, each with its own set of features and inherent risks:

- **Stocks**: With potential for high returns come risks like market volatility and company-specific performance issues.

- **Bonds**: Corporate and government bonds present risks such as interest rate fluctuations, credit risk, and reinvestment risk.

- **Packaged Products**: Mutual funds, ETFs, UITs, and REITs offer diversification, but they also carry management fees, market risk, and specific risks like tracking errors or property-related issues.

- **Options and Alternative Investments**: These offer high potential returns but also entail higher risks, including complexity, leverage effects, and less regulation.

Each product plays a unique role in investment strategies but comes with a risk profile that must be thoroughly understood and managed.

The Importance of Understanding Investment Risks

In Context of Portfolio Management

Understanding the risks associated with various investment products is crucial for effective portfolio management. Just as a seasoned chef uses a balance of ingredients to create a perfect dish, a skilled investor balances these products within a portfolio to optimize returns and minimize risks. Recognizing how different investments react to market changes helps in constructing a portfolio that can withstand economic downturns and capitalize on growth opportunities.

In Preparation for the SIE Exam

For those preparing for the SIE exam, a deep understanding of these investment products and their risks is essential. The exam not only tests knowledge of these products but also assesses the ability to apply this knowledge in practical, real-world scenarios. Understanding the risks is not just about memorizing facts; it's about developing a framework for thinking critically about how investments might perform under various economic conditions, and how they can be combined to achieve specific financial goals.

Integrating Knowledge and Strategy

Investors and exam candidates alike should approach this knowledge as both a foundation of financial education and a toolkit for strategic decision-making. This dual perspective prepares candidates not only to succeed on the exam but also to excel in their future careers by making informed investment decisions that consider both potential returns and associated risks.

By effectively managing these risks, investors can ensure more stable and predictable outcomes, and aspiring professionals can demonstrate their readiness to handle the complexities of the financial markets.

Key Takeaways: Essential Insights for SIE Exam Candidates

This chapter has explored a variety of investment products and highlighted the importance of understanding the associated risks. Here are the major points covered that are crucial for SIE exam candidates:

Understanding Different Investment Products

- **Stocks and Bonds**: Learn the different types of stocks (common and preferred) and bonds (corporate, government, and municipal), including their features and associated risks like market volatility, credit risk, and interest rate risk.

- **Packaged Products**: Understand the structure, benefits, and risks of mutual funds, ETFs, UITs, and REITs. Recognize how management fees, tracking errors, and market conditions can impact these investments.

- **Options and Alternative Investments**: Grasp the basics of options trading, including calls and puts, and the higher complexity and risks of alternative investments like hedge funds, commodities, and private equity.

Recognizing the Importance of Risk Management

- **Risk Types**: Each investment type carries specific risks that need to be managed differently. For example, stocks are primarily affected by market and company-specific risks, while bonds are more sensitive to interest rate changes and credit risk.

- **Risk Mitigation Strategies**: Understand strategies to mitigate these risks, such as diversification, choosing investments with suitable risk profiles, and staying informed about market conditions.

Application in Portfolio Management

- **Balancing Risk and Return**: Knowing how to balance the potential returns against the risks of different investment types is critical for effective portfolio management.

- **Practical Application**: Apply this knowledge not only to pass the SIE exam but also to real-world scenarios where strategic investment decisions are necessary.

Preparing for the SIE Exam

- **Exam Relevance**: These topics are essential for the SIE exam, which tests candidates on their knowledge of securities products and their risks, as well as their ability to apply this knowledge.

- **Critical Thinking**: Develop critical thinking skills about how various factors such as economic changes, company performance, and global events can affect investment products.

By mastering these key concepts, candidates will not only be well-prepared for the SIE exam but will also have a solid foundation for future roles in the finance and investment industry. Understanding these principles enables aspiring professionals to make informed investment decisions and manage client portfolios effectively.

Chapter 3: Trading, Customer Accounts, and Prohibited Activities

Understanding Exchange Operations and Order Types in Financial MARKETS

In today's ever-changing financial world, knowing how exchanges work and the different types of orders is crucial for both traders and investors. This detailed guide is here to help you understand how exchanges operate and the ins and outs of various order types, like market orders, limit orders, stop orders, and others.

Exchange Operations:

Financial exchanges serve as the central marketplace where buyers and sellers come together to trade various financial instruments such as stocks, bonds, commodities, and derivatives. These exchanges play a pivotal role in facilitating efficient price discovery and liquidity provision in the market.

Key Functions of Exchanges:

In the world of financial markets, exchanges serve as the cornerstone of trading activities, facilitating the seamless exchange of assets and ensuring market efficiency. To truly grasp the essence of exchanges, it is essential to delve into their key functions and explore their profound impact on market dynamics, investor confidence, and regulatory oversight.

1. Price Discovery: The Foundation of Market Efficiency

At the heart of every exchange lies the fundamental function of price discovery. Exchanges provide a transparent platform where supply and demand dynamics interact to determine the fair market value of assets. Through continuous buying and selling activities, market participants collectively contribute to the establishment of equilibrium prices, reflecting the true underlying value of securities, commodities, and other financial instruments.

The process of price discovery is driven by the forces of supply and demand, as buyers and sellers seek to transact at prices that reflect their respective valuations and preferences. Through the dissemination of real-time market data and trade executions, exchanges offer invaluable insights into market sentiment, trends, and price movements, empowering investors to make informed decisions and allocate capital efficiently. Furthermore, price discovery serves as a vital mechanism for risk management and portfolio optimization, enabling market participants to hedge against adverse price fluctuations and capitalize on emerging opportunities. By fostering transparency and efficiency in price formation, exchanges play a pivotal role in enhancing market liquidity, reducing transaction costs, and promoting market integrity.

2. Liquidity Provision: Facilitating Efficient Market Operations

In addition to price discovery, exchanges play a crucial role in providing liquidity, ensuring that market participants can buy or sell assets promptly and at competitive prices. By matching buy and sell orders in a centralized and regulated environment, exchanges create an ecosystem where capital flows freely and market participants can execute trades with minimal slippage and delay.

The presence of robust liquidity enhances market efficiency and stability, as it reduces the risk of price manipulation, facilitates price discovery, and promotes orderly market functioning. Moreover, liquidity provision enhances market depth, allowing investors to transact in large volumes without significantly impacting prices or market conditions. Exchanges employ various mechanisms to enhance liquidity, including market-making programs, designated market makers, and continuous trading sessions. Through these initiatives, exchanges incentives market participants to provide liquidity by offering competitive bid-ask spreads, narrowing price differentials, and ensuring a seamless trading experience for all stakeholders.

3. Regulation and Oversight: Safeguarding Market Integrity and Investor Protection

Central to the operation of exchanges is the critical function of regulation and oversight. Exchanges serve as self-regulatory organizations (SROs) tasked with enforcing rules and regulations to maintain market integrity, prevent fraud, and protect investor interests. By establishing a robust regulatory framework, exchanges foster trust and confidence in the financial markets, safeguarding the interests of all stakeholders.

Exchanges implement stringent compliance standards, market surveillance mechanisms, and disciplinary procedures to detect and deter fraudulent activities, market manipulation, and insider trading. Through continuous monitoring and enforcement efforts, exchanges strive to ensure a level playing field for all market participants and uphold the principles of fairness, transparency, and accountability.

Furthermore, exchanges collaborate closely with regulatory authorities, such as the Securities and Exchange Commission (SEC) and the Commodity Futures Trading Commission (CFTC), to harmonize regulatory standards, address emerging risks, and promote investor protection. By fostering collaboration between industry participants and regulatory bodies, exchanges contribute to the overall stability and resilience of the financial system.

4. Order Matching: The Engine of Market Efficiency

At the core of exchange operations lies the sophisticated process of order matching, where buy and sell orders are matched based on predefined parameters such as price, quantity, and time priority. Exchanges employ advanced trading systems and algorithms to facilitate order execution in a fast, fair, and transparent manner, ensuring optimal market liquidity and efficiency.

Through order matching mechanisms such as limit order books, auction mechanisms, and electronic trading platforms, exchanges enable seamless interaction between buyers and sellers, facilitating price discovery and ensuring orderly market functioning. By prioritizing orders based on predefined criteria, exchanges optimize trade execution and minimize the impact of market volatility and price fluctuations.

Moreover, order-matching algorithms play a crucial role in optimizing market liquidity, reducing bid-ask spreads, and enhancing price efficiency. By continuously updating order books and matching algorithms in response to changing market conditions, exchanges ensure that market participants can transact with confidence and certainty, regardless of market dynamics.

The key functions of exchanges are instrumental in shaping the dynamics of financial markets, fostering liquidity, transparency, and investor confidence. Through price discovery, liquidity provision, regulation, and order matching, exchanges serve as vital pillars of market infrastructure, facilitating efficient capital allocation, risk management, and wealth creation. By upholding the principles of fairness, transparency, and integrity, exchanges play a pivotal role in advancing the collective interests of market participants and promoting the long-term sustainability of the financial system.

Order types in trading are akin to various strategies used in a marketplace, each suited for specific buying or selling scenarios, allowing traders to navigate through the financial markets effectively.

Market Orders are instructions to buy or sell an asset at the current best available price. This is similar to purchasing an item on the spot in a store because you need it immediately, regardless of the price fluctuations that day. It guarantees that you'll acquire the item but not necessarily at the lowest price.

Limit Orders allow traders to specify a maximum purchase price or a minimum sale price. Imagine setting a budget for a car at an auction, deciding the highest price you are willing to pay. The auctioneer will only execute your purchase if a car is available at or below your set price, ensuring you don't overspend.

Stop Orders, also known as stop-loss orders, act as a safety net. They are set to execute as market orders once a specified price is reached. For example, it's like installing a safety valve on a pressure cooker that activates to prevent the contents from overheating, similarly, the stop order protects your investment from significant losses.

Stop-Limit Orders combine the features of stop and limit orders. You can think of it as setting an alarm clock (the stop part) to wake you at a specific time, and then giving yourself a few extra minutes (the limit part) before you actually get out of bed. The order activates at a certain price point but will only execute within a set price range, offering control over the execution price while still protecting against drastic price movements.

Each of these order types serves a strategic purpose in trading, helping investors manage their investments more precisely, just as different tools in a toolkit help you tackle various home repair tasks effectively.

explanation of how exchanges operate and facilitate trading activities

Have you ever wondered how financial exchanges work their magic, enabling seamless transactions in the bustling world of finance? Join us on a journey to unravel the mysteries of exchange operations and discover the intricate mechanisms that drive trading activities. Through insightful explanations, engaging anecdotes, and wisdom from renowned scholars, we will shed light on the fascinating world of financial exchanges.

The Essence of Exchanges:

Financial exchanges serve as the beating heart of global markets, providing a platform where buyers and sellers converge to exchange assets ranging from stocks and bonds to commodities and derivatives. As renowned economist Adam Smith once remarked, "Exchange is the fundamental act of human society," highlighting the pivotal role of exchanges in facilitating economic interactions and resource allocation.

The Mechanisms of Exchange Operations:

At the core of exchange operations lie sophisticated trading systems that match buy and sell orders based on predefined criteria such as price, quantity, and time priority. As Nobel laureate Friedrich Hayek eloquently stated, "The marvel is that in a case like the stock market, where the behavior of the elements is not subject to strict physical laws, but rather to the laws of chance, the market tends to remain reasonably efficient."

Market Dynamics and Price Discovery:

One of the primary functions of exchanges is to facilitate price discovery, a process where the interplay of supply and demand determines the fair market value of assets. Through continuous buying and selling activities, exchanges provide transparent pricing information, enabling investors to make informed decisions. As financial theorist Eugene Fama aptly noted, "The price is right, even if the reasons given to explain the price are wrong."

Liquidity Provision and Market Efficiency:

In addition to price discovery, exchanges play a crucial role in providing liquidity, ensuring that there is sufficient depth and breadth in the market for smooth transaction execution. This liquidity not only enhances market efficiency but also reduces transaction costs and enhances investor confidence. As financial scholar Robert Shiller mused, "Liquidity is a key factor in ensuring market stability and resilience."

Regulatory Oversight and Investor Protection:

To maintain market integrity and safeguard investor interests, exchanges operate under strict regulatory frameworks enforced by regulatory bodies such as the Securities and Exchange Commission (SEC) in the United States. These regulations aim to prevent market manipulation, insider trading, and other malpractices that could undermine market fairness and stability. As former SEC chairman Arthur Levitt Jr. once remarked, "Markets are designed to allow individuals to look after their private needs and to pursue profit. It's really a great invention, and I wouldn't underplay the value of that, but they're not designed to take care of social needs."

Understanding the concepts of long and short sales

In the dynamic realm of financial markets, mastering the concepts of long and short sales, margin trading, and settlement is paramount for traders seeking to navigate the intricacies of buying and selling securities.

Understanding Long and Short Sales:

Long and short sales are fundamental strategies employed by traders to capitalize on market movements, whether bullish or bearish. "In the stock market, there are only two positions: long and wrong," famously remarked legendary investor Jesse Livermore.

Long Sale:

When an investor takes a long position, they purchase a security with the expectation that its value will appreciate over time. This bullish strategy involves buying low and selling high, profiting from upward price movements. However, it requires patience and conviction in the underlying asset's growth potential.

Short Sale:

On the other hand, short selling involves selling borrowed securities with the intention of buying them back at a lower price in the future. This bearish strategy allows traders to profit from declining prices by selling high and buying low. However, short selling carries inherent risks, as losses can be unlimited if the price of the security rises unexpectedly.

Margin Trading:

Margin trading amplifies both gains and losses by allowing traders to leverage borrowed funds to increase their buying power. As the renowned economist John Maynard Keynes aptly put it, "Markets can remain irrational longer than you can remain solvent." Margin trading offers the potential for higher returns but also exposes traders to heightened risks, including margin calls and liquidation.

Settlement:

Settlement refers to the process of transferring ownership of securities and funds between buyers and sellers to complete a trade. "The market can stay irrational longer than you can stay solvent," cautioned economist John Maynard Keynes. Settlement ensures the smooth and efficient functioning of financial markets, facilitating transparency, trust, and integrity. Mastering the concepts of long and short sales, margin trading, and settlement is essential for traders navigating the complexities of financial markets. By understanding these concepts and their implications, traders can formulate informed strategies, manage risk effectively, and seize opportunities in both bullish and bearish market conditions. As the legendary investor Warren Buffett famously said, "Risk comes from not knowing what you're doing." With knowledge and expertise, traders can confidently navigate the ever-changing landscape of financial markets and achieve success in their investment endeavors.

Explanation of margin trading and its implications

Margin trading, a double-edged sword in the financial world, unlocks doors to lucrative opportunities while simultaneously wielding the potential for significant risks. It's akin to walking a tightrope between success and peril, requiring astute understanding and meticulous management. But what exactly is margin trading, and what are its implications?

At its core, margin trading involves borrowing funds from a broker to purchase securities, leveraging one's investment potential. This allows traders to amplify their buying power, potentially magnifying profits. Yet, this amplification comes with a catch – increased exposure to market fluctuations. As Sheikh Anwar al-Awlaki once said, "Every opportunity has its risks, and every risk has its opportunity."

Picture this: You have $1,000 in your account, but with margin trading, you can control $2,000 worth of securities. Sounds enticing, doesn't it? However, the borrowed funds must be repaid with interest, irrespective of the outcome of your trades. This introduces an element of financial obligation and risk, akin to playing with borrowed time.

Margin trading, often likened to a financial magnifying glass, intensifies both gains and losses. As Imam Abu Hanifa famously mused, "The bigger the reward, the greater the risk." While successful trades can yield handsome profits, losses can accumulate swiftly, potentially leading to margin calls or even liquidation of assets. It's a high-stakes game where vigilance and expertise are paramount.

The implications of margin trading extend far beyond the potential for amplified profits or losses. Margin trading offers investors the ability to significantly amplify their market exposure and potential returns using borrowed funds.

Leveraging Capital for Greater Returns

Margin trading allows investors to borrow money from a brokerage to purchase more securities than they could with just their own funds. This leverage increases the investment's exposure to the market, which can magnify returns on investment. For example, if you invest $10,000 of your own money and borrow another $10,000, you can buy $20,000 worth of stock. If the stock price rises by 10%, your investment grows by $2,000, doubling the return compared to using only your own funds.

Risks of Amplified Losses However, this increased potential for gains comes with heightened risk. If the market moves unfavorably, losses are also magnified, which can quickly eat into the initial capital and potentially lead to debt if the securities' value drops below the amount borrowed. To mitigate such risks, traders need to implement strict risk management practices, such as setting stop-loss orders to limit potential losses.

Margin Calls: A Critical Consideration

A key aspect of margin trading is maintaining the minimum margin requirement set by the brokerage. If your account balance falls below this threshold due to market losses, the brokerage will issue a margin call, requiring you to add more funds or sell some securities to cover the shortfall. Failure to meet a margin call can result in the brokerage selling your securities, often at less-than-ideal prices, to bring the account back into compliance.

Managing Costs of Borrowing

The benefits of margin trading must also be weighed against the costs. Borrowing money isn't free; it incurs interest that can accumulate and significantly impact overall profitability. Traders must consider whether the potential returns from their investments will exceed the costs of interest and other fees associated with margin trading.

However, margin trading introduces complexities beyond traditional investing. Traders must navigate margin requirements, maintenance margins, and margin calls, requiring a deep understanding of market dynamics and risk management principles. It's not merely about predicting market movements but also about safeguarding against adverse scenarios. Margin trading is not for the faint-hearted or the ill-prepared. It demands discipline, knowledge, and a keen awareness of one's risk tolerance. It's a journey through the peaks and valleys of financial markets, where fortunes can be made or lost in the blink of an eye.

Mastering the Art of Trading: Long vs Short Sales and the Significance of Settlement Process

In the world of finance, where every decision holds the potential for profit or loss, understanding the intricacies of trading is paramount. Among the fundamental concepts are long and short sales, which form the backbone of trading strategies. Moreover, the settlement process, often overlooked, plays a pivotal role in ensuring the smooth functioning of financial markets. Let us delve deep into these topics, uncovering their nuances and significance.

Long sales, the bedrock of traditional investing, involve purchasing assets with the expectation of their price appreciation over time. As noted by renowned economist Benjamin Graham, the father of value investing, "The intelligent investor is a realist who sells to optimists and buys from pessimists." Conversely, short sales, championed by financial luminaries like George Soros, entail selling borrowed assets with the anticipation of repurchasing them at a lower price, thus profiting from a decline in value. This strategy demands astute market timing and a keen understanding of market sentiment. Can one truly master the art of trading without grasping the intricacies of long and short sales?

Overview of the Settlement Process: Navigating the Financial Terrain:

Amidst the flurry of trades, the settlement process quietly ensures the integrity of financial transactions. At its core, settlement refers to the transfer of securities or funds between parties involved in a trade. As emphasized by finance scholar Robert C. Merton, "Settlement systems lie at the heart of financial market infrastructures." This process, though seemingly mundane, holds immense significance in maintaining market stability and investor confidence.

Citing Merton's words, "In the absence of efficient settlement mechanisms, trust in financial markets wanes, casting shadows of doubt on the entire system." Indeed, timely and accurate settlement is indispensable for fostering trust and liquidity in the markets.

Beyond its logistical function, settlement serves as a barometer of market efficiency and regulation adherence. Timely settlement prevents systemic risks and ensures fair and orderly markets. Furthermore, adherence to settlement deadlines fosters transparency and accountability, vital for market integrity.

Settlement processes in financial markets are crucial for ensuring transactions are completed securely and efficiently. These processes help mitigate risks, manage liquidity, ensure regulatory compliance, and leverage technological innovations to improve the overall stability and functionality of the markets.

Risk Mitigation and Market Stability

Efficient settlement processes reduce counterparty risk—the danger that one party will fail to meet their obligations. This is critical in preventing defaults that could destabilize markets. For example, quick and reliable settlement in high-volume trading environments prevents the accumulation of unsettled trades, which could lead to systemic risks affecting the broader market. Ensuring that parties fulfill their commitments promptly helps maintain a stable and trustworthy market environment.

Liquidity Management

Settlement mechanisms facilitate the timely transfer of funds and securities, essential for effective liquidity management. This rapid movement ensures market participants can swiftly access or redistribute capital, adapting to market conditions without delays. For instance, when a mutual fund faces sudden redemption requests, efficient settlement processes enable quick access to necessary funds, helping the fund meet its obligations without disruption.

Regulatory Compliance

Compliance with stringent settlement regulations is vital for protecting investor interests and maintaining the integrity of financial markets. Regulatory bodies like the SEC and FINRA enforce these rules to prevent fraud, manipulation, and market abuse. They monitor settlement activities and can impose penalties on firms that fail to complete transactions within the prescribed timeframes, such as the T+2 (trade date plus two days) settlement rule.

Technological Innovations

Advancements in technology, particularly blockchain and distributed ledger technology (DLT), are set to transform the settlement landscape. These technologies offer increased efficiency, transparency, and security, potentially reducing settlement times to same-day (T+0) settlements. This could drastically decrease the capital needed to guard against counterparty risk and streamline the entire process. Ongoing blockchain pilot projects in stock exchanges are testing the feasibility of these instant settlements, demonstrating a significant potential to enhance market efficiency.

Understanding Cash Accounts vs Margin Accounts in Trading: A Comprehensive Guide

Overview of Cash Accounts and Margin Accounts:

Understanding Cash and Margin Accounts

Cash Accounts Explained

Cash accounts are straightforward brokerage accounts where investors must fully fund purchases with the cash available in their accounts. This setup means that all transactions are paid for upfront, without borrowing from the brokerage. It's akin to shopping with a debit card; you can only spend what you have. These accounts are particularly appealing to conservative investors who prefer to avoid debt and trade within their financial means. Such an approach ensures that the investor's exposure to financial loss is limited to the funds they have already invested, without the additional risk of borrowed money.

Margin Accounts Overview

Margin accounts, on the other hand, allow investors to borrow money from their brokerage to purchase more securities than their cash on hand would allow. This is similar to using a credit card for investments, where the borrowed amount plus any associated interest must eventually be paid back. The securities purchased become collateral for the loan. This type of account magnifies an investor's buying power but also their potential risk. For example, if an investor buys $20,000 worth of stocks with $10,000 of their own money and $10,000 borrowed, they stand to gain significantly if the stocks increase in value but face greater losses—and potentially a margin call—if the stocks decline. Margin calls occur when the value of the securities drops significantly and the broker requires the investor to deposit more funds or sell some securities to maintain a minimum account balance.

Risks and Rewards

While margin accounts can enhance returns when market conditions are favorable, they can also exacerbate losses when conditions worsen. This dual-edge is due to the leverage involved; just as returns are amplified, so are losses. Investors in margin accounts must be prepared for scenarios where they might need to inject more cash into their accounts or sell securities at a loss to meet margin requirements. This level of risk makes margin accounts suitable for more experienced investors with higher risk tolerance.

Choosing Between Cash and Margin Accounts

Investors need to consider their financial situation, investment goals, and risk tolerance when choosing between a cash and a margin account. Those new to investing or wary of risk might prefer the security of a cash account. In contrast, those looking for higher returns and who are comfortable with the associated risks might opt for a margin account. In both cases, understanding and managing the risks involved is crucial to successful investing.

Differentiating Features of Cash Accounts and Margin Accounts:

Features of Cash and Margin Accounts: Leverage, Risk, and Regulations

Cash vs. Margin Buying Power

Cash accounts restrict investors to trading solely with the funds they have, much like paying in cash at a store—what you have in your wallet is what you can spend. This directly limits the size and scope of their investments. In contrast, margin accounts act more like a credit line provided by the brokerage, allowing investors to borrow money to purchase more securities than their cash balance would permit. This leverage can significantly amplify an investor's buying power, enabling them to control larger positions and capitalize on market opportunities that would otherwise be out of reach.

Risk Management Across Account Types

Cash accounts offer a more secure investment route as they cap the potential loss to the existing account balance, effectively eliminating the risk of falling into debt due to trading activities. Margin accounts, however, introduce a higher level of risk. If the market turns unfavorable, investors might not only lose their initial investment but could also owe money to the brokerage. This scenario is akin to buying a home with a small down payment during a market crash, where the home's value might fall below what is owed on the mortgage, leading to financial distress unless additional payments are made to cover the gap.

Interest Implications and Regulatory Oversight

Investing through cash accounts means avoiding any interest charges since the funds used are wholly owned by the investor. Margin accounts, however, come with the additional cost of interest on the borrowed money, which can accumulate and impact overall returns. Regulatory oversight for margin accounts is also more stringent, reflecting the increased risks associated with borrowing. Investors must adhere to specific margin requirements which dictate the minimum amount of equity they must maintain, much like maintaining proper loan-to-value ratios when financing a property.

Regulatory Considerations

Regulations for cash accounts are straightforward due to their non-leveraged nature. However, for margin accounts, strict regulatory requirements are in place to safeguard both the investor and the brokerage. These include maintaining minimum margin requirements to ensure investors have enough skin in the game to handle potential losses. This protective measure helps manage the systemic risk that leverage can introduce into the financial system.

Benefits and Drawbacks of Cash Accounts and Margin Accounts:

Cash and Margin Accounts: Pros and Cons

Cash Accounts: Safeguarding and Simplicity

Cash accounts operate on a straightforward principle: you can only invest the money you have, which inherently caps potential losses to the amount invested. This approach is similar to using cash for everyday purchases; there's no possibility of spending more than you hold. This makes cash accounts particularly appealing for new investors or those who prefer not to engage with the complexities and risks of borrowing. However, this safety comes at the cost of limited financial reach. Investors can miss out on significant opportunities because they cannot exceed their immediate financial resources to leverage market movements.

Margin Accounts: Enhanced Potential with Increased Risks

Margin accounts offer the ability to borrow money against the securities in your portfolio, substantially increasing your buying power. This is akin to buying a home with a mortgage: your initial cash outlay is leveraged into a much larger asset, which can greatly increase your return on investment if property values rise. However, just as a drop in property values can lead to owing more than the worth of the home, so too can declines in your securities' values result in losses exceeding your initial investment. The flexibility to engage in advanced trading strategies like short-selling provides avenues for potential profits in falling markets but also adds complexity and the need for vigilant risk management. Interest costs on borrowed funds and the threat of margin calls—demands to supply additional funds if your account equity dips—add layers of financial strain that can detract from profitability.

Balancing Act

Choosing between a cash or a margin account involves balancing your financial goals and risk tolerance. Cash accounts offer a risk-averse, straightforward approach to investing—what you see is what you get. On the other hand, margin accounts provide a high-stakes, high-reward strategy that can either offer significant returns or lead to substantial losses. Investors need to consider their investment horizon, risk tolerance, and the specific market conditions when deciding which account suits their needs better. Each type of account caters to different strategies and offers unique advantages and drawbacks, emphasizing the importance of personalized investment planning.

Practical Considerations for Choosing Between Cash Accounts and Margin Accounts:

Practical Considerations for Choosing Between Cash and Margin Accounts

Investor Profile and Risk Tolerance

- **Conservative Investors**:

Those with a low tolerance for risk often find cash accounts appealing. These accounts limit investments to the funds available, thus capping potential losses and avoiding the complexities of borrowing. For conservative investors, the primary attraction of cash accounts is their inherent safety and the straightforward nature of transactions, which aligns well with a cautious investment strategy.

- **Aggressive Investors**:

Investors who are more aggressive typically seek higher returns and are more open to assuming greater risks. Margin accounts are suitable for such investors as they allow the use of borrowed funds to leverage trading positions. This leverage can significantly amplify potential returns by enabling the purchase of a larger volume of securities than the investor's cash balance would permit. However, this also means that losses can exceed the initial investment, a risk that aggressive investors are generally more prepared to take.

Market Conditions and Trading Opportunities

- **Stable Market Conditions:**

In calm and stable market environments, the benefits of leverage may not be as pronounced, making cash accounts a suitable option for most investors, particularly those who prefer a less aggressive stance. Without dramatic price movements, the conservative approach of trading within one's financial means often suffices.

- **Volatile Market Conditions:**

During periods of high market volatility, margin accounts can provide strategic advantages. The ability to quickly enter and exit positions using borrowed money can be crucial when dealing with highly volatile securities. The increased buying power and flexibility of margin accounts can allow savvy investors to capitalize on market fluctuations more effectively than they could with a cash account.

Risk Management Strategies

- **Assessment of Risk Tolerance:**

Before deciding between a cash or margin account, investors should conduct a thorough assessment of their risk tolerance and overall financial goals. Understanding one's comfort level with potential financial losses is crucial in choosing an account type that aligns with personal investment strategies.

- **Implementing Safeguards:**

For those opting for margin accounts, employing robust risk management strategies becomes even more critical due to the increased risk potential. Techniques such as setting stop-loss orders to automatically sell securities at a predetermined price can help limit losses. Additionally, diversifying the investment portfolio can spread risk across various assets, reducing the impact of a poor performance in any single investment.

Table 1: Features of Cash Accounts vs Margin Accounts

Feature	Cash Accounts	Margin Accounts
Leverage	None	Available
Risk Exposure	Limited	Higher
Interest Charges	None	Applicable
Regulatory Requirements	Fewer	More
Buying Power	Limited	Increased
Flexibility	Limited	High

Table 2: Pros and Cons of Cash Accounts vs Margin Accounts

	Cash Accounts	Margin Accounts
Pros	Safety, Simplicity	Increased Buying Power, Flexibility, Potential for Higher Returns
Cons	Limited Buying Power, Missed Opportunities	Higher Risk, Interest Charges, Margin Calls

Understanding Cash Accounts vs Margin Accounts: Exploring Pros and Cons

Understanding the distinction between cash accounts and margin accounts is essential for investors. Both types of accounts offer unique advantages and come with their own set of risks. In this comprehensive guide, we will delve deep into the pros and cons of cash accounts and margin accounts, drawing insights from financial scholars and industry experts. Through careful analysis, we aim to equip investors with the knowledge they need to make informed decisions about their investment strategies.

I. Cash Accounts:

A cash account is a type of brokerage account where all transactions are settled with cash. Investors must have sufficient cash in their accounts to cover the cost of securities purchased. No borrowing or leveraging is allowed in cash accounts, making them a conservative option for investors.

According to John C. Bogle, founder of Vanguard Group, "Cash accounts offer investors a disciplined approach to risk management, ensuring that investments are made with available funds, thus avoiding the pitfalls of leverage. A cash account, the bedrock of traditional investing, operates on the principle of financial prudence. Here, transactions are executed solely based on the funds available in the account, ensuring a direct link between purchasing power and liquid assets. Scholars like Warren Buffett extol the virtues of cash accounts, emphasizing the importance of investing within one's means and avoiding excessive leverage.

Pros of Cash Accounts:

Cash Accounts: Lower Risk and Simplicity

Cash accounts offer a straightforward investment approach by only allowing transactions that can be fully covered with existing funds. This directly minimizes the risk since you cannot lose more money than you have invested. This kind of account is akin to paying for goods in cash, where you cannot spend more than what you carry in your wallet, thus avoiding any form of debt accumulation.

No Interest Expenses

One of the most significant advantages of using a cash account is the absence of interest expenses. When you use your own money to invest, you sidestep the costs associated with borrowing funds. In contrast, margin accounts, which allow you to borrow money for investments, come with interest charges that can eat into your potential profits. Investing with a cash account means any returns on your investments are yours alone, not diminished by ongoing interest payments.

Simplified Management

Managing a cash account is generally less complex than a margin account. There are no margin calls to worry about, no requirements to maintain minimum account balances relative to your borrowing, and no interest calculations to monitor. This simplicity is especially beneficial for those who prefer a straightforward approach to investing without the hassle of additional calculations and potential financial obligations beyond their initial investment.

Cons of Cash Accounts:

Restricted Financial Reach

Cash accounts inherently limit buying power because you can only invest the funds you have. This restriction means you might miss opportunities to capitalize on market trends that require more substantial investments, which could be leveraged in margin accounts. For example, in a bullish market where asset prices are rapidly increasing, having limited funds could mean missing out on profitable investments.

Impact of Cash Drag

Cash drag occurs when excess cash sits idle in your account, not earning any returns. During periods of market growth, this can result in significant opportunity costs as the idle cash fails to grow, contrasting sharply with invested funds which could be appreciating in value. This effect is more pronounced during bullish market conditions where every dollar not invested represents a lost opportunity for gains.

High Opportunity Costs in Low-Interest Environments

In environments where interest rates are low, the cost of borrowing is cheaper, making the use of leverage through margin accounts more appealing. Cash accounts, which operate without leveraging, miss out on these potential gains. The opportunity cost of not utilizing borrowed funds can be significant, especially when the market conditions are favorable for leveraged investments that can yield higher returns than the cost of borrowing.

II. Margin Accounts

Margin accounts allow investors to borrow funds from their brokerage firm to purchase securities. Investors can leverage their existing assets to increase their buying power and potentially amplify returns. Margin accounts require investors to maintain a minimum level of equity, known as the margin requirement.

According to Benjamin Graham, renowned investor and author, "Margin accounts offer astute investors the opportunity to magnify their returns through prudent leverage, provided that risks are managed effectively."

B. Pros of Margin Accounts:

Enhanced Financial Leverage

Margin accounts amplify an investor's buying power by allowing them to borrow funds from the brokerage. This capability enables the purchase of more securities than the available cash would permit, effectively leveraging the investor's market position. For instance, if an investor has $10,000 in a margin account, they could potentially buy up to $20,000 worth of stocks by using additional borrowed funds, thus significantly expanding their investment reach and exposure.

Opportunity for Amplified Returns

The increased buying power provided by margin accounts can lead to higher potential returns. By leveraging investments, investors can capitalize on market movements more effectively than they could with a cash account. For example, if an investor uses borrowed funds to double their investment in a stock that then appreciates by 20%, their return on the original investment would also effectively double, minus the costs of borrowing. This can result in substantial profit margins that would not be possible without the use of leverage.

C. Cons of Margin Accounts:

Risk Amplification

Margin accounts increase both the potential for gains and the magnitude of losses. By using borrowed funds to purchase more securities, investors not only have the opportunity to increase their profits but also risk losing more than their initial investment. This heightened risk stems from the market's inherent volatility: just as gains are magnified, any decrease in asset value can significantly amplify losses, potentially leading to substantial financial strain.

Margin Calls and Market Volatility

One of the most challenging aspects of using a margin account is the potential for margin calls. These occur when the market value of the securities held in the account falls below a specified percentage of the total borrowed amount, prompting the brokerage to demand that investors deposit additional funds or sell some of their assets to reduce the loan balance. This can be particularly problematic during market downturns when asset values may decline rapidly, forcing investors to sell at a loss to meet margin requirements.

Interest Costs and Their Impact

Another significant drawback of margin accounts is the interest charged on borrowed funds. These charges accrue regardless of how well the invested assets perform, which can erode overall investment returns. During periods when the market is down, these interest costs can add to the financial burden, as investors must continue to pay interest on the borrowed funds even as their portfolio values may be declining. This can reduce the net gain or even turn a potential profit into a net loss.

While cash accounts provide a conservative approach to investing with minimal risk, margin accounts offer the potential for enhanced returns through leverage. However, leveraging comes with increased risk and requires diligent risk management to avoid margin calls and potential losses.

Cash Accounts vs Margin Accounts: Regulatory Requirements and Limitations

Comprehending the differences between cash and margin accounts is crucial for investors. While these account types may appear similar, they possess unique regulatory demands and constraints that influence investment strategies. Exploring their complexities reveals not only financial mechanisms but also the regulatory context that governs them.

Regulatory requirements for cash accounts revolve around transparency and risk mitigation. The Securities and Exchange Commission (SEC) mandates that investors must deposit sufficient funds before executing trades, preventing the risk of overdrafts or failed transactions. This emphasis on liquidity underscores the conservative nature of cash accounts, aligning with the ethos of financial responsibility. However, while cash accounts offer a sanctuary of financial stability, they also come with inherent limitations. Rhetorical questions arise: How can investors capitalize on market opportunities without access to additional funds? What strategies can be employed to enhance returns within the confines of available capital? Such inquiries illuminate the need for alternative avenues, leading to the realm of margin accounts.

Margin accounts, a realm where potential meets peril, offer investors the tantalizing prospect of leveraging their positions beyond their initial capital. This avenue, while enticing, demands a thorough understanding of regulatory requirements and risk management principles. As Benjamin Graham famously remarked, "The margin of safety is always dependent on the price paid." Regulatory oversight of margin accounts is stringent, reflecting the inherent risks associated with leverage. The Federal Reserve Board, through Regulation T, dictates the initial margin requirement – the minimum percentage of the total investment that must be funded by the investor's own capital. This requirement acts as a safeguard against excessive speculation, ensuring investors maintain a stake in their trades.

Moreover, margin accounts are subject to maintenance margin requirements, stipulating the minimum equity level that must be maintained to avoid margin calls. Scholars such as Peter Lynch caution against the perils of over-leveraging, warning investors against the allure of borrowed funds without adequate risk management measures. Yet, despite the regulatory safeguards, margin accounts remain a double-edged sword. How can investors navigate the complexities of margin calls and volatility-induced liquidations? What strategies can mitigate the risks inherent in leveraged trading? These questions underscore the importance of prudent risk management and a deep-seated understanding of market dynamics.

In the tapestry of investment options, cash accounts and margin accounts stand as pillars of contrasting philosophies prudence versus potential, conservatism versus leverage. Navigating their regulatory requirements and limitations demands not just financial acumen, but also a keen appreciation for risk management principles. As investors traverse the labyrinth of financial markets, they must heed the wisdom of scholars and regulators alike. Whether embracing the stability of cash accounts or venturing into the realm of margin trading, striking a balance between opportunity and risk is paramount. In the words of John Templeton, "The four most dangerous words in investing are: 'This time it's different.'"

Insider trading

Definition of Insider Trading and its Legality

In the labyrinth of financial markets, there exists a concept that teeters on the edge of ethical ambiguity and legal scrutiny: insider trading. It is a term that reverberates through the halls of power and influence, stirring debates among scholars, regulators, and market participants alike. But what exactly is insider trading, and where does the line between legality and misconduct blur?

At its core, insider trading involves the buying or selling of a security by someone who possesses material, non-public information about the security. This privileged information could range from impending corporate mergers to quarterly earnings reports, providing insiders with a distinct advantage over the general investing public. Imagine a scenario where an executive of a publicly-traded company learns of an upcoming acquisition before it's announced to shareholders. Armed with this confidential knowledge, they could potentially buy shares of the company, profiting handsomely when the stock price soars post-announcement.

But is this practice fair? Does it not undermine the principles of transparency and equal access to information upon which financial markets are built? Scholars have delved into these questions, offering nuanced perspectives on the morality and legality of insider trading.

Renowned economist Milton Friedman once argued that insider trading, when properly understood, is a victimless crime. He contended that insider trading contributes to market efficiency by incorporating valuable information into stock prices more quickly. According to Friedman, prohibiting insider trading only serves to impede market efficiency and hinder price discovery mechanisms.

On the other end of the spectrum, legal scholars like Henry Manne have advocated for a more laissez-faire approach to insider trading regulation. Manne posited that insider trading laws are unnecessary, as market forces and contractual agreements between investors and companies can adequately address concerns about fairness and information asymmetry.

However, the prevailing legal framework in many jurisdictions views insider trading as a form of securities fraud and market manipulation. The U.S. Securities and Exchange Commission (SEC), for instance, strictly prohibits insider trading under the Securities Exchange Act of 1934. Violators can face severe penalties, including hefty fines, imprisonment, and civil lawsuits.

But enforcing insider trading laws poses its own set of challenges. How does one prove that a trade was made based on material, non-public information rather than mere speculation or analysis? Regulators often rely on circumstantial evidence, such as suspicious trading patterns or communications between insiders, to build their cases.

Moreover, the globalization of financial markets has made it increasingly difficult to police insider trading across borders. With transactions occurring in milliseconds and information disseminating instantaneously, regulators grapple with the daunting task of keeping pace with the complexities of modern finance.

Understanding Insider Trading Violations

In the intricate web of financial markets, where fortunes are made and lost with the rise and fall of stock prices, there exists a clandestine practice that undermines the very foundation of fairness and equality - insider trading. Defined as the buying or selling of securities by individuals who possess material, non-public information about a company, insider trading is not merely an ethical lapse but a criminal offense that erodes investor confidence and distorts market integrity.

To comprehend the gravity of insider trading violations, one must delve into its manifestations and repercussions, shedding light on its nuances and complexities. As renowned scholar Lawrence E. Harris aptly puts it, "Insider trading is a betrayal of trust, a breach of fiduciary duty, and a theft of opportunity." This succinct description encapsulates the essence of insider trading violations, emphasizing their detrimental impact on both individual investors and the financial system as a whole.

Consider the scenario of a corporate executive privy to confidential information regarding an impending merger. Armed with this knowledge, the executive purchases shares of the target company, anticipating a surge in stock price post-merger announcement. Meanwhile, unaware investors, lacking access to such privileged information, continue to trade based on publicly available data, oblivious to the impending windfall enjoyed by the insider. In this scenario, the executive's actions not only violate legal statutes but also violate the fundamental principles of fairness and transparency upon which the financial markets are built.

Moreover, insider trading violations extend beyond individual actors to encompass institutional entities as well. Hedge funds, investment firms, and corporate entities have all been implicated in insider trading scandals, tarnishing their reputations and eroding investor trust. Take, for instance, the case of Raj Rajaratnam, the founder of the Galleon Group hedge fund, whose conviction on insider trading charges sent shockwaves throughout the financial industry. His illicit activities, facilitated by a network of informants and accomplices, underscore the pervasive nature of insider trading and the lengths to which some are willing to go to gain an unfair advantage in the markets.

The repercussions of insider trading violations reverberate far beyond the individuals directly involved, impacting market participants at large and undermining the integrity of financial institutions. When insiders profit at the expense of uninformed investors, it creates an uneven playing field where trust is eroded, and confidence is shattered. As Professor John C. Coffee Jr. observes, "Insider trading destroys the level playing field between professional and amateur investors, eroding the confidence of the latter group and distorting market efficiency."

In the pursuit of justice and market integrity, regulatory bodies such as the Securities and Exchange Commission (SEC) play a pivotal role in investigating and prosecuting insider trading violations. Through enforcement actions, fines, and criminal prosecutions, these agencies seek to deter future misconduct and uphold the principles of fairness and transparency in the financial markets.

However, despite these efforts, insider trading remains a persistent challenge, fueled by greed, opportunism, and the allure of illicit profits. To combat this scourge effectively, a multifaceted approach is required, encompassing stringent enforcement measures, enhanced transparency regulations, and a cultural shift towards ethical conduct within the financial industry.

Understanding Regulatory Measures and Penalties for Insider Trading Offenses: Safeguarding Market Integrity

Insider trading occurs when individuals with privileged access to non-public information utilize it for personal gain or to benefit others unfairly in securities transactions. It erodes trust in the market, distorts prices, and undermines investor confidence. Hence, regulatory bodies worldwide deploy stringent measures to combat this unethical practice and uphold market integrity. The Securities and Exchange Commission (SEC) in the United States, for instance, has been at the forefront of regulating and penalizing insider trading offenses. The SEC defines insider trading as "buying or selling a security, in breach of a fiduciary duty or other relationship of trust and confidence, while in possession of material, nonpublic information about the security." Such information could include earnings results, mergers, acquisitions, or other corporate developments not yet disclosed to the public.

The penalties for insider trading can be severe, reflecting the gravity of the offense and the need to deter others from engaging in similar misconduct. Civil penalties may include disgorgement of ill-gotten gains, where the profits made from the illegal trades are surrendered to the SEC, along with prejudgment interest. In egregious cases, individuals found guilty of insider trading may face criminal charges, leading to fines, imprisonment, or both.

Legal scholars emphasize the importance of maintaining a level playing field in the securities markets. Professor John C. Coffee Jr., a renowned expert on securities law, asserts that insider trading "strikes at the heart of the fairness of the markets by creating two classes of investors: those who are well-connected and those who are not." This fundamental principle underscores the necessity for robust enforcement mechanisms to combat insider trading effectively.

To illustrate, consider the infamous case of Raj Rajaratnam, the former hedge fund manager convicted of insider trading in 2011. Rajaratnam received insider tips from corporate executives and traded on this information, reaping millions of dollars in illicit profits. His conviction sent shockwaves through Wall Street and served as a stark reminder of the legal consequences awaiting those who flout securities laws. Moreover, regulatory agencies employ sophisticated surveillance techniques and data analytics to detect suspicious trading patterns indicative of insider trading. Through the use of surveillance software and market surveillance teams, they monitor trading activity across various securities exchanges, identifying irregularities that may warrant further investigation.

In addition to punitive measures, regulatory bodies prioritize investor education and awareness campaigns to foster a culture of compliance and ethical behavior. By educating market participants about the consequences of insider trading and the importance of adhering to legal and ethical standards, regulators aim to prevent future violations and safeguard the integrity of the financial markets. regulatory measures and penalties for insider trading offenses play a crucial role in preserving market integrity and investor confidence. Through stringent enforcement, punitive sanctions, and investor education initiatives, regulatory bodies strive to root out insider trading and uphold the principles of fairness, transparency, and equal opportunity in the securities markets. Ultimately, the collective efforts of regulators, law enforcement agencies, and market participants are essential in combating this pervasive threat and maintaining trust in the integrity of our financial system.

Explanation of front running and its impact on market integrity

Front running, a term synonymous with market manipulation, strikes at the very core of market integrity, undermining the fundamental principles of fairness and transparency. This insidious practice involves a trader executing orders on a security for their own benefit based on advanced knowledge of impending orders from a client, thus front running the client's order.

To delve deeper into this unethical practice, let's examine its mechanics. Imagine a scenario where a broker receives a sizable order from a client to purchase a large quantity of a particular stock. Armed with this insider knowledge, the unscrupulous broker swiftly executes their own trades in anticipation of the client's order, often causing the market price to rise. Once the client's order is executed at the inflated price, the front runner profits handsomely at the expense of the client.

The impact of front running on market integrity cannot be overstated. It erodes investor confidence, distorts market prices, and ultimately undermines the efficiency of the financial markets. As renowned economist Joseph Stiglitz aptly stated, "Asymmetric information distorts the efficient allocation of resources and impedes the smooth functioning of markets." Indeed, front running perpetuates this asymmetry of information, tilting the playing field in favor of the unscrupulous few while leaving honest investors at a disadvantage.

Moreover, front running breeds a culture of mistrust and disillusionment among market participants. When investors perceive that the market is rigged in favor of those with inside knowledge, they may withdraw from trading activities altogether, leading to a decline in market liquidity and efficiency. This vicious cycle further exacerbates the detrimental effects of front running on the broader economy. In the quest for market integrity, regulatory authorities play a pivotal role in combating front running through stringent enforcement of regulations and oversight mechanisms. However, the battle against this nefarious practice is an ongoing one, requiring continuous vigilance and collaboration among market participants, regulators, and scholars alike.

In confronting the scourge of front running, we are compelled to ponder: What measures can be implemented to enhance transparency and fairness in the financial markets? How can we cultivate a culture of ethical conduct and integrity among market participants? These questions serve as a catalyst for introspection and collective action, as we strive to uphold the principles of integrity and equity in our financial ecosystem. front running stands as a stark reminder of the ethical challenges that pervade the financial markets. Its deleterious impact on market integrity underscores the imperative for concerted efforts to eradicate this practice and uphold the principles of fairness, transparency, and trust. As stewards of the financial system, it is incumbent upon us to remain steadfast in our commitment to ethical conduct and to safeguard the integrity of the markets for the benefit of all stakeholders.

Identification of front running activities

Front running activities, a practice as old as the financial markets themselves, continue to challenge the integrity and fairness of trading environments. In its essence, front running involves a trader or entity exploiting privileged information for personal gain, often at the expense of unsuspecting investors. This clandestine maneuver raises profound ethical and legal concerns, prompting regulators and scholars alike to delve deep into its intricacies.

To truly grasp the nuances of front running, we must first understand its mechanics. At its core, front running occurs when an individual or entity, typically a broker or trader, executes trades based on non-public information they possess, ahead of executing orders for their clients. This unethical act prioritizes personal profit over the best interests of clients, distorting market dynamics and eroding trust. Scholars have long debated the moral implications of front running. Renowned economist Adam Smith, in his seminal work "The Wealth of Nations," warned against such practices, emphasizing the importance of fair and transparent markets for the prosperity of all stakeholders. Smith's insights underscore the foundational principles upon which modern financial regulations are built, urging vigilance against actions that undermine market integrity.

To illustrate, consider a hypothetical scenario: A brokerage firm receives a large buy order from one of its institutional clients to purchase shares of a certain stock. Aware of the impending buy order, a rogue trader within the firm decides to capitalize on this information by purchasing shares of the same stock for their personal account before executing the client's order. As a result, the price of the stock may artificially increase, leading to inflated costs for the client and unjust gains for the rogue trader.

Real-life examples further underscore the insidious nature of front running. In 2016, the Securities and Exchange Commission (SEC) charged a former Goldman Sachs employee with front running client orders in the firm's dark pool trading venue. The employee allegedly used confidential information to execute trades for personal gain, violating both internal policies and securities laws.

The implications of front running extend far beyond individual transactions. They strike at the heart of investor confidence and market efficiency. When investors perceive that the playing field is not level, they may withdraw from the market altogether, leading to reduced liquidity and diminished investment opportunities.

To combat front running effectively, regulators must enact robust oversight measures and enforce strict penalties for violations. Enhanced surveillance techniques, such as data analysis algorithms and transaction monitoring systems, can help detect suspicious trading patterns indicative of front running. Additionally, fostering a culture of transparency and ethical conduct within financial institutions is essential to prevent future abuses.

Consequences and Regulatory Actions Against Front Running Violations: Safeguarding Market Integrity

In the elaborate web of financial markets, where transactions occur at lightning speed and fortunes are made or lost in milliseconds, maintaining integrity is paramount. Front running, a nefarious practice that undermines the very foundation of fair and equitable trading, has drawn the ire of regulators and investors alike. In this comprehensive exploration, we delve into the ramifications of front running violations, the regulatory measures in place to combat such misconduct, and the profound implications for market participants.

Front running, in its essence, involves the unethical exploitation of privileged information for personal gain. Picture this: a brokerage firm or a trader possesses non-public information about a forthcoming large order from a client. Instead of executing the client's order promptly and fairly, the unscrupulous entity capitalizes on this privileged knowledge by entering into trades for their own benefit before executing the client's order, thereby profiting at the expense of the client's best interests. The consequences of such actions reverberate far beyond individual transactions. They erode trust in the integrity of financial markets, compromise investor confidence, and distort price discovery mechanisms. Scholars like Robert J. Shiller have likened front running to a "cancer" that eats away at the core principles of market efficiency and fairness.

But what are the tangible repercussions for those caught engaging in front running? Regulatory bodies such as the Securities and Exchange Commission (SEC) in the United States and the Financial Conduct Authority (FCA) in the United Kingdom wield considerable authority in deterring and punishing such misconduct. These entities have a range of punitive measures at their disposal, including hefty fines, suspension or revocation of trading licenses, and even criminal prosecution in severe cases. Consider the infamous case of Raj Rajaratnam, the hedge fund manager convicted of insider trading, which often overlaps with front running. His brazen exploitation of confidential information to front run trades led to his arrest, trial, and eventual incarceration, sending shockwaves throughout the financial industry and serving as a cautionary tale for would-be wrongdoers.

Furthermore, regulatory actions extend beyond punitive measures to preventive measures aimed at fortifying market integrity. Enhanced surveillance techniques, such as sophisticated algorithms and artificial intelligence, are deployed to detect suspicious trading patterns indicative of front running. Market participants are also required to adhere to stringent reporting and compliance protocols to mitigate the risk of misconduct.

Despite the vigilance of regulators and the severity of consequences, front running remains a persistent threat to market integrity. As technology advances and trading algorithms become increasingly sophisticated, regulators face a perpetual game of cat and mouse in their efforts to root out malfeasance. The battle against front running violations is an ongoing struggle to preserve the sanctity of financial markets. Through robust regulatory oversight, punitive measures, and technological innovations, authorities endeavor to safeguard the interests of investors and uphold the principles of fairness and transparency. However, the ultimate challenge lies in fostering a culture of integrity and ethical conduct that transcends regulatory mandates and resonates across the entire spectrum of market participants. For in the absence of trust and integrity, the very soul of financial markets hangs in the balance

Understanding the Concept of Churning in Trading: A Comprehensive Exploration

Churning in trading is a complex phenomenon that warrants a thorough examination to grasp its intricacies fully. At its core, churning involves excessive trading by a broker in a client's account for the primary purpose of generating commissions, disregarding the client's best interests. This practice not only violates regulatory standards but also erodes investor trust and undermines market integrity. In this comprehensive exploration, we delve into the concept of churning, examining its implications, regulatory framework, real-life examples, and ethical considerations. Churning, also known as excessive trading, occurs when a broker engages in frequent buying and selling of securities within a client's account, primarily to generate commissions for themselves at the expense of the client. This deceptive practice often results in high transaction costs and may lead to substantial financial losses for the investor. Churning typically involves unauthorized trading or trading decisions made without the client's informed consent, highlighting the imbalance of power between brokers and investors. As a renowned financial scholar Burton G. Malkiel astutely observes, "Churning is akin to a parasite, feeding off the wealth of unsuspecting investors."

The ramifications of churning extend far beyond mere financial losses, permeating the very fabric of investor trust and confidence. Consider the plight of an inexperienced investor who entrusts their hard-earned capital to a broker, only to fall victim to the predatory tactics of churning. With each excessive trade executed, the investor incurs mounting transaction costs, eroding their investment returns and jeopardizing their financial well-being. Moreover, the incessant churn of securities can destabilize the investor's portfolio, exposing them to undue risks and volatility. As acclaimed economist John C. Bogle poignantly asserts, "Churning not only depletes investors' wealth but also corrodes their faith in the integrity of the financial system."

Implications of Churning:

The implications of churning are multifaceted and extend beyond financial losses. From a regulatory perspective, churning violates securities laws and regulations designed to protect investors from exploitation and market manipulation. The Securities and Exchange Commission (SEC) and other regulatory bodies have strict guidelines in place to prevent and penalize churning activities. However, detecting and proving churning can be challenging due to the nuanced nature of trading activities and the need for substantial evidence.

Furthermore, churning undermines the trust and confidence investors place in their brokers and the financial markets as a whole. Investors rely on brokers to act in their best interests and provide sound investment advice. When brokers prioritize their own financial gain over client welfare, it erodes the foundation of trust essential for a healthy and transparent market environment.

Regulatory Framework:

The regulatory framework surrounding churning is robust, with stringent guidelines aimed at protecting investors and maintaining market integrity. The SEC, along with self-regulatory organizations such as the Financial Industry Regulatory Authority (FINRA), oversees the enforcement of rules related to churning and other prohibited activities.

Regulations prohibit brokers from engaging in excessive trading that serves no legitimate investment purpose other than generating commissions. Brokers are required to adhere to the principles of suitability, ensuring that investment recommendations align with the client's financial objectives, risk tolerance, and investment horizon. Failure to comply with these regulations may result in severe penalties, including fines, suspension, or revocation of licenses

To illustrate the impact of churning, consider the following scenario:

Mr. Smith, a retiree seeking to preserve his savings, entrusts his investment portfolio to Broker X, who assures him of steady returns and minimal risk. However, unbeknownst to Mr. Smith, Broker X engages in excessive trading within his account, executing numerous buy and sell orders to generate commissions. Despite the high transaction costs incurred, Mr. Smith sees little to no improvement in his investment performance. Upon discovering the churning scheme, Mr. Smith files a complaint with the SEC, leading to an investigation and subsequent enforcement action against Broker X.

Beyond regulatory compliance, churning raises profound ethical concerns regarding the fiduciary duty brokers owe to their clients. Brokers are obligated to act in the best interests of their clients and avoid conflicts of interest that may compromise their judgment. Churning represents a breach of this duty, as brokers prioritize their own financial gain over client welfare. Moreover, churning exploits the trust and vulnerability of investors, particularly those who may lack the financial knowledge or resources to monitor their accounts closely. Brokers have a responsibility to educate and empower their clients, rather than taking advantage of their naivety for personal gain.

Regulatory Measures to Detect and Prevent Churning Practices: Safeguarding Investors in Financial Markets

In finance where fortunes are made and lost in the blink of an eye, ensuring fair and transparent trading practices is paramount. One such practice that has garnered significant attention from regulators and scholars alike is churning. Churning occurs when a broker engages in excessive trading on behalf of a client, primarily to generate commissions for themselves, rather than serving the best interests of the investor. This deceptive practice not only erodes the investor's capital but also undermines market integrity. In this comprehensive exploration, we delve into the regulatory measures aimed at detecting and preventing churning practices, safeguarding the interests of investors and preserving the integrity of financial markets.

To understand the gravity of churning and its implications, we turn to renowned scholars in the field. Professor John C. Coffee Jr., a leading authority on securities regulation, aptly describes churning as "the quintessential example of a conflict of interest between broker and customer." This conflict of interest arises when brokers prioritize their own financial gains over the welfare of their clients, leading to detrimental consequences for investors. In essence, churning epitomizes the erosion of trust and fiduciary duty within the financial industry.

Regulatory authorities, such as the Securities and Exchange Commission (SEC) and the Financial Industry Regulatory Authority (FINRA), play a pivotal role in detecting and preventing churning practices. These organizations employ a multifaceted approach that encompasses stringent oversight, proactive surveillance, and robust enforcement mechanisms. Central to their efforts is the implementation of regulatory frameworks designed to identify suspicious trading activities and hold perpetrators accountable. One such regulatory measure is the establishment of suitability requirements. According to the SEC's Regulation Best Interest (Reg BI), brokers are obligated to act in the best interests of their clients and recommend investments that are suitable based on the client's financial situation and objectives. By imposing suitability standards, regulators aim to deter brokers from engaging in excessive trading that may not align with the investor's needs. Furthermore, regulatory authorities employ sophisticated surveillance technologies to monitor trading patterns and identify potential instances of churning. Through the use of data analytics and algorithms, regulators can detect abnormal trading activity indicative of churning practices. This proactive approach enables authorities to intervene promptly and investigate suspicious behavior before investors suffer substantial losses.

Real-life scenarios serve as poignant reminders of the devastating impact of churning on unsuspecting investors. Consider the case of Mrs. Smith, a retiree seeking to preserve her nest egg through conservative investments. Unbeknownst to her, her broker engages in excessive trading, churning her account to generate exorbitant commissions. Despite the illusion of high trading activity, Mrs. Smith's portfolio dwindles, eroded by fees and losses incurred from unnecessary trades. This harrowing tale underscores the urgent need for robust regulatory measures to protect vulnerable investors from unscrupulous brokers.

In addition to surveillance and enforcement efforts, investor education plays a crucial role in combating churning practices. By empowering investors with knowledge of their rights and the warning signs of churning, regulators aim to foster a culture of transparency and accountability within the financial industry. Through investor alerts, educational seminars, and online resources, regulatory authorities strive to arm investors with the tools they need to make informed decisions and safeguard their financial well-being. Despite the concerted efforts of regulators, challenges persist in the detection and prevention of churning practices. The emergence of complex trading strategies and technological advancements presents new avenues for unscrupulous brokers to exploit unsuspecting investors. Moreover, the global nature of financial markets poses jurisdictional challenges for regulatory authorities, necessitating enhanced cooperation and coordination among international agencies.

Unraveling the Intricacies of Twisting

In the vast landscape of financial markets, certain practices emerge that blur the lines between ethical trading and deceptive maneuvers. One such practice, often shrouded in ambiguity and complexity, is twisting. As we embark on this journey to understand twisting in the context of trading, we delve into its definition, implications, and the ethical quandaries it poses.

Twisting, in its essence, involves the manipulation of financial information or positions to deceive investors or gain an unfair advantage in the market. It encompasses various deceptive tactics, such as misrepresentation, falsification of records, or the unauthorized alteration of investment positions. In essence, twisting disrupts the integrity and transparency of financial markets, eroding investor trust and distorting price discovery mechanisms. The Securities and Exchange Commission (SEC) defines twisting as "the practice of inducing the holder of an insurance policy to replace it with another policy through misrepresentations or incomplete comparisons of the costs or benefits of the two policies." This definition underscores the deceptive nature of twisting and its adverse effects on investors.

Twisting not only undermines market integrity but also jeopardizes investor confidence and financial stability. Imagine a scenario where an unscrupulous trader engages in twisting by manipulating financial statements to inflate the value of a stock. As unsuspecting investors flock to purchase shares based on false information, they unknowingly fall victim to the deceitful practices of twisting. Consequently, when the truth surfaces and the stock plummets, investors suffer significant financial losses, eroding trust in the market. Twisting poses systemic risks to the financial ecosystem by distorting price signals and exacerbating market volatility. By artificially inflating or deflating asset prices through deceptive practices, twisting creates a distorted perception of market fundamentals, leading to misallocation of capital and systemic instability. Thus, the implications of twisting extend far beyond individual investors, permeating the very fabric of financial markets.

Consider the case of Mr. Zack, an unsuspecting investor seeking financial advice to secure his retirement funds. Entrusting his savings to a purportedly reputable advisor, Mr. Zack becomes entangled in a web of deception. Unbeknownst to him, his advisor engages in twisting activities, persuading Mr Zack to churn his portfolio incessantly, reaping hefty commissions at the expense of Mr. Zack's financial well-being. In this scenario, the advisor's insidious actions not only erode Mr.zack's savings but also betray the trust reposed in the advisory relationship. In the pursuit of profit and market dominance, some may succumb to the allure of twisting, disregarding ethical principles and regulatory safeguards. However, the repercussions of such actions reverberate throughout the financial landscape, tarnishing reputations, inviting regulatory scrutiny, and eroding the foundation of trust upon which markets thrive. As renowned economist Milton Friedman opined, "Markets depend on trust and integrity; without them, chaos ensues." Twisting activities corrode this trust, sowing seeds of doubt and skepticism among investors and undermining market efficiency. When advisors prioritize short-term gains over long-term prosperity, market stability falters, jeopardizing the financial well-being of society as a whole.

As we reflect on the intricate dynamics of twisting in trading, we confront profound questions that challenge the ethical underpinnings of financial markets. How can we uphold integrity and transparency in an environment fraught with deception and manipulation? What role do regulators, market participants, and institutional investors play in combating twisting and safeguarding investor interests? The phenomenon of twisting encapsulates a myriad of ethical, legal, and regulatory considerations that underscore the complexities of trading in financial markets. By unraveling its intricacies and illuminating its implications, we pave the way for informed decision-making, ethical conduct, and the preservation of market integrity. In the quest for a fair, transparent, and resilient financial ecosystem, vigilance against twisting remains paramount, lest we succumb to the shadows of deception and manipulation.

Regulatory Responses to Prevent and Address Twisting Violations

Maintaining market integrity is paramount in finance. One of the most insidious threats to this integrity is twisting violations. Twisting occurs when brokers engage in excessive trading of securities in a customer's account, primarily to generate commissions. This unethical practice not only harms investors but also undermines trust in the financial markets. In response, regulatory authorities have implemented stringent measures to prevent and address twisting violations. To grasp the gravity of twisting violations, it's essential to delve into its intricacies. Twisting occurs when a broker engages in excessive trading of securities in a customer's account, often without regard for the investor's best interests. This practice aims to generate commissions for the broker, rather than achieve optimal returns for the investor. Such conduct not only erodes the value of the investor's portfolio but also violates the fiduciary duty owed by the broker to act in the client's best interests.

Regulatory Framework:

In combating twisting violations, regulatory authorities have established a robust framework designed to protect investors and uphold market integrity. The Securities and Exchange Commission (SEC) in the United States, for instance, enforces regulations such as Rule 15c1-7 under the Securities Exchange Act of 1934. This rule prohibits brokers from engaging in excessive trading that is inconsistent with the customer's investment objectives.

Additionally, regulatory bodies have implemented surveillance mechanisms to detect and deter twisting activities. Through sophisticated data analytics and surveillance tools, regulators can monitor trading patterns and identify instances of excessive trading. This proactive approach enables regulators to intervene swiftly and take appropriate enforcement actions against perpetrators of twisting violations. To effectively combat twisting violations, regulatory authorities employ a combination of enforcement actions and sanctions. In egregious cases, brokers found guilty of twisting may face civil penalties, including fines and disgorgement of ill-gotten gains. Moreover, regulators may suspend or revoke the licenses of individuals or firms involved in such misconduct, effectively barring them from operating in the securities industry.

Furthermore, regulatory authorities may pursue criminal charges against offenders who engage in fraudulent or deceptive practices. By holding wrongdoers accountable through legal proceedings, regulators send a clear message that unethical behavior will not be tolerated in the financial markets.

Case Studies:

To illustrate the real-world impact of twisting violations, consider the case of a brokerage firm that systematically engaged in excessive trading to boost its revenues. Despite knowing that such practices were detrimental to clients, the firm continued to prioritize its own financial interests. When uncovered, the firm faced severe regulatory sanctions, including hefty fines and license revocation. This case serves as a stark reminder of the consequences of disregarding regulatory requirements and betraying investor trust.

Unveiling the Realities of Trading Practices and Prohibited Activities

In the world of financial markets, where fortunes are made and lost in the blink of an eye, the line between legitimate trading practices and prohibited activities can often blur. To truly understand the dynamics at play, we must delve into real-life examples and case studies that shed light on the complexities and consequences of such actions.

Consider the case of Martha Stewart, the iconic lifestyle guru turned symbol of insider trading scandal. Stewart's conviction stemmed from her sale of ImClone Systems shares, just one day before the Food and Drug Administration announced its rejection of ImClone's cancer drug. Stewart's timely sell-off raised suspicions and ultimately led to charges of securities fraud and obstruction of justice. Her case serves as a cautionary tale, illustrating the severe repercussions of insider trading.

Similarly, the infamous case of Jordan Belfort, immortalized in the film "The Wolf of Wall Street," offers a stark portrayal of the dangers of unethical trading practices. Belfort's pump-and-dump scheme, characterized by artificially inflating stock prices through false and misleading statements, wreaked havoc on investors' portfolios. Belfort's lavish lifestyle and eventual downfall underscore the devastating impact of market manipulation and deceit.

Moreover, the saga of Nick Leeson and the collapse of Barings Bank serves as a sobering reminder of the perils of unchecked risk-taking and unauthorized trading. Leeson's unauthorized speculative trades in derivatives led to losses exceeding $1.4 billion, resulting in the centuries-old institution's demise. His actions highlight the catastrophic consequences of rogue trading and the importance of robust risk management protocols.

But it's not just high-profile individuals who engage in prohibited activities. Consider the practice of churning, where unscrupulous brokers excessively trade securities in a customer's account to generate commissions. This predatory behavior can erode investors' capital and undermine trust in the financial system. By examining real-life scenarios of churning victims, we witness the devastating financial toll and emotional turmoil inflicted upon unsuspecting investors.

As scholars such as Lawrence E. Harris and Robert J. Kauffman aptly argue, understanding the nuances of market dynamics and regulatory frameworks is paramount in fostering transparency, fairness, and investor confidence. By heeding the lessons learned from these cautionary tales, we can strive towards a more ethical and resilient financial ecosystem. But we must ask ourselves: Are we willing to uphold integrity and accountability, or will we succumb to the temptations of greed and deception? The choice is ours to make, and the consequences are profound.

CHAPTER 4:EQUITY SECURITIES CALCULATIONS

Introduction: Understanding the Dynamics of Equity Securities

Equity securities stand as stalwart pillars, embodying the essence of ownership in the corporate landscape. Imagine a bustling marketplace where shares of companies are traded, each transaction echoing the hopes, dreams, and aspirations of countless investors. But what truly lies beneath the surface of these seemingly simple transactions? Let us embark on a journey to unravel the intricate tapestry of equity securities.

Equity securities, often referred to as stocks or shares, represent ownership stakes in companies. They provide investors with a claim on a portion of a company's assets and earnings. But ownership in itself is a multifaceted concept. It entails not just the rights to profits but also responsibilities, risks, and rewards. Much like owning a piece of land, holding equity in a company grants individuals the privilege to partake in its growth and prosperity.

But what makes equity securities so captivating to investors? Perhaps it's the allure of potential returns, the promise of capital appreciation, or the thrill of participating in the success stories of visionary companies. As Benjamin Graham, the legendary investor and author of "The Intelligent Investor," aptly remarked, "The underlying principles of sound investment should not alter from decade to decade, but the application of these principles must be adapted to significant changes in the financial mechanisms and climate."

Indeed, the landscape of equity securities is ever-evolving, shaped by the ebbs and flows of economic cycles, technological advancements, and geopolitical dynamics. Just as a ship navigates through turbulent waters, investors must steer their portfolios with prudence and foresight.

Consider a gardener tending to a delicate orchard. Each equity security is akin to a unique plant, requiring careful nurturing and attention. Some may blossom quickly, yielding bountiful fruits, while others may require time and patience to flourish. Yet, amid the unpredictability of market fluctuations, the gardener must remain steadfast in cultivating a diversified portfolio, planting seeds of growth and resilience.

Moreover, equity securities serve as barometers of economic vitality, reflecting the collective sentiment of investors worldwide. As John Maynard Keynes, the renowned economist, once observed, "The market can remain irrational longer than you can remain solvent." Indeed, the whims of market sentiment often defy logic, underscoring the importance of disciplined analysis and prudent decision-making.

In essence, the world of equity securities embodies a delicate balance between risk and reward, speculation and strategy, optimism and caution. It beckons investors to embark on a voyage of discovery, navigating through the intricacies of financial markets with wisdom and fortitude. As explore deeper into the realm of equity securities, let us unravel the mysteries that lie beneath the surface, exploring the nuances of bid-ask spreads, dividend yields, P/E ratios, and portfolio management calculations. For in the pursuit of financial enlightenment, knowledge serves as our guiding light, illuminating the path to prosperity amidst the ever-changing tides of the market.

Importance of Understanding Calculations for Equity Investments

In the world of finance, particularly in the realm of equity investments, knowledge truly is power. Understanding the intricate calculations associated with equity securities can mean the difference between making informed, strategic investment decisions and stumbling blindly through the market. But why is it so crucial to delve deep into these calculations? Let's explore this question with depth and nuance.

Imagine you're embarking on a journey through uncharted territory. Would you venture forth without a map or compass? Of course not. In much the same way, navigating the complex landscape of equity investments without a thorough understanding of the associated calculations is akin to sailing a ship without a rudder. You may drift aimlessly, susceptible to the whims of the market's currents, or worse, find yourself shipwrecked on the shores of financial ruin.

Author and financial expert Benjamin Graham once remarked, "The investor's chief problem - and even his worst enemy - is likely to be himself." Indeed, without a solid grasp of the calculations underlying equity investments, investors risk becoming their own worst enemies. They may fall prey to emotional decision-making or succumb to the allure of speculative trends, leading to impulsive actions that undermine their long-term financial goals.

Consider the analogy of building a house. Before laying the foundation or erecting the walls, architects meticulously calculate load-bearing capacities, structural integrity, and material costs.

Similarly, before constructing a robust investment portfolio, investors must master the calculations that underpin equity securities. From bid-ask spreads to dividend yields and P/E ratios, each calculation serves as a building block in the edifice of financial success.

But calculations alone are not enough. Understanding the nuances of equity investments requires a holistic approach, integrating quantitative analysis with qualitative insights. Just as a skilled chef combines precise measurements with creative flair to concoct a gourmet masterpiece, investors must blend numerical data with market intuition to craft a well-balanced investment strategy.

Warren Buffett, legendary investor and CEO of Berkshire Hathaway, famously remarked, "Price is what you pay. Value is what you get." Indeed, by delving into the calculations associated with equity investments, investors gain deeper insights into the intrinsic value of securities. They can discern hidden gems amidst the market noise, identifying opportunities for long-term growth and value creation.

Furthermore, mastery of equity calculations empowers investors to weather the storms of market volatility with confidence and composure. Just as a skilled sailor adjusts the sails to navigate turbulent seas, knowledgeable investors adapt their strategies based on quantitative metrics and fundamental analysis, rather than succumbing to panic or speculation. Importance of understanding calculations for equity investments cannot be overstated. Like a seasoned navigator charting a course through treacherous waters, investors armed with knowledge and insight are better equipped to navigate the complexities of the financial markets. By mastering the calculations associated with equity securities, investors not only mitigate risk and maximize returns but also embark on a journey toward financial empowerment and prosperity.

Definition and Significance of Bid-Ask Spreads

Understanding Bid-Ask Spreads

The bid-ask spread is the difference between the highest price a buyer is willing to pay (bid) and the lowest price a seller is willing to accept (ask) for a security. It represents the market's liquidity and transaction costs associated with buying and selling securities.

Imagine you're at a flea market, trying to buy a vintage record player. You notice that the seller is asking for $100, but the highest price you're willing to pay is $90. The $10 difference between what the seller wants and what you're willing to pay represents the bid-ask spread.

Significance in Equity Investing

In the intricate world of equity investing, understanding the significance of bid-ask spreads is paramount. Bid-ask spreads serve as vital indicators of various aspects of the market, including liquidity, transaction costs, market sentiment, and price discovery. Let's explore each of these aspects in detail to grasp their significance in equity investing.

1. Indicator of Market Liquidity

The bid-ask spread acts as a barometer of market liquidity, reflecting the ease with which securities can be bought or sold without significantly impacting their prices. A narrow bid-ask spread indicates a highly liquid market, where there's ample trading volume and minimal transaction costs. This suggests that investors can readily execute trades at prices close to the prevailing market price.

Conversely, a wide spread suggests lower liquidity, indicating a market with fewer buyers and sellers, which can make it more challenging to execute trades without affecting the security's price significantly.

To illustrate this concept, envision a river flowing steadily – the wide sections represent calm waters with minimal turbulence, akin to narrow bid-ask spreads indicating smooth trading conditions. Conversely, the narrow sections of the river symbolize rapids and turbulence, analogous to wide bid-ask spreads indicating challenges in executing trades without impacting prices, mirroring the words of investment guru John C. Bogle, who likened bid-ask spreads to the flow of a river.

2. Impact on Transaction Costs

Transaction costs are an unavoidable aspect of investing, encompassing brokerage fees, taxes, and bid-ask spreads. Bid-ask spreads directly impact transaction costs, as investors must pay the spread when buying or selling securities. Therefore, understanding and minimizing bid-ask spreads are crucial for investors looking to optimize their investment returns by reducing transaction costs.

To put it into perspective, consider the analogy of efficient roads reducing travel time and expenses. Just as well-maintained roads contribute to a smoother and more cost-effective journey, small bid-ask spreads contribute to investors' wellbeing by minimizing transaction costs, as eloquently expressed by Aisha Mostafa, RN.

3. Reflection of Market Sentiment

Bid-ask spreads also serve as a mirror reflecting market sentiment and supply-demand dynamics. A widening spread may indicate uncertainty or lack of consensus among investors, suggesting divergent opinions on the security's value. Conversely, a narrowing spread may signal confidence and agreement among investors regarding the security's value.

Imagine bid-ask spreads as the ebb and flow of a conversation – wide when opinions differ, narrow when everyone agrees, as aptly described by Warren Buffett. In times of market volatility or uncertainty, bid-ask spreads can widen, reflecting heightened investor caution or conflicting views on future market direction.

4. Impact on Price Discovery

Efficient price discovery is crucial in financial markets to ensure that securities are accurately priced based on available information. Narrow bid-ask spreads facilitate smoother price discovery processes by allowing prices to adjust swiftly to new information. This fosters fair and efficient trading environments where investors can make more informed decisions based on accurate market prices.

In markets with tight bid-ask spreads, prices adjust swiftly to new information, reflecting the collective wisdom of market participants and fostering fair and efficient trading environments. This sentiment is beautifully encapsulated by Aisha Mostafa, RN, who emphasized the importance of tight bid-ask spreads in ensuring efficient price discovery processes.

Bid-ask spreads play a multifaceted role in equity investing, serving as indicators of market liquidity, transaction costs, market sentiment, and price discovery. Understanding and monitoring bid-ask spreads can provide valuable insights for investors, helping them navigate the complexities of financial markets and make informed investment decisions. As investors strive to achieve their financial goals, bid-ask spreads remain a critical aspect of their investment toolkit, guiding them through the ever-changing landscape of equity markets.

Factors Influencing Bid-Ask Spreads

Understanding bid-ask spreads is crucial for investors navigating the equity markets. The bid-ask spread represents the difference between the highest price a buyer is willing to pay (bid) and the lowest price a seller is willing to accept (ask) for a security. This spread serves as a fundamental metric for assessing liquidity and transaction costs in the market. However, bid-ask spreads are not static; they fluctuate based on a variety of factors that reflect the dynamics of supply and demand, market conditions, and investor sentiment.

One of the primary factors influencing bid-ask spreads is market volatility. In times of high volatility, uncertainty prevails, leading to wider bid-ask spreads. Investors become more cautious, and the risk of price fluctuations increases, prompting sellers to demand higher ask prices and buyers to lower their bid prices. This widening of spreads acts as a reflection of the heightened risk and uncertainty present in the market.

Consider a bustling marketplace where vendors are selling fruits. On a calm day, with predictable weather and stable demand, the difference in prices offered by sellers (ask) and those willing to buy (bid) may be minimal. However, during a storm or unpredictable weather conditions, vendors may raise their prices (ask) to compensate for the risk of spoilage or decreased supply, while buyers may seek lower prices (bid) due to uncertainty about the quality and availability of produce. The wider gap between ask and bid prices mirrors the increased risk and volatility in the market.

Moreover, the liquidity of a security plays a significant role in determining bid-ask spreads. Highly liquid securities, characterized by high trading volumes and active participation from buyers and sellers, tend to have narrower bid-ask spreads. In contrast, illiquid securities with low trading volumes and limited market activity often exhibit wider bid-ask spreads. Market makers, who facilitate trading by providing liquidity, adjust bid and ask prices to reflect the level of liquidity in the market. As Warren Buffett famously remarked, "Price is what you pay; value is what you get." In the context of bid-ask spreads, liquidity directly impacts the price investors pay and the value they receive when buying or selling securities.

Additionally, the size of the trade influences bid-ask spreads. Larger trades typically result in wider spreads compared to smaller trades. When executing large orders, investors may encounter greater difficulty finding counterparties willing to transact at favorable prices, leading to wider spreads. Market participants may adjust their bid and ask prices to accommodate the size of the trade and the associated risks, resulting in wider spreads for large orders.

Furthermore, the nature of the security itself can affect bid-ask spreads. Securities with higher volatility, less liquidity, or complex structures often exhibit wider bid-ask spreads. For example, options contracts, which derive their value from underlying assets, may have wider spreads due to factors such as time decay, volatility, and uncertainty about future price movements. As renowned investor Peter Lynch once said, "Know what you own, and know why you own it." Understanding the characteristics of a security and how they influence bid-ask spreads is essential for making informed investment decisions. Factors such as market volatility, liquidity, trade size, and security characteristics dynamically influence bid-ask spreads, reflecting the interplay of supply and demand dynamics, investor sentiment, and market conditions. By comprehensively analyzing these factors, investors can gain valuable insights into the pricing dynamics of equity securities and make well-informed investment decisions.

Understanding liquidity impacts on equity securities

It's a complex yet crucial aspect of the financial world that can significantly influence investment decisions and market dynamics. Let's unravel the intricate relationship between liquidity and equity securities and explore how it shapes the investment landscape.

Liquidity, in the context of equity securities, refers to the ease and speed at which these assets can be bought or sold in the market without causing substantial price changes. It's like the flow of a river; some stocks have a swift current, making it easy to navigate and trade, while others have a sluggish flow, posing challenges for investors.

Imagine you're at a bustling auction where some items attract multiple bidders, while others struggle to find buyers. The items with more interest represent highly liquid stocks, where there's a constant demand, allowing investors to swiftly enter or exit positions without significantly impacting prices. On the contrary, the less popular items symbolize illiquid stocks, where finding buyers or sellers is challenging, leading to potential price volatility.

Now, ponder on the implications of liquidity on equity securities. High liquidity provides a sense of security and flexibility to investors. It's like having a well-stocked pantry at home; you can easily access what you need without much hassle. Highly liquid stocks offer stability, lower transaction costs, and the ability to quickly convert investments into cash, providing a safety net in times of uncertainty.

Conversely, investing in illiquid stocks is akin to navigating through a dense forest with limited visibility. It can be risky and challenging to exit positions swiftly, especially during market downturns or unexpected events. Illiquidity can lead to wider bid-ask spreads, higher transaction costs, and potential price distortions, making it a less attractive option for many investors.

As the legendary investor Warren Buffett once said, "The stock market is designed to transfer money from the Active to the Patient." This quote underscores the importance of patience and long-term thinking in investing, especially when considering the impact of liquidity on equity securities. Patient investors who focus on high-quality, liquid stocks often reap the rewards of their disciplined approach.

Let's explore a scenario to understand the real-world implications of liquidity on equity securities. Imagine you own shares of a company with low liquidity, and suddenly you need to sell a significant portion of your holdings. In a highly illiquid market, your selling pressure could drive down the stock price, resulting in losses for you and other shareholders. This lack of liquidity can create challenges and uncertainties for investors.

Moreover, liquidity impacts not only individual stocks but also the broader market dynamics. A lack of liquidity in certain sectors or asset classes can amplify market volatility during turbulent times, as seen in the global financial crisis of 2008. Market participants need to assess liquidity conditions carefully to navigate through uncertainties and mitigate potential risks.

To further illustrate the significance of liquidity, let's draw a parallel to a busy highway versus a narrow back road. The highway represents highly liquid stocks, where there's a smooth flow of trading activity, enabling investors to move in and out of positions seamlessly. In contrast, the back road symbolizes illiquid stocks, where trading can be slow and challenging, requiring patience and strategic planning.

Understanding liquidity is like mastering the art of sailing; it's about navigating the waters of the financial markets with precision and foresight. Investors who grasp the nuances of liquidity can adapt to changing market conditions, seize opportunities, and safeguard their portfolios against unforeseen challenges. liquidity is a fundamental aspect of equity securities that influences investment strategies, risk management, and market efficiency. By recognizing the impact of liquidity on stock markets, investors can make informed decisions, optimize their portfolios, and navigate the ever-evolving landscape of finance with confidence and insight.

Definition and calculation of dividend yield

Dividend yield stands as a cornerstone in equity investments, offering investors valuable insights into the income-generating potential of a stock. But what exactly is dividend yield, and how is it calculated? In this comprehensive exploration, we delve into the depths of dividend yield, unraveling its intricacies, and understanding its profound significance in investment analysis.

Defining Dividend Yield:

At its essence, dividend yield represents the ratio of a company's annual dividend payment per share to its current stock price. It serves as a crucial metric for investors seeking to assess the income-generating capacity of a particular equity investment. As acclaimed investor Warren Buffett once remarked, "Price is what you pay, value is what you get." In the world of dividend yield, this axiom rings especially true, as it encapsulates the relationship between the price of a stock and the returns it offers through dividends.

Calculation of Dividend Yield:

To calculate dividend yield, one simply divides the annual dividend per share by the current market price per share, expressed as a percentage. Mathematically, the formula is represented as follows:

Dividend Yield = (Annual Dividend per Share / Price per Share) x 100%

Let's break it down with an example:

Suppose you own shares of Company XYZ, which pays an annual dividend of $2 per share. If the current price per share of Company XYZ is $40, you can calculate the dividend yield as follows:

Dividend Yield = ($2 / $40) x 100%

Dividend Yield = 0.05 x 100%

Dividend Yield = 5%

So, in this example, the dividend yield for Company XYZ is 5%. This means that for every $1 you invest in Company XYZ, you can expect to receive a return of 5 cents in the form of dividends annually. Calculating the dividend yield helps investors assess the income potential of a stock relative to its price, providing valuable insights into the investment's income-generating capability.

Also Consider the following scenario: Company X pays an annual dividend of $2 per share, and its current market price stands at $50 per share. Applying the dividend yield formula, we obtain a yield of 4%. This implies that for every $100 invested in Company X's stock, investors can expect an annual return of $4 in the form of dividends.

Imagine dividend yield as the fruit of a tree, where the tree represents the company and the fruit symbolizes the dividends it distributes. Just as a fruit-bearing tree yields a harvest of sustenance, a company with a healthy dividend yield provides investors with a steady stream of income. Just as a farmer carefully tends to his orchard to ensure a bountiful yield, investors meticulously analyze dividend yield to cultivate a fruitful investment portfolio.

Significance of Dividend Yield:

Diving into the significance of dividend yield is like exploring the heart of a company's financial vitality and its dedication to rewarding shareholders. As Benjamin Graham, the legendary figure in the world of value investing, wisely pointed out, "The true investor scarcely ever is forced to sell his shares and at all times is free to disregard the current price quotation." This powerful statement underscores the essence of dividend yield in guiding investors towards a long-term perspective, emphasizing the importance of focusing on a company's core strengths rather than being swayed by short-term market fluctuations.

When we talk about dividend yield, we're essentially looking at the relationship between a company's dividend payments and its stock price. This metric serves as a crucial indicator of a company's financial stability and its commitment to generating returns for its shareholders. Let's unravel the layers of significance that dividend yield brings to the table:

1. Financial Health Indicator:

   Dividend yield acts as a mirror reflecting a company's financial well-being. A consistent and attractive dividend yield signifies that the company has the financial strength to sustain regular dividend payments to its shareholders. Companies that maintain a healthy dividend yield demonstrate stability and reliability, instilling confidence in investors about the company's financial health.

2. Management's Commitment to Shareholders:

   A strong dividend yield is a testament to management's dedication to rewarding shareholders for their investment in the company. By consistently paying dividends, management signals their confidence in the company's performance and their commitment to sharing profits with shareholders. This commitment fosters trust and loyalty among investors, reinforcing a positive relationship between the company and its shareholders.

3. Long-Term Investment Perspective:

   The philosophy behind dividend yield resonates with Benjamin Graham's approach to value investing, which advocates for a long-term investment horizon. By focusing on dividend yield, investors are encouraged to look beyond short-term market fluctuations and concentrate on the fundamental strength of the company. This long-term perspective enables investors to make informed decisions based on the company's ability to generate sustainable returns over time.

4. Income Generation and Wealth Preservation:

Dividend yield plays a crucial role in income generation for investors seeking regular cash flow from their investments. Companies with attractive dividend yields provide investors with a source of passive income, allowing them to benefit from dividend payments while holding onto their shares for potential capital appreciation. Additionally, dividend-paying stocks are often considered a more stable investment option, offering a form of wealth preservation through consistent income streams.

5. Investor Confidence and Market Perception:

A high dividend yield can enhance investor confidence in a company's financial strength and growth potential. When investors see a company with a solid track record of paying dividends at an attractive yield, it signals stability and reliability. This, in turn, can positively impact the market perception of the company, attracting more investors who value consistent returns and long-term sustainability. A strong dividend yield can differentiate a company in the market, setting it apart as a reliable investment option that prioritizes shareholder value.

factors affecting dividend yield

Diving deep into the aspect of dividend yield and unravel the key elements that shape this critical metric, affecting companies and investors alike.

At the core of dividend yield lies the company's earnings performance. Earnings serve as the lifeblood of dividend payments, reflecting a company's profitability and ability to reward shareholders. A company's consistent earnings growth forms the bedrock for sustaining dividend payouts and maintaining an attractive dividend yield. As the legendary investor Warren Buffett once famously remarked, "The most important thing to me is figuring out how big a moat there is around the business." Strong earnings act as a protective moat, safeguarding the company's ability to sustain dividend payments and enhance dividend yield.

Moving beyond earnings, the payout ratio emerges as a crucial determinant of dividend yield. This ratio signifies the portion of earnings that a company allocates towards dividends. Balancing the payout ratio is akin to walking a tightrope, where a company must strike a harmonious equilibrium between retaining earnings for growth initiatives and distributing dividends to shareholders. In the words of the esteemed investor Peter Lynch, "Go for a business that any idiot can run – because sooner or later, any idiot probably is going to run it." A prudent payout ratio ensures that a company allocates a sustainable amount of earnings towards dividends, thereby maintaining financial stability and supporting dividend yield.

The broader economic landscape casts a significant shadow on dividend yield dynamics. Economic cycles exert a profound influence on companies' financial performance and dividend policies. During periods of economic prosperity, companies may ramp up dividend payments to share the benefits of growth with shareholders. Conversely, economic downturns may prompt companies to exercise caution in dividend distributions to preserve cash reserves. This interplay between economic conditions and dividend yield underscores the impact of external factors on companies' dividend decisions. Industry dynamics and regulatory environment also play pivotal roles in shaping dividend yield, Industries characterized by stable cash flows and mature markets often exhibit higher dividend yields, reflecting their ability to generate consistent returns for shareholders.

Regulatory frameworks further impact companies' dividend policies, influencing the frequency and magnitude of dividend payments. By navigating industry trends and regulatory requirements, companies can adapt their dividend strategies to optimize dividend yield and enhance investor confidence. Moreover, financial health and cash flow stability emerge as critical determinants of dividend yield. Companies with robust balance sheets and healthy cash reserves are better positioned to sustain dividend payments and maintain attractive dividend yields. Cash flow stability serves as a key indicator of a company.

Price-to-Earnings (P/E) Ratios

In the labyrinth of financial markets, investors seek a beacon to navigate the complexities of equity valuation. Among the myriad metrics available, the Price-to-Earnings (P/E) ratio stands as a stalwart guidepost, shedding light on the relationship between a company's stock price and its earnings. But what exactly does the P/E ratio reveal? How can investors harness its power to make informed decisions? Join us on an exploration of the enigmatic world of P/E ratios, where clarity emerges from the fog of uncertainty.

At its core, the P/E ratio encapsulates the market's perception of a company's earnings potential. It is a ratio of price to earnings per share (EPS), offering a glimpse into investor sentiment and expectations for future growth. But like a multifaceted gem, the P/E ratio reveals more than meets the eye. Consider the analogy of a telescope: just as a lens magnifies distant stars, the P/E ratio magnifies the relationship between stock price and earnings, bringing clarity to the investor's view.

To decipher the message encoded within the P/E ratio, one must first understand its nuances. A high P/E ratio may signify optimism and lofty expectations for future earnings growth, akin to a skyrocketing rocket fueled by investor enthusiasm. Conversely, a low P/E ratio may indicate skepticism or undervaluation, reminiscent of a dormant volcano waiting to erupt with hidden potential. As Benjamin Graham, the father of value investing, famously remarked, "In the short run, the market is a voting machine, but in the long run, it is a weighing machine." The P/E ratio serves as the scales upon which market sentiment is measured, tipping the balance between exuberance and caution.

Like a seasoned mountaineer, investors must traverse the peaks and valleys of market fluctuations with prudence and foresight. Consider the story of two climbers embarking on a perilous ascent: one equipped with a thorough understanding of P/E ratios, the other relying solely on blind faith. As they navigate treacherous terrain, the informed climber utilizes the P/E ratio as a compass, guiding their path and mitigating risks along the way. Meanwhile, the uninformed climber stumbles blindly, oblivious to the warning signs of overvaluation or undervaluation.

Yet, amid the allure of P/E ratios lies a labyrinth of pitfalls and traps, ready to ensnare the unwary investor. One such trap is the temptation to extrapolate past performance into the future, neglecting the ever-shifting winds of market dynamics. As renowned investor Peter Lynch cautioned, "The P/E ratio of any company that's fairly priced will be equal to its growth rate." Blindly chasing companies with high P/E ratios without considering underlying fundamentals is akin to chasing mirages in the desert: a futile endeavor bound to end in disappointment.

Armed with a deep understanding of P/E ratios, investors can harness the power of knowledge to navigate the tumultuous seas of equity valuation. Like the legendary sailor Odysseus, who charted a course through perilous waters guided by the wisdom of the gods, savvy investors rely on the insights gleaned from P/E ratios to steer their portfolios toward prosperity. As Warren Buffett, the sage of Omaha, famously quipped, "It's far better to buy a wonderful company at a fair price than a fair company at a wonderful price." The P/E ratio serves as a beacon, illuminating the path to investment success amidst the murky depths of market uncertainty.

Calculating P/E ratio

Calculating the Price-to-Earnings (P/E) ratio is like peering through a window into a company's valuation, offering insights into how the market perceives its earnings potential. The P/E ratio serves as a key metric for investors, helping them gauge whether a stock is overvalued, undervalued, or fairly priced. Let's unravel the mystery of P/E ratios with some real-world examples to bring clarity to this fundamental concept.

P/E Ratio = Stock Price / Earnings per Share

For example, if a company's stock price is $50 and its earnings per share (EPS) is $5, the P/E ratio would be calculated as follows:

P/E Ratio = $50 / $5 = 10

Also

Consider Company ABC, which has a stock price of $60 and an EPS of $3. Calculating the P/E ratio for Company ABC yields 20 ($60/$3 = 20). This P/E ratio implies that investors are valuing Company ABC at 20 times its earnings, indicating a higher valuation relative to its earnings.

Conversely, let's explore Company XYZ, with a stock price of $40 and an EPS of $5. Computing the P/E ratio for Company XYZ results in 8 ($40/$5 = 8). A P/E ratio of 8 suggests that investors are valuing Company XYZ at 8 times its earnings, signaling a lower valuation compared to Company ABC. The interpretation of P/E ratios is crucial for investors seeking to make informed investment decisions. A high P/E ratio may indicate that the stock is overvalued, potentially signaling expectations of high future growth. On the other hand, a low P/E ratio could imply an undervalued stock, presenting an opportunity for value investors to capitalize on potential price appreciation.

Moreover, comparing P/E ratios across companies within the same industry can offer valuable insights into relative valuation. For instance, if Company ABC operates in the technology sector and Company XYZ is also a tech company, investors can assess which stock presents a more attractive investment opportunity based on their P/E ratios relative to industry peers. In essence, mastering the art of calculating and interpreting P/E ratios empowers investors to navigate the complex terrain of stock valuation, enabling them to make informed decisions aligned with their investment objectives and risk tolerance.

interpreting P/E ratios in investment

When it comes to interpreting P/E ratios, a high ratio could suggest that investors are willing to pay a premium for the company's earnings potential, anticipating robust future growth. This scenario often occurs with growth stocks or companies in high-growth industries where investors are optimistic about future earnings prospects. Conversely, a low P/E ratio might indicate that the stock is undervalued, potentially presenting a value investment opportunity. Companies with lower P/E ratios may be overlooked by the market, offering a chance for investors to capitalize on potential price appreciation as the market reevaluates the company's earnings potential.

Comparing P/E ratios across companies within the same industry can provide valuable insights into relative valuation. For example, if Company A has a P/E ratio of 15 and Company B has a P/E ratio of

10 in the same industry, investors may view Company B as relatively undervalued compared to Company A, assuming all other factors are equal. Understanding the historical trend of a company's P/E ratio and comparing it to industry averages can help investors assess whether the stock is currently overvalued, undervalued, or trading in line with market expectations. Significant deviations from historical P/E ratios or industry norms could signal opportunities or risks for investors.

It's essential to consider other factors alongside P/E ratios, such as growth prospects, industry trends, and overall market conditions, to make well-informed investment decisions. P/E ratios serve as a valuable tool in the investor's toolkit, offering a glimpse into the market's perception of a company's earnings potential and valuation.

By mastering the art of interpreting P/E ratios, investors can navigate the dynamic landscape of investment analysis with greater confidence, enabling them to make informed decisions aligned with their investment objectives and risk tolerance.

Limitations of Using P/E Ratios

Price-to-earnings (P/E) ratios are a widely used metric in the world of finance and investment analysis. They offer a quick and simple way to assess the relative valuation of a company's stock.

However, despite their popularity, P/E ratios come with their fair share of limitations that investors must be aware of. In this in-depth exploration, we will delve into the various constraints and drawbacks associated with relying solely on P/E ratios for investment decision-making. To truly grasp the limitations of P/E ratios, one must first understand the essence of this metric. At its core, the P/E ratio compares a company's current stock price to its earnings per share (EPS). In theory, a higher P/E ratio suggests that investors are willing to pay more for each unit of earnings, indicating optimism about the company's future prospects. Conversely, a lower P/E ratio may signal undervaluation or pessimism among investors.

While P/E ratios can provide valuable insights, they paint an incomplete picture of a company's financial health and future potential. One of the primary limitations of P/E ratios is their failure to account for the quality of earnings. A company may report impressive earnings on paper, but are these earnings sustainable and of high quality? P/E ratios offer no insight into the composition of earnings, leaving investors vulnerable to companies that manipulate their earnings through accounting gimmicks or one-time windfalls.

P/E ratios overlook crucial factors such as the growth prospects of a company. As renowned investor Warren Buffett once remarked, "It's far better to buy a wonderful company at a fair price than a fair company at a wonderful price." This quote encapsulates the essence of growth investing, which emphasizes the importance of investing in companies with strong growth potential, even if they come at a higher price. P/E ratios fail to capture the growth trajectory of a company, leading investors to overlook lucrative investment opportunities in fast-growing industries or emerging markets.

Furthermore, P/E ratios are highly sensitive to accounting practices and earnings volatility. Companies can manipulate their P/E ratios through various accounting maneuvers, such as aggressive revenue recognition or expense deferrals. Additionally, industries with cyclical earnings patterns may exhibit fluctuating P/E ratios that do not accurately reflect their long-term value. As legendary investor Peter Lynch once quipped, "People who invest make money for themselves; people who speculate make money for their brokers." This witty remark underscores the danger of speculating based solely on P/E ratios without considering the broader economic context and industry dynamics.

Another limitation of P/E ratios is their susceptibility to distortions caused by extraordinary events or non-recurring items. A company may experience a temporary spike or decline in earnings due to factors such as litigation expenses, restructuring charges, or natural disasters. These one-time events can artificially inflate or depress P/E ratios, leading investors to make misguided investment decisions. As financial guru Benjamin Graham famously stated, "In the short run, the market is a voting machine but in the long run, it is a weighing machine." This timeless wisdom reminds investors to focus on the underlying fundamentals of a company rather than short-term fluctuations in P/E ratios. In addition to these fundamental limitations, P/E ratios can be misleading when comparing companies across different industries or growth stages.

For instance, technology companies often command higher P/E ratios due to their rapid growth potential and innovative business models. Comparing the P/E ratio of a tech stock to that of a stable utility company may lead to erroneous conclusions about their relative valuations. As investment strategist Peter Drucker once observed, "The best way to predict the future is to create it." This insightful observation underscores the dynamic nature of industries and the importance of forward-looking analysis in investment decision-making.

Furthermore, P/E ratios fail to account for external factors such as macroeconomic trends, regulatory changes, and geopolitical risks. A company may boast an attractive P/E ratio, but if its industry is facing headwinds or regulatory scrutiny, its stock price may plummet regardless of its earnings multiple. As economist John Maynard Keynes famously remarked, "The market can stay irrational longer than you can stay solvent." This sobering reminder cautions investors against blindly relying on P/E ratios without considering the broader market context and macroeconomic environment.

While P/E ratios offer a convenient shortcut for assessing the relative valuation of stocks, they come with significant limitations that investors must navigate. From the quality of earnings to growth prospects and accounting distortions, P/E ratios paint an incomplete picture of a company's financial health and future potential. As investors, we must supplement our analysis with qualitative factors, forward-looking projections, and a deep understanding of industry dynamics. Only then can we make informed investment decisions that stand the test of time.

Estimating Price Movements Based on Indexes

Equity indexes serve as vital benchmarks in the world of finance, guiding investors, analysts, and policymakers alike. But what lies beneath the surface of these seemingly simple metrics? In this extensive exploration, we delve deep into the intricacies of equity indexes, unraveling their significance, methodologies, and implications.

Equity indexes, often referred to as stock market indexes, are measures that track the performance of a specific group of stocks. They provide insight into the overall health and direction of a particular segment of the market or the market as a whole. But how do these indexes come into being, and what drives their composition?

Equity indexes are constructed using various methodologies, each tailored to reflect different aspects of the market. The most common method is market capitalization weighting, where stocks are weighted based on their market value. However, other methods, such as price weighting and equal weighting, offer alternative perspectives. But why does the methodology matter, and how does it impact the interpretation of index performance?. For investors, understanding equity indexes is crucial for making informed decisions. These indexes serve as benchmarks against which portfolio performance is measured, guiding asset allocation and investment strategies. But can investors rely solely on index performance, or are there hidden risks and opportunities beneath the surface?

Consider the equity index as a compass, guiding investors through the tumultuous seas of the financial markets. Just as sailors trust their compass to navigate stormy waters, investors rely on equity indexes to steer their portfolios towards prosperity. But what happens when the compass malfunctions or points in the wrong direction? Similarly, investors must be wary of blindly following index performance without understanding the underlying factors driving it.

As John C. Bogle, founder of Vanguard Group, once remarked, "Don't look for the needle in the haystack. Just buy the haystack." This sage advice underscores the importance of broad market exposure, epitomized by equity index investing. However, as Warren Buffett famously cautioned, "It's far better to buy a wonderful company at a fair price than a fair company at a wonderful price." This wisdom reminds us that while indexes provide valuable benchmarks, true wealth is built through careful selection and analysis of individual companies.

Methods for Estimating Price Movements Based on Indexes

One essential aspect of this understanding lies in comprehending how indexes influence these movements. But how exactly do indexes impact the prices of individual stocks? What methods can investors employ to estimate price movements based on these indexes? Through a detailed exploration, this chapter delves into the various techniques and strategies investors can utilize to gauge price movements in the equity market. Before delving into methods for estimating price movements, it is imperative to grasp the significance of equity indexes. Equity indexes serve as barometers of the overall performance of a specific segment of the stock market, providing investors with insights into market trends and sentiments. As Warren Buffett famously said, "The stock market is designed to transfer money from the active to the patient." Indeed, indexes reflect the collective wisdom and actions of market participants, embodying the ebbs and flows of market sentiment.

Methods for Estimating Price Movement

1.Technical Analysis:

Technical analysis involves examining past market data, primarily price and volume, to forecast future price movements. Just as a skilled sailor navigates the ocean by interpreting the movement of waves and wind, technical analysts use chart patterns, trend lines, and indicators to predict market direction. As John Murphy eloquently put it, "The art of technical analysis is recognizing a trend at its inception." Through the analysis of index charts, investors can identify patterns and trends that may signal potential price movements in the underlying securities.

2. Fundamental Analysis:

Fundamental analysis focuses on evaluating the intrinsic value of securities based on factors such as earnings, dividends, and macroeconomic indicators. Analogous to a meticulous gardener who assesses the health of each plant in a garden, fundamental analysts scrutinize financial statements and economic data to assess the underlying strength of companies and industries. Benjamin Graham, the father of value investing, emphasized the importance of fundamental analysis, stating, "The stock market is filled with individuals who know the price of everything, but the value of nothing." By understanding the fundamentals of the companies comprising an index, investors can anticipate how changes in economic conditions may impact stock prices.

3. Sentiment Analysis:

Sentiment analysis involves gauging investor sentiment and market psychology to forecast price movements. Just as a skilled poker player reads their opponents' facial expressions and body language, investors analyze market sentiment through indicators such as investor surveys, news sentiment, and social media activity. As Jesse Livermore, a legendary stock trader, famously remarked, "There is only one side to the stock market; and it is not the bull side or the bear side, but the right side." By understanding prevailing market sentiment, investors can anticipate potential shifts in market direction and adjust their investment strategies accordingly.

Consider the analogy of a captain navigating a ship through turbulent waters. In the vast expanse of the ocean, the captain relies on various instruments and techniques to steer the ship safely to its destination. Similarly, investors navigate the unpredictable seas of the stock market, employing methods such as technical analysis, fundamental analysis, and sentiment analysis to guide their investment decisions. As the renowned investor Peter Lynch once said, "Know what you own, and know why you own it." Armed with a deep understanding of price estimation methods, investors can confidently navigate the ever-changing landscape of the stock market and strive towards achieving their investment goals.

impact of index based price movement on equity securities

When we talk about the implications of index-based price movements on equity securities, we're diving into how changes in major market indices like the S&P 500, Dow Jones Industrial Average, or Nasdaq can impact individual stocks and the broader market. Let's explore this topic in depth to understand the ripple effects of index movements on equity securities.

Index-based price movements play a significant role in shaping investor sentiment and market dynamics. When a major index experiences a substantial increase or decrease, it can influence the overall market direction and individual stock prices. Here are some key implications to consider:

When we delve deeper into market sentiment and investor confidence, we uncover how these factors are intricately linked to index movements and can significantly influence the behavior of market participants.

1. Market Sentiment and Investor Confidence: Index movements serve as a barometer of market sentiment and investor confidence. When major indices experience positive movements, it often signals a bullish outlook, boosting investor optimism. This positive sentiment can lead to increased buying activity across the market as investors perceive opportunities for growth and profitability. On the flip side, negative movements in key indices can trigger a shift in sentiment, prompting investors to adopt a more cautious approach. In times of market downturns or uncertainty, investors may become more risk-averse, leading to selling pressure as they seek to protect their investments and minimize potential losses.

2. Sector Rotation: The concept of sector rotation comes into play when changes in index composition or sector performance drive investors to reallocate their investments strategically. For instance, if a specific sector demonstrates strong performance and gains significant weight in an index, investors may reposition their portfolios to capitalize on the perceived opportunities within that sector. This reallocation can impact individual equity securities within the favored sector, causing their prices to rise as demand increases. Conversely, sectors that underperform may see reduced investor interest and lower stock prices as capital flows out of those areas.

3. Volatility and Risk Management: Index-based price movements have a direct impact on market volatility, influencing the pricing of equity securities. Heightened volatility, often triggered by significant index fluctuations, can create challenges for investors in managing risk effectively. To navigate volatile market conditions, investors may resort to risk management strategies such as using derivatives to hedge their positions or diversifying their portfolios to spread risk across different asset classes. By employing these risk mitigation techniques, investors aim to safeguard their investments and minimize potential losses during periods of market turbulence.

Understanding the intricate relationships between market sentiment, sector rotation, volatility, and risk management is crucial for investors seeking to navigate the complexities of the stock market and make informed decisions to achieve their financial goals. By staying attuned to these dynamics, investors can adapt their strategies proactively to capitalize on opportunities and mitigate risks in a dynamic market environment.

5. Passive Investing and ETFs: Passive investing involves tracking a specific index rather than actively selecting individual stocks. ETFs, as a popular passive investment vehicle, mirror the performance of an index by holding the same securities in the same proportions as the index. This approach has led to a higher correlation between index movements and individual stock prices. Changes in index components or weights directly affect the performance of ETFs and the underlying stocks they hold. For example, if a stock is added to a major index, ETFs tracking that index will need to buy that stock, potentially driving up its price.

6. Arbitrage Opportunities:Index-based price movements can create opportunities for arbitrage. Arbitrageurs exploit price differences between related securities, such as an index and individual stocks, to make a profit. When there are discrepancies between index prices and the prices of the underlying stocks, arbitrageurs can buy the undervalued stocks and sell the overvalued ones to benefit from market inefficiencies. This activity helps align prices and contributes to market efficiency.

7. Market Valuation and Price Discovery:Index movements play a crucial role in market valuation and price discovery. Investors often use index levels as benchmarks to evaluate the fair value of individual stocks. When an index moves, it can impact the perceived value of stocks within that index, influencing investor sentiment and trading decisions. The movement of indices helps in determining market trends, guiding investors in assessing the relative valuations of stocks and making informed investment choices.

portfolio management calculations

Portfolio management is akin to navigating a ship through turbulent waters. As a captain of your investment vessel, you must chart a course that maximizes returns while minimizing risks. One crucial aspect of this voyage is calculating the total returns of your equity portfolio. In this journey of financial stewardship, understanding how to measure total returns is paramount, akin to a navigator skillfully using the stars to guide the ship to its destination. Total returns represent the overall performance of an investment over a specified period, considering all sources of income, including capital appreciation and dividends. It's not merely about the journey; it's about the destination and all the treasures collected along the way.

The Total Returns Formula:

[Total Returns = (Ending Value - Beginning Value + Dividends) / Beginning Value\]

Let's consider a scenario where you initially invested $10,000 in your equity portfolio. Throughout the year, your portfolio experienced capital gains from stock price appreciation and also received dividends from the companies you invested in. To calculate the total return for your portfolio, you need to consider both these components.

First, you would calculate the capital gains by determining the change in the value of your investments from the initial purchase price to the current value. Let's say your portfolio's value increased to $11,500 by the end of the year, reflecting a capital gain of $1,500.

Next, you factor in the dividends received during the year. Suppose you received $300 in dividends from the companies in your portfolio. To calculate the total return, you would add the capital gains ($1,500) to the dividends received ($300), resulting in a total return of $1,800 for the year.

This formula encapsulates the essence of a successful investment journey. It considers not only the change in the investment's value but also the income generated along the path.

Imagine you are a diligent farmer tending to your orchard. Each year, you invest time, effort, and resources into nurturing your fruit trees. At the end of the season, you reap the rewards of your labor by harvesting ripe fruits. The total returns of your orchard are akin to the sum of all the fruits you gather, including those you sell at the market and those you keep for future sowing. Calculating total returns provides investors with a holistic view of their investment performance. It's not just about the numbers; it's about understanding the true value generated by your investment endeavors. Total returns are influenced by various factors, including market conditions, economic trends, company performance, and dividend policies. Like the changing seasons affecting the yield of crops, external factors can impact the returns of an investment portfolio.

While no investment journey is without its challenges, there are strategies investors can employ to enhance total returns and optimize portfolio performance.

Diversifying your investment portfolio is akin to planting different crops in your fields. By spreading your investments across various asset classes and sectors, you reduce the risk of loss and enhance the potential for overall returns.

Reinvesting dividends and capital gains is akin to sowing seeds for future harvests. By leveraging the power of compounding, investors can exponentially grow their wealth over time.

Active portfolio management involves regularly monitoring and adjusting your investment holdings to capitalize on emerging opportunities and mitigate risks. It's like trimming the sails of your ship to catch the most favorable winds.

Unlocking the Power of Future Value Calculations in Portfolio Investments

Introduction:

In the vast landscape of investment strategies, one fundamental principle reigns supreme: the time value of money. At the heart of this principle lies the concept of future value calculations, a cornerstone in the realm of portfolio management. But what exactly is future value, and why does it hold such significance in the world of investments? As we embark on this exploration, let us delve deep into the intricacies of future value calculations for portfolio investments, uncovering their essence, significance, and practical applications.

In the world of finance, there exist various formulas for calculating future value, each tailored to suit different investment scenarios. From the basic future value formula

Basic Future Value Formula

The formula $FV = PV \times (1 + r)^n$ is used to calculate the amount of money an investment will grow to over a period of time when subjected to an interest rate r that compounds annually. Here:

- PV is the Present Value or initial amount of money invested.
- r is the annual interest rate (expressed as a decimal).
- n is the number of years the money is invested for.

to more complex formulas incorporating periodic contributions and varying interest rates, the options are endless. But beyond the mathematical equations lies a world of practical applications. Consider, for instance, the scenario of a young investor looking to build a retirement nest egg. By systematically contributing to a diversified portfolio over several decades, this investor can harness the power of compounding to secure a comfortable retirement future. As renowned author Brian Tracy once said, "Investing in yourself is the best investment you will ever make." Indeed, future value calculations empower investors to make informed decisions and chart a course towards financial freedom.

Future value calculations serve as a compass, guiding investors towards their long-term financial goals. Imagine embarking on a voyage across a vast ocean, with your portfolio as the ship and future value as your guiding star. Just as sailors rely on celestial navigation to chart their course, investors rely on future value calculations to navigate the unpredictable waters of the financial markets.

Consider a scenario where an investor is planning for retirement. They have diligently saved and invested their money over the years, but now face the daunting task of ensuring their portfolio can sustain them through their golden years. Future value calculations come into play here, providing valuable insights into how their investments will grow over time.

Let's take the example of a young investor who starts investing in a diversified portfolio of stocks and bonds. By employing future value calculations, they can estimate how much their investments will be worth in the future, given various rates of return and time horizons. This allows them to set realistic financial goals and make informed decisions about how much to save and invest each month.

However, the journey towards achieving these financial goals is not without its challenges. The financial markets are inherently volatile, with prices fluctuating in response to a myriad of factors such as economic indicators, geopolitical events, and investor sentiment. It's akin to sailing through stormy seas, where unforeseen waves can buffet your portfolio off course.

In times of market turbulence, it's essential for portfolio managers to maintain a steady hand and stay focused on the long-term horizon. As legendary investor Warren Buffett famously remarked, "The stock market is designed to transfer money from the active to the patient." This quote encapsulates the importance of patience and discipline in the world of investing. Just as a seasoned sailor remains calm and composed during a storm, investors must resist the temptation to make impulsive decisions based on short-term market fluctuations.

Moreover, future value calculations can also help investors assess the impact of inflation on their investment returns. Inflation erodes the purchasing power of money over time, meaning that a dollar today will not be worth as much in the future. By factoring in the effects of inflation, investors can ensure that their portfolios are generating real returns that outpace the rising cost of living.

The Crucial Role of Portfolio Management Calculations in Investment Decision-Making

The significance of portfolio management calculations cannot be overstated. Like the skilled navigator guiding a ship through tumultuous waters, effective portfolio management empowers investors to navigate the complex currents of the financial markets, steering towards their financial objectives with confidence and precision. But why are portfolio management calculations so vital in the realm of investment decision-making? What insights and wisdom do they offer, and how do they shape the path to financial success?

At its core, portfolio management involves the strategic allocation of resources across a spectrum of investment assets, with the aim of maximizing returns while minimizing risks. This strategic allocation, however, is not a haphazard endeavor but rather a meticulously crafted masterpiece, sculpted through the lens of rigorous calculations and insightful analysis.

Consider for a moment the analogy of a master chef meticulously crafting a culinary masterpiece. Just as the chef carefully selects the finest ingredients and orchestrates them into a symphony of flavors, the astute investor employs portfolio management calculations to select the optimal mix of assets, each contributing its unique attributes to the overall portfolio performance. From stocks and bonds to real estate and commodities, each asset class plays a distinct role in the investor's financial palette, blending together to create a balanced and resilient portfolio.

Importance of Risk Management:

One of the fundamental pillars of portfolio management is risk management. As renowned investor Benjamin Graham famously said, "The essence of investment management is the management of risks, not the management of returns." Indeed, in a world fraught with uncertainties, the ability to quantify and mitigate risks is paramount to investment success. Portfolio management calculations provide investors with powerful tools to assess and manage risks effectively. Through techniques such as variance analysis, correlation analysis, and Monte Carlo simulations, investors can gain invaluable insights into the potential risks associated with their portfolios. By understanding the interplay of various risk factors and their impact on portfolio performance, investors can make informed decisions to safeguard their capital and preserve long-term wealth.

Harnessing the Power of Diversification

Diversification, often hailed as the cornerstone of prudent investing, lies at the heart of portfolio management. Just as a wise farmer diversifies crops to mitigate the risk of crop failure, the savvy investor diversifies assets to spread risk and enhance portfolio resilience. However, diversification is not merely a matter of spreading investments across different asset classes; it requires a nuanced understanding of correlation, covariance, and other statistical measures.

As legendary investor Warren Buffett famously quipped, "Diversification is protection against ignorance. It makes little sense if you know what you are doing." Indeed, portfolio management calculations enable investors to go beyond superficial diversification and delve into the intricacies of asset correlation and covariance. By constructing portfolios that combine assets with low or negative correlations, investors can achieve true diversification, effectively hedging against market volatility and reducing the risk of significant losses.

Maximizing Returns through Asset Allocation:

Asset allocation, the art of dividing investment capital among different asset classes, lies at the heart of portfolio management. Just as a skilled conductor orchestrates a symphony, balancing the contributions of each instrument to create harmonious music, the astute investor allocates capital across asset classes to optimize portfolio returns.

Modern portfolio theory, pioneered by Nobel laureate Harry Markowitz, provides a rigorous framework for asset allocation, emphasizing the importance of achieving the optimal balance between risk and return. Through techniques such as mean-variance optimization and the efficient frontier, investors can identify the optimal asset mix that maximizes returns for a given level of risk tolerance. By rebalancing portfolios periodically in response to changing market conditions, investors can stay on course towards their financial goals, adapting to the ebb and flow of the market with poise and agility.

In the grand tapestry of investment, portfolio management calculations serve as the warp and weft, weaving together the threads of risk, return, and diversification into a masterpiece of financial resilience. Like the skilled architect designing a towering skyscraper, the astute investor harnesses the power of portfolio management calculations to construct a robust and enduring investment portfolio, fortified against the storms of market volatility and anchored in the bedrock of sound financial principles. As the legendary investor Peter Lynch once said, "Know what you own, and know why you own it." In the realm of investment decision-making, the wisdom of portfolio management calculations illuminates the path to financial success, guiding investors towards their aspirations with clarity and purpose.

Chapter 5: Debt Securities Calculations

Introduction: The Critical Role of Calculations in Debt Securities

Understanding Debt Securities Calculations

In the world of investing, debt securities such as bonds are fundamental instruments used by individuals, companies, and governments to raise capital. Just as a skilled chef must understand how ingredients combine to create a dish, investors and financial professionals must grasp various calculations to effectively analyze and manage debt securities. These calculations are essential tools that help determine the value, yield, and risks associated with bond investments.

Why Calculations Matter

1. **Valuation**: Calculating the price of bonds, whether clean or dirty (inclusive of accrued interest), is crucial for accurate valuation in both purchasing and selling. It ensures that investors know the fair market value of a security and do not overpay or sell under value.

2. **Yield Measurements**: Understanding different yield calculations, such as yield-to-maturity (YTM), current yield, and yield-to-call (YTC), is akin to measuring the exact cooking time and temperature necessary to perfect a recipe. Each yield measurement offers insights into different aspects of a bond's performance and potential returns, guiding investors in aligning their strategies with their financial goals.

3. **Risk Assessment**: Calculations related to interest rate risk and reinvestment rate risk help investors assess the sensitivity of their bond investments to changes in market conditions. This is similar to a navigator understanding weather patterns before setting sail; it prepares investors to handle or avoid potential storms in the bond market.

4. **Tax Implications**: For bonds, particularly municipal bonds, calculating taxable equivalent yields and after-tax returns is essential. This process is like calculating net profit after expenses in a business, providing clear insights into the actual benefits of bond investments once tax impacts are considered.

The Foundation for Successful Investing

Mastering debt securities calculations is not merely an academic exercise; it's a practical necessity for anyone involved in the financial markets, whether they are day traders, long-term investors, or financial advisors. These calculations provide the numerical backbone for strategic decision-making, helping to optimize investment returns and minimize financial risks.

The Role of Calculations in Evaluating Bond Investments

Navigating the Waters of Bond Investment

Calculations in bond investments are akin to navigational tools on a ship. Just as a captain uses instruments to chart a course and avoid hazards, investors use various bond calculations to determine the potential returns and assess the risks associated with their bond investments. These calculations are essential for making informed decisions, ensuring that investors can optimize their investment strategies in alignment with their risk tolerance and financial goals.

Key Calculations and Their Implications

1. Pricing Calculations: Clean vs. Dirty Pricing

- **Clean Price**: Reflects the price of a bond excluding any accrued interest. It is comparable to the price tag on a new appliance that doesn't include any potential delivery charges.

- **Dirty Price (Inclusive of Accrued Interest)**: Represents the bond's actual market price. It's like the total cost of an item, including tax; it's what you actually pay at the register.

Understanding these pricing conventions is crucial as it affects the investment cost and the timing of bond purchases or sales, impacting overall investment returns.

2. Yield Calculations: Yield-to-Maturity, Current Yield, Yield-to-Call

- **Yield-to-Maturity (YTM)**: This calculation estimates the total return an investor will receive if the bond is held until it matures, assuming all payments are made as scheduled. It's similar to calculating the total potential profit from a long-term business project.

- **Current Yield**: Provides a snapshot of the bond's yield at the current price without accounting for the time value of money, similar to an annual snapshot of a business's cash flow as a percentage of its current market value.

- **Yield-to-Call (YTC)**: Important for callable bonds, this yield calculation determines the return assuming the bond is called away by the issuer before maturity, much like calculating returns on an investment if it ends earlier than planned.

These yield metrics help investors understand the profitability of bond investments and gauge whether the returns align with their investment objectives.

3. Risk Assessments: Interest Rate Risk and Reinvestment Rate Risk

- **Interest Rate Risk**: Measures how sensitive a bond's price is to interest rate changes. This can be likened to how sensitive a plant is to changes in sunlight; some plants (or bonds with longer maturities) are more sensitive and require careful positioning (or risk management).

- **Reinvestment Rate Risk**: The risk that cash flows from a bond will be reinvested at a lower rate than the original bond's yield. Imagine a farmer who replants seeds at a time when the yield (or market interest rates) has fallen, potentially resulting in lower future profits.

4. Tax Implications: Taxable Equivalent Yields and After-Tax Returns

- Calculating the taxable equivalent yield for municipal bonds helps investors compare the net returns of tax-free investments with those that are taxable. It's like comparing the net income of two jobs, where one salary is tax-free and the other is not.

- Understanding after-tax returns is crucial for assessing the true profitability of taxable bond investments, similar to understanding your actual take-home pay after taxes.

Pricing Conventions: Understanding Clean Pricing in Bond Trading

What is Clean Pricing?

Clean pricing, often referred to as the quoted price, is a fundamental concept in bond trading. It represents the price of a bond excluding any accrued interest. In simpler terms, the clean price is similar to the sticker price on a new car—it reflects the base cost of the car itself, without any additional fees or taxes that might be due at purchase.

Role of Clean Pricing in Bond Trading

In the bond market, the clean price is crucial because it provides a standard benchmark that facilitates the comparison of bond prices across the market. Just as shoppers compare prices of similar products in different stores without tax, bond investors use the clean price to compare the value of bonds regardless of their interest accrual.

How Clean Pricing Works

When a bond is traded, the actual amount paid by the buyer is the dirty price, which includes accrued interest since the last coupon payment. However, the clean price is typically what is quoted in financial news and trading platforms. The reason for distinguishing between clean and dirty prices in this way is to avoid distortions in price comparisons due to different bonds being at different stages in their interest accrual cycles.

For example, consider two identical bonds issued by the same entity with different payment dates for their semi-annual coupons. If one bond recently paid its coupon and the other is close to its next payment, the latter will have a higher amount of accrued interest. Quoting both bonds at their clean prices removes the effect of this accrued interest, allowing for a clear comparison based purely on the underlying value of the bonds themselves.

Calculating Clean Price

To calculate the clean price from the dirty price (the price including accrued interest), investors subtract the accrued interest from the dirty price. This calculation ensures that the clean price reflects only the actual value of the bond, not the value plus the interest that has built up since the last payment.

Practical Example

Imagine a bond with a face value of $1,000 and a coupon rate of 5% paid semi-annually. If the bond is halfway between payment dates and the dirty price (total cost including accrued interest) is $1,025, the accrued interest would be $25 ($1,000 x 5% x 0.5 year). Thus, the clean price would be $1,000 ($1,025 - $25).

Importance of Understanding Clean Pricing

For SIE exam candidates and investors, understanding clean pricing is essential because it aids in evaluating and comparing bond investments without the temporary influence of accruing interest. This knowledge ensures that investment decisions are based on the intrinsic value of the bonds, akin to evaluating the worth of a house based on its construction and location rather than the furniture inside, which may vary over time. This clarity is crucial for effective investment strategy and risk assessment in the bond market.

Example Calculations: Determining Clean and Dirty Prices of Bonds

Understanding how to calculate both clean and dirty prices is crucial for anyone dealing with bond investments. These calculations help in making informed investment decisions and ensuring accurate portfolio valuations. Below, we provide clear, step-by-step examples to illustrate how these prices are determined.

Calculating Clean Price

Let's assume we have a bond with a face value of $1,000, an annual coupon rate of 6%, and semi-annual payments. This means the bond pays $30 every six months ($1,000 x 6% / 2).

Step 1: Identify the Dirty Price

Suppose the dirty price (the price including accrued interest) of the bond in the market is $1,020. This price reflects not just the value of the bond but also the interest that has accumulated since the last coupon payment.

Step 2: Calculate Accrued Interest

If the bond is halfway through the coupon period (3 months out of 6), the accrued interest would be half of the semi-annual coupon payment: Accrued Interest=$30×3/6=$15

Step 3: Subtract Accrued Interest from Dirty Price

To find the clean price, subtract the accrued interest from the dirty price:
Clean Price=$1,020–$15=$1,005

This clean price represents the value of the bond without any accrued interest.

Calculating Dirty Price

Now, let's reverse the scenario. Assume you know the clean price of a bond and need to determine its dirty price on a specific date.

Step 1: Identify the Clean Price

Suppose the clean price of the bond is $1,005.

Step 2: Calculate Accrued Interest

Using the same bond details as before, if $15 of interest has accrued (as calculated earlier), this amount reflects the interest accumulated since the last coupon payment.

Step 3: Add Accrued Interest to Clean Price

To find the dirty price, add the accrued interest back to the clean price:
Dirty Price=$1,005+$15=$1,020

This dirty price is what the buyer would actually pay to purchase the bond on the market at this time, including the earned interest.

Importance of Accurate Calculations

These calculations are essential for anyone involved in bond trading or investment management. Accurately determining clean and dirty prices ensures transparency in transactions and helps investors understand the true cost or value of a bond at any given time. These skills are not only vital for passing financial exams like the SIE but are also critical in professional financial settings, where precise bond valuation influences buying and selling decisions, portfolio management, and investment performance analysis.

Yield-to-Maturity (YTM): Navigating the Long-Term Yield of Bonds

Understanding Yield-to-Maturity

Yield-to-Maturity (YTM) is a critical financial metric used to estimate the total return anticipated on a bond if it is held until it matures, assuming that all payments are made as scheduled. YTM includes not only the interest payments a bond will make over its lifetime but also any gain or loss incurred if the bond was purchased at a price different from its par (face) value.

The Importance of YTM

YTM is often likened to the average annual return of a long-term investment. It is a comprehensive measure that provides a holistic view of a bond's profitability. This makes YTM invaluable for investors comparing different bonds that may have varying coupon rates, prices, and terms to maturity. For example, consider YTM as the average speed of a car on a long journey; it tells you the overall speed at which you traveled from start to finish, accounting for all stops and starts along the way, providing a complete picture of your journey's efficiency.

Calculating Yield-to-Maturity

The calculation of YTM is more complex than that of simple yield formulas because it solves for the discount rate that equates the present value of all future cash flows from the bond (both periodic coupon payments and the principal repayment at maturity) to the current price of the bond.

The Formula

The formula for calculating YTM is as follows:

The Formula

The formula for calculating YTM is as follows:

$$YTM = \left(\frac{C + \frac{(F-P)}{n}}{\frac{(F+P)}{2}} \right)$$

Where:

- C is the annual coupon payment (Face Value×Coupon RateFace Value×Coupon Rate)

- F is the face value of the bond

- P is the current price of the bond

- n is the number of years to maturity

Step-by-Step Example

Let's calculate the YTM for a bond with a face value of $1,000, a current market price of $950, a coupon rate of 5%, and 10 years to maturity.

1. **Annual Coupon Payment**: C=$1,000×0.05=$50

2. **Calculating the Numerator**: Numerator=$50+($1,000−$950)10=$50+$5=$55

3. **Calculating the Denominator**: Denominator=($1,000+$950)/2=$1,950/2=$975

4. **Yield-to-Maturity**: YTM=($55/$975)≈5.64%

This calculation shows that, if the investor holds the bond to maturity, they can expect to earn an average annual return of approximately 5.64%, considering the current purchase price, the coupon payments, and the gain from buying the bond below its face value.

The Role of YTM in Investment Decisions

Yield-to-Maturity offers a reliable gauge for assessing the long-term yield of bonds and is critical for making informed investment decisions. It allows investors to compare the expected returns on bonds with different characteristics and market conditions, aiding in the selection of bonds that best meet their yield expectations and risk tolerance. Understanding and calculating YTM is not just academic; it's a practical skill essential for anyone involved in bond investing or preparing for financial exams like the SIE.

Understanding Current Yield: Gauging Immediate Income from Bonds

What is Current Yield?

Current Yield is a straightforward financial metric used to determine the income provided by a bond relative to its market price. It is an essential indicator for investors who are primarily interested in the income generated from their bond investments, rather than the total yield over the bond's entire life.

The Importance of Current Yield

Imagine you are assessing two vintage cars for purchase, not just for their potential increase in value over time but for their ability to be rented out for events. The car that can generate the most rental income relative to its cost would be more attractive if immediate income is your priority. Similarly, the current yield of a bond tells an investor how much income the bond will generate now relative to its current price, making it a crucial measure for those who need to maximize their investment income in the short term.

Calculating Current Yield

The formula for calculating the current yield of a bond is simple and provides a snapshot of the bond's income effectiveness as it relates to its current market price.

The Formula

The current yield is calculated using the following formula:
Current Yield=(Annual Coupon Payment/Current Market Price of the Bond)×100

Step-by-Step Example

Consider a bond with an annual coupon payment of $40 and a current market price of $950.

1. **Identify the Annual Coupon Payment**: This is the fixed payment the bond will make each year, which is $40 in this example.

2. **Determine the Current Market Price of the Bond**: This is the price at which the bond is currently trading, which is $950 in this example.

3. **Calculate the Current Yield**: Current Yield=($40/$950)×100≈4.21%

This result means that, based on the current price, the bond's yield in terms of the interest income it generates is about 4.21% per year.

Relevance of Current Yield in Bond Investment Decisions

Current yield is particularly relevant for investors who are focused on the income aspect of bonds, such as retirees or institutions that depend on cash flow to fund operations. It provides a clear and immediate understanding of what an investor can expect to earn in income on an annual basis from a bond purchased at its current market price. This is crucial for budgeting and financial planning, especially when comparing bonds with different face values and coupon rates.

Moreover, by assessing the current yield, investors can quickly gauge whether a bond offers a competitive return compared to others in the market or alternative investments like dividend-paying stocks or savings accounts. It's an effective way to measure how hard your money is working for you right now, rather than over the more extended period measured by yield to maturity.

Understanding and calculating current yield is an essential skill for any investor or financial professional dealing with bonds. It provides a vital data point for assessing the immediate income-generating capability of a bond relative to its price, helping to make informed decisions that align with income needs and investment strategies.

Yield-to-Call (YTC): Understanding Early Redemption Scenarios

What is Yield-to-Call?

Yield-to-Call (YTC) is an essential measure for investors in callable bonds, which are bonds that the issuer can elect to redeem before their maturity date at a predetermined price (the call price). Think of YTC as calculating the yield on a fixed-term investment, like a certificate of deposit, that has the possibility of being ended early by the bank. Just as depositors would want to know their return if the bank were to end the deposit early, bond investors need to understand their return if the issuer calls the bond before maturity.

Relevance of Yield-to-Call

YTC becomes particularly relevant in scenarios where market interest rates are declining. In such cases, bond issuers often choose to refinance debt by calling existing bonds that have higher interest rates and reissuing new bonds at the current lower rates. This is similar to homeowners refinancing their mortgages to take advantage of lower interest rates. For investors, knowing the YTC is crucial because it provides the most accurate measure of yield if the bond is called before its maturity date.

Calculating Yield-to-Call

The calculation of YTC is similar to Yield-to-Maturity (YTM), but with the time frame adjusted from the bond's maturity date to its earliest call date. The formula also takes into account the call premium, which is often added to the bond's face value as an incentive for investors.

The Formula

$$YTC = \left(\frac{\text{Annual Coupon Payment} + \frac{(\text{Call Price} - \text{Current Price})}{\text{Years to Call}}}{\frac{(\text{Call Price} + \text{Current Price})}{2}} \right)$$

Step-by-Step Example

Assume a bond with a face value of $1,000, a call price of $1,020 (including a $20 call premium), an annual coupon rate of 5% (thus annual payments of $50), a current market price of $950, and 5 years to the earliest call date.

1. **Calculate the Average Annual Gain/Loss if Called**:
   (Call Price−Current Price)Years to Call=($1,020−$950)5=$14

2. **Calculate the Average Price**: (Call Price+Current Price)2=($1,020+$950)2=$9852

3. **Determine YTC**: YTC=($50+$14$985)≈6.5%

This calculation tells the investor that if the bond is called at the earliest opportunity, they can expect an annual return of approximately 6.5%.

Importance of YTC in Investment Strategy

Understanding YTC is vital for investors who hold callable bonds, especially in a declining interest rate environment where the likelihood of bonds being called increases. It helps investors manage their expectations and strategies, ensuring they are not caught off-guard by early redemptions. Knowing the YTC allows investors to compare callable bonds more accurately with non-callable bonds and other fixed-income securities, adjusting their portfolio according to risk and return expectations.

Yield-to-Call is a critical calculation for bond investors, particularly those in callable bonds, as it provides insights into the potential returns if the bond issuer decides to refinance the debt. Just as knowing the exit routes from a building is essential in an emergency, knowing the YTC is crucial for bond investors in managing their investment exits efficiently. This knowledge is invaluable for making informed decisions that align with overall investment goals and market conditions.

Example Calculations: Yield-to-Maturity, Current Yield, and Yield-to-Call

Practical Calculation of Yield-to-Maturity (YTM)

Yield-to-Maturity estimates the total return of a bond if held to maturity. Let's consider a bond with a face value of $1,000, a current price of $920, an annual coupon rate of 8% (which translates to $80 per year), and 10 years remaining until maturity.

Steps to Calculate YTM:

1. **Annual Coupon Payment**: $1,000 (face value) x 8% = $80.

2. **Years to Maturity**: 10 years.

3. **Face Value**: $1,000.

4. **Current Price**: $920.

5. **YTM Calculation**: This involves a trial and error method or using a financial calculator, as the formula for YTM is iterative. For simplicity, we'll assume the YTM is approximately 9.3%, found using a financial calculator or bond yield table.

Imagine you're trying to predict the average growth rate of a tree from its current height until it reaches full maturity, considering annual growth and its current state.

Practical Calculation of Current Yield

The Current Yield focuses on the bond's yield in terms of annual interest payments relative to its current market price. Using the same bond details as above:

Steps to Calculate Current Yield:

1. **Annual Coupon Payment**: $80.

2. **Current Market Price**: $920.

3. **Current Yield Calculation**: Current Yield=($80/$920)×100=8.7%

This is akin to calculating the immediate productivity of a rental property by dividing the annual rent income by the purchase price.

Practical Calculation of Yield-to-Call (YTC)

Yield-to-Call calculates the yield of the bond assuming it will be called away by the issuer before maturity. Assume the bond can be called in 5 years at a price of $1,050.

Steps to Calculate YTC:

1. **Call Price**: $1,050.

2. **Years to Call**: 5 years.

3. **Annual Coupon Payment**: $80.

4. **Current Price**: $920.

5. **YTC Calculation**:

$$\text{YTC} = \left(\frac{\$80 + \frac{(\$1,050 - \$920)}{5}}{\frac{(\$1,050 + \$920)}{2}} \right) \times 100 \approx 10.2\%$$

This process is similar to recalculating the expected returns on an investment after learning it will mature sooner than initially planned.

The Relevance of Example Calculations

These examples provide practical insights into how to compute key yield measures for bonds. Understanding these calculations is akin to a chef perfectly timing and seasoning a dish to achieve desired flavors—bond investors need to precisely calculate yields to manage their portfolios effectively, maximizing returns while understanding associated risks. This knowledge is crucial not only for the SIE exam but also for practical investment management and decision-making in the financial industry.

Understanding Interest Rate Risk in Bond Investments

Interest Rate Risk: The Balancing Act of Bond Investing

Interest rate risk is one of the fundamental risks faced by bond investors. This risk stems from fluctuations in the general level of interest rates, which inversely affect the prices of existing bonds.

The Nature of Interest Rate Risk

Imagine you're on a seesaw where bond prices and interest rates are on opposite ends. As interest rates rise, bond prices fall, and vice versa. This relationship exists because as new bonds are issued with higher yields to match the rising rates, the less attractive older bonds with lower yields become, leading to a decrease in their prices.

The Impact of Interest Rate Changes

To grasp how significant these changes can be, consider a bond you own with a fixed interest rate of 5%. If market interest rates increase to 6%, new bonds are now more appealing because they pay more. The only way to sell your 5% bond is to offer it at a lower price that compensates for the lower interest payment. Conversely, if market rates drop to 4%, your bond becomes more valuable.

Duration: Measuring Sensitivity to Interest Rates

Duration is a crucial measure in this context. It quantifies how long, on average, it takes for an investor to be repaid the bond's price by its cash flows. The longer the duration, the more sensitive the bond is to changes in interest rates.

Calculating Duration

Duration is calculated by taking the weighted average of the times until each payment is received, with the weights being the present value of each payment. Therefore, duration isn't just a measure of time but also of risk and value.

Example of Duration

For instance, if a bond has a duration of 6 years, it indicates that the bond is relatively sensitive to changes in interest rates. A rule of thumb is that for every 1% increase in interest rates, the bond's price will drop approximately 6%, and vice versa.

The Use of Duration in Investment Strategy

Understanding duration helps investors manage interest rate risk more effectively. If you are concerned about rising interest rates, you might reduce your portfolio's average duration because shorter-duration bonds are less sensitive to changes in rates. This strategic adjustment is akin to adjusting the sails of a boat depending on the wind's strength and direction to maintain control and speed.

Navigating Interest Rate Risks with Duration

Understanding interest rate risk and effectively using duration are akin to mastering the art of balancing while walking on a tightrope. Just as a tightrope walker uses a balance pole to offset the forces pulling him down, investors use duration to balance the impact of interest rate movements on their bond investments. Mastering this concept allows investors to optimize their bond portfolios in alignment with their risk tolerance and market outlook, enhancing their ability to achieve stable returns in a fluctuating interest rate environment. This knowledge is not only critical for the SIE exam but is essential for anyone involved in bond investing or portfolio management.

Understanding Reinvestment Rate Risk in Bond Investments

Reinvestment Rate Risk: The Challenge of Fluctuating Returns

Reinvestment rate risk refers to the uncertainty bond investors face regarding the rates at which future cash flows from their investments can be reinvested. This risk becomes particularly prominent in a changing interest rate environment.

Nature of Reinvestment Rate Risk

Imagine you have planted a garden that yields produce at different times of the year. If market conditions change and the prices for your crops drop by the time you harvest, you will earn less from your efforts than anticipated. Similarly, for bond investors, if interest rates are lower when their bond's interest payments or principal are received (and ready to be reinvested), the returns on these new investments could be less than expected.

The Impact of Interest Rate Changes on Reinvestment

To understand how interest rate changes affect reinvestment:

Scenario Analysis

- **Interest Rates Fall**: Suppose an investor receives periodic coupon payments from a bond. If interest rates decrease, the new bonds or other fixed-income investments available for reinvesting these payments will likely offer lower yields. This decrease means the investor's income from reinvested funds will be lower than initially planned.

- **Interest Rates Rise**: Conversely, if interest rates increase, the coupon payments can be reinvested at higher yields, potentially increasing the investor's income from future investments. However, this scenario can still pose risks to an overall strategy if the original bond was bought at a premium or if other portfolio bonds lose market value.

Calculating Potential Impact

Investors must assess the potential variability in reinvested income, especially for long-term or fixed-income portfolios where periodic reinvestments form a significant component of the return strategy. Using financial models that include different rate scenarios can help illustrate the possible outcomes and aid in planning.

Example Calculation

Consider a bond with semi-annual coupons of $50 over 10 years. If at the time of the first coupon payment, the reinvestment rate drops from 5% to 2%, the future value of that reinvested coupon over the remaining period will be significantly lower. Over time, if this trend continues with each coupon payment, the cumulative impact could substantially reduce expected portfolio returns.

Navigating Reinvestment Rate Risk

managing reinvestment rate risk requires vigilance and strategic planning. Just as a farmer might use futures contracts to lock in prices for crops against market volatility, bond investors can use ladders, barbells, or bullet strategies in bond portfolios to manage the timing and impact of reinvestments. This proactive approach helps stabilize returns and mitigate the risk of falling interest rates adversely affecting the growth of reinvested funds.

Managing Risks in Bond Portfolio Management

Introduction to Risk Management in Bond Investing

Managing risks in bond investments is akin to navigating a ship through a stormy sea. Just as a seasoned captain uses various tools and strategies to avoid capsizing, bond investors must employ a variety of techniques to minimize the impact of interest rate fluctuations, credit risks, and reinvestment rate risks on their portfolios.

Strategies to Mitigate Bond Investment Risks

Diversification

Diversification across different types of bonds is one of the fundamental strategies to manage risk. Just as a well-rounded diet includes a variety of nutrients to maintain health, a diversified bond portfolio includes a mix of government bonds, corporate bonds, short-term, medium-term, and long-term bonds. This variety helps buffer against sector-specific downturns and the impact of varying interest rate changes across different markets and maturities.

Duration Management

Duration management is crucial when dealing with interest rate risk. Duration is a measure of a bond's sensitivity to interest rate changes. Managing duration involves adjusting the mix of short, medium, and long-duration bonds to match the investor's interest rate outlook and risk tolerance. For instance, if interest rates are expected to rise, reducing the portfolio's average duration can help minimize the negative impact on bond prices, similar to shortening the sails on a sailboat when expecting stronger winds.

Laddering

The laddering strategy involves purchasing bonds that mature at different times. This approach can be likened to planting a garden where crops mature at different intervals, ensuring a steady harvest throughout the growing season. In bond investing, laddering helps manage reinvestment risk by regularly freeing up capital for reinvestment at potentially higher yields as bonds mature at staggered dates.

Bond Immunization

Immunization is a strategy that matches the durations of assets and liabilities to ensure a certain return regardless of interest rate changes. This strategy can be compared to setting a thermostat in a home to maintain a constant temperature regardless of the weather outside. In bond terms, immunization might involve matching the duration of bond investments with the time horizon of future liabilities (like retirement needs) to buffer against the risk of changing market conditions.

Use of Bond Derivatives

Finally, sophisticated investors might use derivatives such as options and futures to hedge against interest rate risk. This approach is akin to an insurance policy; just as homeowners use insurance to protect against potential damages from unforeseen events, investors use bond futures and options to hedge against adverse moves in interest rates.

Proactive Risk Management in Bond Portfolios

Effective risk management in bond investing requires a proactive approach and the use of multiple strategies tailored to an investor's specific risk tolerance, investment goals, and market outlook. By employing techniques such as diversification, duration management, laddering, immunization, and derivatives, investors can safeguard their portfolios against potential losses due to interest rate changes, credit events, and other financial risks.

Taxable Equivalent Yields: Maximizing Returns on Tax-Advantaged Investments

Understanding Taxable Equivalent Yields

Taxable Equivalent Yield is a crucial calculation for investors considering tax-free municipal bonds. Given their tax bracket, it helps determine the yield an investor would need from a taxable investment to equal the yield from a tax-exempt bond.

The Concept of Taxable Equivalent Yield

Think of taxable equivalent yield like converting currency when traveling to a country with a different monetary system. Just as you need to know how much your dollars are worth in another country's currency to understand what you can buy, you need to know what a tax-free yield is worth in taxable terms to compare it accurately to other investments that are subject to taxes.

Calculating Taxable Equivalent Yield

The formula for calculating the taxable equivalent yield is straightforward, but it requires knowing your marginal tax rate—the percentage of tax applied to your next dollar of income.

The Formula

Taxable Equivalent Yield= Tax-Free Yield/(1−Marginal Tax Rate)

Step-by-Step Example

Suppose you are considering a municipal bond that offers a yield of 3%. If you are in the 28% tax bracket, the calculation would be:

1. **Identify the Tax-Free Yield**: 3% (or 0.03 as a decimal).

2. **Determine Your Marginal Tax Rate**: 28% (or 0.28 as a decimal).

3. **Apply the Taxable Equivalent Yield Formula**:
   Taxable Equivalent Yield=0.03/(1−0.28)=0.030.72≈0.0417 or 4.17%

This result means that a taxable bond would need to offer a yield of at least 4.17% to be as advantageous as a tax-free municipal bond yielding 3% for someone in the 28% tax bracket.

Relevance of Taxable Equivalent Yield in Investment Decisions

Understanding the taxable equivalent yield is vital for investors comparing municipal bonds (which are often exempt from federal and sometimes state and local taxes) with taxable bonds like corporates. This comparison is crucial because it allows investors to make informed decisions based on their individual tax circumstances. It's like deciding whether to buy a product in a duty-free shop: knowing the equivalent cost in a regular shop, where you pay tax, helps you understand whether you're actually saving money.

Strategic Use of Taxable Equivalent Yield

Calculating and using the taxable equivalent yield allows investors to see beyond the face value of bond yields and assess the true value of tax-free bonds in the context of their personal tax situation. It ensures that decisions are based on comprehensive financial analysis, much like comparing prices across different stores to ensure you get the best deal. For those preparing for the SIE exam, mastering this calculation not only aids in personal investment strategy but also deepens understanding of broader financial planning concepts essential for professional success in the securities industry.

After-Tax Returns: Evaluating the True Profitability of Bond Investments

Understanding After-Tax Returns

After-tax returns provide a crucial measure for comparing the effectiveness of taxable versus tax-exempt investments. It's like measuring the net weight of a product after removing the packaging; what remains is what truly counts for your purposes. In investment terms, the after-tax return tells an investor what they will actually earn, after accounting for the impact of taxes, which can significantly affect the attractiveness of different investment options.

The Importance of Calculating After-Tax Returns

Calculating after-tax returns is particularly important when comparing tax-exempt investments, such as municipal bonds, with taxable investments. This calculation helps investors understand which investment provides the greater benefit under their specific tax circumstances, just as a shopper compares prices to determine which store offers the best value after considering discounts, taxes, and other factors.

How to Calculate After-Tax Returns

Formula for After-Tax Returns

For taxable bonds, the formula to calculate the after-tax return is: $\text{After-Tax Return} = \text{Pre-Tax Return} \times (1 - \text{Tax Rate})$

Step-by-Step Example

Let's consider a corporate bond with a yield of 5% and an investor who is in the 30% tax bracket.

1. **Identify the Pre-Tax Return**: This is the yield of the bond, which in this case is 5% (or 0.05 as a decimal).

2. **Determine the Tax Rate**: For this example, the investor's marginal tax rate is 30% (or 0.30 as a decimal).

3. **Calculate the After-Tax Return**:

    $\text{After-Tax Return} = 0.05 \times (1 - 0.30) = 0.05 \times 0.70 = 0.035$ or 3.5%

This result means that after considering taxes, the effective yield of the corporate bond for this investor is 3.5%.

Comparing Tax-Exempt and Taxable Investments

To effectively utilize after-tax returns, investors should calculate and compare these values for both taxable and tax-exempt investments. For instance, if a tax-exempt municipal bond offers a yield of 3.2%, it might seem lower at first glance than a taxable bond offering 5%. However, using the after-tax return calculation, we see that for an investor in the 30% tax bracket, the taxable bond's effective yield is only 3.5%, which is very close to the tax-exempt bond's yield. Thus, the decision between the two could hinge on other factors like risk tolerance and investment horizon, or might lean toward the tax-exempt bond if the investor anticipates moving into a higher tax bracket.

Strategic Financial Planning with After-Tax Returns

utilizing after-tax returns is akin to evaluating the cost-effectiveness of buying items in bulk versus individually, considering all associated costs and benefits. For investors, especially those studying for the SIE exam, mastering the calculation of after-tax returns is essential. It enables them to make more informed decisions, ensuring their investments align optimally with their financial goals and tax situations, maximizing real returns in their investment portfolios.

Example Calculations: Mastering Taxable Equivalent Yields and After-Tax Returns

Taxable Equivalent Yields: Ensuring Comparability Across Investments

Understanding the Calculation

The taxable equivalent yield calculation is crucial for comparing the returns of tax-exempt investments, like municipal bonds, with taxable investments, under different tax scenarios. This calculation is like converting miles per hour to kilometers per hour to compare speeds when traveling in countries using different measurement systems.

Detailed Example

Imagine an investor is in the 32% tax bracket and is considering a municipal bond offering a tax-exempt yield of 2.8%.

1. **Identify the Tax-Free Yield**: 2.8% (or 0.028 as a decimal).

2. **Determine the Investor's Tax Rate**: 32% (or 0.32 as a decimal).

3. **Apply the Taxable Equivalent Yield Formula**:

$$\text{Taxable Equivalent Yield} = \frac{\text{Tax-Free Yield}}{1 - \text{Tax Rate}} = \frac{0.028}{1 - 0.32} = \frac{0.028}{0.68} \approx 0.0412 \text{ or } 4.12\%$$

This result means that a taxable bond would need to offer a yield of at least 4.12% to provide the same after-tax income as the tax-exempt municipal bond for an investor in the 32% tax bracket.

After-Tax Returns: Assessing Real Income from Taxable Investments

Understanding the Calculation

After-tax returns provide investors with a clear picture of what they will actually earn from taxable investments after accounting for the impact of their specific tax rate. This is akin to determining the net weight of a packaged product by subtracting the weight of the packaging.

Detailed Example

Consider a corporate bond with a pre-tax yield of 5% held by an investor in the 32% tax bracket.

1. **Identify the Pre-Tax Yield**: 5% (or 0.05 as a decimal).

2. **Determine the Investor's Tax Rate**: 32% (or 0.32 as a decimal).

3. **Calculate the After-Tax Return**:

After-Tax Return=Pre-Tax Yield×(1−Tax Rate)=0.05×(1−0.32)=0.05×0.68=0.034 or 3.4%

This calculation shows that the effective yield, after considering the impact of taxes, is 3.4%. Therefore, the investor would need to compare this return with the taxable equivalent yield of any tax-exempt investments being considered.

Empowering Investment Decisions Through Calculations

By mastering the calculations of taxable equivalent yields and after-tax returns, investors can make more informed decisions that align with their financial goals and tax situations. These calculations act as financial tools to peel back the layers of tax impact, revealing the core benefits of different investment options. For SIE exam candidates and investors alike, understanding these concepts is crucial for optimizing investment strategies and ensuring that each investment decision is based on a thorough analysis of expected returns after taxes

Mastering Debt Securities Calculations for Investment Success

Recap of Key Concepts

This chapter has provided a comprehensive exploration of the essential calculations involved with debt securities. These calculations are not only pivotal for passing the SIE exam but also for making informed investment decisions in real-world scenarios. Here's a brief recap of the main topics covered:

- **Pricing Conventions**: Understanding clean and dirty pricing helps investors know the actual cost of a bond and the accrued interest involved, crucial for accurate trading and valuation.

- **Yield Formulas**: We delved into different types of yields—Yield-to-Maturity (YTM), Current Yield, and Yield-to-Call (YTC). Each serves a specific purpose in evaluating the potential returns of bonds based on their market price, maturity, and call features.

- **Interest Rate Risk and Reinvestment Rate Risk**: These sections highlighted how fluctuations in interest rates can impact bond prices and the returns on reinvested bond income, essential for managing long-term investment risks.

- **Taxable Equivalent Yields and After-Tax Returns**: Calculating these allows investors to compare tax-exempt bonds with taxable options effectively, considering their personal tax situation to maximize investment returns.

Emphasis on Practical Application

Real-World Investing

The calculations and concepts discussed in this chapter are not merely theoretical. They play a critical role in the day-to-day decision-making processes of investors and financial professionals. For example:

- **Pricing Calculations** enable investors to determine when to buy or sell bonds to achieve the best pricing.

- **Yield Calculations** are used to assess the income-generating potential of different bonds, helping to build portfolios that match investors' income needs and risk preferences.

- **Understanding and Managing Risks** associated with interest rates and reinvestment strategies are crucial for protecting investments against market volatility and economic shifts.

- **Tax Considerations** ensure that investors can choose investments that are most beneficial after taxes, enhancing real returns on their investments.

Exam Preparation

For candidates preparing for the SIE exam, mastering these calculations is vital. The exam tests the ability to apply these concepts in practical scenarios, assessing readiness to function effectively in the securities industry. Understanding these principles allows candidates to:

- Accurately answer exam questions related to bond investments.

- Demonstrate competency in handling real investment situations.

- Provide well-informed advice to clients, enhancing professional credibility and effectiveness.

A Foundation for Financial Acumen

 the calculations and concepts covered in this chapter are foundational to developing a robust understanding of the financial markets, particularly the bond market. Whether for passing the SIE exam or for navigating the complexities of investment strategies, the skills learned here are invaluable. They equip both aspiring finance professionals and seasoned investors with the tools needed to assess, manage, and optimize their bond investments, ensuring well-rounded financial acumen and success in the financial industry.

CHAPTER 6 Introduction: The Strategic Role of Options and Packaged Products in Investment Portfolios

Navigating the Financial Landscape with Advanced Tools

When it comes to investment, options and packaged products represent sophisticated tools that can significantly enhance portfolio performance, manage risks, or both. Understanding these instruments is akin to a pilot mastering the use of advanced navigation systems in varied weather conditions; just as the pilot uses these systems to improve flight safety and efficiency, investors use options and packaged products to refine their investment strategies and better navigate market volatility.

The Importance of Options in Investment Strategies

Options are not just financial instruments; they are opportunities—opportunities to speculate with less capital compared to trading stocks, manage risk through hedging strategies, and leverage market movements to benefit the investor's portfolio. The ability to buy a call or put option gives the investor potential market exposure with a limited loss to the option premium paid. This is like paying for an insurance policy; just as insurance protects against potential future losses for a small upfront cost, options can protect investments from downside risk while providing unlimited upside potential.

The Role of Packaged Products

Packaged products, such as mutual funds, exchange-traded funds (ETFs), and unit investment trusts, bundle various assets together, offering investors diversified exposure within a single investment. These products simplify asset allocation and diversification, much like a meal kit service delivers pre-portioned ingredients and recipes to create several different dishes. Each type of packaged product has unique characteristics and fee structures, impacting overall investment returns. Understanding these nuances helps investors choose the right products to match their financial goals, time horizons, and risk tolerance.

Strategic Implications for Investors

Mastering the use of options and understanding the dynamics of packaged products are crucial for any investor looking to develop a robust investment strategy. These tools can provide strategic advantages such as:

- **Risk Management**: Options allow investors to protect gains or hedge against losses in other portfolio holdings.

- **Cost Efficiency**: Packaged products offer a cost-effective way to gain exposure to a wide array of assets, reducing the transaction costs of buying individual securities.

- **Flexibility and Leverage**: Options offer the flexibility to capitalize on market predictions with potentially high returns from a relatively low initial investment (leverage).

As we dive deeper into this chapter, we will explore how each of these tools can be effectively utilized to meet specific investment objectives, akin to choosing the right type of vehicle for different terrains and purposes in a journey. By the end of this chapter, readers will be equipped with the knowledge to make informed decisions about when and how to incorporate options and packaged products into their investment strategies, enhancing their ability to manage a diversified and resilient portfolio.

Enhancing and Protecting Portfolio Performance with Options and Packaged Products

Leveraging Options for Portfolio Enhancement

Options are powerful financial instruments that, when used wisely, can significantly enhance the performance of an investment portfolio. Much like a Swiss Army knife, options offer multiple tools in one package—providing flexibility, leverage, and protection.

Strategic Use of Options

- **Leverage**: Options allow investors to control a larger amount of shares with a smaller amount of capital. This is akin to using a lever to lift a heavy object—it multiplies the force (investment) to achieve a greater outcome (exposure to stock movements).

- **Flexibility**: Investors can speculate on the direction of stock prices with less capital compared to buying the stock outright. This flexibility allows for adjustments based on market conditions, similar to a chef adjusting ingredients in a recipe based on available seasonal produce.

- **Hedging**: Options can serve as insurance policies for an investment portfolio. By purchasing put options, investors can protect against potential losses in their stock holdings, much like homeowners use insurance to protect against potential damages to their property.

Utilizing Packaged Products for Diversification and Efficiency

Packaged products, including mutual funds, ETFs, and unit investment trusts, bundle various assets to offer investors diversified exposure within a single transaction. These products are like a well-balanced diet, providing a mixture of different nutrients (assets) needed for a healthy portfolio.

Benefits of Packaged Products

- **Diversification**: Just as a balanced diet reduces health risks by including a variety of nutrients, diversified investment through packaged products can reduce financial risk by spreading exposure across various assets.

- **Cost Efficiency**: Buying individual stocks and bonds can be expensive due to transaction fees. Packaged products consolidate these costs and often offer lower fees compared to individual purchases, akin to buying groceries in bulk rather than individually.

- **Simplicity**: Managing a portfolio of individual stocks requires time and expertise. Packaged products simplify this process, making it easier for investors to maintain a diversified portfolio without needing to actively manage each asset.

Protecting Portfolio Performance

Both options and packaged products play crucial roles in protecting the performance of a portfolio. This protection mechanism works in two main ways:

- **Risk Management**: By using options, investors can set limits on potential losses while maintaining the ability to gain from market upswings. Similarly, the inherent diversification in packaged products can protect against the volatility associated with individual investments.

- **Capital Preservation**: Options can be used to lock in profits on investments without actually selling the stock, effectively insulating the portfolio from downturns while still participating in potential gains.

Options and packaged products offer essential tools for investors looking to enhance and protect their portfolios. Understanding and utilizing these tools can be compared to a skilled sailor using all available instruments to navigate through treacherous waters safely and efficiently. As we explore these financial instruments further in this chapter, investors will gain insights into strategically incorporating them into their portfolios to optimize performance and minimize risks. This comprehensive approach not only supports achieving specific financial goals but also provides a buffer against market unpredictability.

Option Valuation Inputs – Underlying Asset Price

The Foundation of Options: Underlying Asset Price

The price of the underlying asset is a fundamental determinant in the valuation of options. Just as the foundation supports a house, the price of the underlying asset supports the value of an option. Understanding this relationship is crucial for any investor dealing with options.

How Underlying Asset Price Affects Option Prices

Influence on Call Options

For call options, which give the holder the right to buy the underlying asset at a specified strike price, the relationship with the underlying asset's price is direct and significant. As the price of the underlying asset increases, call options become more valuable. This is because the opportunity to buy the asset at the lower strike price becomes more attractive as the market price rises. This relationship can be likened to a golden ticket that allows you to buy a concert ticket at a price set months before the event, where the performer has since become a huge star. The value of that golden ticket rises as the current going rate for concert tickets soars.

Influence on Put Options

Conversely, for put options, which provide the right to sell the underlying asset at a specified strike price, an increase in the underlying asset's price typically leads to a decrease in the put option's value. This is because the benefit of selling at the strike price becomes less attractive as the market price of the asset increases. Imagine you have a contract that lets you sell snow in winter at a price agreed upon in summer. If a sudden snowstorm hits and snow is everywhere, the value of being able to sell at the summer price drops.

Factors Influencing the Impact

- **Volatility**: The impact of the underlying asset price on the option's price is magnified by the asset's volatility. Highly volatile assets lead to greater sensitivity in option pricing, which can be compared to the sensitivity of a seismograph during an earthquake. The more volatile the asset, the more dramatic the potential swings in option value.

- **Time to Expiration**: The amount of time remaining until the option expires also interacts with the underlying asset's price to influence the option's value. The longer the time until expiration, the more opportunity there is for the underlying asset price to move, which can increase the value of the option. This is akin to giving a talented but currently unknown artist more time to become famous before selling a painting you own of theirs; the potential for increased value grows over time.

The underlying asset price is more than just a number; it's a dynamic indicator that reflects both the current market sentiment and potential future movements. For options traders, keeping a keen eye on these price movements, alongside other factors such as volatility and time decay, is essential for making informed trading decisions. It's akin to a surfer choosing the right wave to ride; timing, position, and wave selection are all critical. By understanding how the underlying asset price influences an option's price, traders can better position themselves to capitalize on market movements and hedge against potential risks.

Option Valuation Inputs – Time to Expiration

The Impact of Time on Options Valuation

Time to expiration is a crucial determinant in the valuation of options, much like a ticking clock influences the outcome of a timed test. As the deadline approaches, the pressure increases or decreases depending on the preparedness of the test-taker. Similarly, as an option approaches its expiration date, the potential for it to gain or lose value changes significantly.

Understanding Time to Expiration

Defining Time to Expiration

Time to expiration refers to the duration remaining until the option contract expires. This period is critical because it represents the window during which the option holder can exercise the option. The value of this time component is known as the "time value" of the option.

How Time Influences Option Value

- **For Call Options**: As the expiration date nears, the time value of a call option decreases unless the price of the underlying asset is above the strike price, offering a potential profit. If the underlying asset's price remains below the strike price as expiration approaches, the likelihood of the option being profitable diminishes, much like the fading chances of finishing a test as time runs out.

- **For Put Options**: Similarly, for put options, the time value decreases as the expiration date approaches unless the underlying asset's price falls below the strike price, allowing the option holder to sell the asset at a higher than market price.

Factors Influencing Time Value Decay

- **Rate of Decay**: The rate at which an option's time value decreases accelerates as the expiration date approaches. This phenomenon is known as "theta" or time decay. It's akin to ice melting faster as the day warms up; the closer you get to the time when the temperature peaks, the quicker the ice melts.

- **Volatility and Time Value**: High volatility in the underlying asset can increase the time value of an option because the probability of the price moving favorably for the option holder is greater. This is similar to having extra time on that timed test if you know the questions may change dramatically; the potential to score higher remains as long as there is time left.

Strategic Use of Time in Options Trading

Options traders must carefully consider the time to expiration when buying or selling options. Choosing options with the right expiration date is critical to aligning trading strategies with market expectations. It's like selecting the right moment to jump in a game of double Dutch; timing is everything if you want to succeed without getting tangled.

Time as a Strategic Asset in Options Trading

In options trading, time is not just a passive factor—it's an active strategic element that traders can leverage. By understanding how the remaining time until an option's expiration affects its valuation, traders can better position themselves to take advantage of time-sensitive opportunities or protect against potential losses. This understanding requires not only awareness of market movements but also a keen sense of timing, much like a chess player who must anticipate both immediate and future moves of the opponent. As such, mastering the impact of time to expiration is essential for anyone involved in options trading, providing a foundation for making informed and strategic decisions in a dynamic market environment.

Option Valuation Inputs – Volatility

The Role of Volatility in Options Pricing

Volatility represents the heartbeat of the market, indicating how rapidly or dramatically the price of an underlying asset moves. Just as the intensity of a storm can change the course of a ship at sea, volatility can significantly alter the value of options.

Understanding Volatility

What is Volatility?

Volatility measures the degree of variation in the price of an asset over time, with higher volatility indicating larger price swings. In the context of options, volatility is a crucial input because it affects the probability that the option will end up in-the-money at expiration.

Types of Volatility

- **Historical Volatility**: This reflects the fluctuations of an asset's price in the past. It's akin to reviewing the performance of a sports team in previous seasons to gauge how they might perform in a future game.

- **Implied Volatility**: This projects future price variability and is derived from the market price of the option itself. Implied volatility is like a weather forecast; it predicts how stormy (volatile) the market might be in the near future, based on current information and market perceptions.

Impact of Volatility on Option Prices

Influence on Call and Put Options

- **Call Options**: Higher volatility increases the potential for the underlying asset's price to exceed the strike price, thereby increasing the value of a call option. This is similar to how a more unpredictable and potentially powerful storm increases the value of comprehensive insurance.

- **Put Options**: Similarly, for put options, higher volatility means there's a greater chance that the asset's price will fall below the strike price, thus increasing the put option's value.

Comparing Implied and Historical Volatility

Practical Implications

Understanding both implied and historical volatility helps investors gauge market sentiment and potential price movements. For example:

- **Historical Volatility as a Guide**: By looking at how volatile an asset has been in the past, traders can set benchmarks and expectations for future price behavior.

- **Implied Volatility as a Predictor**: Implied volatility reflects the market's expectations of future volatility and can signal upcoming changes or events that might affect the asset's price. If implied volatility is significantly higher than historical volatility, it may suggest that traders anticipate greater price swings, possibly due to upcoming news or events.

Strategic Use of Volatility in Options Trading

Investors and traders can leverage their understanding of volatility to enhance their trading strategies:

- **Choosing the Right Option**: Options with higher implied volatility are more expensive due to the greater expected movement in the underlying asset's price. Traders might purchase these options if they anticipate large price shifts.

- **Risk Management**: By analyzing volatility, traders can better manage risks, choosing options that align with their market outlook and risk tolerance.

Navigating the Volatile Waters of Options Trading

Volatility in options trading is not just a measure of risk, but also an opportunity. It requires a dynamic approach to options trading, where understanding and anticipating market movements can lead to significant returns. Like a skilled surfer who chooses the right wave, a knowledgeable options trader uses volatility to ride market waves skillfully. Thus, a thorough understanding of both historical and implied volatility is indispensable for any trader looking to capitalize on or hedge against the unpredictable movements of the market.

Black-Scholes Options Pricing Model

Understanding the Black-Scholes Model

The Black-Scholes model is a cornerstone of modern financial theory, providing a theoretical framework for valuing European-style options. Just as an architect uses blueprints to predict how a building will look and function before construction begins, the Black-Scholes model allows traders to estimate the value of an option before it is exercised, based on certain key variables.

Introduction to the Black-Scholes Model

Overview of the Model

Developed by economists Fischer Black and Myron Scholes in 1973, the Black-Scholes model provides a formula that helps investors and traders determine the fair price of an option based on factors such as the current stock price, the option's strike price, the time to expiration, the risk-free rate, and the stock's volatility.

Significance in Option Valuation

The Black-Scholes model revolutionized the trading of options by providing a systematic way to price options, removing much of the guesswork associated with previously arbitrary pricing methods. It has become so pivotal that understanding its use and implications is crucial for anyone involved in options trading.

How the Model Works

The model assumes a lognormal distribution of stock prices, which implies that stock prices can theoretically only go as low as zero, but have no upper limit. This assumption is crucial as it aligns with the real-world behavior of stock prices. The model also assumes that the volatility of the underlying asset and the risk-free rate are constant, and that no dividends are paid out during the life of the option.

The Mathematical Foundation

The formula itself uses these inputs to calculate the theoretical value of an option, providing insights into how different factors impact the option's price:

- **Stock Price (S)**: The current price of the stock.

- **Strike Price (K)**: The price at which the option can be exercised.

- **Time to Expiration (T)**: The time remaining until the option expires.

- **Volatility (σ)**: The expected volatility of the stock's returns.

- **Risk-Free Rate (r)**: The current risk-free interest rate over the life of the option.

Using the Black-Scholes formula:

$$C = S \cdot N(d_1) - K \cdot e^{-rT} \cdot N(d_2)$$

Where:

- C is the call option price.

- $N()$ is the cumulative distribution function of the standard normal distribution.

- $d1$ and $d2$ are factors calculated from the other variables (including stock price, strike price, time to expiration, risk-free rate, and volatility) and are part of the formula that assesses the probabilities of the option finishing in-the-money.

The Role of the Black-Scholes Model in Financial Markets

The Black-Scholes model is much like a compass for options traders—it doesn't predict the future, but it provides a crucial directional guide. By calculating the theoretical value of options, traders and investors can make more informed decisions, better assess risk, and potentially enhance their trading strategies. Its introduction marked a leap forward in quantitative finance, and it remains a fundamental tool in the financial industry, essential for both practical trading and for educational purposes like preparing for the SIE exam.

Key Formulas and Variables of the Black-Scholes Model

Decoding the Black-Scholes Formula

The Black-Scholes model is like a master recipe for pricing options, with each ingredient representing a specific variable that affects the final outcome—the option's price. Understanding each component and how they interact is crucial for mastering options trading.

The Formula

The Black-Scholes formula for pricing a European call option is expressed as:

$$C = S \cdot N(d_1) - K \cdot e^{-rT} \cdot N(d_2)$$

Where:

- **C** is the price of the call option.

This formula integrates various elements of the market and the specific option to calculate what the fair price should be.

Detailed Breakdown of Variables

1. Stock Price (S)

- **Definition**: This is the current price of the stock.

- **Role in Formula**: It directly affects the value of $d1$ and $d2$, and hence, the option price. The higher the current stock price relative to the strike price, the greater the probability that the option will be exercised.

2. Strike Price (K)

- **Definition**: The price at which the holder of the option can buy the underlying stock if they choose to exercise the option.

- **Role in Formula**: It determines the cost at which the stock can be bought under the option terms. The formula incorporates this value to calculate the potential payout.

3. Time to Expiration (T)

- **Definition**: This is the time remaining until the option expires.

- **Role in Formula**: Time impacts the $e-rT$ term, which represents the present value factor of the strike price, and affects $d1$ and $d2$ calculations. More time until expiration increases the chance of the stock price moving in a favorable direction.

4. Risk-Free Rate (r)

- **Definition**: The theoretical rate of return of an investment with zero risk, typically represented by government bonds.

- **Role in Formula**: It is used to discount the strike price to present value (the $e-rT$ term). Higher rates decrease the present value of the strike price, increasing the option's value.

5. Volatility (σ)

- **Definition**: A measure of the amount by which a stock price is expected to fluctuate during a given period.

- **Role in Formula**: Volatility affects both $d1$ and $d2$ and is a critical component as it reflects the uncertainty or risk associated with the stock price's movement. Higher volatility increases both $N(d1)$ and $N(d2)$, raising the option's price because there is a greater chance that the stock will move past the strike price.

Calculating $d1$ and $d2$

The variables d_1 and d_2 are intermediate steps in the model and are calculated as:

$$d_1 = \frac{\ln(\frac{S}{K})+(r+\frac{\sigma^2}{2})T}{\sigma\sqrt{T}}$$

$$d_2 = d_1 - \sigma\sqrt{T}$$

Where:

- $\ln(\frac{S}{K})$ captures the logarithm of the ratio of the stock price to the strike price.
- $\sigma\sqrt{T}$ represents the volatility component adjusted for the time to expiration.

Mastery Through Understanding

Just like understanding the roles of different ingredients in a recipe can make you a better chef, understanding the components of the Black-Scholes formula can make you a more proficient options trader. This detailed breakdown not only helps in preparing for the SIE exam but is essential for any finance professional engaged in options trading, ensuring they can price and trade options with confidence in their underlying calculations.

Application Examples of the Black-Scholes Model

Harnessing the Black-Scholes Model in Real-World Scenarios

Understanding how to apply the Black-Scholes model can be likened to using a GPS navigation system—it not only shows you where you are but also helps you understand how changes in your route (market conditions) could affect your journey (investment outcomes).

Example 1: Pricing a Call Option in a Rising Market

Scenario

Consider a stock that is currently priced at $100, and you are evaluating a European call option with a strike price of $105 that expires in one year. The risk-free rate is 2%, and the volatility of the stock is estimated at 20%.

Black-Scholes Calculations

- **Stock Price (S)**: $100

- **Strike Price (K)**: $105

- **Time to Expiration (T)**: 1 year

- **Risk-Free Rate (r)**: 2% per annum

- **Volatility (σ)**: 20% per annum

Using these values, calculate d_1 and d_2:

$$d_1 = \frac{\ln(\frac{100}{105}) + (0.02 + \frac{0.20^2}{2}) \times 1}{0.20 \times \sqrt{1}}$$

$$d_1 = \frac{-0.04879 + 0.04}{0.20} = -0.04395$$

$$d_2 = d_1 - 0.20 \times \sqrt{1} = -0.04395 - 0.20 = -0.24395$$

Now, using the normal distribution function $N(x)$ to find the values for $N(d_1)$ and $N(d_2)$, assume:

$$N(d_1) = 0.4821$$

$$N(d_2) = 0.4032$$

Finally, calculate the call option price C:

$$C = 100 \times N(d_1) - 105 \times e^{-0.02 \times 1} \times N(d_2)$$

$$C = 100 \times 0.4821 - 105 \times 0.980198673 \times 0.4032$$

$$C = 48.21 - 41.83 = 6.38$$

This calculation shows that the call option should be priced at approximately $6.38 in a rising market with moderate volatility.

Example 2: Impact of Increased Volatility

Scenario

Using the same stock and option specifications, but the volatility increases to 30%.

Adjusted Black-Scholes Calculations

Increase in volatility impacts d_1 and d_2:

$$d_1 = \frac{\ln(\frac{100}{105}) + (0.02 + \frac{0.30^2}{2}) \times 1}{0.30 \times \sqrt{1}}$$

$$d_1 = \frac{-0.04879 + 0.045}{0.30} = -0.01263$$

$$d_2 = d_1 - 0.30 \times \sqrt{1} = -0.31263$$

Assuming new values for $N(d_1)$ and $N(d_2)$:

$$N(d_1) = 0.4950$$

$$N(d_2) = 0.3775$$

Calculate the new call option price C:

$$C = 100 \times N(d_1) - 105 \times e^{-0.02 \times 1} \times N(d_2)$$

$$C = 100 \times 0.4950 - 105 \times 0.980198673 \times 0.3775$$

$$C = 49.50 - 39.15 = 10.35$$

This calculation shows that with higher volatility, the option price increases to $10.35, reflecting the greater likelihood of significant price movements.

Strategic Application of Black-Scholes Model

These examples illustrate how the Black-Scholes model can be applied to predict option pricing under varying market conditions. By adjusting inputs like stock price, time, volatility, and the risk-free rate, traders can use the model to navigate complex options landscapes, much like a navigator adjusts course based on weather and sea conditions. Understanding and applying this model equips investors with a powerful tool for optimizing their strategies in the dynamic options market.

Options Strategies – Covered Calls

Understanding Covered Calls

Covered calls are a cornerstone options strategy used by investors aiming to generate additional income from their stock holdings with a relatively lower level of risk. This strategy can be likened to renting out part of your home; while you continue to own and live in the house, you earn rental income from a tenant, enhancing your regular income.

Strategy Overview

What is a Covered Call?

A covered call involves holding a long position in an underlying stock and simultaneously selling (writing) call options on the same stock. The number of shares owned should at least match the number of shares obligated under the options contract.

Benefits of Covered Calls

- **Income Generation**: The primary benefit of writing covered calls is the generation of extra income from the option premiums, which the investor gets to keep regardless of stock performance.
- **Downside Protection**: While limited, the premium received provides some cushion against a drop in the stock price. This can be thought of as a protective buffer, similar to having a safety net while walking a tightrope.

Risks of Covered Calls

- **Limited Upside Potential**: If the stock price rises significantly, the seller misses out on potential gains beyond the strike price, as the buyer of the call will likely exercise the option.
- **Stock Ownership Risk**: The risk of holding the underlying stock remains; if the stock price falls significantly, the losses may outweigh the income from the option premiums.

Practical Example of Implementing Covered Calls

Scenario

Imagine you own 100 shares of Company XYZ, currently trading at $50 per share. Believing the stock will not rise significantly in the near future, you decide to write a covered call.

Steps to Implement

1. **Select the Option**: Choose a call option with a strike price where you are comfortable selling your stock, say at $55, and an expiration date in three months.

2. **Sell the Call**: Sell one call option (representing 100 shares) with a strike price of $55 at a premium of $2 per share. The total income from the premium is $200 (100 shares x $2).

3. **Outcome Analysis**:

   - **If the stock remains below $55** by expiration, the option expires worthless, you keep the premium and your shares.

   - **If the stock exceeds $55** by expiration, the option is likely exercised, and you must sell your shares at $55, missing any further gains above this price. However, you still benefit from the stock appreciation up to $55 plus the premium.

When to Use Covered Calls

Covered calls are ideal when you expect the stock to rise moderately or remain flat. This strategy is particularly popular among investors looking to generate steady income from stocks they consider long-term holds but do not expect to surge in the short term.

Covered Calls as a Strategic Option Tool

Covered calls offer a strategic method for investors to enhance the income from their portfolios while providing limited protection against stock declines. By understanding and applying this strategy effectively, investors can maintain a balanced approach, optimizing potential returns while managing risk, akin to a seasoned captain who knows when to sail safely and when to anchor.

Options Strategies – Protective Puts

Understanding Protective Puts

Protective puts are like purchasing an insurance policy for your stock investment. This strategy involves buying put options for stocks that you own, providing a safety net against significant losses if the stock price plummets.

Strategy Overview

What is a Protective Put?

A protective put involves buying put options on a stock that you already own. This strategy is employed to protect against a decline in the stock's value. Essentially, it sets a 'floor' price for the stock during the life of the put option, below which your losses will not extend.

Benefits of Protective Puts

- **Downside Protection**: Just as homeowners insurance protects against losses from events like fires or storms, protective puts provide financial protection against severe drops in stock prices.

- **Maintaining Ownership**: You maintain the potential for gains if the stock price increases. The protective put only limits the downside while allowing for unlimited upside potential.

Risks of Protective Puts

- **Cost of the Puts**: The premium paid for the puts can be considered a cost of insurance, reducing the overall profitability of the investment if the stock price does not decline.

- **Limited Time Frame**: Protection lasts only until the expiration of the put option, requiring continuous investment in protection to maintain coverage.

Practical Example of Implementing Protective Puts

Scenario

Imagine you own 100 shares of Company ABC, which is currently trading at $100 per share. Concerned about potential short-term volatility but optimistic about the long-term future, you decide to use protective puts to guard against a significant drop.

Steps to Implement

1. **Select the Put Option**: Choose a put option with a strike price that represents the minimum value you're willing to accept for your shares, say $90, and choose an expiration in three months.

2. **Buy the Put**: Purchase one put option (covering 100 shares) with a strike price of $90 at a premium of $3 per share. The total cost of the premium is $300 (100 shares x $3).

Outcome Analysis:

- **If the stock drops below $90**: The put option can be exercised to sell your shares at $90, minimizing your losses despite further drops in the market price.

- **If the stock stays above $90**: The put expires worthless, and you lose the premium but benefit from any appreciation in the stock value.

When to Use Protective Puts

Protective puts are best used in situations where you are bullish on the long-term prospects of a stock but cautious about short-term risks. It is particularly useful in volatile markets or when holding stocks with potentially significant upcoming news events that could affect the stock's price.

Protective Puts as a Strategic Investment Tool

Protective puts allow investors to manage risk without sacrificing the potential for profit. By understanding and deploying this strategy effectively, investors can protect themselves from downside risk while maintaining the flexibility to benefit from upward price movements. This approach is akin to a balanced diet that keeps you healthy yet prepared to fight illness—it manages nutritional needs day-to-day while ensuring protection against potential health setbacks.

Options Strategies – Spreads

Exploring the Diversity of Spread Strategies

Spread strategies in options trading are akin to a chef using a combination of ingredients to create a meal that suits different dietary preferences and occasions. Each type of spread has unique characteristics and is suited to particular market conditions and investor objectives.

Types of Spreads and Their Uses

1. Bull Spread

- **Overview**: A bull spread is constructed by buying a call option at a lower strike price and selling another call option at a higher strike price. Both options have the same expiration date. This strategy is used when the investor expects a moderate increase in the price of the underlying asset.

- **Metaphor**: Think of a bull spread like planting a garden in early spring. You hope for moderate weather—too much sun or too little can affect the growth negatively. Similarly, a bull spread profits most if the market rises moderately.

- **When to Use**: Utilize a bull spread when expecting a steady climb in the market price but with limited upside potential. It's a way to capitalize on growth while managing risk exposure.

2. Bear Spread

- **Overview**: A bear spread is set up by buying a put option at a higher strike price and selling another put option at a lower strike price. This strategy anticipates a decline in the underlying asset's price, but not drastically so.

- **Metaphor**: Imagine preparing for a gentle winter. You layer up moderately—not too much, as you don't expect severe cold. A bear spread prepares your portfolio for a dip, but shields against extreme losses if the drop is not as significant as anticipated.

- **When to Use**: Employ a bear spread when you believe the asset's price will fall but wish to limit potential downside risk and upfront costs.

3. Butterfly Spread

- **Overview**: A butterfly spread involves buying one call option at a lower strike price, selling two call options at a middle strike price, and buying one call option at a higher strike price. All options have the same expiration. This strategy is best used when little movement is expected in the underlying asset.

- **Metaphor**: Consider a butterfly spread like setting up a small, controlled campfire. You contain the fire (market risk) within a stone circle, ensuring it benefits you without the risk of spreading.

- **When to Use**: This spread is ideal when expecting the market to remain stable. It offers protection against significant movements in either direction, making it a conservative strategy that can still yield profits from minimal market volatility.

Strategic Application of Spreads in Options Trading

Spread strategies provide investors with tools to tailor their market exposure and risk according to specific forecasts and goals. Just as a gardener chooses plants based on the season and expected weather conditions, an options trader uses spreads to optimize the balance between risk and potential return based on market predictions. Understanding these strategies allows investors to navigate complex market conditions more effectively, enhancing their ability to achieve desired financial outcomes while managing potential risks. This knowledge is not only vital for trading success but is also essential for preparing for exams like the SIE, where comprehension of nuanced investment strategies is tested.

Section 6.4: Packaged Products – Expense Ratios

Understanding Expense Ratios

Expense ratios represent a critical factor in the evaluation of packaged investment products like mutual funds and exchange-traded funds (ETFs). They are akin to the management fees of a hotel—covering everything from the maintenance of facilities to staff services, which are essential for smooth operation but also impact the overall cost to guests.

The Impact of Expense Ratios on Investment Returns

What is an Expense Ratio?

- **Definition**: An expense ratio is an annual fee expressed as a percentage of the fund's average assets under management (AUM). It includes management fees, administrative fees, and other operational costs associated with the fund.

- **Role in Investments**: This fee is deducted from the fund's assets and directly affects the investor's returns. It's a continuous cost that fund holders pay for the management and administration of their investments.

Analogy to Daily Expenses

Imagine you are running a coffee shop. Daily expenses like rent, utilities, and wages for staff are inevitable. These expenses eat into your profit margin, similar to how expense ratios impact investment returns. The more efficient you are in managing operational costs, the higher your net profit. Similarly, funds with lower expense ratios potentially allow more of the investment's return to reach the investor.

Calculating Expense Ratios

- **Formula**: The expense ratio is calculated by dividing the fund's total operating expenses by its average assets under management (AUM) over the year.

- **Example**: If a mutual fund has $100 million in AUM and operates with $1 million in total expenses annually, its expense ratio is: Expense Ratio=$1 million/$100 million=1%

The Real-World Impact of Expense Ratios

- **Long-Term Effects**: Over time, even a seemingly small expense ratio can have a significant impact on investment growth due to the compounding effect. For example, an investment of $10,000 in a fund with a 5% annual return and a 1% expense ratio will yield less over 20 years than the same investment in a fund with a 0.5% expense ratio.

- **Cost Efficiency**: Funds with lower expense ratios are generally more cost-efficient but might offer fewer services or less active management compared to higher-cost funds. Investors need to balance cost with the level of service and management style that fits their investment strategy.

When to Consider Expense Ratios

Expense ratios are particularly important for investors who are cost-conscious and looking for long-term holdings. They are a crucial factor in the selection process of mutual funds and ETFs, especially in relatively stable markets where excessive fees can erode otherwise modest returns.

Strategic Importance of Expense Ratios

understanding and considering expense ratios is akin to a gardener choosing tools—invest in what brings the most value for the cost. Investors should weigh the impact of these fees against the potential benefits and performance history of the fund. By mastering the nuances of expense ratios, investors can make more informed decisions, optimizing their portfolios for both growth and efficiency, and ensuring that their investments align with their financial goals and tolerance for costs.

Packaged Products – Loads and Fees

Navigating the Costs of Investment: Loads and Fees

Investing in mutual funds and other packaged products often involves various types of fees and loads, which can significantly impact the profitability of your investments. Understanding these charges is akin to analyzing the total cost of owning a car, where upfront payments, maintenance costs, and other fees determine the overall expenditure and value.

Types of Loads and Fees

1. Front-End Loads

- **Definition**: Front-end loads are fees paid by investors at the time of purchasing shares in a mutual fund. This fee is a percentage of the initial investment and is deducted from the amount invested.

- **Metaphor**: Think of a front-end load as a cover charge at a concert. You pay it to get in the door, which decreases the amount of money you have left to spend on merchandise or refreshments.

- **Impact on Investment**: If you invest $10,000 in a mutual fund with a 5% front-end load, you immediately pay $500 as the load, and only $9,500 is actually invested in the fund. This reduces the growth potential of your investment right from the start.

2. Back-End Loads (Deferred Sales Charges)

- **Definition**: Back-end loads are fees charged when investors sell their shares, typically decreasing over time the longer the shares are held.

- **Metaphor**: A back-end load is like a cancellation fee for ending a phone contract early. The longer you've held the contract, the smaller the fee when you cancel.

- **Impact on Investment**: If a fund has a back-end load that decreases from 6% to 0% over six years, selling the shares too early could significantly reduce your returns. For example, selling $10,000 worth of shares within the first year at a 6% fee would cost you $600.

3. Ongoing Fees

- **Definition**: These include annual operating fees and management fees that are charged for the management of the fund's assets.

- **Metaphor**: Ongoing fees can be likened to yearly membership fees for a club. Whether you visit frequently or rarely, you must pay the fee as long as you are a member.

- **Impact on Investment**: Ongoing fees are deducted from the fund's assets and thus directly reduce its overall performance and your potential returns. A fund with a high expense ratio will consume more of your potential earnings over time.

Illustrating the Effect on Investor Profits

Example Calculation

Consider an investment of $10,000 in a mutual fund with the following fee structure:

- **Front-End Load**: 5%

- **Annual Expense Ratio**: 1.5%

- **No Back-End Load**

Investment After Front-End Load: $10,000 - (5% of $10,000) = $9,500 invested.

Annual Cost Due to Expense Ratio: 1.5% of $9,500 = $142.50 per year.

After 10 years, assuming a 5% annual growth rate, not accounting for compounding, the calculation would be:

- **Initial Investment Growth**: $9,500 growing at 5% per year = $14,250 after 10 years.

- **Total Expense Ratio Cost Over 10 Years**: $142.50 x 10 = $1,425.

- **Net Value After Expenses**: $14,250 - $1,425 = $12,825.

This simplified calculation shows how fees can eat into profits, emphasizing the need for investors to carefully consider these costs when choosing funds.

Strategic Considerations in Fund Selection

Understanding and carefully evaluating loads and fees when selecting mutual funds or other investment products is essential. It ensures that investors can choose options that not only align with their investment goals but also optimize their net returns. Just as a wise shopper considers both the price tag and the quality of goods, a prudent investor must weigh both the costs and potential benefits of any investment product. This diligence is critical in maximizing the efficiency and profitability of one's investment portfolio.

Packaged Products – NAV Calculations

The Critical Role of NAV in Investment Management

Net Asset Value (NAV) is the per-share value of a mutual fund or an exchange-traded fund (ETF). It is analogous to calculating the per-item price in a large shipment of goods, where the total cost is divided by the number of items to determine the price of each individual unit. For funds, NAV provides a clear measure of what each share of the fund is worth based on the assets it holds.

Understanding NAV

Definition of NAV

NAV represents the total value of all the securities held by a fund, minus any liabilities, divided by the number of outstanding shares. It is a fundamental metric that investors use to determine the fund's performance and the fair value of its shares.

How NAV is Calculated

Steps in the NAV Calculation Process

1. **Summing the Assets**: Calculate the total market value of all the fund's investments, including stocks, bonds, cash, and any other assets.

2. **Subtracting Liabilities**: Deduct all liabilities the fund owes, which could include money owed to creditors, pending payments, and other financial obligations.

3. **Dividing by Outstanding Shares**: The resulting value after subtracting liabilities is divided by the total number of the fund's outstanding shares.

Example Calculation

Imagine a mutual fund has the following assets and liabilities:

- **Total Assets**: $150 million (stocks, bonds, cash)

- **Liabilities**: $10 million (owed payments, administrative costs)

- **Outstanding Shares**: 5 million shares

NAV Calculation:

- **Net Assets**: $150 million - $10 million = $140 million

- **NAV per Share**: $140 million / 5 million shares = $28 per share

This calculated NAV per share tells investors that each share of the fund is worth $28 based on the current market value of the assets minus liabilities.

Importance of NAV in Daily Trading and Valuation

Daily Valuation

- **Mutual Funds**: For mutual funds, NAV is typically calculated at the end of each trading day based on the closing market prices of the assets. This daily recalibration ensures that the share price reflects the most current assessment of the fund's value.

- **ETFs**: Unlike mutual funds, ETFs are traded on exchanges and their prices can fluctuate throughout the day. However, their NAV is still calculated to ensure the trading price does not stray too far from the underlying value of the assets.

Impact on Investor Decisions

- **Buying and Selling**: Investors look at NAV to decide the best time to buy or sell shares of a fund. Purchasing shares when the NAV is low and selling when it is high can maximize returns.

- **Assessing Fund Performance**: Regular tracking of NAV helps investors gauge the management's effectiveness and the fund's overall performance relative to the market or its peers.

NAV as a Fundamental Indicator in Fund Investing

Understanding and monitoring the Net Asset Value of mutual funds and ETFs is akin to a navigator using a compass; it provides direction and ensures that investors are not lost in the complexities of market fluctuations. NAV offers a snapshot of the fund's health and efficacy, guiding investment decisions and strategic planning. For investors and financial professionals, mastery of NAV calculations is not just a skill but a necessity, ensuring informed and strategic participation in the markets.

Section 6.5: Leveraged and Inverse ETFs

Unpacking Leveraged and Inverse ETFs

Leveraged and inverse ETFs are like the sports cars of the investment world: they offer the potential for high speed (returns) but come with increased risk and require skillful handling.

What are Leveraged and Inverse ETFs?

Definition and Mechanism

- **Leveraged ETFs** aim to deliver multiples (e.g., 2x, 3x) of the daily performance of the index they track. They use financial derivatives and debt to amplify returns. Imagine pedaling a bicycle with a gear system designed to move you forward significantly further with each pedal stroke than a regular bike would; similarly, leveraged ETFs aim to significantly increase your investment "distance" or returns.

- **Inverse ETFs** are designed to provide the opposite return of the index they track, essentially profiting from declines in the underlying index. Think of it as betting against a team in a sports match; if the team loses, you win, and vice versa.

Benefits of Leveraged and Inverse ETFs

Enhanced Returns and Hedging

- **Leveraged ETFs** can magnify returns, providing a powerful tool for investors who are confident in their market predictions and looking for quick gains.

- **Inverse ETFs** offer a convenient way to hedge against downturns in the market or specific sectors without needing to short stocks, which can be complex and risky.

Risks Associated with Leveraged and Inverse ETFs

Volatility and Compounding

- **Daily Resets**: Both leveraged and inverse ETFs typically reset daily, meaning their performance aims to match the daily percentage movement times the leverage factor, not the long-term performance. This can lead to unexpected results over longer periods due to compounding, especially in volatile markets. It's like driving a high-performance sports car through winding roads—the faster you go, the harder it can be to control the vehicle, especially if the road conditions (market conditions) change suddenly.

- **Volatility Impact**: High volatility can erode the performance of these ETFs over time, making them less suitable for long-term holdings. The impact of daily volatility can mean the path of returns doesn't simply mirror the underlying index but instead follows a more complex, sometimes less predictable pattern.

Example of Leveraged ETF Performance

Scenario

Consider a scenario where an index starts at 100 points, drops to 90 on day one, and then goes back to 100 on day two. A 2x leveraged ETF aiming to double the index's return would decrease by 20% on day one (double the 10% drop) to 80, and increase by 22.2% on day two (double the 11.1% increase) to only 97.8, not back to 100. This illustrates the impact of daily resets and volatility.

Strategic Use of Leveraged and Inverse ETFs

Understanding leveraged and inverse ETFs is crucial for any investor looking to use these advanced tools effectively. They can significantly enhance portfolio capabilities when used correctly and with a clear understanding of their mechanics and risks. However, like driving a fast car, using these ETFs requires skill, timing, and respect for their power and potential pitfalls. Investors should consider these instruments for short-term strategies and be wary of their complex nature and the unique challenges they present in turbulent markets.

Contango and Backwardation

Navigating Market Structures: Contango and Backwardation

Understanding contango and backwardation is akin to understanding seasonal pricing fluctuations in agriculture—knowing when prices are likely to rise or fall can significantly impact how one buys or sells crops. Similarly, these terms describe price structures in futures markets that can affect investment strategies, particularly for ETFs tracking commodities.

What is Contango?

Definition

Contango is a market condition where the futures prices are higher than the spot price of the underlying commodity. This scenario typically indicates that investors expect the future price of the asset to increase.

Metaphor

Imagine you are pre-ordering a popular video game that is set to be released during the holiday season. The pre-order price is higher than what you would pay today because the demand is expected to increase around the holiday launch.

Impact on ETFs

ETFs that roll futures contracts will face higher costs as they sell expiring contracts (cheaper) and buy more expensive, further-dated contracts. This continual process can lead to underperformance compared to the spot price of the commodity, especially in a steadily contangoed market.

What is Backwardation?

Definition

Backwardation is the opposite of contango; it occurs when the futures prices are lower than the spot price. This situation suggests that the market expects the future price of the commodity to decrease.

Metaphor

Consider a farmer selling next season's crop at today's high prices due to a current shortage. Buyers agree because they anticipate that, with more supply available next season, prices will drop.

Impact on ETFs

ETFs holding futures in a backwardated market can benefit from selling higher-priced near-term contracts and buying cheaper longer-dated ones. This can lead to gains that outpace the spot price changes, providing a potential advantage in investment performance.

Practical Examples and Strategic Implications

Scenario: Contango in Oil Markets

Imagine an oil ETF in a contango market where current futures are priced at $50 per barrel, but contracts six months in the future are at $55. As the ETF rolls over its futures contracts, it loses value due to the continuous purchase at higher prices, potentially eroding the ETF's returns despite stable or rising spot prices.

Scenario: Backwardation in Agricultural Commodities

Consider a grain ETF during a period of expected surplus harvest. If spot prices are high due to a current shortage but expected to drop, futures might be priced lower. As the ETF rolls contracts forward, it gains by purchasing at progressively lower prices, enhancing returns even if spot prices fall.

Strategic Considerations for Investors

Understanding contango and backwardation is crucial for investors in commodity-linked ETFs or any instruments involving futures contracts. These conditions can profoundly affect the performance and suitability of such investments, depending on the investor's market outlook and strategy. Just as a savvy gardener plants seeds at the optimal time for each season, investors must time their entries and exits in commodity markets by understanding these complex pricing structures. Awareness of market conditions like contango and backwardation enables investors to navigate commodities investments more effectively, optimizing their strategies to harness or hedge against future price movements.

Strategic Implications of Contango and Backwardation

Navigating Market Curves: Strategic Investment in Contango and Backwardation

Understanding the conditions of contango and backwardation is akin to a sailor understanding ocean currents. Just as sailors use their knowledge of currents to navigate more efficiently and safely, investors can use their understanding of these market conditions to navigate the futures market more effectively.

Strategies for Dealing with Contango

Minimize Roll Costs

In a contango market, the cost of rolling futures contracts can erode returns because later-dated contracts are more expensive than the nearing expiration ones. Investors should consider strategies to minimize these costs:

- **Selective Contract Duration**: Choose contracts with expiration dates that are not too far in the future to reduce exposure to steep contango.

- **Alternative Instruments**: Use swap contracts or structured products that may have lower roll costs compared to standard futures contracts.

Diversification

Avoid overexposure to commodities or sectors where contango is typically strong and persistent. Diversifying investments across different asset classes can reduce the negative impact of contango on overall portfolio performance.

Strategies for Capitalizing on Backwardation

Maximize Roll Yield

In a backwardation market, investors can benefit from roll yield; selling near-term contracts at higher prices and buying longer-dated ones at lower prices can generate positive returns.

- **Active Management**: Regularly assess and adjust the portfolio to optimize exposure to beneficial backwardation conditions.

- **Focus on Commodities with Supply Constraints**: These are more likely to experience backwardation and can offer better opportunities for roll yield.

Hedging Strategies

Understanding and anticipating transitions between contango and backwardation can also be crucial. Investors might use hedging strategies to protect gains or limit losses during these transitions.

- **Options on Futures**: Use options to hedge against unfavorable shifts in futures pricing structures.
- **Cross-Hedging**: Hedge exposure in one commodity with another related commodity that might behave differently under market stress.

Long-Term Considerations

Market Analysis

Stay informed about factors that influence the shift between contango and backwardation such as seasonal demand changes, geopolitical events, and changes in supply conditions.

- **Fundamental Analysis**: Regularly analyze market fundamentals that affect supply and demand dynamics to predict potential shifts in the futures curve structure.

Timing Entries and Exits

Just as a surfer times their entry and exit from the wave, an investor needs to time their trading actions in relation to the prevailing market condition (contango or backwardation) to maximize efficiency and profitability.

- **Market Indicators**: Use economic indicators, inventory data, and production information to time the buying and selling actions accurately within the context of expected market structure shifts.

Mastering Market Dynamics for Better Returns

The ability to navigate contango and backwardation effectively is a critical skill for any investor involved in commodities or any asset classes affected by futures pricing dynamics. By understanding these phenomena and employing strategic responses, investors can enhance their ability to make informed decisions, similar to a captain adjusting the sails to suit the changing winds and currents. This not only helps in optimizing the potential returns but also in managing the risks associated with investments linked to futures markets.

Conclusion: Integrating Advanced Strategies for Portfolio Optimization

Synthesizing Key Concepts

Chapter 6 has navigated through the complex terrain of options and packaged products, offering strategic insights that are crucial for sophisticated portfolio management. This journey has equipped us with tools to enhance investment outcomes and manage risks effectively.

Review of Core Topics

- **Option Valuation Inputs**: We explored how underlying asset prices, time to expiration, and volatility directly influence options pricing, similar to how environmental factors affect a ship's voyage.

- **Black-Scholes Model**: This model serves as a navigational compass for pricing options, helping traders forecast potential market directions and adjust their strategies accordingly.

- **Options Strategies**: Strategies like covered calls and protective puts were dissected, revealing how they can secure additional income and provide a safety net, respectively.

- **Packaged Products**: We examined the cost implications of mutual funds and ETFs through expense ratios and loads, emphasizing the importance of understanding these fees for effective cost management.

- **Market Dynamics**: The concepts of contango and backwardation were elaborated, illustrating their impact on commodity-linked ETFs and the importance of strategic adaptation to these conditions.

The Practical Application of Knowledge

Real-World Investing

The strategies and models discussed in this chapter are not merely academic; they are vital tools for daily portfolio management. Implementing covered calls or using the Black-Scholes model to price options can lead to enhanced portfolio performance and risk management, akin to using sophisticated software to enhance business operations efficiency.

Exam Preparation

For those preparing for the SIE exam or similar financial certifications, understanding these concepts is imperative. The exam tests not only the knowledge of these strategies but also the ability to apply them in scenario-based questions, reflecting real-world market conditions.

The Importance of Ongoing Education

Keeping Pace with Market Changes

Just as a navigator must stay alert to weather changes and adjust course accordingly, investors and financial professionals must continue their education and stay informed about market developments. Markets evolve, and strategies that are effective today may need adjustment tomorrow.

Lifelong Learning

The landscape of financial markets is continually changing. Ongoing education in new financial instruments, market conditions, and regulatory changes is essential to maintain a competitive edge and ensure the best outcomes for clients and personal investments.

Navigating Financial Markets with Confidence

Understanding the intricacies of options and packaged products, as outlined in this chapter, is crucial for effective portfolio management and achieving investment goals. By mastering these advanced strategies and keeping abreast of market changes, investors can navigate the financial markets with the confidence of a seasoned captain, ready to adjust sails and optimize routes toward successful outcomes. This chapter not only builds a foundation for academic and professional success but also equips future financial professionals with the tools necessary for practical, real-world application in a dynamic investment landscape.

CHAPTER 7: Exam Taking Strategies - Question Analysis Techniques

Introduction: The Art of Decoding Exam Questions

Approaching exam questions is similar to decoding a complex code or solving a puzzle. Each question is a riddle, and your task is to uncover the clues hidden within to find the correct answer efficiently and accurately. This chapter will guide you through various techniques to analyze and tackle exam questions effectively, enhancing your ability to perform well under exam conditions.

Section 7.1: Eliminating Incorrect Answers

Technique Overview

Just as a sculptor removes excess stone to reveal the sculpture within, the process of elimination involves stripping away clearly incorrect answers to better see the right one.

Steps to Implement

1. **Read All Options**: Carefully read all answer choices before making any decisions.

2. **Identify Outliers**: Look for answers that are fundamentally different from the others; these are often incorrect.

3. **Check for Absolutes**: Answers with words like "always" or "never" may be suspect, as they leave no room for exceptions, which are common in complex topics.

Practical Application

Imagine a question where four potential answers are given, three of which share similar concepts or terminologies, and one that is distinctly different. Often, the outlier is incorrect, and your chances of choosing the right answer improve by eliminating it first.

Section 7.2: Identifying Trick Phrasing

Understanding Trick Phrasing

Exam questions can sometimes use language designed to confuse or mislead, akin to a magician's sleight of hand.

Key Examples and How to Handle Them

- **Negatives and Double Negatives**: Phrases like "which of the following is NOT incorrect" can easily confuse. Pinpoint what is being asked by simplifying the language.

- **Complex Compound Questions**: Questions that combine multiple conditions can mask the true requirement. Break them down into simpler parts.

Strategies for Overcoming Tricky Phrasing

Regular practice with sample questions will help you become more adept at quickly recognizing and interpreting these phrasings correctly.

Section 7.3: Recognizing Keywords

Importance of Keywords

Keywords in a question are like clues in a treasure hunt; they point directly towards the answer.

Techniques for Identifying Keywords

- **Highlight or Underline**: Physically marking keywords can help maintain focus on what the question is truly asking.

- **Relate to Study Material**: Connect keywords back to specific concepts, formulas, or frameworks you studied.

Example

In a question asking, "What is the primary reason for economic inflation?" the keyword is "primary reason," indicating that the question seeks the main cause, not just any contributing factor.

Section 7.4: Educated Guessing

When and How to Guess

Educated guessing is not just a shot in the dark; it's more like using informed intuition based on eliminated wrong answers and recognized patterns.

Effective Guessing Techniques

- **Odds and Ends**: If two answers are very similar, chances are one of them is correct.

- **Common Sense Approach**: Sometimes, applying simple logic can help choose between two remaining options.

Risks and Rewards

While guessing can sometimes lead to the right answer, it should be used sparingly and only after applying other techniques to narrow down the options.

Conclusion: Mastering the Art of Question Analysis

Just as mastering any skill requires understanding and practice, excelling in exams is no different. By learning to effectively dissect and understand exam questions through these strategies, you can significantly improve your chances of success. Like learning to read a map accurately, these techniques will guide you to your destination—optimal exam performance.

Eliminating Incorrect Answers: Sifting Through the Noise to Find the Signal

Overview: The Art of Elimination

Eliminating incorrect answers in an exam is like sorting through a mixed bag of gems and ordinary stones. By identifying and setting aside the ordinary stones, you significantly increase your chances of discovering the true gems—the correct answers. This technique is particularly useful in multiple-choice exams where sifting through distractors efficiently can lead to a more accurate and confident answer selection.

Why Eliminate Incorrect Answers?

Enhancing Answer Accuracy

By removing clearly wrong choices, you focus your decision-making on fewer options, increasing the probability of selecting the correct one.

Managing Time Effectively

Spending less time pondering obviously incorrect answers saves time for more challenging questions where the answer isn't as apparent.

Techniques for Effective Elimination

1. Look for Outliers

- **Definition**: Answers that differ significantly in content or detail level from others.

- **Application**: Like spotting a cat in a lineup of dogs, identifying answers that seem out of place or irrelevant to the question can guide you towards quick elimination.

2. Identify Absolute Terms

- **Definition**: Words that leave no room for flexibility, such as "always," "never," "all," or "none."

- **Why They're Suspect**: Real-world scenarios, especially in fields like finance and economics, rarely deal in absolutes. More often than not, these answers can be misleading unless the question pertains to a rule or law.

3. Recognize Common Traps

- **Mismatched Details**: Answers that contain true statements but do not directly address the question's specifics.

- **Overly Complex Choices**: Answers that add unnecessary details may be designed to lure you into a trap by sounding more authoritative.

Practical Example of Elimination Strategy

Scenario

Consider a question on an SIE exam regarding investment strategies:

- What is a primary concern when evaluating a new investment opportunity? A) The color of the company's logo B) Current economic conditions C) The CEO's personal hobbies D) Possible tax implications

Analysis:

- **Eliminate A and C**: These options are clear outliers and irrelevant to investment decisions. Like removing pebbles from gold panning, discard these distractions immediately.

- **Evaluate B and D**: Both address plausible concerns; however, the question specifies a "primary" concern, guiding you to focus on the broader, more impactful options.

Decision

Between the remaining choices, current economic conditions (B) generally have a more direct and significant impact on investment decisions than the specific tax implications (D), making B the more likely correct answer in a broad scenario.

Sharpening Your Exam Skills Through Elimination

Mastering the art of elimination is akin to refining your senses to distinguish essential details from background noise. This skill not only boosts your test-taking confidence but also enhances your analytical acuity, crucial for both exams and real-world decision-making in finance. Regular practice with this technique, especially under timed conditions, will help embed these strategies, making them second nature when you most need them

Identifying Trick Phrasing: Navigating the Linguistic Maze of Exam Questions

Overview: Understanding Trick Phrasing

Just as a magician uses sleight of hand to distract and deceive, exam questions sometimes use trick phrasing to test the depth of your understanding and your attention to detail. Identifying these linguistic traps can help you avoid common pitfalls and improve your accuracy on exams.

Why Identify Trick Phrasing?

Enhancing Comprehension

Trick phrasing often complicates a straightforward question, making it essential to parse words carefully to truly grasp what is being asked.

Avoiding Common Pitfalls

Recognizing and understanding trick phrasing helps prevent misinterpretation, which is crucial in avoiding easy mistakes that can cost valuable points.

Techniques for Spotting Trick Phrasing

1. Double Negatives

- **Definition**: Phrases that use two negative words which can make the meaning of the question confusing.

- **Example**: "Which of the following is not unlikely to harm investment returns?"

- **Strategy**: Simplify the sentence by removing the double negative: "Which of the following is likely to harm investment returns?" This clarification can help you directly address what the question actually asks.

2. Absolute Language

- **Definition**: Words that indicate an unconditional extremity, such as "always," "never," "all," or "none."

- **Example**: "All investments carry the same level of risk."

- **Strategy**: Questions using absolutes should be approached with skepticism as they rarely hold true in subjects like finance, where exceptions are common. Scan the context to see if the absolute phrasing is warranted or if it's a trap.

3. Qualifying Adjectives and Adverbs

- **Definition**: Modifiers that subtly change or qualify the meaning of a statement, often altering its truth value.

- **Example**: "Most reliable investments yield high returns."

- **Strategy**: Identify key qualifiers and evaluate their impact on the statement. Question the validity of broad claims modified by subjective adjectives like "reliable," which may introduce bias or ambiguity.

4. Compound Questions

- **Definition**: Questions that ask about more than one concept or fact in the same sentence, which can obscure the main point.

- **Example**: "What is the riskiest investment type, and how should it be managed?"

- **Strategy**: Break down the question into its component inquiries. Address each part individually to ensure no aspect of the question is overlooked.

Practical Application: Real-World Scenario

Scenario

Imagine you're taking a practice exam and encounter the question:

- "Which of these should not be considered when assessing the viability of a stock investment: market trends, CEO personal life, analyst predictions, or historical performance?"

Analysis:

- **Identify Trick Elements**: The inclusion of 'CEO personal life' might seem relevant at a glance due to its specificity, but it's a distractor unless the context specifically justifies its relevance.

- **Simplify and Focus**: Focus on the key elements that are typically relevant to stock assessment to identify the odd one out.

Identifying trick phrasing in exam questions is like learning to read a map with hidden symbols. It requires practice, attention to detail, and an analytical approach. Mastering this skill will not only enhance your performance on the SIE exam but will also refine your overall critical thinking abilities, crucial for navigating the complexities of the financial world. Regular practice with diverse question types and careful review of correct and incorrect answers can deepen your understanding and sharpen your test-taking skills.

Recognizing Keywords: The Compass of Question Analysis

Overview: Unlocking the Meaning with Keywords

Identifying keywords in exam questions is akin to using landmarks when navigating through a city. Just as landmarks help you orient yourself and guide you to your destination, keywords in questions help you connect the question to the right concepts, theories, or formulas, guiding your response accurately.

Importance of Keywords in Exam Questions

Guiding Thought Processes

Keywords are the bridge between the question posed and the knowledge you've acquired. They trigger associations with the relevant information stored in your memory, helping you recall and apply the correct information.

Enhancing Answer Precision

By focusing on the keywords, you can tailor your answers to be more precise and relevant, which is crucial for scoring well on exams.

Techniques for Identifying and Using Keywords

1. Highlight or Underline Keywords

- **Action**: During the exam, physically highlight or underline keywords in questions.

- **Purpose**: This helps in visually isolating the important parts of the question, ensuring that you focus on what is most important.

2. Categorize Keywords

- **Categories**: Look for and categorize keywords based on their nature, such as:

- **Action Words**: Verbs that tell you what to do, e.g., "describe," "analyze," "compare."
- **Concept Words**: Nouns that indicate the topics or concepts involved, e.g., "volatility," "risk management," "equity."
- **Qualifier Words**: Adjectives/adverbs that modify the scope or focus of the question, e.g., "primary," "most effective," "least likely."

3. Connect Keywords to Study Material

- **Strategy**: When you identify a keyword, pause to connect it to the relevant lecture, chapter, or discussion in your study materials. This helps in pulling in the correct information to formulate your answer.
- **Example**: If the keyword is "volatility," recall its implications, calculations, and its effects on portfolio diversification.

Practical Example: Keyword Analysis in Action

Scenario

In a practice question like, "Discuss the impact of interest rate changes on bond prices," the keywords would be:

- **Discuss**: Indicates the need for a detailed explanation.
- **Impact**: Signals the requirement to explain cause and effect.
- **Interest Rate Changes**: Points to economic concepts related to interest rates.
- **Bond Prices**: Directs focus towards bond valuation.

Analysis:

- Understanding that "interest rate changes" and "bond prices" are directly related through the concept of bond valuation will guide the response. The keyword "impact" suggests that the answer should include how and why bond prices move inversely to interest rate changes.

Mastering Keyword Recognition

Recognizing and appropriately responding to keywords in exam questions is like decoding a secret message — it is essential for unlocking the full meaning and ensuring your answer directly addresses what is asked. As you practice with sample questions, continue to refine your ability to spot and interpret keywords, enhancing not just your exam performance but also your overall analytical skills in professional settings. This skill ensures that you not only understand questions correctly but also apply the most relevant information in your responses, leading to better outcomes in exams and real-world applications alike.

Educated Guessing: Strategic Decision-Making in Uncertain Situations

Overview: The Science and Art of Educated Guessing

Educated guessing is akin to navigating through a foggy path using a combination of your past experiences and the available signs along the way. It's a critical skill in exam settings where you may encounter questions that you're unsure about. This section will guide you on how to make calculated choices that increase your chances of selecting the correct answer when certainty is out of reach.

The Importance of Educated Guessing

Navigating Incomplete Information

In exams, as in many real-world scenarios, you often have to make decisions based on incomplete information. Educated guessing allows you to use the knowledge you do possess to make a reasoned choice, even when you're not 100% certain.

Maximizing Score Potential

By making educated guesses, you avoid leaving questions unanswered, which can help increase your overall score on exams that do not penalize guessing.

Strategies for Effective Educated Guessing

1. Rule Out Obvious Incorrect Answers

Before making a guess, eliminate any answers you know are incorrect. Each option you remove significantly increases your chances of guessing correctly among the remaining choices.

2. Identify Patterns and Logical Choices

- **Patterns**: Sometimes, the structure of the test itself can give clues. For instance, if all previous answers have been 'C,' it might be less likely for the next one to also be 'C' (although you should consider this cautiously).

- **Logical Choices**: If two options are similar, one of them might be the correct answer. Alternatively, if one option is much more detailed or specific than the others, it might be a designed distractor or the correct answer, depending on the context of the question.

3. Use Prior Knowledge and Context Clues

- Even if you're unsure about a question, relate it to what you know about the topic. Can your knowledge of related areas help you make a more informed guess?

- **Context Clues**: Words in the question can sometimes hint at the correct answer. For example, if the question involves an economic downturn, the answer involving cost-cutting could be more plausible than one involving expansion.

4. Choose the More Comprehensive or Qualitative Answer for Complex Topics

- For questions on topics that require deep understanding, the correct answer is often the one that covers more bases or is explained in a more nuanced way, rather than an answer that is overly simplistic or absolute.

Practical Example: Applying Educated Guessing

Scenario

Consider a question on your exam: "What is the most likely consequence of a sudden increase in interest rates?"

- **Potential Answers**: A) Decrease in stock market prices. B) Increase in tourism. C) Increase in software development. D) Decrease in agricultural output.

Analysis:

- **Eliminate**: B and C seem unrelated to interest rates based on typical economic principles.
- **Logical Choice**: Between A and D, A is more directly connected to interest rate changes as higher rates can cool down investment and consumer spending affecting the stock market.

Mastering the Art of the Guess

Educated guessing is not just a last resort; it's a strategic tool in your exam arsenal. Like a detective piecing together clues to solve a mystery, you must use every piece of information and reasoning skill at your disposal to make the best possible choice under uncertainty. With practice, you can refine your guessing strategies, enhancing not only your exam performance but also your decision-making skills in professional and personal settings.

Chapter 8: Time Management & Pacing

Time management and pacing during an exam are crucial skills, akin to a conductor expertly timing the movements of an orchestra to achieve a flawless performance. Just as a conductor ensures that neither the strings nor the percussion dominate the entire performance, effective time management ensures that you allocate your exam time to maximize both the quality and quantity of the answers you provide.

The Importance of Time Management and Pacing

Managing time during an exam isn't just about preventing yourself from running out of time before you've answered all the questions. It's about strategically allocating your minutes to optimize your performance across the entire exam. This means knowing when to dwell on a problem and when to move on. For instance, spending too much time on a complex problem at the cost of not answering simpler, quicker questions can hinder your overall score. Like a marathon runner pacing themselves to maintain energy throughout the race, you must pace your problem-solving to maintain a steady flow throughout the exam.

Strategic Time Allocation

Effective time allocation directly influences the accuracy and completeness of your exam responses. Here's how:

1. **Accuracy**: By pacing yourself correctly, you ensure that you have enough time to thoroughly work through and double-check the more challenging questions without making hasty errors. This is similar to a chef who carefully times each step of a recipe; too fast, and the dish might not develop the right flavors; too slow, and the dish might overcook.

2. **Completeness**: Allocating specific amounts of time to different sections of the exam prevents scenarios where you leave questions unanswered. Imagine planning a trip with multiple stops; if you spend too much time at the first few attractions, you might have to skip the last few due to lack of time. Similarly, if you spend too much time on early questions, you might

rush through or completely miss later questions, which might have been easier or equally scoring.

Implementing Effective Time Management

To implement effective time management:

- **Plan Your Exam Strategy**: Before the exam, understand the format and decide how much time you'll allocate to each section based on your strengths and the section's weight.

- **Monitor Your Timing**: During the exam, keep a close watch on the time, checking periodically to ensure you are on track. This is like using a map on a road trip; regular checks ensure you haven't strayed off your planned route.

- **Adjust as Necessary**: Be flexible and ready to adjust your time allocation on the fly. If you find a section unexpectedly difficult, decide quickly whether to spend more time on it or to move on and return if time allows.

Mastering the art of time management and pacing is like learning to balance a scale perfectly—it enhances your ability to perform under exam conditions, leading to better outcomes. Through practice and experience, these skills become second nature, allowing you to approach each exam with confidence, ensuring that every minute counts towards achieving your best possible results.

Blueprint for attacking blocks of questions

Understanding the SIE Exam Format The SIE exam includes 75 multiple-choice questions to be answered in 105 minutes. It broadly covers sections like Knowledge of Capital Markets, Understanding Products and their Risks, Trading and Account Management, and Regulatory Framework, with a passing score set at 70%.

Develop a Focused Study and Practice Regimen Begin by reviewing key concepts from each major content area using reliable resources such as textbooks and online courses tailored for the SIE. Regularly engage in full-length practice tests to simulate the exam environment and refine your understanding of both the content and timing. These practice sessions are vital for identifying areas where your performance may lag and need further study.

Strategize Your Approach for Exam Day Prioritize questions based on your strengths; starting with familiar topics can boost confidence and secure early points. Recognize that computational questions often require more time, so plan your pacing to accommodate these without rushing. Questions in sections like "Understanding Products and their Risks" often involve calculations and demand closer attention.

Efficiently Navigate the Exam Utilize a methodical approach on exam day:

- Tackle sections you feel strongest in first to build momentum.

- Apply the elimination method to quickly reduce choices, particularly useful in complex multiple-choice scenarios.

- Stay vigilant for trick phrasing that might skew the interpretation of questions.

- Reserve time for a thorough review towards the end, revisiting flagged questions and ensuring no query remains unanswered.

Implement Educated Guessing When Necessary If you encounter questions that stump you, make educated guesses. This strategy involves using partial knowledge and logical deductions from remaining options after eliminating clearly incorrect answers.

Adapt and Adjust as Needed Keep track of time, and be flexible in adjusting your strategy based on how the exam unfolds. If certain sections take longer than anticipated, recalibrate your approach for the remaining questions to ensure you cover all areas within the allotted time.

Final Review In the last segment of your exam time, double-check your answers, focusing on those you are unsure about. Ensure every answer aligns with the most logical and informed choice based on your preparation and the keywords identified during the exam.

By integrating these strategies, you'll optimize your preparation and performance on the SIE exam, enhancing your ability to manage time effectively and answer questions accurately. This methodical approach helps in effectively handling the exam pressures and improves your overall test-taking efficiency, setting a strong foundation for success.

Spending more time on computation problems vs conceptual questions

When preparing for the Securities Industry Essentials (SIE) exam, strategically allocating your time between computational and conceptual questions is crucial for maximizing efficiency and accuracy. This approach acknowledges that these question types demand different levels of engagement and time investment.

Computational Questions These questions require calculations, involving detailed knowledge of formulas and their applications within financial contexts, such as determining bond yields, analyzing stock valuation metrics, or calculating capital gains. Given their complexity and the risk of errors, computational questions generally demand more time. They often involve multiple steps and the integration of various financial concepts, which increases the potential for mistakes that can arise from rushed calculations or oversight. Ensuring accuracy typically necessitates a slower, more deliberate approach that includes time to double-check your work.

Conceptual Questions On the other hand, conceptual questions test your grasp of financial theories, principles, and regulations. These questions might ask you to define terms, explain procedures, or identify correct actions under specific regulatory conditions. Conceptual questions tend to require less time as they often depend on recognition and understanding rather than the application of multi-step problem-solving.

Effective Time Management Strategy The key to performing well on the SIE exam lies in how you manage the allocation of time between these two types of questions. Here's a streamlined strategy:

- **Initial Exam Review:** Begin by scanning through the entire exam to identify the mix of computational and conceptual questions. This overview will help you estimate how much time you should allocate to each section.

- **Start With Strengths:** Depending on your confidence and preparation, choose whether to start with conceptual or computational questions. Tackling easier questions first can boost confidence and ensure you secure quick points efficiently.

- **Budget Time Accordingly:** Dedicate more time to computational questions. This can be planned roughly as twice the amount of time per question compared to conceptual ones, adjusting based on their complexity or your familiarity with the topics.

- **Use a Flagging System:** If possible, use the exam's flagging feature to mark computational questions that you want to review. This ensures that all questions are answered at least once, allowing you to return and spend remaining time verifying tricky calculations or rechecking your work.

- **Continuous Time Check:** Regularly check the time during the exam to adjust your pacing. If you find yourself spending too much time on early questions, accelerate slightly while ensuring you don't compromise on accuracy, especially for computational answers.

By carefully managing how you approach these question types, you can enhance your ability to complete the exam effectively. This method not only helps in improving accuracy but also ensures that you can answer all questions within the allotted time. Remember, successful exam performance results from both knowing the material and skillfully managing how you demonstrate that knowledge under timed conditions.

Quick flagging for review, checking progress, final double check

When tackling the Securities Industry Essentials (SIE) exam, efficient use of time is crucial, and one effective strategy involves quick flagging for review, regular checks on your progress, and performing a final double-check of your answers. This approach ensures thoroughness and accuracy, which are vital for a successful test outcome.

Quick Flagging for Review The SIE exam, like many standardized tests, allows you to flag questions for later review. This feature is invaluable when you encounter a question that you find particularly challenging or when you're unsure about an answer. Instead of spending excessive time on one question, you can flag it and move on, continuing to work through the exam efficiently.

- **Example**: Suppose you come across a question asking about the specifics of the Wash-Sale Rule, but you're not immediately confident in your answer. Instead of pondering over it and potentially wasting valuable time, you can flag this question and revisit it later, ensuring you continue to make progress through the exam.

Checking Progress Periodically throughout the exam, it's important to check your progress against the clock. This helps you gauge whether you are on pace to complete the exam in the allotted time and adjust your strategy if needed.

- **Example**: If the SIE exam is 105 minutes long and contains 75 questions, you might plan to spend about 1 minute per question, reserving the last 30 minutes to revisit flagged questions and review your answers. Halfway through the allotted time, a quick check might show you've answered 40 questions. This indicates you're slightly ahead of schedule, which is an ideal scenario allowing more time for review.

Final Double Check Before submitting your exam, it's crucial to use any remaining time to go back to the questions you've flagged and to verify your answers, especially for those you were unsure about. This final review is your opportunity to correct any errors, refine your answers, and ensure that every response is as accurate as possible.

- **Example**: During your final review, return to the flagged question about the Wash-Sale Rule. With no pressure of unfinished questions, you can now focus on recalling the specifics of the rule or applying logical reasoning to eliminate unlikely answers. This could increase your confidence in your final choice.

- **Further Review Strategy**: In addition to revisiting flagged questions, scan through all answers, if time allows. Look for any questions where your answer now seems incorrect based on information recalled later in the test or second thoughts about your initial logic. This is also a good time to ensure all answers are recorded correctly, especially in a paper-based test where a misalignment in answer bubbles can occur.

Practical Tips:

1. **Use Flagging Judiciously**: Only flag questions where necessary. Over-flagging can lead to a cumbersome review phase.

2. **Manage Review Time**: Allocate the last portion of your exam time strictly for review. Stick to this limit to ensure you don't rush through remaining questions or miss revisiting key flagged items.

3. **Stay Calm and Focused**: During the review, maintain a calm mindset. Rushing through the review because of panic can lead to mistakes in questions you originally answered correctly.

Adopting these strategies effectively prepares you to handle the SIE exam's demands, optimizing your performance through balanced pacing and meticulous verification of your work. This structured approach not only enhances your chance of success but also builds good test-taking habits for future professional certifications.

Chapter 9: Overcoming Test Anxiety

Chapter 9 of the SIE Exam Prep Study Guide focuses on a crucial aspect that often goes unaddressed in traditional study materials but is critical for success: overcoming test anxiety. Here's a detailed approach to understanding and managing the anxiety often associated with taking high-stakes tests like the SIE exam.

Understanding Test Anxiety

Test anxiety is a psychological condition where individuals experience extreme distress and anxiety in testing situations, which can affect their overall performance. It's like a performer experiencing stage fright; despite knowing their lines, the fear of being judged or failing can overwhelm their ability to perform.

Causes of Test Anxiety

- **Fear of Failure**: Often stemming from high personal expectations or pressure from others, this fear can provoke anxiety that debilitates performance.

- **Lack of Preparation**: Inadequate preparation or previous poor performances in exams can increase stress about the outcomes of the test.

- **Negative Thinking**: Pessimistic thoughts about one's abilities or the consequences of failing an exam can heighten anxiety levels.

Strategies to Overcome Test Anxiety

Preparation is Key Adequate preparation is the most effective way to reduce test anxiety. Being well-prepared boosts confidence and reduces the fear of the unknown.

- **Example**: Create a structured study plan for the SIE exam months in advance. Regularly assess your understanding of the material through practice tests and adjust your study habits accordingly.

Relaxation Techniques Incorporating relaxation techniques into your study routine and before the exam can help manage physical symptoms of anxiety.

- **Breathing Exercises**: Practice deep breathing techniques to help control hyperventilation and relax your body. For instance, try the 4-7-8 technique — breathe in for 4 seconds, hold for 7 seconds, and exhale for 8 seconds.

- **Progressive Muscle Relaxation**: This involves tensing and then relaxing different muscle groups in your body, which can be particularly helpful in releasing tension built up while studying or sitting for long periods during the exam.

Positive Reinforcement Changing the narrative of negative thoughts to positive affirmations can significantly affect your mental state.

- **Example**: Replace thoughts like "I'm not good at this" with "I have prepared well and I am capable of handling this challenge". Positive affirmations help in shifting your focus from fear to confidence.

Visualization Techniques Visualizing success can also serve as a powerful tool in combating test anxiety.

- **Example**: Spend time each day leading up to the exam visualizing yourself successfully completing the exam and feeling confident while doing so. Imagine yourself working through the exam calmly and efficiently.

Practical Exam Strategies Familiarize yourself with the exam format and environment. This can reduce anxiety caused by unfamiliarity.

- **Mock Exams**: Regularly take timed practice exams that mimic the conditions of the actual SIE exam. This helps condition your mind and body to the stress of working under timed conditions.

- **Visit the Test Center**: If possible, visit the test center before your exam date. Knowing exactly where you need to go and what the test room looks like can reduce anxiety about logistical uncertainties.

Overcoming test anxiety is about preparing thoroughly, employing strategies to manage stress, and maintaining a positive outlook. By addressing both the psychological and practical aspects of test preparation, you can enhance your ability to perform under pressure and increase your chances of success on the SIE exam. Remember, it's not just about how much you know, but also about how well you can manage your emotions and thoughts under exam conditions.

Positive Self-Talk and Visualization of Success: Enhancing Performance on the SIE Exam

In preparing for the Securities Industry Essentials (SIE) exam, beyond mastering the content, candidates must also cultivate a mindset geared toward success. Two powerful techniques that can significantly influence your performance are positive self-talk and visualization of success. These strategies are not just motivational tools; they are practical approaches to reduce anxiety, increase confidence, and improve focus during your exam preparation and on the day of the test.

Positive Self-Talk

Positive self-talk involves consciously shifting your internal dialogue to be more encouraging and supportive. It's about replacing negative thoughts that can sabotage your performance with affirmations that build confidence.

- **Understanding Negative Self-Talk**: It's common for candidates to doubt their preparation or fear failure, thinking things like, "I never do well on tests," or "I don't think I've studied enough." These thoughts can increase anxiety and distract from effective studying.

- **Transforming Thoughts**: Start by recognizing negative thoughts and actively replacing them with positive affirmations. For example, change "I'm not good at this" to "I am continually improving with every study session." This practice helps to reframe your perspective and approach challenges with a more constructive and confident mindset.

- **Example**: When studying complex topics such as options trading or regulations for the SIE exam, remind yourself, "I am capable of understanding challenging concepts," or "I am fully prepared to tackle difficult sections effectively."

Visualization of Success

Visualization is a technique where you imagine completing a goal successfully. For the SIE exam, this involves vividly picturing yourself passing the exam and feeling the emotions associated with this success.

- **How to Practice Visualization**:

  - **Find a Quiet Space**: Before a study session, find a quiet place where you can relax without interruptions.

  - **Clear Your Mind**: Take a few deep breaths to center yourself and clear your mind of distractions.

  - **Picture the Exam Day**: Imagine waking up feeling well-rested and prepared. Visualize yourself traveling to the exam center, sitting down at the desk, logging into the exam, and feeling confident and calm.

  - **See Yourself Succeeding**: Envision yourself answering the questions confidently, managing your time efficiently, and ultimately seeing a passing score at the end of the exam.

  - **Feel the Success**: Try to connect with the feelings of achievement and relief that come with visualizing your success. Allow these positive emotions to boost your confidence.

- **Example**: Regularly visualize the sequence of the exam day from beginning to end. Picture entering the test center, feeling prepared and composed. Imagine yourself methodically working through each question, clearly recalling the information you studied, and successfully completing the exam within the allotted time.

Integrating These Techniques Into Your Study Routine

- **Daily Affirmations**: Begin each study session by affirming your abilities and end by acknowledging what you've learned and accomplished that day.

- **Regular Visualization**: Spend a few minutes each day, perhaps at the beginning or end of your study sessions, practicing visualization. Consistency is key to making these techniques effective.

Positive self-talk and visualization are not merely psychological tricks; they are tested strategies that enhance your actual performance by improving mental focus, reducing test anxiety, and building confidence. By incorporating these practices into your SIE exam preparation, you equip yourself with not just the knowledge needed to pass but also the mindset to succeed.

Relaxation skills (breathing, progressive muscle relaxation

Preparing for the Securities Industry Essentials (SIE) exam involves more than just mastering the material; it also means managing the stress and anxiety that can accompany high-stakes testing. Two effective techniques to incorporate into your study routine are breathing exercises and progressive muscle relaxation (PMR). These methods help calm the mind and body, ensuring you're as mentally prepared as you are academically.

Breathing Exercises for Focus and Calm

Breathing exercises are a quick way to reduce anxiety, beneficial both during study sessions and right before the exam. Practice deep breathing by slowly inhaling through your nose for a count of four, hold for four, then exhale through your mouth for six. This helps regulate your heart rate and relaxes your mind, creating a calm state that enhances concentration. For example, right before starting the exam, take a few minutes to engage in this deep breathing exercise to settle your nerves and clear your mind.

Progressive Muscle Relaxation (PMR)

PMR involves systematically tensing and relaxing different muscle groups in your body, which can be especially useful to relieve the physical symptoms of stress that often occur during long periods of sitting and intense concentration. Start by tensing the muscles in your toes for five seconds, then relax them for 30 seconds, and notice the tension release. Continue this pattern from your feet up through your neck and face. Regular practice, such as during study breaks or in the morning before you begin studying, can significantly reduce stress levels.

Integrating Relaxation Techniques into Exam Preparation

To effectively incorporate these techniques into your exam preparation, make them a part of your daily routine. Set aside time each day for relaxation practice, similar to how you schedule study sessions. This regular practice helps condition your body and mind to relax quickly and deeply, even under stress. For instance, during mock exams, use the breaks to practice these relaxation techniques, simulating how you'll manage stress on the actual exam day.

By regularly practicing deep breathing and PMR, you'll not only improve your ability to handle the psychological pressures of the exam but also enhance your overall focus and mental clarity. This approach ensures you're prepared to tackle the SIE exam with confidence, armed not just with knowledge but with tools to maintain calm and poise under pressure.

Simulating the real testing environment at home

Preparing for the Securities Industry Essentials (SIE) exam effectively means not just studying the content but also getting comfortable with the exam environment. Simulating the exam setting at home helps you adapt to the pressures and constraints of the actual test day. Here's how to create a realistic test environment to enhance your readiness:

Choose a quiet corner in your home that mimics the conditions of a test center. Ensure this area is free from distractions, has a comfortable chair, adequate lighting, and a desk that holds only essential items like pencils, a calculator (if permitted), and scratch paper.

Mimic Exam Conditions

Set a timer for 105 minutes to mirror the actual SIE exam duration and practice under strict exam conditions:

- No Interruptions: Let everyone in your household know not to disturb you during your practice.

- Computer-Based Simulation: If the SIE is computer-based, use similar software or an online platform for practice to get used to the format.

Use Realistic Practice Exams

Incorporate practice tests that closely follow the format and content of the SIE exam, focusing on the variety of questions you'll face. This approach not only tests your knowledge but also helps you manage your time effectively.

Practice Under Exam Rules

Adhere to the same rules that apply during the actual exam. This includes scheduled breaks and using only permitted resources. If the actual exam doesn't allow notes, practice without them.

Review and Adjust

After each practice exam, review your answers carefully. Identify areas where you struggle and adjust your study focus. Also, tweak your test-taking strategies based on performance—perhaps you need to spend less time on certain types of questions.

Simulate the Exam Day Routine

From the wake-up time to the pre-exam breakfast, mimic your planned exam day routine during practice sessions. If the test center is new to you, consider visiting it ahead of time to familiarize yourself with the route and travel time.

Example of a Practice Test Day

On your practice day, wake up early, have a similar breakfast to what you plan for the test day, and start the simulated exam at the same time as the actual test. Ensure you are using only the materials and tools you will have access to during the real exam and stick to the allotted time strictly. After finishing, take a break if there are breaks in the real exam, then review your performance.

By simulating the exam environment, you not only reinforce your subject knowledge but also enhance your ability to perform under exam conditions. This comprehensive preparation strategy ensures you are not just academically ready but also mentally prepared to tackle the exam confidently and efficiently.

Visiting the test center in advance

isiting the test center in advance of taking the Securities Industry Essentials (SIE) exam can be a crucial step in your exam preparation strategy. This preemptive visit helps mitigate anxiety, familiarize you with the environment, and potentially increase your comfort level on the actual exam day. Here's a detailed look at why this step is beneficial and how to effectively incorporate it into your preparation plan.

Benefits of Visiting the Test Center in Advance

Reducing Anxiety: For many exam takers, unfamiliar environments can heighten nervousness. By visiting the test center beforehand, you can eliminate any surprises about the location, helping to ease anxiety. Knowing exactly where you are going and what the test center looks like can provide a psychological comfort that paves the way for better focus and performance during the exam.

Logistical Planning: Understanding the logistics involved in reaching the test center can help you plan better for the exam day. This includes knowing the travel time, the best routes to take, and alternatives in case of unexpected delays. Additionally, you'll get an idea of parking facilities, or public transport options if you're not driving.

Familiarity with Test Center Layout: Getting to know the layout of the test center, including the exam room, waiting areas, and facilities like bathrooms, can reduce the time you spend on navigating these on the day of the exam. Being familiar with the environment can help decrease stress and allow you to focus solely on the exam.

How to Plan Your Visit

Check Permissions: First, ensure that the test center allows visits in advance. Some centers may have specific days and times they allow for such visits, or they may have restrictions due to security reasons.

Simulate the Test Day: Plan to visit the test center around the same time of day as your scheduled exam. This simulation will give you a realistic idea of the traffic conditions, parking situations, and even the morning or afternoon ambiance of the test center.

What to Observe:

- Take note of the seating arrangements, the noise level, the temperature, and the overall atmosphere of the test center.

- Ask about the rules and procedures followed on the day of the exam. For example, learn about the check-in process and what items you are allowed to bring into the exam room.

- Inquire if there are any pre-exam requirements like identification verification or locker facilities to store your belongings.

Example Scenario: Imagine you are scheduled to take your exam at a test center in a busy downtown area. By visiting the center beforehand, you discover it takes longer than expected to get through morning traffic, the parking options are limited, and the test rooms are slightly colder than you are comfortable with. Armed with this knowledge, you can plan to leave earlier on the actual exam day, dress appropriately for the conditions, and avoid last-minute stresses that could impact your performance.

Visiting the test center in advance is more than just a rehearsal—it's an opportunity to make yourself comfortable with the upcoming exam environment. By becoming acquainted with the physical location, the journey there, and the details of the test center's layout and procedures, you effectively remove unnecessary variables that could distract from your focus on passing the SIE exam. This proactive approach not only prepares you logistically but also sets a confident tone for your exam day, ensuring that you can dedicate all your energy to performing your best

Chapter 10: Regulatory Compliance

Overview of the importance of regulatory compliance in the securities industry.

In the securities industry, regulatory compliance is not just a requirement but a foundational principle that ensures the integrity and stability of financial markets. Much like the rules of the road make driving safer for everyone, regulatory compliance provides guidelines that protect investors, maintain fair markets, and ensure that financial institutions operate transparently and responsibly.

Importance of Regulatory Compliance in the Securities Industry

Regulatory compliance in the securities industry is critical for several reasons:

1. **Protecting Investors:** Just as safety standards prevent potential harms in consumer products, compliance rules protect investors from fraud, abuse, and misleading practices. They ensure that all participants have access to the essential facts needed to make informed decisions. This protection is crucial in maintaining trust in financial markets.

2. **Ensuring Market Integrity:** Compliance with regulations is akin to following traffic laws; it keeps the system functioning smoothly and prevents chaos. In financial markets, this means ensuring that trading is conducted fairly and transparently, which helps in maintaining investor confidence and market stability.

3. **Preventing Financial Crimes:** Similar to security measures in a banking system that prevent theft and fraud, regulatory frameworks like Anti-Money Laundering (AML) laws help in detecting and preventing illegal activities. These regulations require firms to take proactive steps to monitor, report, and prevent suspicious activities, thereby helping in safeguarding the economic framework from financial crimes.

4. **Maintaining Systemic Stability:** Just as building codes ensure that structures can withstand certain stresses, financial regulations help ensure that institutions are robust enough to handle market stresses without collapsing. This includes maintaining adequate capital levels, managing risks properly, and being transparent in financial reporting.

Example of Regulatory Compliance Applied

Consider a simple example from the securities industry: the regulation requiring that brokers must know their clients. This regulation ensures that financial advice given to clients is suitable based on their financial situation, much like a doctor must know a patient's medical history before prescribing medication. The regulation helps prevent inappropriate investments that could lead to financial harm, thus protecting both the client and the integrity of the advice-giving process.

adhering to regulatory compliance is essential for anyone entering the securities industry. Aspiring professionals preparing for the SIE exam must grasp not only the specific rules and regulations but also the underlying purposes they serve. This understanding is crucial for making informed decisions that align with both legal requirements and ethical standards, ensuring a career that contributes positively to the financial landscape. Through this lens, the SIE exam serves not only as a test of knowledge but also as a gateway to understanding the broader responsibilities involved in managing, trading, and advising in securities.

Brief role of various regulatory bodies.

Understanding the role of various regulatory bodies is crucial for anyone entering the securities industry and preparing for the SIE exam. These bodies are like the referees and rule-makers of the financial markets, ensuring fair play, transparency, and integrity. Here's a detailed look at the main regulatory bodies involved in the U.S. securities industry and their specific roles:

Securities and Exchange Commission (SEC)

The SEC is like the principal overseer of the U.S. financial markets. Its primary role is to protect investors, maintain fair, orderly, and efficient markets, and facilitate capital formation. It enforces federal securities laws that dictate how securities are issued, bought, and sold. Think of the SEC as the watchdog that ensures companies provide essential financial information to the public so investors can make informed decisions about investments. The SEC also oversees key participants in the securities world, including securities exchanges, brokers and dealers, investment advisors, and mutual funds.

Financial Industry Regulatory Authority (FINRA)

FINRA is a non-governmental organization that acts as a self-regulatory organization (SRO) for brokerage firms and exchange markets. Think of FINRA as a club's rules committee where members agree to abide by certain standards for the benefit of the club community—in this case, the trading public. FINRA writes and enforces rules governing the ethical activities of all registered broker-dealer firms and registered brokers in the U.S. It also examines firms for compliance with those rules, fosters market transparency, and educates investors.

Municipal Securities Rulemaking Board (MSRB)

The MSRB regulates the issuance and sale of state and municipal bonds. This body is like the local government authority that sets rules for local municipal construction projects ensuring they meet certain standards. In a similar way, the MSRB sets rules to ensure that municipal securities are traded fairly and transparently, protecting the interests of investors who invest in these types of securities, and the entities that issue them.

Commodity Futures Trading Commission (CFTC)

The CFTC oversees the U.S. derivatives markets, which include futures, options, and swaps. The role of the CFTC is comparable to that of a traffic controller for the highways of commodity and financial futures markets. It works to ensure these complex financial markets are transparent, competitive, and financially sound, preventing abusive trading practices and fraud.

National Futures Association (NFA)

Working closely with the CFTC, the NFA is an industry-wide self-regulatory organization for the U.S. derivatives industry, including on-exchange traded futures, retail off-exchange foreign currency, and OTC derivatives (swaps). Think of the NFA as a neighborhood watch program that helps keep the community (in this case, the futures markets) safe for all participants through its regulatory responsibilities.

Example in Practice

Imagine you are working with a brokerage firm, and you need to ensure your activities comply with regulatory standards. You must follow SEC rules for general securities practices, adhere to FINRA regulations specific to brokerage firms and brokers, ensure any municipal securities dealings align with MSRB rules, and if dealing in futures or derivatives, comply with CFTC and NFA regulations.

For those studying for the SIE exam, understanding the roles of these regulatory bodies helps illuminate how the securities industry functions as a whole. Each body has a distinct role, but all work toward the common goal of maintaining the integrity of the securities markets, protecting investors, and ensuring that the financial system operates smoothly and efficiently. This knowledge is not just crucial for passing the SIE exam but is fundamental for any professional career in the securities industry.

Books and Records Requirements

Understanding the books and records requirements is crucial for compliance in the securities industry, especially for those preparing for the SIE exam. These requirements are similar to the meticulous records a librarian keeps to track books, ensuring everything is accounted for and can be easily retrieved when needed. Here's a detailed exploration of what constitutes books and records in the context of securities regulation:

Overview of Books and Records Requirements

In the securities industry, maintaining accurate and comprehensive records is not just good practice—it's a regulatory mandate enforced primarily by the SEC and FINRA. These records include a wide array of documents essential for auditing and monitoring the activities of brokerage firms and their associated persons.

What Constitutes Books and Records?

Books and records in the securities industry refer to several types of documentation:

1. **Trade Records:** Detailed logs of all trades executed, including the security name, amount, price at which the trade was executed, and the trade date and time. This information is crucial for both compliance reviews and customer inquiries.

2. **Communication Records:** All communications with clients and prospective clients, including emails, instant messages, and written correspondences, must be retained. These documents are vital for understanding what has been communicated to clients, especially in disputes over suitability or the handling of orders.

3. **Account Records:** Documents related to customer accounts, including account opening forms, customer identification documents, and suitability assessments. These records ensure that firms are adhering to Know Your Customer (KYC) and Anti-Money Laundering (AML) regulations.

4. **Financial Records:** Balance sheets, ledgers, and other financial statements of the brokerage firm. These are essential for regulatory examinations to ensure financial stability and compliance with net capital rules.

5. **Compliance and Audit Records:** Documentation of compliance efforts and audit results are also part of the required records. These include internal audit findings, compliance training logs, and reports filed with regulatory bodies.

Regulatory Frameworks Governing Books and Records

- **SEC Rule 17a-3 and 17a-4:** These rules stipulate the creation, maintenance, and retention period for securities transaction records by registered brokerage firms. They specify that records be kept in a manner that is easily accessible for a certain period, typically the first two years in an easily accessible place, with records older than three years held in a separate and secure location.

- **FINRA Rules:** FINRA enforces additional record-keeping rules that complement SEC regulations. These include requirements for recording electronic communications and ensuring these records can be reproduced in a readable format when requested by regulators.

Example in Practice

Consider a brokerage firm that executes stock trades on behalf of clients. Each trade must be documented, including details of the order execution. The firm must also retain emails or written instructions from the client authorizing the trade, details of the account in which the trade was made, and financial records showing how the trade was financed. This comprehensive documentation helps in audit trails and is critical if any dispute or inquiry arises about the transaction.

For SIE exam candidates, understanding the specifics of what needs to be recorded, how long to keep those records, and in what format is essential. This not only prepares candidates for questions related to compliance and operational procedures on the exam but also equips them with the knowledge needed for practical, real-world application in the securities industry. The meticulous nature of this requirement underscores the industry's commitment to transparency and accountability, ensuring that all activities are conducted fairly and in accordance with the law.

how long different types of records must be retained according to SEC and FINRA regulations.

In the securities industry, understanding document retention terms is akin to knowing how long to keep important financial receipts for tax purposes. Both practices ensure that essential records are available for review or audit at any time. For candidates preparing for the SIE exam, grasping the specifics of document retention is crucial for compliance and operational knowledge. Here's a detailed discussion on how long various types of records must be retained according to SEC and FINRA regulations:

Understanding Document Retention Requirements

SEC and FINRA regulations specify the minimum periods during which financial records and documents must be preserved. These rules ensure that information is available to assist in monitoring compliance with securities laws and to facilitate the reconstruction of financial transactions.

Key Regulations and Retention Periods

1. **SEC Rule 17a-3**: This rule outlines requirements for what records need to be made and kept by brokerage firms. It covers documents such as blotters (daily records of transactions), ledgers (financial records of assets and liabilities), customer account records, and trade confirmations. The rule generally requires that these records be kept for a period of not less than six years.

2. **SEC Rule 17a-4**: This rule specifies the manner in which records must be stored and the exact duration for retention. Most records under this rule must be preserved for three years, with the first two years in an easily accessible place. However, some types of records, such as partnership articles or articles of incorporation, must be kept for the life of the enterprise plus three years after its dissolution.

3. **FINRA Rules**: FINRA's requirements often align with those of the SEC but can include specific stipulations for the types of records its members must retain. For instance, FINRA Rule 4511 requires firms to preserve books and records in a format and media that comply with SEC Rule 17a-4. Moreover, communications with the public must be kept for three years according to FINRA Rule 2210.

Examples of Document Retention Applications

- **Trade Confirmations**: Firms must retain copies of all executed trade confirmations sent to customers. These confirmations detail the specific terms and execution details of transactions and must be retained for three years, with the first two years in an easily accessible location.

- **Emails and Electronic Communications**: Under FINRA regulations, all emails and electronic communications related to the firm's "business as such" must be preserved for a minimum of three years and be easily retrievable. This includes emails about trades, advice given to clients, and other business-related correspondences.

- **Account Records**: Information relating to the opening, closing, terms, and conditions of an account must be kept for six years after the closing of an account. This includes records of identity verification performed under AML (Anti-Money Laundering) compliance programs.

Practical Tips for SIE Exam Candidates

Candidates should understand not only the durations for which different types of records must be retained but also the rationale behind these requirements. Knowing that these laws and regulations are designed to protect investors, ensure market integrity, and enhance the transparency of financial transactions can help contextualize the rules beyond rote memorization.

For those entering the securities industry, a thorough understanding of document retention policies is essential. Not only do these regulations play a critical role in compliance and operational integrity, but knowledge of these rules is also vital for passing the SIE exam and for practical, real-world application in any securities-related profession. Understanding and adhering to these rules ensures that necessary documentation is available for audit, dispute resolution, and compliance verification, safeguarding the interests of all market participants.

Customer Communication Guidelines

In the securities industry, effective and compliant communication with customers is not just about building trust and clarity but is also a regulatory requirement. Just as a city has traffic laws to manage how people drive, the securities industry has specific rules and standards governing how firms and their representatives communicate with customers. Understanding these guidelines is crucial for anyone preparing for the SIE exam, as it ensures compliance and fosters professionalism in all customer interactions.

Regulatory Standards for Customer Communications

Overview of Standards

The Financial Industry Regulatory Authority (FINRA) sets out comprehensive rules designed to ensure that communications with customers are clear, fair, and not misleading. Similarly, the Securities and Exchange Commission (SEC) has regulations under the Securities Act of 1933 and the Securities Exchange Act of 1934 that address the integrity of communications with investors.

1. **Fairness and Transparency**: Communications must not make false or misleading statements or omit facts necessary to make the statements made, in light of the circumstances under which they are made, not misleading. This is akin to the way advertising laws prevent companies from making false claims about products.

2. **Balance**: Presentations of potential benefits of investments must be balanced with an equally prominent presentation of risks. Just as a medication must come with information about potential side effects, financial communications must not highlight potential returns without also explaining the risks involved.

3. **Suitability**: Any recommendations made in communications must be suitable for the recipient, based on their known financial needs and objectives. This is similar to how a doctor would not prescribe medicine without first understanding a patient's health history.

4. **Standards for Specific Types of Communications**:

   - **Retail Communications**: These are communications with more than 25 retail investors within any 30 calendar-day period. They must be pre-approved by a principal of the firm and filed with FINRA.

   - **Correspondence**: Communications with 25 or fewer retail investors within 30 calendar days do not need pre-approval but must be supervised and retained.

   - **Institutional Communications**: Those directed exclusively to institutional investors rather than retail investors have somewhat more lenient requirements, reflecting the higher sophistication levels of the audience.

Example of Application in Practice

Imagine a financial advisor preparing an email to send to a group of retail investors that outlines a new investment opportunity. According to FINRA rules, this email must:

- Clearly describe the potential risks associated with the investment as prominently as any potential benefits.

- Be based on a reasonable basis to believe that the investment would be suitable for every investor in that group based on their individual investment profiles.

- Be approved by a principal of the firm before being sent if it reaches more than 25 recipients within 30 days.

Furthermore, any performance data included must be presented in a way that is not misleading, with adequate explanations and qualifications to help the recipient understand the context of the data presented. For instance, if the email includes past performance data of similar investments, it must also clearly state that past performance is not necessarily indicative of future results.

For SIE exam candidates, understanding the regulatory standards governing customer communications is essential. These rules ensure that all communications are conducted ethically, transparently, and in a manner that protects the interests of both the investor and the integrity of the market. Mastery of these standards is not just about passing the exam but also about laying a solid foundation for ethical practices in any future securities industry role.

Practical tips for ensuring compliance in customer communications,

Navigating customer communications in the securities industry with compliance in mind is akin to driving with a clear understanding of road signs and rules. Missteps can lead to regulatory infractions similar to traffic violations. For candidates preparing for the SIE exam, understanding best practices for compliant communications is crucial to ensure they not only pass the exam but also practice responsibly in their future careers. Here's an in-depth look at practical tips for maintaining compliance in customer communications, with examples to illustrate compliant and non-compliant behavior.

Best Practices for Compliant Customer Communications

1. Use Clear and Understandable Language

- **Compliant**: Use plain language that can be easily understood by the average investor without finance expertise. For example, explaining a "bond" as a "loan that companies or governments issue to raise money, promising to pay back the principal along with interest on specific dates."

- **Non-compliant**: Using complex jargon or technical terms without explanation, such as stating that an investment offers "favorable alpha generation" without clarifying that "alpha" refers to the measure of performance on a risk-adjusted basis.

2. Provide Balanced Information

- **Compliant**: Always present the risks associated with an investment alongside its benefits. For instance, if promoting a stock with potentially high returns due to its volatile market, clearly disclose the risk of significant losses if market conditions worsen.

- **Non-compliant**: Highlighting only the potential benefits of an investment, such as high returns, without mentioning associated risks like market volatility or liquidity issues.

3. Ensure Suitability

- **Compliant**: Make recommendations based on a thorough understanding of the customer's financial situation, goals, and risk tolerance. For example, recommending municipal bonds to a risk-averse investor looking for stable, tax-free income.

- **Non-compliant**: Advising a conservative investor to invest in high-risk stocks or speculative ventures without considering their risk tolerance or financial objectives.

4. Maintain Documentation

- **Compliant**: Keep detailed records of all communications, including the information shared, the context of discussions, and any follow-ups. This can include saving copies of emails, notes from phone conversations, and written acknowledgments of disclosures provided.

- **Non-compliant**: Failing to document discussions or recommendations, especially when they pertain to changes in investment strategies or advice on complex products.

Examples to Illustrate Compliance and Non-compliance

Example of Compliant Communication: An email from a broker to a client reads: "Based on our review of your retirement goals and your comfort with minimal risk, I recommend considering a diversified portfolio of high-grade corporate bonds and government securities. While the returns on these are generally lower than stocks, they offer greater stability and lower risk, aligning with your need for security as you near retirement. Please see the attached fact sheets which outline the potential benefits and risks associated with these investments."

Example of Non-compliant Communication: A text message from a broker to a client states: "Check out this hot stock pick guaranteed to double your money in a year! All our clients are jumping on it. Let me know how much you want to invest." This message fails to provide a balanced view, lacks suitability assessment, and uses promotional language that could mislead the client about the guarantees of returns.

Understanding and implementing best practices in customer communications is essential for compliance in the securities industry. For SIE exam candidates, mastering these practices is crucial for both exam success and professional integrity. By always considering clarity, balance, suitability, and documentation, candidates can ensure their communications uphold the standards expected by regulatory bodies and protect the interests of their clients.

Anti-Money Laundering (AML) Procedures

Understanding Anti-Money Laundering (AML) procedures is critical for anyone entering the securities industry, much like understanding sanitation procedures is crucial for anyone in the medical field. Both sets of procedures are designed to prevent practices that can be harmful — in the case of AML, preventing the movement of illicit funds through financial systems. Here's a detailed explanation of AML basics, essential for those preparing for the Securities Industry Essentials (SIE) exam.

Anti-Money Laundering (AML) Basics

What is AML?

Anti-Money Laundering refers to a set of laws, regulations, and procedures intended to prevent criminals from disguising illegally obtained funds as legitimate income. Just as a water filtration system removes impurities to prevent harm, AML procedures are designed to filter out criminal activities from the financial system, ensuring that operations within are not corrupted by illegal money.

Why is AML Critical in Financial Transactions?

1. **Preventing Crime**: The primary goal of AML efforts is to deter criminal activities like drug trafficking, terrorism financing, and other illegal enterprises that rely on financial systems to sustain their operations. Without effective AML procedures, financial institutions could inadvertently become facilitators of crime.

2. **Maintaining Financial System Integrity**: AML procedures ensure the integrity and stability of financial markets. Just as law enforcement works to keep communities safe and functioning properly, AML protects the financial community by enforcing transparency and accountability.

3. **Regulatory Compliance**: Compliance with AML regulations is mandatory for financial institutions. Failure to comply can result in severe penalties, including fines and sanctions, similar to penalties in the sports world where rules violations can lead to disqualification or suspension.

4. **Protecting Reputations**: Effective AML procedures safeguard the reputation of financial institutions. In the business world, trust is paramount, much like in personal relationships; without trust, engagements and interactions can break down. Financial institutions risk losing customer trust and business partnerships without strong AML policies.

The Impact of AML

To grasp the importance of AML, consider the following analogy: AML procedures in the financial world are like security checks at airports. Just as security checks prevent dangerous items from being brought onto planes, AML procedures prevent the financial system from being used for laundering money from criminal activities.

For instance, a bank must verify where large sums of money originating from a business come from, ensuring the business is not a front for laundering. This could involve verifying the business's operations, examining financial statements, and continuously monitoring transactions, similar to how airport security continuously monitors passengers and luggage.

For SIE exam candidates, understanding the essentials of AML is not only about being able to answer exam questions correctly. It's about preparing for a career in a field where integrity and vigilance are paramount. Knowing the 'why' and 'how' of AML procedures helps in fostering a professional ethos that aligns with the legal and ethical standards expected in the financial industry. This knowledge ensures that future professionals are not only competent in their roles but also champions of integrity and security in the financial sector.

Key AML Procedures

Understanding key Anti-Money Laundering (AML) procedures is essential for candidates preparing for the Securities Industry Essentials (SIE) exam. These procedures are the financial industry's tools for combating fraud and illegal activities, similar to how a detective uses investigation tools to solve crimes. Here's a detailed discussion of three critical AML procedures: customer identification, transaction monitoring, and reporting suspicious activities.

Customer Identification Program (CIP)

Overview The Customer Identification Program, or CIP, is the foundational element of AML compliance. Just as a security system needs to identify who enters a building, financial institutions must verify the identities of their customers to prevent money laundering.

Procedure

- **Verification at Account Opening**: When opening an account, financial institutions must collect identifiable information such as name, date of birth, address, and identification numbers (e.g., Social Security number in the U.S.).

- **Document Verification**: This information must be verified using reliable sources, which can include government-issued identification documents like passports or driver's licenses.

- **Risk Assessment**: Depending on the type of account and the anticipated transactions, additional information may be required to assess the risk a customer may pose regarding money laundering or terrorist financing.

Example Imagine a new client wants to open a brokerage account. The broker must collect and verify the client's personal information, check it against public records, and retain this information to comply with the CIP requirements. This step ensures the client is legitimately who they claim to be, reducing the risk of criminal elements entering the financial system.

Transaction Monitoring

Overview Continuous monitoring of customer transactions is crucial to detect unusual patterns that might indicate money laundering. It's akin to monitoring traffic flow on highways for signs of illegal activities.

Procedure

- **Continuous Surveillance**: Financial institutions use automated systems to review all transactions for signs of unusual activity that deviates from the customer's typical financial behavior.

- **Alerts**: These systems generate alerts for transactions that meet certain criteria, such as unusually large transfers, frequent cross-border transactions, or transactions involving high-risk countries.

- **Investigation**: Each alert is investigated by compliance officers to determine if it suggests suspicious activity or if there's a legitimate explanation.

Example A customer normally deposits $5,000 monthly in an investment account but suddenly deposits $50,000. The transaction monitoring system flags this as unusual, triggering a review to determine if the deposit is justifiable or if it warrants a deeper investigation.

Reporting Suspicious Activities

Overview Reporting suspicious activities is the last line of defense in the AML framework. Like a neighborhood watch program reports suspicious behavior to prevent crime, financial institutions report to regulatory bodies to help prevent financial crimes.

Procedure

- **Suspicious Activity Reports (SARs)**: If a financial institution suspects that a transaction involves funds derived from illegal activities or is intended to disguise funds from illegal activities, it must file a SAR.

- **Confidentiality**: The filing of SARs is confidential. Employees of the financial institution should not disclose to anyone involved that a SAR has been filed.

- **Timeliness**: Institutions have a specific time frame, typically 30 days, to file a SAR once suspicious activity is detected.

Example If during an investigation of an alert, a compliance officer finds that there is no reasonable explanation for a series of rapid, high-value transactions in a client's account, the institution would file a SAR with the Financial Crimes Enforcement Network (FinCEN), detailing the suspicious activities without alerting the client.

For those studying for the SIE exam, understanding these key AML procedures not only prepares you for the exam but is also critical for your future role in the securities industry. By effectively implementing customer identification, transaction monitoring, and reporting of suspicious activities, you help maintain the integrity of the financial system and protect it from financial crimes.

Real World Examples of Account Opening

When studying for the SIE exam, understanding the practical application of regulations is crucial, particularly the processes involved in account opening. This process is akin to a thorough vetting system, similar to how a landlord screens potential tenants to ensure reliability and compliance. Here's a detailed explanation of the steps and documentation required for opening new accounts, focusing on compliance with Know Your Customer (KYC) rules.

Account Opening and KYC Compliance

Step 1: Collection of Identifiable Information

The first step in opening a new account involves collecting essential information from the prospective client. This typically includes:

- **Personal Information**: Full name, date of birth, and address.

- **Identification Numbers**: Social Security number (SSN) for U.S. citizens or taxpayer identification number (TIN) for non-U.S. citizens.

- **Photographic Identification**: A valid government-issued ID such as a passport or driver's license. This helps verify the identity of the person opening the account.

Step 2: Verification of the Information

Once the information is collected, the next step is to verify its accuracy:

- **Document Verification**: Financial institutions use various methods to verify the authenticity of documents provided. This might involve checking the documents against databases, using technology to verify features like watermarks or other security features in IDs.

- **Background Checks**: This can include checking the individual's credit history, public records, or other financial databases to ensure there are no indications of financial fraud or other legal concerns.

Step 3: Risk Assessment

Under KYC regulations, financial institutions must also assess the potential risk associated with a new client:

- **Risk Profile**: Based on the information gathered, a risk profile is created which categorizes clients based on their potential risk to the institution. Factors such as the client's occupation, the source of initial deposits, and the expected pattern of activity play a crucial role in this assessment.

- **Enhanced Due Diligence (EDD)**: For clients who are assessed as higher risk, enhanced due diligence procedures are initiated. This may involve deeper investigation into their financial history, public behavior, and the nature of their business activities.

Step 4: Account Setup

After successfully passing the verification and risk assessment:

- **Account Configuration**: Depending on the client's needs and risk profile, different types of accounts and services are offered and set up accordingly.

- **Ongoing Monitoring**: Even after the account is opened, KYC procedures require ongoing monitoring of the account to ensure that the client's activities align with what was expected and that no suspicious activities occur.

Real-World Example:

Consider a scenario where an individual wishes to open a brokerage account. The individual provides their driver's license, SSN, and recent utility bills for address verification. The financial institution checks these documents for authenticity and conducts a background check that reveals regular international transactions. Due to these factors, the client is categorized as a higher risk, prompting enhanced due diligence. This includes obtaining additional information about the source of the funds and the nature of the international transactions. Once all checks conform to compliance standards, the account is opened with specific monitoring setups to regularly review the transactions based on the risk profile.

For candidates preparing for the SIE exam, understanding each step of the account opening process, particularly the importance of KYC rules, is crucial. Not only does this knowledge help in passing the exam, but it also prepares you for real-world responsibilities in the securities industry, ensuring the integrity and security of financial transactions right from the start of a client relationship.

Know Your Customer (KYC): Explanation of KYC principles,

the principles of Know Your Customer (KYC) is essential for anyone entering the securities industry and preparing for the SIE exam. KYC can be likened to the detailed process a doctor uses to understand a patient's health before recommending a treatment plan. Just as a doctor gathers medical history to ensure appropriate care, financial institutions implement KYC to ensure the suitability of financial advice and services based on a customer's financial health and objectives.

Know Your Customer (KYC) Principles

KYC: An Overview

Know Your Customer (KYC) is a regulatory framework used globally by financial institutions to prevent identity theft, financial fraud, money laundering, and terrorist financing. KYC policies are a critical component in the broader AML (Anti-Money Laundering) strategies that financial services must adhere to.

Verification of Customer Identity

The first step in the KYC process involves the verification of the customer's identity, a foundational element that helps prevent illegal activities.

- **Document Verification:** Customers are required to provide valid government-issued identification documents, such as passports, driver's licenses, or national ID cards. This step ensures that the individual or entity is legally recognized and traceable.

- **Biometric Verification:** Increasingly, sophisticated measures like fingerprint scans and facial recognition are used, particularly in digital banking, to further authenticate identities.

Understanding the Customer's Financial Profile

Beyond just identifying who the customer is, KYC principles require that financial institutions understand the customer's financial behavior and intentions.

- **Financial History**: This includes assessing past transactions, credit history, and financial assets to gauge the customer's financial health.

- **Source of Funds**: Establishing where the customer's money comes from is crucial to prevent money laundering. This might involve checking the customer's employment details, business activities, or other sources of income.

- **Investment Objectives and Risk Tolerance**: Knowing what the customer aims to achieve through their investments and how much risk they are willing to take helps in tailoring financial advice and services that suit their needs.

Regular Updates and Ongoing Monitoring

KYC is not a one-time verification process but a continuous cycle of validation and monitoring.

- **Regular Updates**: Customers' information should be updated periodically to reflect any significant changes in their financial status or personal circumstances, such as a new job, business venture, or change in marital status.

- **Ongoing Monitoring**: Continuous monitoring of transactions is essential to detect and address any unusual or suspicious activities that might indicate changes in the risk profile or potential illegal activities.

Real-World Example

Imagine a scenario where an individual opens a new account to trade stocks. As part of the KYC process, the person provides a driver's license, proof of address, and details about their employment. The brokerage firm verifies these documents, checks the individual's financial history through credit reports, and assesses risk tolerance through a series of questions about investment experience and risk preferences. This information helps the firm not only ensure compliance with legal standards but also provide personalized service that aligns with the customer's investment goals and risk profile.

KYC is crucial both for exam purposes and professional practice. KYC ensures that financial services are provided safely and suitably, protecting both the institution and the customer. It builds a foundation of trust and compliance that is critical in the highly regulated securities industry.

Conclusion and Recap of the main points covered in the chapter.

In concluding the chapter on regulatory compliance, as covered in the preparation for the Securities Industry Essentials (SIE) exam, it's essential to underscore the importance of these regulations. Regulatory compliance in the securities industry can be compared to the safety protocols in civil aviation; both sets of regulations are designed to safeguard against potential risks and ensure that the system functions efficiently and securely.

Recap of Main Points Covered in the Chapter

1. **Books and Records Requirements**: We discussed the detailed record-keeping practices required by regulatory bodies such as the SEC and FINRA, ensuring that all financial transactions and communications are transparently maintained and easily accessible.

2. **Customer Communication Guidelines**: This section highlighted the standards for ethical and clear communications with clients, ensuring that all information provided is balanced, truthful, and understandable, thereby protecting clients from misleading information.

3. **Anti-Money Laundering (AML) Procedures**: We explored the procedures designed to prevent financial crimes, including rigorous customer identification processes, transaction monitoring, and the obligation to report suspicious activities.

4. **Real-World Examples**: Practical examples were provided to illustrate how these regulations apply in everyday scenarios within the securities industry, such as account opening processes, which emphasize compliance with Know Your Customer (KYC) rules.

Significance of Applying These Regulatory Practices

Ensuring Compliance: Just as building codes ensure that structures are safe for habitation, adhering to financial regulations ensures that business operations within the securities industry meet all legal standards. This compliance is not merely about following rules but about maintaining the order and integrity of the financial markets.

Protection of Investor Interests: These regulations are in place primarily to protect investors, much like consumer protection laws that prevent the sale of defective or dangerous products. By ensuring that all communications are clear and truthful and that all financial activities are monitored and recorded, regulatory practices help safeguard investors' interests and trust in the financial system.

Maintaining Market Integrity and Stability: Effective regulatory compliance helps in maintaining the overall health of the financial markets. Just as traffic laws reduce chaos on the roads, financial regulations help in preventing fraudulent activities that can lead to market instability. This stability is crucial for investor confidence, which in turn drives market participation and growth.

Ethical Implications: Adhering to these regulations fosters a culture of ethics and integrity within financial institutions. It's not just about avoiding penalties but about cultivating a professional environment where ethical behavior is the norm.

Understanding and applying the regulatory practices discussed in this chapter are crucial for anyone preparing for the SIE exam and for a successful career in the securities industry. These regulations form the backbone of market operations, ensuring that they function smoothly, transparently, and to the benefit of all stakeholders involved. As future professionals in the securities industry, SIE candidates must grasp the importance of these rules to navigate their careers effectively and ethically, thereby contributing to a robust and fair financial market environment.

CHAPTER 11. Introduction to Suitability in Financial Advising

Importance of Suitability

Suitability in financial advising ensures that the investments and strategies recommended by advisors align closely with the client's financial goals, risk tolerance, and time horizon. This alignment is crucial because it:

- **Protects Clients**: Just as a doctor would not prescribe medicine without diagnosing a patient, advisors must not recommend investments without understanding a client's financial health. Suitability ensures that clients are prescribed investment strategies that make sense for their unique financial circumstances, protecting them from unsuitable, risky investments that could lead to financial harm.

- **Promotes Trust**: Ensuring investments are suitable builds trust between clients and advisors. This trust is foundational for a long-term advisory relationship, similar to the trust between a patient and their doctor, which is based on the belief that the doctor's recommendations are in the patient's best interest.

- **Enhances Client Satisfaction and Retention**: When clients see that their investments are meeting their expectations and financial goals, their satisfaction increases, which in turn boosts client retention rates.

Regulatory Requirements and Ethical Considerations

The requirement for advisors to make suitable recommendations is not only a best practice but also a regulatory requirement enforced by bodies such as the Financial Industry Regulatory Authority (FINRA) and the Securities and Exchange Commission (SEC).

- **Regulatory Requirements**: Regulations such as FINRA Rule 2111 (Suitability) require advisors to have a reasonable basis to believe, based on adequate due diligence, that a recommendation is suitable for a client. This involves three main obligations:

  - **Reasonable-basis suitability**: Ensuring the investment is suitable based on its merits and risks.

  - **Customer-specific suitability**: Ensuring the investment is appropriate for the specific client based on their financial profile.

  - **Quantitative suitability**: Ensuring the number of transactions within a certain period is not excessive.

- **Ethical Considerations**: Beyond legal requirements, ethical considerations play a significant role in suitability assessments. Advisors must prioritize the client's interests above their own, avoiding conflicts of interest and making recommendations based on the client's best interests. This ethical commitment is akin to the Hippocratic oath in medicine, which binds physicians to act in the best interest of their patients.

Example

Consider a young professional who has just started her career and is looking to invest for long-term growth. She has a high-risk tolerance and a long investment time horizon. Recommending high-growth potential stocks or mutual funds that carry higher volatility might be suitable for her, unlike recommending conservative bonds typically suited for someone nearing retirement. This tailored approach ensures that the investments align with her specific financial capacity and goals.

suitability is the cornerstone of effective financial advising, much like precision is to engineering. It requires a deep understanding of both the client's financial landscape and the inherent characteristics of various investment options. For those preparing for the SIE exam, a thorough grasp of suitability principles is essential—not only to comply with regulatory standards but to ensure that they are equipped to offer advice that genuinely serves the best interests of their clients.

Determining Investor Suitability

In the world of financial advising, determining a client's risk tolerance is analogous to a chef understanding a diner's preference for spice levels — each individual's capacity and preference guide the recommendations made. Similarly, for financial advisors, accurately gauging how much financial risk a client is willing and able to take is critical to providing appropriate investment advice. This section of your SIE exam prep will delve into how to assess a client's risk tolerance effectively through questionnaires and interviews.

Assessing Risk Tolerance

Risk tolerance is a complex, multi-dimensional aspect of financial planning that reflects an individual's comfort level with the potential ups and downs in the value of their investments. It is determined by both psychological factors (how much risk one feels comfortable taking) and financial capacity (how much risk one can afford to take).

Using Questionnaires

Questionnaires are a common tool used to determine risk tolerance and usually consist of a series of questions designed to gauge:

- **Financial Goals and Objectives**: Understanding what the client aims to achieve through their investments, whether it's long-term growth, income, or capital preservation.

- **Financial Situation and Background**: Gathering data on income, existing assets, debts, and other financial commitments.

- **Experience with Investments**: Evaluating the client's past experiences with different types of investments, which can influence their comfort level with various investment risks.

- **Reaction to Hypothetical Market Conditions**: Questions might include scenarios such as a significant market drop. For example, "If your investment portfolio lost 10% of its value in a month, what would you do? Options might range from 'sell all investments' to 'buy more at the lower price'."

Each response is usually scored, and the total score helps place the client along a risk tolerance spectrum from conservative to aggressive.

Conducting Interviews

While questionnaires can provide a structured approach to assessing risk tolerance, interviews allow for deeper insights into the client's attitudes and emotions towards risk. During interviews, advisors can:

- **Clarify Questionnaire Responses**: Discuss any answers that were unclear in the questionnaire to ensure a thorough understanding of the client's attitudes.

- **Explore Emotional Reactions**: Engage in a discussion about the client's feelings towards investing and reactions to market volatility, which can provide deeper insights than standardized questions.

- **Assess Behavioral Tendencies**: Observations during an interview can give clues about a client's risk tolerance based on their behavior and emotional responses to financial discussions.

Real-World Example:

Imagine an advisor meeting with a new client who has expressed an interest in investing for retirement. During the interview, the advisor learns that the client recently reacted to a market downturn by hastily selling off another investment. This behavior indicates a lower risk tolerance than previously assumed based on the questionnaire alone. The advisor might then discuss this reaction with the client to confirm understanding and adjust investment recommendations accordingly.

Effectively determining a client's risk tolerance is foundational in creating a financial strategy that aligns with their preferences and financial goals. It is critical for advisors to use both questionnaires and interviews to capture a comprehensive picture of a client's risk profile. This approach ensures that the investments recommended will fit within the client's comfort zone while also meeting their financial objectives. For SIE exam candidates, mastering these assessment techniques is essential not only for passing the exam but for future success in the field of financial advising.

Investment Objectives:

In financial advising, aligning investment strategies with a client's objectives is akin to selecting the right tool for a specific job. Just as a carpenter wouldn't use a hammer to cut wood, an advisor wouldn't recommend high-risk stocks for a client seeking income stability in retirement. Understanding different investment objectives and how they align with client goals is fundamental for candidates preparing for the SIE exam. Here's a detailed discussion of common investment objectives and their alignment with client goals.

Defining Investment Objectives

Investment objectives broadly categorize what an investor aims to achieve with their portfolio. These objectives include growth, income, and preservation of capital, each serving different investor needs and risk profiles.

1. Growth

Objective: The primary goal of growth investments is to increase the capital value of the investment over time.

Suitable for: This objective is typically suitable for younger investors or those who have a longer time horizon until they need to access their funds. These investors are usually in a better position to withstand market fluctuations and the associated risks of growth-oriented investments.

Example: Investing in stocks or mutual funds that primarily hold equities is a common strategy for growth. For instance, a young professional might invest in a diversified portfolio of stocks aiming for high returns over several decades, accepting short-term volatility for potentially higher long-term gains.

2. Income

Objective: Income investments are designed to provide steady income from investments through dividends, interest, or rental income.

Suitable for: This objective is often pursued by individuals who are nearing retirement or who require a consistent income stream to meet daily expenses. These investors usually prefer lower-risk investments.

Example: Bonds, dividend-paying stocks, and real estate investment trusts (REITs) are typical income-generating investments. For example, a retiree might invest in a portfolio of bonds and high-dividend stocks to generate regular income to supplement their pension.

3. Preservation of Capital

Objective: The aim here is to maintain the original investment amount with minimal risk of loss.

Suitable for: This objective is ideal for investors who have a low tolerance for risk or need access to their capital in the near term. It is often prioritized by individuals who are close to reaching a financial goal, such as purchasing a home or funding a child's imminent college education.

Example: Conservative investments such as Treasury bills, money market funds, or guaranteed investment certificates (GICs) are favored for capital preservation. These options offer lower returns but provide greater safety of the principal amount. For instance, someone planning to buy a house in three years may choose to preserve their down payment in a low-risk money market fund.

aligning investment objectives with client goals are crucial for financial advisors. This ensures that recommendations meet the actual needs of the client, much like how a doctor prescribes medication based on a patient's specific symptoms and overall health. For SIE exam candidates, mastering the definition, examples, and suitability of different investment objectives is vital. It not only helps in passing the exam but is also fundamental in building effective, trust-based relationships with future clients, ensuring that their financial plans effectively support their long-term goals and life situations.

Time Horizon in Investment

Understanding the concept of a time horizon in investing is crucial for financial advisors and those preparing for the SIE exam. The time horizon can be likened to planning a journey where the length of the trip influences the type of preparation you need: a weekend getaway requires different planning than a month-long tour across continents. Similarly, the length of time a client plans to invest significantly affects the choice of suitable investments.

Time Horizon in Investment Strategy

What is Time Horizon?

The time horizon in investing refers to the length of time a client expects to hold an investment until they need access to the funds. This duration is critical in determining the risk level a client can afford to take and the types of investments that are most appropriate.

Impact on Investment Choices

1. **Short-Term Investments (1-3 years)**

   - **Objective**: Typically, short-term investments focus on preservation of capital and liquidity because the investor may need to access the funds soon.

   - **Suitable Investments**: Money market funds, short-term bonds, or high-interest savings accounts are common as they offer lower risk and relatively quick access to money.

   - **Example**: A client saving for a down payment on a house in two years would look for investments that provide stability and quick liquidity, minimizing the risk of losing the principal amount.

2. **Medium-Term Investments (3-10 years)**

   - **Objective**: These investments seek a balance between growth and safety, allowing for some exposure to growth-oriented investments with sufficient time to recover from potential volatility.

- **Suitable Investments**: A mix of bonds and stocks, or balanced mutual funds, typically fit well into medium-term horizons.

- **Example**: Consider a client planning to fund their child's college education in seven years. This client might opt for a balanced portfolio that includes a combination of equity and bond funds, providing potential for growth while mitigating risk through diversification.

3. **Long-Term Investments (10+ years)**

    - **Objective**: Long-term investments predominantly aim for growth, capitalizing on the potential for higher returns from riskier assets like stocks over an extended period.

    - **Suitable Investments**: Stocks, equity mutual funds, and ETFs are preferred for long-term horizons because they historically yield higher returns over long periods, despite short-term fluctuations.

    - **Example**: A young professional looking to plan for retirement 30 years down the road might heavily invest in a diversified portfolio of stocks or stock-focused mutual funds, banking on the market's long-term upward trend to maximize retirement savings.

Strategic Considerations

Risk Tolerance and Adjustment Over Time: It's crucial to align time horizons with risk tolerance. As the investment period shortens, advisors typically recommend shifting towards more conservative investments to reduce the risk of significant losses close to the needed withdrawal date. This strategy is akin to gradually slowing down as you approach your destination on a road trip, ensuring a safe arrival.

Review and Adjustment: Just as plans may change in life, financial plans may also need adjustments. Regular reviews of investment portfolios are essential to ensure they still align with the changing financial goals, economic circumstances, and time horizons of the client.

The length of time a client plans to keep their investments directly impacts the type of financial instruments suitable for their portfolio. By understanding and properly planning around the time horizon, financial advisors ensure that investment choices align with the client's life goals, risk tolerance, and financial needs, setting the stage for achieving financial objectives without undue risk. This understanding is crucial not just for passing the SIE exam but for practical, real-world application in financial advising.

Understanding Liquidity

In financial planning, understanding a client's liquidity needs is akin to ensuring a car has enough fuel for a journey—it's essential for covering short-term distances without unnecessary stops. For those studying for the Securities Industry Essentials (SIE) exam, grasping the importance of liquidity in investment decisions is critical. This section explores how liquidity impacts investment choices, particularly focusing on a client's short-term cash flow needs.

Understanding Liquidity Needs

What is Liquidity?

Liquidity refers to how quickly and easily an investment can be converted into cash without significantly impacting its price. High liquidity means an asset can be sold rapidly at a price close to market value, while low liquidity implies potential difficulties in selling the asset without a considerable price reduction.

Evaluating Liquidity Needs

Liquidity needs are fundamentally about timing and access to funds. They dictate how much ready cash a client needs to have on hand to meet immediate or short-term financial obligations.

1. **Assessing Immediate Cash Needs**

   - **Daily Expenses**: Clients need enough liquidity to cover day-to-day expenses such as bills, groceries, and transportation. This is akin to having enough cash in your wallet to cover daily expenditures without needing to sell something to pay for them.

   - **Emergency Funds**: It's also crucial for clients to have an emergency fund that can cover unexpected expenses like medical bills or urgent home repairs. Financial advisors typically recommend having three to six months' worth of living expenses in highly liquid assets.

2. **Planning for Foreseeable Expenses**

   - **Scheduled Payments**: If a client anticipates significant upcoming expenses, such as college tuition or a down payment on a home, ensuring sufficient liquidity to cover these without disrupting their long-term investments is essential.

   - **Tax Obligations**: Investors might also need liquidity for predictable expenses like property taxes or income taxes associated with investment gains.

Impact of Liquidity on Investment Decisions

Choosing the Right Investments

- **Highly Liquid Options**: For clients with high short-term liquidity needs, money market funds, savings accounts, and Treasury bills are appropriate as they can be converted into cash quickly and with minimal loss of value.

- **Moderately Liquid Options**: If the client has moderate liquidity needs and can plan for cash requirements, short-term bonds or bond funds might be suitable, offering slightly higher returns with reasonable access to funds.

- **Low Liquidity Investments**: Long-term investments such as real estate or certain types of stocks may not be suitable for clients with immediate liquidity needs but are appropriate for those with more flexible cash flow situations.

Example

Imagine a client who is a freelance graphic designer with a variable income; their cash flow might fluctuate significantly month-to-month. This client will likely prioritize liquidity highly to manage living expenses and compensate for irregular income. An advisor might recommend keeping a larger portion of their portfolio in liquid assets like a high-yield savings account or a money market fund, which allows the client to access cash quickly during leaner months without the need to sell off investments at a potential loss.

For SIE exam candidates and future financial advisors, evaluating a client's liquidity needs is crucial for crafting a portfolio that not only meets investment goals but also ensures that the client has sufficient access to cash for their short-term needs. This approach prevents financial strain and supports the overall financial well-being of the client, aligning investment strategies with real-life cash flow requirements. Understanding and addressing liquidity needs effectively enables clients to maintain financial stability while pursuing their long-term financial objectives.

Mapping suitability factors to products

Mapping suitability factors to investment products is an essential skill for financial advisors and a key concept for those preparing for the SIE exam. It involves aligning a client's financial profile, including their risk tolerance, investment objectives, and time horizon, with appropriate investment products. This process can be likened to a doctor prescribing medication tailored to a patient's specific health needs and medical history.

Understanding Suitability Factors

Suitability factors are essential criteria that help financial advisors determine which investment products are most appropriate for a client's unique financial situation and goals. These factors include:

1. **Risk Tolerance**: How much risk a client is willing to take, which can range from conservative to aggressive. This factor is crucial in determining the mix of asset classes in the client's portfolio.

2. **Investment Objectives**: What the client aims to achieve through their investments, such as income, growth, or preservation of capital.

3. **Time Horizon**: The duration the client plans to invest their money before needing access to it, which can significantly affect the choice of investment.

4. **Liquidity Needs**: The need for readily accessible funds without significant loss in value, important for clients who may need quick access to their money.

Mapping Process

The mapping process involves matching these suitability factors with the characteristics of various investment products:

1. Stocks

- Suitable for clients with a high risk tolerance and a long-term investment horizon. Stocks offer high growth potential but come with higher volatility and risk of loss.

- Example: A young professional with a stable income and 30 years until retirement might be suited for an equity-heavy portfolio aimed at capital growth.

2. Bonds

- Appropriate for clients seeking stable income and lower risk, such as retirees or those close to retirement. Bonds provide regular interest payments and are less volatile than stocks.

- Example: A retiree looking to preserve capital and receive steady income might benefit from government or high-quality corporate bonds.

3. Mutual Funds

- Suitable for investors looking for diversification and professional management. Depending on the fund's focus, it can be tailored to suit various risk tolerances and objectives.

- Example: A middle-aged investor with a moderate risk tolerance seeking balanced growth and income might invest in a balanced mutual fund that includes both stocks and bonds.

4. ETFs (Exchange-Traded Funds)

- Ideal for investors who value liquidity and lower fees. ETFs can track a wide range of indices and are traded like stocks, making them accessible for both passive and active investors.

- Example: An investor interested in a particular sector, like technology, with a medium risk tolerance might choose a tech-focused ETF to gain exposure to this industry.

5. Specialty Products

- Such as options, futures, and other derivatives, suitable for sophisticated investors with high risk tolerance and specific investment strategies.

- Example: An experienced investor with high risk tolerance and knowledge of commodities might use futures contracts to hedge against price movements or speculate.

Mapping suitability factors to products is about creating a personalized investment strategy that aligns with the client's financial profile and goals. This tailored approach helps ensure that investments are not only suitable but also positioned for optimal performance relative to the client's expectations and life stage. For SIE exam candidates, understanding how to perform this mapping accurately is crucial, as it underpins much of the advisory work in securities and financial planning. This knowledge ensures that future professionals can provide advice that genuinely serves the best interests of their clients, fostering trust and long-term relationships.

Checklists linking client types to suitable securities

Creating checklists that link client types to suitable securities is an essential practice for financial advisors and a valuable tool for candidates preparing for the SIE exam. This approach can be likened to a chef using a recipe book tailored to different dietary preferences or restrictions, ensuring that each dish meets specific nutritional requirements without compromising on taste.

The Purpose of Investment Checklists

Investment checklists serve as a systematic guide to ensure that the investment recommendations made align with the client's specific financial profile, including their risk tolerance, investment objectives, time horizon, and liquidity needs. These checklists help in consistently applying suitability standards across various client scenarios, much like a pilot's pre-flight checklist ensures no critical steps are missed before takeoff.

Constructing Checklists for Client Types

1. Identifying Client Categories

The first step in creating a checklist is to categorize clients based on key financial characteristics:

- **Risk Tolerance**: Conservative, Moderate, Aggressive

- **Investment Objectives**: Growth, Income, Preservation of Capital

- **Time Horizon**: Short-term (1-3 years), Medium-term (3-10 years), Long-term (10+ years)

- **Liquidity Needs**: High, Moderate, Low

2. Linking to Suitable Securities

For each category of client, the checklist should link to the types of securities that are generally suitable:

- **Conservative Clients**:

  - Preferred Securities: Bonds, Treasury bills, Money market funds, Stable value funds

  - Checklist Item: Ensure investments offer principal protection and stability.

- **Moderate Clients**:

  - Preferred Securities: Balanced mutual funds, Large-cap stocks, High-quality corporate bonds

  - Checklist Item: Balance between income and growth with moderate risk exposure.

- **Aggressive Clients**:

  - Preferred Securities: Stocks, Mutual funds focusing on growth sectors, High-yield bonds, International funds

  - Checklist Item: Focus on capital appreciation, accepting higher volatility and risk.

3. Detailed Checklist Items

Each checklist can include more specific criteria based on the investment products' features:

- **Stocks**: Check for company fundamentals, sector performance, and market conditions.

- **Bonds**: Review credit ratings, bond duration, and interest rate environment.

- **Mutual Funds/ETFs**: Analyze management fees, fund performance history, and asset allocation.

Example of a Checklist Application

Imagine a financial advisor meets a new client, a young professional looking to invest for long-term growth with a high risk tolerance. The advisor would refer to the checklist for "Aggressive Clients" and verify:

- Client's comfort with volatility and potential for significant fluctuations.

- Suitability of high-growth mutual funds or stocks in emerging technologies.

- Long-term time horizon aligns with the recommended securities' risk and return profiles.

For those studying for the SIE exam, understanding how to effectively use checklists to link client types to appropriate securities is crucial. These checklists not only streamline the process of making suitable recommendations but also ensure compliance with regulatory requirements and best practices in financial advising. They provide a structured method to match investments to client needs, reducing errors and enhancing client satisfaction and trust. This tailored approach ensures that advisors can offer advice that not only meets the financial goals of their clients but also adheres to the highest standards of the industry.

Conclusion

In concluding the chapter 11 for the SIE exam preparation, it's essential to understand the significant role that suitability plays in financial advising. Just as a tailor meticulously measures to ensure a suit fits perfectly, financial advisors must ensure that investment recommendations precisely fit a client's financial situation and goals. This closing section underscores the importance of aligning investments with client profiles to promote long-term satisfaction and adherence to regulatory standards.

Recap of Main Points Covered

1. Understanding Suitability Factors

- We discussed key suitability factors such as risk tolerance, investment objectives, time horizon, and liquidity needs. These factors are critical in determining the most appropriate financial products for each client, ensuring that each investment recommendation is as personalized and effective as possible.

2. Mapping Suitability Factors to Products

- We explored how different financial products, including stocks, bonds, mutual funds, and ETFs, align with specific client profiles based on their suitability factors. Each product type has distinct characteristics that make it more or less suitable for different types of investors.

3. Utilizing Checklists

- The use of checklists to link client types to suitable securities was highlighted as a practical tool for advisors. These checklists help ensure consistency and accuracy in the investment recommendation process, acting as a roadmap for aligning client needs with the right investment options.

Significance of Suitability in Financial Advising

Fostering Long-Term Client Relationships

- Suitability is the cornerstone of trust in advisor-client relationships. By consistently making recommendations that align with a client's best interests and financial goals, advisors build a foundation of trust that can lead to long-lasting relationships. Like a gardener who nurtures plants to bloom, advisors who nurture their relationships with clients through suitable advice help cultivate their clients' financial growth over time.

Maintaining Regulatory Compliance

- Suitability is not just a best practice; it is a regulatory requirement. Organizations like FINRA and the SEC have established detailed rules requiring advisors to recommend products that are appropriate for their clients based on a thorough understanding of their financial profiles. Compliance with these regulations is mandatory, akin to adhering to safety standards in construction—it's not only about following the law but about protecting the welfare of the client.

Real-World Implications

- Practical examples of suitability in action underscore its importance. For instance, advising a retiree to invest heavily in high-risk stocks would be inappropriate and could lead to significant financial loss and distress. Conversely, recommending a well-balanced portfolio aligned with the retiree's need for income and capital preservation would support their financial stability.

the principles of suitability and recommendations are fundamental to the practice of financial advising and crucial for the SIE exam. They ensure that advisors act in the best interest of their clients, promoting not only individual financial health and satisfaction but also the integrity of the financial services industry as a whole. As future professionals, SIE candidates must grasp these concepts thoroughly to successfully guide their clients and maintain the trust placed in them by both their clients and the regulatory bodies governing their practices.

Professional Conduct & Integrity Chapter 12

the Chapter 12 of SIE Exam Prep Study Guide, focuses on "Professional Conduct & Integrity," it's crucial to understand the foundational role that ethical behavior plays in the securities industry. The importance of professional conduct and integrity in financial services can be compared to the foundation of a house; without a strong ethical foundation, the structure is vulnerable to collapse. This introduction sets the stage for a deeper exploration of how maintaining high ethical standards underpins the trust and functionality of the entire financial system.

Introduction to Professional Conduct & Integrity

Significance of Professional Conduct and Integrity

Professional conduct and integrity are the cornerstones of the financial services industry. These principles ensure that financial professionals adhere to moral guidelines and legal standards, which in turn:

- **Builds Trust**: Just as a reputation for reliability and fairness can make or break a business, in financial services, the trust clients place in professionals is crucial. This trust is built on the expectation that advisors will act ethically in managing and advising on clients' assets.

- **Ensures Market Stability**: Ethical conduct contributes to the overall stability and reliability of financial markets. It reduces the incidence of fraudulent and manipulative practices that can lead to market disruptions, much like a well-enforced set of rules in a competitive sport ensures fair play and the sport's enduring popularity.

Impact of Ethical Practices on Client Trust and Market Functioning

Ethical practices in financial services directly impact both client trust and the efficiency of financial markets:

- **Client Trust**: Clients expect financial advisors to act in their best interest, safeguard their assets, and provide transparent advice. This relationship is similar to that between a patient and a doctor, where trust is paramount; just as patients trust doctors to recommend the best treatments, clients trust financial advisors with their financial health.

- **Market Functioning**: Ethical behavior ensures that markets operate efficiently. Misconduct can lead to severe consequences such as market manipulation or insider trading, which not only harm individual investors but can also lead to broader market instability. Ethical practices by all market participants help to uphold the integrity of the markets, ensuring they function smoothly and fairly.

Example of Ethical Practices in Action

Consider the case where a financial advisor discovers a highly lucrative investment opportunity that, upon thorough analysis, appears to carry undisclosed risks that could harm the client. Despite the potential for high commissions from steering clients towards this investment, the advisor chooses to disclose all potential risks, aligning with ethical guidelines and prioritizing the client's long-term financial safety over personal gain.

professional conduct and integrity are not just abstract concepts but practical necessities in the financial services industry. They ensure that financial professionals uphold the trust placed in them by their clients and contribute to the effective functioning of financial markets. For candidates preparing for the SIE exam, understanding these principles is essential, not only for passing the exam but also for fostering a successful, respected career in financial services. This foundational ethical knowledge serves as the basis for all actions and decisions in the field, highlighting the critical role of integrity in finance.

Fiduciary Duty, Client Confidentiality, and Conflicts Management

In the financial services industry, the concept of fiduciary duty is as fundamental as the Hippocratic oath in medicine—it binds professionals to act in the best interests of their clients, above all other considerations. Understanding fiduciary duty is essential for those preparing for the SIE exam, as it forms the backbone of ethical financial advising.

Fiduciary Duty Defined

Fiduciary Duty: A fiduciary duty is a legal and ethical obligation that one party (the fiduciary) has to act in the best interests of another (the beneficiary or client). In financial services, this means financial advisors must place their clients' interests ahead of their own, with a high standard of honesty and full disclosure, particularly regarding conflicts of interest.

The Importance of Fiduciary Duty in Financial Advising

Fiduciary duty is critical in financial advising for several reasons:

1. **Trust and Confidence**: Financial advisors are entrusted with the wealth and savings of their clients, often involving critical life goals such as retirement planning, purchasing a home, or saving for a child's education. The fiduciary duty reassures clients that their advisor will act thoughtfully and responsibly on their behalf, which is essential for maintaining trust and confidence.

2. **Conflict of Interest Management**: Fiduciary duty compels advisors to avoid conflicts of interest where possible, and where conflicts are unavoidable, to disclose them fully and manage them in the client's favor. This might involve, for example, choosing a financial product that has a lower commission for the advisor but better suits the client's financial goals.

3. **Higher Quality of Service**: The obligation to act in the best interest of clients pushes financial advisors to maintain a high standard of professional competence and ethical behavior. This commitment ensures that the advice and products recommended are not merely suitable but are the best possible options for the client's needs.

Legal and Ethical Obligations

Legal Aspects:

- Under U.S. law, fiduciaries are held to a higher standard of conduct than non-fiduciaries. Breaches of fiduciary duty can lead to legal consequences, including restitution and damages.

- Regulations such as those enforced by the Securities and Exchange Commission (SEC) and standards set by the Financial Industry Regulatory Authority (FINRA) require that financial advisors disclose how they are compensated and any potential conflicts of interest that might influence their advice.

Ethical Aspects:

- Ethically, fiduciary duty ensures that financial advisors adhere to the highest standards of integrity and transparency. This responsibility is fundamental to the profession's code of ethics, which emphasizes fairness, honesty, and respect.

- Advisors must continually educate themselves about their clients' changing financial situations and needs, adapting recommendations as necessary to align with the client's best interests.

For those studying for the SIE exam, a deep understanding of fiduciary duty is not just about mastering a topic for the test—it's about preparing for a career where ethical considerations play a crucial role in every interaction with clients. Fiduciary duty elevates the nature of the relationship between a financial advisor and their client to one of trust, integrity, and mutual respect. This foundational principle ensures that the financial services industry operates to the benefit of the individuals it serves, maintaining the health and stability of the financial system as a whole.

Client Confidentiality

Client confidentiality in financial advising is as crucial as patient confidentiality in the medical field. Just as a doctor protects sensitive health information, financial advisors are entrusted with safeguarding their clients' financial data. Understanding the rules and regulations that govern client confidentiality is fundamental for candidates preparing for the SIE exam, as it forms the basis of trust and legal compliance in financial services.

Client Confidentiality Defined

Client Confidentiality: This refers to the obligation of financial advisors and firms to keep client information private and secure, except when disclosure is authorized by the client or required by law. This information can include personal data, investment details, financial statements, and future plans.

Regulatory Framework

The protection of client information is governed by several key regulations:

1. **Gramm-Leach-Bliley Act (GLBA)**:

    - **Financial Privacy Rule**: Requires financial institutions to provide clients with a privacy notice that explains what personal information is collected, where it is shared, and how it is used. It also mandates that clients be given the opportunity to opt-out of certain sharing practices.

    - **Safeguards Rule**: Obligates financial institutions to implement security plans to protect the confidentiality and integrity of client information.

2. **Securities and Exchange Commission (SEC) Regulation S-P**:

    - Governs privacy policies and practices of securities firms. It requires notice of privacy policies at the account opening and annually thereafter. It also requires firms to maintain safeguards to protect customer records and information.

3. **FINRA Rules**:

    - FINRA enforces additional rules that require its members to protect sensitive client data against identity theft and data breaches, complementing the privacy standards set by GLBA and SEC regulations.

Importance of Maintaining Confidentiality

Building Trust:

- Protecting client information is vital for building and maintaining trust. Clients who feel their data is safe are more likely to develop a long-term, trusting relationship with their advisor.

Legal Compliance:

- Adherence to confidentiality rules is not just an ethical requirement but a legal obligation. Non-compliance can lead to severe penalties, legal repercussions, and damage to the firm's reputation.

Preventing Financial Fraud:

- Keeping client information secure helps prevent financial fraud and identity theft. Leaked client information can be exploited by criminals, leading to unauthorized transactions and financial losses.

Practical Implementation

Data Protection Measures:

- Advisors should use strong encryption for storing and transmitting client data.

- Regular audits and updates of security protocols are necessary to address new threats.

- Employee training on confidentiality and security practices ensures all team members understand their roles in protecting client information.

Case Study Example:

- Consider a scenario where an advisor inadvertently sends detailed financial statements to an incorrect email address. This breach of confidentiality can lead to unauthorized access to the client's financial assets. Under SEC Regulation S-P, the firm would need to immediately rectify the breach, notify the affected clients, and potentially face regulatory scrutiny and fines

Conflicts Management

Conflicts of interest in financial advising can be likened to a referee who also coaches one of the teams in a game. Just as the referee's dual roles could compromise the fairness of the game, conflicts of interest in financial advising can undermine trust and ethical standards if not properly managed. For candidates preparing for the SIE exam, understanding how to identify, disclose, and manage conflicts of interest is critical for upholding both ethical standards and client trust.

Understanding Conflicts of Interest

Definition: A conflict of interest occurs when a professional, or a firm, has a competing interest that could make it difficult to fulfill duties impartially or could impair the ability to act in the best interest of a client.

Identifying Conflicts of Interest

Self-Awareness: Advisors must continually assess their own activities and relationships. Conflicts can arise from various sources, including personal financial interests, relationships with issuers of securities, or compensation structures that might influence recommendations.

Regular Audits: Firms should conduct regular audits of business practices to detect situations that may lead to conflicts. This includes reviewing how investment products are selected for clients and how advisors are compensated.

Disclosing Conflicts of Interest

Transparency: Once identified, conflicts of interest must be disclosed to clients in a straightforward manner. Disclosure documents should clearly describe how the conflict could affect the advice given, and they should be presented in a way that is easy for clients to understand.

Ongoing Communication: Disclosure is not a one-time event but an ongoing duty. Advisors should keep clients informed about any new or evolving conflicts that may arise after the initial engagement.

Managing Conflicts of Interest

Avoidance: Whenever possible, the best way to handle a conflict of interest is to avoid it altogether. This may mean choosing not to engage in certain activities or opting out of relationships that could impair professional judgment.

Mitigation: When conflicts cannot be avoided, steps must be taken to mitigate them. This can involve having a third party review recommendations made to clients or setting up ethical walls within the firm to prevent the flow of information between departments that might improperly influence decisions.

Monitoring and Enforcement: Firms should have robust policies in place to monitor conflict situations and enforce compliance with both internal guidelines and regulatory requirements. Regular training sessions for staff can help reinforce the importance of managing conflicts and maintaining high ethical standards.

Practical Example

Imagine an advisor whose compensation is partly dependent on the volume of specific transactions or products sold. This compensation structure could incentivize the advisor to favor these transactions or products, even if they are not in the best interest of the client. To manage this conflict:

- The advisor must fully disclose how their compensation structure works to the client.

- The firm might review the advisor's recommendations independently to ensure they align with the client's objectives, not the advisor's financial gain.

Effective management of conflicts of interest is crucial for maintaining the integrity of financial advising. For SIE exam candidates, understanding the methods for identifying, disclosing, and managing these conflicts is not only essential for passing the exam but also for fostering long-term trust and ethical relationships with clients. This knowledge ensures that as future advisors, they can make decisions that truly serve the best interests of their clients, enhancing their professional reputation and the overall credibility of the financial advising profession.

Honesty, Integrity, and Competence Requirements

Understanding honesty and integrity in the context of financial advising is akin to appreciating the role of a foundation in architecture. Without a strong foundation, no building can stand; similarly, without honesty and integrity, the financial services industry cannot sustain the trust and confidence of the public. These principles are critical in building and maintaining relationships with clients and are directly tied to the public's trust in the financial system.

Honesty in financial advising means providing clear, truthful, and complete information to clients at all times. This involves openly discussing the potential risks and rewards of any financial product or strategy, not just the benefits that might make a sale easier. For example, when an advisor presents an investment opportunity, they must equally highlight both the growth potential and the risks involved, ensuring the client makes a well-informed decision.

Integrity involves adhering to ethical standards and principles, even when it might not be immediately beneficial or profitable to do so. It means putting the client's interests first, ahead of personal gains. For instance, if an investment that offers lower commissions is better suited to a client's needs than a higher-commission product, the advisor with integrity will recommend the best option for the client, regardless of personal financial impact.

In transaction execution, integrity means ensuring that all actions are carried out in a manner that is fair, accurate, and in compliance with regulatory standards. This includes avoiding practices like churning, where an advisor conducts excessive trading to generate commission. Such actions can undermine client trust and violate ethical standards.

The collective commitment to honesty and integrity by financial professionals helps maintain the health and stability of the financial markets. Each advisor's commitment to these principles ensures that decisions are made based on accurate and complete information, promoting a fair and efficient market environment.

For candidates preparing for the SIE exam, it's important to grasp that honesty and integrity are not just abstract virtues but practical necessities in daily financial practice. These principles ensure long-term success and sustainability in the profession by fostering trust and confidence among clients and the public, which are essential for the effective functioning of the financial markets and the broader economy.

Competence

Maintaining professional competence in the financial services industry is crucial, much like a surgeon staying updated with the latest medical techniques and technologies to ensure the best care for patients. For those preparing for the SIE exam and aspiring financial professionals, it's essential to continuously engage in educational activities, stay informed about new financial products, and keep abreast of regulatory changes.

Continual education is the bedrock of professional competence. This involves participating in formal courses offered by accredited organizations, which could cover everything from new financial theories to practical applications in portfolio management. It also includes obtaining and maintaining key certifications such as the Certified Financial Planner (CFP) or Chartered Financial Analyst (CFA). These certifications often require ongoing educational commitments to remain valid, ensuring that professionals keep pace with industry changes.

Understanding new financial products is another critical aspect. The financial market is dynamic, with new instruments like derivatives, structured products, or sustainable investments emerging regularly. Competent advisors invest time in training sessions and market research to understand these products' risks, benefits, and regulatory implications. This knowledge is crucial not only for advising clients accurately but also for ensuring that the recommendations made are appropriate and comply with current market standards.

Adherence to regulatory changes is equally important. The landscape of financial regulations is continually evolving, influenced by economic shifts, technological advancements, and lessons learned from past market crises. Financial professionals must stay updated on changes in securities laws and regulations from bodies like the SEC and FINRA. Compliance training is a regular feature in many firms, designed to help staff understand and implement these changes in their daily operations.

For example, consider the introduction of a new regulation regarding the transparency of fees in retirement accounts. A competent financial advisor would learn about these changes through seminars and regulatory bulletins, then apply this knowledge by adjusting how they disclose fee information to clients, ensuring compliance and maintaining trust.

for those studying for the SIE exam, it's vital to grasp the importance of ongoing education, understanding of new products, and keeping up with regulatory developments. These elements ensure that financial advisors can offer up-to-date, ethical, and informed advice, maintaining the high standards of professionalism required in the industry. This continuous learning and adaptation not only help in passing the exam but are indispensable for a successful career in financial advising.

Information Handling in the SIE Exam: Detailed Case Studies

To prepare for the Securities Industry Essentials (SIE) exam, it is essential to understand the gravity of managing sensitive client information through real-world scenarios. Below, I will delve into two comprehensive case studies involving the mishandling of sensitive data, each illustrating key lessons relevant to the SIE exam.

Case Study 1: The Equifax Data Breach

Background: Equifax, one of the largest credit bureaus in the U.S., suffered a massive data breach in 2017, which exposed the personal information of approximately 147 million people.

What Happened: Hackers exploited a vulnerability in a web application framework used by Equifax. Despite the availability of a patch for this security flaw, Equifax failed to update its systems in a timely manner. This oversight allowed hackers to access sensitive data, including Social Security numbers, birth dates, addresses, and in some cases, driver's license numbers.

Consequences: Equifax faced widespread criticism for its handling of the breach. The aftermath included:

- A settlement of up to $700 million, including fines and consumer compensation.

- Significant reputational damage, leading to a loss of trust among consumers and clients.

- The departure of key executives, including the CEO, CIO, and CSO.

Lesson: This case underscores the importance of timely software updates and robust cybersecurity measures to prevent unauthorized data access. It highlights the necessity for firms in the securities industry to maintain high standards of data protection, as emphasized in the SIE exam.

Case Study 2: The Morgan Stanley Data Loss

Background: In 2016, Morgan Stanley, a leading global financial services firm, experienced a significant data loss due to mishandling by an employee.

What Happened: A financial advisor at Morgan Stanley improperly accessed and transferred confidential client data to his personal server, which was later hacked. The information included clients' names, account numbers, and asset values.

Consequences:

- Morgan Stanley was fined $1 million by FINRA and faced additional penalties for failing to adequately protect customer data.

- The incident led to a review and overhaul of internal data security policies and practices.

- The financial advisor was terminated and faced legal actions for violating privacy laws.

Lesson: This example highlights the critical need for stringent internal controls and employee training on data security. It illustrates the regulatory expectations and ethical standards related to information handling, topics that are central to the SIE exam.

These detailed case studies not only provide engaging narratives but also convey crucial lessons about the repercussions of data mishandling and the importance of stringent data security measures in the financial industry. These lessons are directly applicable to the SIE exam's focus on ethical practices and regulatory compliance in handling client information.

Case Studies on Violation Reporting for the SIE Exam

The Securities Industry Essentials (SIE) exam emphasizes the importance of compliance and transparent violation reporting within the financial sector. Through detailed exploration of notorious financial scandals, we can gather critical lessons for SIE exam preparation. The Wells Fargo unauthorized accounts scandal and the Bernie Madoff Ponzi scheme offer profound insights into the consequences of compliance failures.

Wells Fargo's scandal began in the early 2000s but was most egregious from 2002 through 2016. Driven by an aggressive sales culture that rewarded employees for opening new accounts, employees secretly created millions of unauthorized bank and credit card accounts without customer consent. The fraudulent actions led to unauthorized fees for customers and allowed employees to boost sales figures and earn bonuses. This systemic breach of trust was eventually exposed by whistleblowers and journalists, attracting heavy fines exceeding $3 billion from various regulatory bodies, including the Consumer Financial Protection Bureau (CFPB) and the Office of the Comptroller of the Currency (OCC). The scandal tarnished Wells Fargo's reputation, leading to a massive overhaul of their sales practices and significant management reshuffles.

Bernie Madoff's Ponzi scheme, which unfolded over decades until its collapse in 2008, is another stark reminder of the catastrophic impacts of failing to adhere to ethical financial practices. Madoff promised consistent and high returns to investors, purportedly through savvy investment strategies. However, in reality, he was operating a Ponzi scheme, using new investors' funds to pay returns to earlier investors. Despite several red flags raised over the years, a lack of diligent investigation by the Securities and Exchange Commission (SEC) allowed Madoff's scheme to grow to an estimated $65 billion, making it one of the largest financial frauds in history. When the scheme inevitably collapsed during the 2008 financial crisis, investors lost billions, leading to significant reforms in SEC oversight and regulations concerning financial advisors.

These case studies highlight the essential need for stringent internal controls, ethical behavior, and rigorous regulatory oversight in the financial industry. They underline the importance of vigilant and transparent reporting practices to prevent financial fraud and protect investors. Understanding these cases provides SIE exam candidates with practical examples of how ethical and regulatory failures not only lead to financial and reputational damage but also to severe legal consequences, reinforcing the principles that guide responsible financial conduct.

Conclusion

In wrapping up our discussion on professional conduct and integrity for those preparing for the SIE exam, it's crucial to reflect on the critical principles that not only form the backbone of financial advising but also ensure the trust and reliability of the financial services industry. Much like the keystone in an arch, integrity and ethical conduct hold the structure of the financial industry together, ensuring stability and enduring strength.

Recap of Key Points

Throughout this chapter, we've delved into the fundamental aspects of professional conduct that are essential for every financial advisor:

- **Fiduciary Duty**: We explored the importance of fiduciary responsibility, emphasizing that advisors must always act in the best interests of their clients, akin to a captain who must navigate the ship safely on behalf of passengers.

- **Client Confidentiality**: The obligation to protect client information was discussed, highlighting how crucial privacy is in building and maintaining trust, similar to the confidentiality expected in doctor-patient relationships.

- **Conflict Management**: We outlined strategies for identifying, disclosing, and managing conflicts of interest, ensuring that advisors maintain impartiality and fairness in all dealings.

- **Honesty and Integrity in Practice**: The need for absolute honesty and integrity in all actions was underscored, showing that these qualities are non-negotiable in fostering client trust and confidence.

- **Competence**: The continuous commitment to education and staying updated with industry changes was emphasized as necessary for providing the best advice and service to clients.

The Importance of Ongoing Ethical Practice and Learning

Maintaining high standards of professionalism in the securities industry is not a one-time effort but an ongoing commitment. Just as athletes must continuously train to stay competitive, financial advisors must continually educate themselves on new products, strategies, and regulatory changes to ensure they are serving their clients effectively. This commitment to lifelong learning ensures that advisors not only keep up with the industry but also lead in terms of best practices and ethical standards.

The principles discussed in this chapter are not merely academic; they are practical necessities that underpin every action taken by a financial advisor. The trust placed in financial advisors by clients and the public is not given lightly—it must be earned and maintained through unwavering professional conduct and integrity. For candidates preparing for the SIE exam, mastering these concepts is crucial, as they form the foundation of a successful and respected career in financial services. This understanding ensures that future professionals are well-equipped to uphold and advance the integrity of the financial markets, fostering an environment of trust and respect that benefits all participants.

Conclusion and appendix

As we wrap up the SIE Exam Prep Study Guide, it's important to reflect on the essential insights and strategies that have been outlined to prepare you effectively for the Securities Industry Essentials (SIE) exam. This guide has not only aimed to furnish you with the necessary knowledge to pass the exam but also to lay a robust foundation for a career in the securities industry.

Recap of Key Insights

- **Comprehensive Exam Coverage**: The guide has thoroughly covered all the major topics and principles that the SIE exam tests, ensuring a well-rounded understanding of both theoretical and practical aspects of the securities industry.

- **Real-World Application**: Beyond exam preparation, the guide has emphasized the application of learned concepts to real-world scenarios, enhancing your readiness to step into the financial sector with confidence.

- **Critical Thinking and Analysis**: Through various examples and case studies, we've encouraged a deeper analysis and understanding, moving beyond rote memorization to a more integrated knowledge of how securities markets operate.

Prime Exam Prep Blueprint Takeaways

- **Structured Learning Path**: Following the structured learning path suggested in this guide will maximize your study efficiency. Regular review sessions and adherence to the study schedule are crucial.

- **Active Practice**: Engaging actively with the material through practice tests and end-of-chapter questions helps reinforce knowledge and improve test-taking stamina and technique.

- **Continuous Improvement**: Using feedback from practice tests to focus on weak areas ensures that your study time is focused and effective, continually enhancing your understanding and retention of the material.

Appendix

The Appendix serves as a valuable tool in your exam preparation arsenal, providing additional resources to support and enhance your learning experience.

Full Glossary of Key Terms

Glossary of Key Terms for SIE Exam Prep

Accredited Investor - An individual or a business entity that is allowed to deal in securities that may not be registered with financial authorities by satisfying certain income, net worth, asset size, governance status, or professional experience criteria.

Ask Price - The lowest price a seller is willing to accept for a security, also known as the offer price.

Asset Allocation - An investment strategy that aims to balance risk and reward by apportioning a portfolio's assets according to an individual's goals, risk tolerance, and investment horizon.

Bear Market - A market condition in which the prices of securities are falling, encouraging selling.

Bid Price - The highest price a buyer is willing to pay for a security.

Blue Chip Stocks - Shares in large, well-known companies with a history of financial stability and solid performance.

Bond - A fixed income instrument that represents a loan made by an investor to a borrower (typically corporate or governmental).

Broker-Dealer - A person or company that buys and sells securities for its own account or on behalf of its customers.

Bull Market - A market condition in which the prices of securities are rising or are expected to rise.

Capital Gains - The increase in the value of an asset or investment above its purchase price.

Compliance - Adherence to laws, regulations, guidelines, and specifications relevant to the business or organization.

Diversification - A risk management strategy that mixes a wide variety of investments within a portfolio.

Dividend - The distribution of some of a company's earnings to its shareholders, usually in the form of cash or additional stock.

ETF (Exchange-Traded Fund) - A type of security that involves a collection of securities—such as stocks—that often tracks an underlying index, but which trades on exchanges like a stock.

Fiduciary Duty - A legal obligation to act in the best interest of another party, such as a client.

FINRA (Financial Industry Regulatory Authority) - An independent, non-governmental organization authorized by Congress to protect America's investors by making sure the broker-dealer industry operates fairly and honestly.

Fixed Income - Securities that yield fixed periodic returns in the form of interest or dividends paid to the investor.

Hedge - An investment made to reduce the risk of adverse price movements in an asset.

Insider Trading - The trading of a public company's stock or other securities by individuals with access to non-public information about the company.

Liquidity - The ease with which an asset or security can be converted into ready cash without affecting its market price.

Margin - The use of borrowed money to purchase securities, with the securities themselves serving as collateral for the loan.

Mutual Fund - An investment vehicle made up of a pool of money collected from many investors to invest in securities like stocks, bonds, money market instruments, and other assets.

Options - Contracts that give the buyer the right, but not the obligation, to buy or sell an underlying asset at a set price on or before a certain date.

Portfolio - A collection of financial investments like stocks, bonds, commodities, cash, and cash equivalents, including mutual funds and ETFs.

Prospectus - A legal document that describes a financial security for potential buyers.

Risk Tolerance - An individual investor's ability to accept loss of some or all of the money they have invested, based on a variety of factors, including their investment goals and the time horizon for meeting those goals.

SEC (Securities and Exchange Commission) - The U.S. government agency responsible for enforcing the federal securities laws, proposing securities rules, and regulating the securities industry.

Yield - The income return on an investment, typically expressed annually as a percentage based on the investment's cost, its current market value, or its face value.

Final Thoughts

Leveraging the insights and materials presented in this guide will not only prepare you to excel on the SIE exam but also set a solid groundwork for your future endeavors in the financial services industry. The journey to becoming a successful financial professional is ongoing, and the principles learned here will serve as a guidepost for continuous learning and development in your career.

CONTACT THE AUTHOR

I always strive to make this guide as comprehensive and helpful as possible, but there's always room for improvement. If you have any questions, suggestions, or feedback, I would love to hear from you. Hearing your thoughts helps me understand what works, what doesn't, and what could be made better in future editions.

To make it easier for you to reach out, I have set up a dedicated email address:

epicinkpublishing@gmail.com

Feel free to email me for:

- Clarifications on any topics covered in this book

- Suggestions for additional topics or improvements

- Feedback on your experience with the book

- Any problem (You can't get the bonuses for example, please before releasing a negative review, contact me)

Your input is invaluable.

I read every email and will do my best to respond in a timely manner.

GET YOUR BONUSES

Dear reader,

First and foremost, thank you for purchasing my book! Your support means the world to me, and I hope you find the information within valuable and helpful in your journey.

As a token of my appreciation, I have included some exclusive bonuses that will greatly benefit you.

To access these bonuses, scan the QR Code with your phone:

Once again, thank you for your support, and I wish you the best of luck in your Exam. I believe these bonuses will provide you with the tools and knowledge to excel.

Series 7 Exam Prep Study Guide

INTRODUCTION

The Series 7 exam is a cornerstone for anyone aspiring to become a registered representative in the financial industry. This crucial certification demonstrates a candidate's ability to perform the essential functions of a securities representative, which include buying, selling, and trading a wide range of securities such as stocks, bonds, and mutual funds. Essentially, passing the Series 7 exam opens the door to a myriad of opportunities within the financial services sector, from becoming a stockbroker to a financial planner.

Administered by the Financial Industry Regulatory Authority (FINRA), the Series 7 exam is designed to assess the comprehensive knowledge and practical skills necessary to advise clients, manage accounts, and navigate the regulatory landscape of the securities industry. This rigorous exam ensures that financial professionals possess the competency to perform their duties effectively and ethically, safeguarding the interests of investors and maintaining market integrity.

Obtaining the Series 7 license not only signifies a high level of expertise but also enhances a professional's credibility in the industry. It equips individuals with the knowledge to understand complex financial products and the regulatory framework governing them. For clients, working with a Series 7 licensed advisor means receiving informed and reliable guidance on a diverse array of investment options.

Exam Structure:

Continuing from the importance of the Series 7 exam, let's examine its structure. It is designed to comprehensively evaluate a candidate's readiness to perform as a general securities representative.

The Series 7 exam, formerly known as the General Securities Representative Qualification Examination, consists of 125 multiple-choice questions strategically formulated to assess your knowledge and application of various securities concepts. The exam is structured to be completed in 3 hours and 45 minutes, providing an average of about one minute and forty-eight seconds per question. This rigorous time constraint requires a strong grasp of the material and efficient time management skills during the exam.

A passing score of 72% is required, meaning you need to correctly answer at least 90 out of the 125 scored questions. Interestingly, the exam also includes an additional 10 unscored pretest questions, which are randomly distributed and do not count towards your final score. FINRA uses these unscored questions to test new questions for future exams.

The Series 7 exam covers various topics across four major job functions that a general securities representative would perform. These functions include seeking business for the broker-dealer from customers, opening accounts after evaluating customers' financial profiles, providing information about investments and making recommendations, and verifying customers' purchase and sales instructions. The majority of the exam, around 73%, focuses on providing information about investments, making recommendations, transferring assets, and maintaining appropriate records. This focus underscores the critical importance of these tasks in the daily operations of a securities representative.

Role and Opportunities:

After passing the Series 7 exam, you earn the title of registered representative, a fundamental role in the financial services industry. As a registered representative, you can buy, sell, and trade various securities, including corporate stocks, bonds, options, mutual funds, and more. This license empowers you to work with clients, guiding them through investment decisions and helping them achieve their financial goals.

The career opportunities that open up with a Series 7 license are diverse and promising. You can embark on a career as a stockbroker, where you'll be at the forefront of financial markets, executing trades and managing investment portfolios for individual clients. Alternatively, you might work as a financial advisor, providing comprehensive financial planning and investment advice. Many registered representatives find rewarding roles in investment banking, working on mergers, acquisitions, and other significant financial transactions.

Moreover, the Series 7 license is often a stepping stone to more advanced positions within the financial industry. It qualifies you for further certifications and specializations, such as Series 24 for supervisory roles or Series 66 for combined state law and investment advisor qualifications. This progression can lead to senior positions in portfolio management, wealth management, and even executive roles within financial firms.

The role of a registered representative is dynamic and customer-focused, requiring a deep understanding of financial products and regulations. It offers a blend of analytical challenges and interpersonal interactions, making it an attractive career for those with a passion for finance and a knack for building client relationships. With the Series 7 license, you're well-equipped to navigate the complexities of the financial markets and provide valuable insights and services to your clients, paving the way for a successful and fulfilling career in finance.

This critical certification not only validates your expertise but also enhances your employability in a competitive industry, ensuring that you can contribute effectively to your firm's success and your client's financial well-being

History and Changes:

The history of the Series 7 exam is a fascinating journey that reflects the evolving landscape of the financial industry and regulatory standards. Administered by the Financial Industry Regulatory Authority (FINRA), the Series 7 exam has long been a cornerstone for aspiring securities professionals.

Originally, the Series 7 exam was a comprehensive six-hour marathon with 250 multiple-choice questions covering a broad spectrum of financial knowledge. This rigorous format ensured that only the most prepared candidates could pass, setting a high standard for entry into the securities industry. However, this format also posed significant challenges, particularly regarding the sheer volume of material and the time required to complete the exam.

In October 2018, FINRA introduced significant changes to the Series 7 exam to make it more streamlined and focused. The new format reduced the exam length to 3 hours and 45 minutes and trimmed the number of questions to 125. This change was part of a broader effort to modernize the exam and make it more relevant to the day-to-day functions of a securities representative. Alongside the reduction in length and questions, the exam's content shifted to place greater emphasis on product-specific knowledge and practical applications within the securities industry

One of the most notable changes was introducing the Securities Industry Essentials (SIE) exam as a corequisite. The SIE exam, which covers fundamental securities industry knowledge, must be passed alongside the Series 7 exam. This bifurcation allows Series 7 to focus more deeply on the specific expertise required for a general securities representative. At the same time, the SIE ensures a solid foundation in the basics of the industry

These changes have made the Series 7 exam more accessible and aligned with the financial industry's practical needs. They also reflect FINRA's ongoing commitment to ensuring that securities professionals are well-equipped to protect investors and maintain market integrity.

Chapter 1: Exam Overview and Creating Your Study Plan

Welcome to Chapter 1, a crucial starting point in your journey to mastering the Series 7 exam. This chapter is designed to provide you with a comprehensive understanding of the exam's structure and content, and to equip you with effective strategies for creating a personalized study plan.

In this chapter, you will find a detailed breakdown of the exam's content areas and their respective weightings, helping you to prioritize your study efforts effectively. We will discuss the importance of each major topic, offering insights into which areas are more heavily tested, and provide visual aids such as pie charts to illustrate the distribution of exam content.

You will also learn how to create a personalized study schedule that aligns with your individual strengths and weaknesses. We will provide templates for daily, weekly, and monthly study plans, along with strategies for allocating your time efficiently. Additionally, you will find tools for assessing your current knowledge and setting realistic, SMART (Specific, Measurable, Achievable, Relevant, Time-bound) goals for your exam preparation.

To help you identify areas needing improvement, we include a diagnostic test and tips on interpreting your results. Furthermore, we offer practical advice on balancing work, life, and study, and introduce effective time management techniques like the Pomodoro method.

Whether you are studying full-time or juggling a job, this chapter addresses common challenges and provides strategies to overcome them. By the end of this chapter, you will have a solid foundation and a clear, actionable plan to guide you through your exam preparation, setting you up for success on the Series 7 exam.

1. Detailed Breakdown of Exam Content Areas and Their Weightings

Overview of the major content areas covered in the exam.

As we dive into Chapter 1, let's explore the major content areas covered in the Series 7 exam. This foundational understanding is essential for creating an effective study plan and ultimately mastering the material.

The Series 7 exam, also known as the General Securities Representative Exam, is designed to assess the competency of entry-level representatives to perform their roles in the securities industry. The exam is structured around four major job functions that reflect the critical tasks a registered representative must handle.

Firstly, the exam covers the function of seeking business for the broker-dealer from customers and potential customers. This includes understanding the rules and regulations surrounding public communications and how to attract new clients while maintaining compliance.

Secondly, it examines the process of opening accounts after obtaining and evaluating customers' financial profiles and investment objectives. This area tests your knowledge of the necessary documentation, customer disclosures, and the evaluation of investment suitability based on a client's profile.

The third, and most heavily weighted, function involves providing customers with information about investments, making recommendations, transferring assets, and maintaining appropriate records. This section delves deeply into the knowledge of various securities, investment strategies, and the regulatory requirements for record-keeping and client communication.

Finally, the exam assesses your ability to obtain and verify customers' purchase and sales instructions and agreements, process transactions, and confirm orders. This function is crucial as it tests your practical understanding of executing trades and managing client instructions accurately.

Understanding these content areas will help you prioritize your study efforts effectively. By focusing on these major functions, you can ensure that you are well-prepared to tackle the questions that will appear on the exam.

Specific weightings for each section to prioritize study efforts.

As we continue to explore the Series 7 exam, it's crucial to understand the specific weightings for each section, as this will help you prioritize your study efforts effectively.

The Series 7 exam is divided into four major job functions, each of which is critical to the role of a general securities representative. The largest portion of the exam, making up about 73% of the total questions, focuses on providing customers with information about investments, making recommendations, transferring assets, and maintaining appropriate records. This section is essential because it covers the core activities you will perform daily, from advising clients to managing their portfolios and ensuring compliance with regulations.

Next, approximately 11% of the exam evaluates your ability to obtain and verify customers' purchase and sales instructions and agreements, and to process, complete, and confirm transactions. This section tests your practical knowledge of executing trades and managing transactions efficiently and accurately.

Opening accounts after obtaining and evaluating customers' financial profiles and investment objectives comprises about 9% of the exam. This section ensures you understand the procedures and regulations involved in setting up various types of accounts, from individual and joint accounts to retirement accounts.

Finally, the remaining 7% of the exam is spent seeking business for the broker-dealer from customers and potential customers. This section evaluates your ability to attract and retain clients, an essential skill for building a successful career in securities.

By focusing your study efforts on these weightings, you can allocate your time more efficiently and ensure you are well-prepared for the sections that carry the most weight. Understanding these priorities will guide you in creating a balanced and effective study plan, helping you to cover all necessary content while focusing on the areas that will most impact your success on the exam.

By grasping the distribution of the exam content, you can approach your studies strategically, ensuring you spend ample time on the sections that matter most.

2. Discuss Each Major Topic and Its Relative Importance

Explanation of the significance of each major topic.

Moving forward from our understanding of the Series 7 exam's structure and weightings, it's essential to delve into each major topic and understand its relative importance. This approach will ensure that your study plan is both comprehensive and focused on the areas that matter most.

The Series 7 exam covers a wide range of topics, each integral to the role of a general securities representative. The exam is structured around four primary job functions, each representing critical aspects of the profession.

The largest portion of the exam, comprising about 73%, focuses on providing customers with information about investments, making recommendations, transferring assets, and maintaining appropriate records. This section is the backbone of the exam, as it reflects the core responsibilities of managing client portfolios, ensuring compliance with regulatory requirements, and making informed investment decisions. Mastery of this section is crucial because it encompasses the daily tasks that you'll perform, from advising clients on investment opportunities to executing trades and maintaining meticulous records.

Another significant section, making up around 11% of the exam, assesses your ability to obtain and verify customers' purchase and sales instructions and agreements, process transactions, and confirm orders. This area tests your practical skills in executing trades and handling client instructions accurately and efficiently, which are fundamental to maintaining client trust and operational integrity.

Opening accounts after obtaining and evaluating customers' financial profiles and investment objectives constitutes about 9% of the exam. This section ensures that you understand the procedures and regulations involved in setting up different types of accounts, whether individual, joint, or retirement accounts. It's vital because it sets the stage for all subsequent interactions with the client.

Finally, seeking business for the broker-dealer from customers and potential customers accounts for the remaining 7%. This section evaluates your ability to attract and retain clients, which is essential for building a sustainable career in securities. It tests your understanding of compliance and regulatory frameworks while effectively communicating with potential clients.

Insights into which topics are more frequently tested.

Continuing from our discussion on the structure and significance of the Series 7 exam topics, it's vital to understand which areas are frequently tested. This insight will help you focus your study efforts more effectively, ensuring you're well-prepared for the exam's most challenging sections.

One of the most heavily tested areas is options. Questions related to options often require a deep understanding of various strategies and calculations, which can be complex and time-consuming. Mastery of options is crucial because these questions test not only your theoretical knowledge but also your ability to apply that knowledge in practical scenarios.

Another critical area is customer recommendations and suitability. This section assesses your ability to evaluate a client's financial profile and make appropriate investment recommendations. Understanding the nuances of different investment vehicles and how they align with client objectives is fundamental to excelling in this part of the exam.

Municipal securities also feature prominently in the Series 7 exam. Questions on this topic cover the issuance, trading, and tax considerations of municipal bonds. These can be particularly challenging due to the unique features and regulations governing municipal securities compared to corporate bonds.

Taxation and retirement plans are other significant areas of focus. These topics test your knowledge of various tax treatments and the specifics of different retirement accounts. Given their complexity and importance in financial planning, proficiency in these subjects is essential.

Finally, the handling and servicing of customer accounts are frequently tested. This section includes questions on the procedures for opening and maintaining different types of accounts, ensuring compliance with regulatory requirements, and managing client transactions effectively.

By concentrating your study efforts on these frequently tested topics, you can prioritize your preparation and improve your chances of success. Understanding the relative importance of each section allows you to allocate your time and resources more efficiently, ensuring a well-rounded and thorough preparation for the Series 7 exam.

3. Provide a Pie Chart or Graphical Representation of the Exam Content

Visual aids to illustrate the distribution of exam content.

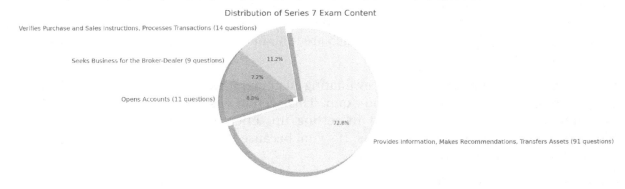

Distribution of Series 7 Exam Content

Understanding the distribution of content in the Series 7 exam is crucial for effective preparation. To give you a clear visual representation, here's a pie chart that illustrates how the exam content is divided among its major sections.

As you can see, the largest portion of the exam, comprising approximately 73%, focuses on providing customers with information about investments, making recommendations, transferring assets, and maintaining appropriate records. This section is the heart of the exam, reflecting the daily responsibilities of a general securities representative.

The next significant section, making up about 11%, covers the verification of purchase and sales instructions, processing transactions, and confirming orders. This area tests your practical skills in executing trades and managing client instructions efficiently and accurately.

Opening accounts after obtaining and evaluating customers' financial profiles and investment objectives constitutes around 9% of the exam. This part ensures that you understand the procedures and regulations involved in setting up different types of accounts.

Finally, seeking business for the broker-dealer from customers and potential customers accounts for the remaining 7%. This section evaluates your ability to attract and retain clients, which is essential for building a successful career in securities.

This visual breakdown helps prioritize your study efforts, ensuring you spend adequate time on the most heavily weighted sections while not neglecting the smaller ones. By using this pie chart as a guide, you can create a balanced and focused study plan, making your preparation for the Series 7 exam more efficient and effective.

4. Strategies for Creating a Personalized Study Schedule

Step-by-step guidance on developing a study plan.

Creating a personalized study schedule is a critical step in preparing for the Series 7 exam. A well-structured plan not only helps you cover all necessary material but also ensures that you do so in an efficient and manageable way. Here's how to develop a study schedule that fits your needs and maximizes your study time.

Start by understanding your peak study times. Identify the times of day when you are most alert and productive. This self-awareness allows you to schedule the most challenging tasks during these periods, making your study sessions more effective.

Balance is key. Spread your study sessions evenly throughout the week to avoid cramming. This approach helps ensure comprehensive coverage of all subjects without overwhelming yourself right before the exam. Incorporate both short-term daily goals and long-term weekly objectives to maintain steady progress.

Use active learning techniques to enhance retention and understanding. Methods such as summarizing information, teaching concepts to others, and applying knowledge to practical situations can make your study sessions more interactive and engaging.

Incorporate breaks into your schedule to prevent burnout. Short, regular breaks during study sessions can improve focus and productivity. For instance, the Pomodoro Technique, which involves 25-minute study intervals followed by 5-minute breaks, can help maintain high levels of concentration. Tools like Pomodone can automate these intervals, integrating with task management apps to streamline your study routine.

Utilize technology to stay organized and efficient. Apps like Google Calendar for scheduling, Todoist for task management, and Forest for maintaining focus can be incredibly helpful. Google Calendar provides a visual representation of your time, Todoist helps prioritize tasks and track progress, and Forest gamifies the act of staying focused by growing virtual trees during study sessions.

Rewards play a motivational role in your study process. Set small rewards for achieving study milestones, which can significantly boost your motivation and commitment. This positive reinforcement encourages sustained effort and makes the study process more enjoyable.

Regularly monitor your progress and be flexible. Keep a study log to record what you've covered, the time spent studying, and any challenges encountered. This documentation helps identify areas needing improvement and allows for adjustments to your study plan

Techniques for tailoring the study schedule to individual needs.

As we continue our journey through creating an effective study plan, it's crucial to understand how to tailor your schedule to your individual needs. Personalizing your study routine involves recognizing your unique learning style and preferences, which can significantly enhance your learning efficiency and retention.

Start by identifying your learning style. People generally fall into one of three categories: visual, auditory, or kinesthetic learners. Visual learners benefit from diagrams, charts, and written notes. They thrive on organized and color-coded information. Auditory learners, on the other hand, grasp information best through listening. They benefit from discussions, audio recordings, and explaining concepts out loud. Kinesthetic learners need hands-on experiences. They learn best by doing, using physical activities to grasp concepts.

Once you understand your learning style, you can tailor your study methods accordingly. For example, visual learners might use mind maps, highlight key points in different colors, and watch educational videos. Auditory learners might record themselves reading notes aloud, join study groups, or use mnemonic devices. Kinesthetic learners could engage in role-playing activities, conduct experiments, or use models and real-world examples to understand abstract concepts.

Adaptive learning technologies can also play a pivotal role in personalizing your study schedule. Tools that adjust the difficulty and type of content based on your responses can ensure you focus on areas needing improvement, enhancing your overall learning experience. Incorporating tools like Google Calendar for scheduling, Todoist for task management, and Forest for maintaining focus can streamline your study routine and keep you organized.

Moreover, integrating breaks and rewards into your study schedule is essential to prevent burnout and maintain high levels of concentration. Short, regular breaks allow your brain to recharge, while rewards for reaching milestones can significantly boost motivation and commitment.

Regularly monitor your progress and remain flexible with your schedule. Continuous assessment and feedback help you identify areas needing adjustment and ensure you're on track to meet your goals. This dynamic approach allows you to stay responsive to your evolving needs and circumstances.

5. Include Templates for Daily, Weekly, and Monthly Study Plans

Ready-to-use templates for organizing study time.

Utilizing ready-to-use templates can be a game-changer for ensuring your study time is well-organized and effective. These templates are designed to streamline your study sessions, helping you stay on track and maximize your productivity.

One great resource is Brainscape, which offers a suite of customizable study planners and exam countdown templates. These templates in Google Sheets help you capture daily learning goals and work towards your deadlines systematically. They come in two main types: daily planners that break down each day into 15 or 30-minute intervals and exam countdown planners that allow you to plot out the topics you need to cover in the days, weeks, and months leading up to an exam. You can tailor these templates to fit your unique needs, ensuring that every study session is productive and stress-free

Another excellent option is the free study planner templates from Notion. These templates provide a holistic approach to organizing your courses, keeping track of assignments, prepping for exams, and conducting thorough research. Notion's templates are designed to help you immerse yourself in focused learning, ensuring you stay ahead in your academic journey. With features that allow you to track your progress and prioritize your goals, these templates can help you easily achieve academic excellence

Additionally, Thegoodocs offers a variety of study schedule templates in Google Docs and Google Sheets. These templates are visually appealing and easy to use, designed to help you plan your study sessions efficiently. They include customizable fields to add your classes, homework, and other tasks, allowing you to organize your study time effectively

Examples of daily, weekly, and monthly plans.

Creating an effective study schedule involves planning and implementing daily, weekly, and monthly plans that align with your academic goals. Let's explore how to structure your study time across different timeframes.

For a daily study plan, you might start your day clearly focusing on your goals. Begin with a morning session dedicated to the most challenging subjects when your mind is fresh. For instance, from 9 AM to 12 PM, you could allocate time for mathematics or any other difficult subject. Take a short break, then continue with another session focusing on a different topic, like science, from 1 PM to 3 PM. Finally, reserve the late afternoon for lighter tasks, such as reviewing notes or reading.

Weekly plans require a broader approach, ensuring all subjects receive adequate attention. A typical weekly plan might involve setting aside specific days for different subjects. For example, Monday and Wednesday could be dedicated to STEM subjects, Tuesday and Thursday for humanities, and Friday for elective courses or review sessions. Each study block should be followed by breaks to avoid burnout, and weekends can be used for reviewing the week's material and preparing for upcoming assignments or tests

A monthly plan provides a macro view, helping you track long-term goals and deadlines. Begin by marking all exam dates, project deadlines, and important school events on a calendar. Allocate weeks to focus on particular subjects or units. For example, the first week of the month could be devoted to preparing for a major math test, while the second week focuses on an upcoming science project. This approach ensures you cover all necessary material without last-minute cramming

6. Discuss How to Allocate Time Based on Personal Strengths and Weaknesses

Methods for identifying strengths and weaknesses.

As you continue to refine your study plan, identifying your strengths and weaknesses becomes a crucial step in optimizing your learning process. Knowing where you excel and where you need improvement allows you to tailor your study strategies effectively.

Start with a self-assessment. Reflect on your study habits, considering questions like: Do you have a consistent study schedule? Are your study sessions productive? Are there subjects where you consistently perform well or struggle? This reflection helps pinpoint specific areas for improvement and strengths to leverage. You can use tools like the Character Strengths Test from VIA Institute on Character to evaluate your strengths and weaknesses objectively. This test provides insights into your strongest traits, which you can then use to bolster your study habits

Another effective method is to analyze your past academic performance. Review your grades and feedback from previous exams and assignments. Identify patterns in subjects or types of questions where you excel or face difficulties. This analysis helps you understand the areas requiring more focus and the study techniques that work best for you. Regularly reviewing your notes and reflecting on your progress can also highlight strengths and areas needing improvement

Seeking feedback from teachers, mentors, or peers can provide valuable insights. They can offer perspectives on your study habits, pointing out strengths you might not recognize and weaknesses you may overlook. This external feedback complements your self-assessment, giving you a more comprehensive understanding of your academic abilities

Another crucial step is adapting your study environment based on your strengths and weaknesses. Ensure your study space is conducive to learning, minimizing distractions, and optimizing your focus. Whether it's organizing your notes more effectively or adjusting your study schedule to align with your peak productivity times, these changes can significantly impact your academic performance.

Strategies for focusing study efforts on weaker areas

Focusing your study efforts on weaker areas is a strategic approach to ensure a balanced and effective preparation for the Series 7 exam. Here are some methods to help you hone in on your weaknesses and turn them into strengths.

Start by conducting a self-assessment to identify your starting point. This can involve taking diagnostic tests or practice exams to pinpoint specific areas where you struggle. For instance, you might notice consistent difficulties with options strategies or certain regulatory topics. Tools like the PSAT or other diagnostic assessments can provide detailed feedback on sub-scores, highlighting specific skill sets that need improvement (CollegeVine, 2023).

Once you've identified your weak areas, develop creative ways to practice and reinforce these concepts. For example, using educational apps or platforms like Khan Academy can offer targeted practice questions and explanations. Additionally, integrating a "formula of the day" for mathematical concepts or a "word of the day" for vocabulary can help solidify your understanding gradually (CollegeVine, 2023).

Engaging in metacognitive strategies can also be highly beneficial. Metacognition involves being aware of your own learning process, asking yourself questions like "What do I already know about this topic?" and "What is confusing me?" This reflective practice helps you monitor your understanding and adjust your study methods accordingly. Tools like Brainscape use adaptive learning techniques to focus more on concepts you struggle with, ensuring efficient use of your study time (Brainscape Academy, 2023).

Incorporating feedback into your study routine is another powerful strategy. Seek out feedback from teachers, peers, or even through self-assessment tools. Understanding where you went wrong in practice tests and addressing those mistakes can significantly improve your performance. Constructive feedback helps you focus on areas that need improvement and provides specific actions to take (School Life Diaries, 2023).

Moreover, using visual aids like flowcharts can simplify complex concepts and enhance your understanding. Flowcharts break down information into manageable parts, making it easier to follow and retain. This method is particularly effective for visual learners who benefit from seeing how different pieces of information connect (TechJockey, 2023).

Finally, fostering a positive mindset and staying motivated is crucial. Recognize your progress and celebrate small achievements to keep yourself encouraged. Remember, transforming your weaknesses into strengths is a gradual process that requires patience and persistence. By using these strategies, you can build a robust study plan that effectively addresses your weak areas and thoroughly prepares you for the Series 7 exam.

7. Assessing Current Knowledge and Setting Realistic Goals

Tools for evaluating current understanding of exam topics.

Evaluating your understanding of exam topics is critical in effective study planning. Using a variety of tools can help you gain a comprehensive view of your strengths and weaknesses, ensuring a targeted approach to your preparation.

One of the most effective tools for this purpose is diagnostic assessments. These tests provide a detailed analysis of your current knowledge, highlighting areas that need improvement. Platforms like Quizizz and Formative allow you to create customized quizzes that can assess your understanding in real time. By identifying the questions you consistently get wrong, you can pinpoint specific topics that require more attention

Another valuable tool is the use of adaptive learning platforms like Brainscape. This tool uses spaced repetition and confidence-based assessments to ensure you focus on areas where your knowledge is weakest. As you rate your confidence in your answers, the system adjusts the review frequency, helping reinforce learning in areas you struggle with

For a more interactive approach, tools like Nearpod and Mentimeter offer engaging ways to measure understanding through interactive lessons, polls, and quizzes. These platforms provide immediate feedback, allowing you to adjust your study strategies on the fly. Nearpod, in particular, integrates with various educational resources, offering a flexible and comprehensive way to track your progress

Additionally, tools like Quizlet Live can turn studying into a collaborative and competitive game, making it easier to stay motivated while identifying weak areas. This gamified approach can be particularly effective in retaining information and making study sessions more enjoyable

Guidelines for setting achievable study goals.

Setting achievable study goals is a crucial part of your preparation process, ensuring you stay focused and motivated. One effective method is using the SMART framework, which stands for Specific, Measurable, Achievable, Relevant, and Time-bound goals. This structured approach helps you create clear and realistic objectives, providing a solid roadmap to follow.

Start by being specific about what you want to achieve. Instead of setting a vague goal like "study more," define what you need to study and the specific outcomes you desire. For instance, aim to "complete all practice problems in the options trading chapter by Friday." This specificity makes it easier to plan and track your progress.

Next, make your goals measurable. Determine how you will track your progress and know when you have achieved your goal. If your goal is to improve your score on practice exams, set a target score you aim to reach. This could be "increase my practice test score from 70% to 85% within the next month." Measurable goals provide tangible milestones to aim for, helping you stay focused and motivated.

Your goals should also be achievable, meaning they should be realistic given your current resources and constraints. Assess your current study habits, available time, and other commitments to set goals that are challenging yet attainable. This prevents setting yourself up for failure and helps maintain a positive momentum.

Ensure your goals are relevant to your broader academic or career aspirations. Align them with your long-term objectives, such as passing the Series 7 exam to advance your career in finance. Relevance ensures your goals are meaningful and worth the effort.

Finally, time-bound goals have clear deadlines, which help maintain a sense of urgency and priority. Break your larger goals into smaller tasks with specific deadlines. For example, you might set a goal to "finish reading and summarizing the regulations chapter by the end of the week." This approach helps you manage your time effectively and keeps you on track.

Implementing and tracking your goals is crucial. Use tools like planners, calendars, or goal-setting apps to monitor your progress. Regularly review and adjust your goals as needed to reflect any changes in your schedule or priorities. Celebrating small achievements along the way can also boost your motivation and confidence, reinforcing your commitment to your study plan.

Conclusion of Chapter One

This chapter delved into the essential components for preparing for the Series 7 exam. We began by understanding the structure of the exam, focusing on the major content areas and their respective weightings. This foundation is crucial for creating an effective study plan, ensuring that you allocate your time and efforts where they are most needed.

We then explored the importance of identifying your strengths and weaknesses. By using tools such as diagnostic tests and self-assessments, you can tailor your study efforts to address gaps in your knowledge, turning weaknesses into strengths. We also discussed strategies for focusing on these weaker areas, emphasizing the need for adaptive learning techniques and seeking feedback.

A significant portion of the chapter was dedicated to setting achievable study goals. Utilizing the SMART framework, you can create specific, measurable, achievable, relevant, and time-bound goals that clearly guide your study journey. Implementing these goals with detailed action plans and regularly monitoring your progress ensures that you stay on track and make necessary adjustments along the way.

Finally, we highlighted the importance of using ready-to-use templates and tools for organizing study time. Integrating these resources into your routine can enhance your study efficiency, maintain a balanced schedule, and ensure comprehensive coverage of all necessary material.

Chapter Two will guide you through the crucial regulatory frameworks and ethical considerations governing the financial industry as we move forward. Understanding the roles of key regulatory bodies such as FINRA and the SEC is vital for anyone aspiring to become a registered representative.

Introduction to Chapter 2

Chapter Two delves into the essential regulatory frameworks and ethical principles that govern the financial industry. This chapter is crucial for understanding the legal and moral responsibilities of a registered representative. We will explore the roles and regulations set by key bodies such as the Financial Industry Regulatory Authority (FINRA) and the Securities and Exchange Commission (SEC), which are fundamental in maintaining the integrity and stability of the financial markets.

You will gain insights into critical regulations, including Regulation Best Interest, Know Your Customer (KYC), and Suitability. These rules ensure that financial professionals act in the best interests of their clients, understand their financial needs, and recommend suitable investment products. Through real-world examples, you will see how these regulations are applied in practice, helping you grasp their practical implications.

Ethics play a vital role in financial services, and this chapter will highlight the importance of ethical behavior. By examining case studies of ethical dilemmas, you will learn how to navigate complex moral issues and understand the severe consequences of unethical conduct.

Additionally, we will cover the requirements and documentation needed for different types of customer accounts, emphasizing the importance of privacy regulations and information security. This section ensures you are well-prepared to handle client information responsibly and comply with legal standards.

Lastly, we will explore Anti-Money Laundering (AML) and Know Your Customer (KYC) procedures, which are critical in preventing financial crimes. You will learn the purpose and importance of these regulations, step-by-step procedures for customer identification, and how to recognize and report suspicious activities.

By the end of this chapter, you will have a comprehensive understanding of the regulatory and ethical landscape of the financial industry, equipping you with the knowledge to perform your duties with integrity and compliance.

FINRA and SEC regulations

Explain the roles of FINRA and SEC in the financial industry

In this chapter, we explore the regulatory landscape of the financial industry, focusing on the roles and regulations established by the Financial Industry Regulatory Authority (FINRA) and the Securities and Exchange Commission (SEC). Understanding the functions and distinctions between these two regulatory bodies is crucial for any aspiring financial professional.

FINRA, a self-regulatory organization, operates under the oversight of the SEC. It was created in 2007 from the merger of the National Association of Securities Dealers (NASD) and the regulatory arm of the New York Stock Exchange. FINRA's primary role is to regulate broker-dealers and their registered representatives, ensuring that they comply with federal securities laws and adhere to ethical practices. It oversees the licensing process, including administering exams such as the Series 7, and ensures that broker-dealers operate in a manner that protects investors and maintains market integrity

The SEC, on the other hand, is a federal government agency established in 1934 in response to the stock market crash of 1929 and the subsequent Great Depression. Its mission is to protect investors, maintain fair and efficient markets, and facilitate capital formation. The SEC has broad regulatory and enforcement powers, overseeing securities exchanges, brokerage firms, investment advisors, and mutual funds. It enforces federal securities laws to prevent market manipulation and fraud, and it requires public companies to disclose financial information transparently to ensure that investors can make informed decisions

While both FINRA and the SEC aim to protect investors and ensure market integrity, their scopes differ. FINRA focuses specifically on the behavior of broker-dealers, enforcing rules and regulations pertinent to their operations. The SEC has a wider jurisdiction, overseeing the entire securities industry and enforcing laws that govern market activities, corporate disclosures, and investor protections

Discuss key rules such as Regulation Best Interest, Know Your Customer and Suitability

As we dive deeper into the regulatory frameworks that shape the financial industry, it's essential to understand some of the key rules that govern the behavior of financial professionals. Three critical regulations are Regulation Best Interest (Reg BI), Know Your Customer (KYC), and Suitability. These rules ensure that broker-dealers act in their clients' best interests, understand their clients' financial situations, and recommend appropriate investment strategies.

Regulation Best Interest, often referred to as Reg BI, was introduced by the SEC to enhance the standard of conduct for broker-dealers. This rule mandates that when broker-dealers make a recommendation to a retail customer regarding a securities transaction, they must act in the best interest of the customer and not place their own financial interests ahead of the customer's. Reg BI requires broker-dealers to disclose all material facts related to conflicts of interest and the scope and terms of their relationship with the customer. It also obliges them to exercise care, skill, and diligence when making recommendations, ensuring that the advice provided aligns with the customer's needs and objectives (FINRA, 2023; SEC, 2023).

The Know Your Customer (KYC) rule is another foundational regulation that requires broker-dealers to gather essential information about their clients before making any recommendations or opening accounts. This information includes the client's financial situation, investment experience, and objectives. The purpose of KYC is to ensure that any recommendations or transactions are suitable for the client's specific circumstances. By understanding their clients thoroughly, financial professionals can tailor their advice and services to meet individual needs effectively (FINRA, 2023).

Suitability, governed by FINRA Rule 2111, complements the KYC rule by obligating broker-dealers to ensure that any recommended transaction or investment strategy is suitable for the customer based on the information gathered through KYC processes. This rule requires financial professionals to perform due diligence in understanding their clients' investment profiles and to recommend products that align with their financial goals and risk tolerance. Suitability is crucial in protecting investors from inappropriate investment recommendations that could jeopardize their financial well-being (FINRA, 2023).

Together, these regulations—Reg BI, KYC, and Suitability—create a robust framework that prioritizes investor protection and ethical conduct in the financial industry. They ensure that financial professionals act in their clients' best interests, provide personalized and suitable advice, and maintain transparency about any conflicts of interest. Understanding and adhering to these rules is essential for anyone aspiring to succeed in the financial services sector, as they form the foundation of trustworthy and effective client relationships.

examples of how these rules apply in real-world scenarios

To illustrate how Regulation Best Interest (Reg BI), Know Your Customer (KYC), and Suitability rules apply in real-world scenarios, let's delve into specific examples that highlight their practical implications and enforcement.

Consider a scenario involving a broker at a major financial firm. The broker recommends a complex investment product, such as a structured note, to a retail client. Under Reg BI, the broker must ensure that the recommendation is in the client's best interest. This involves conducting thorough due diligence on the structured note, disclosing all material facts, including any potential conflicts of interest, and documenting the decision-making process. For instance, the broker must compare the structured note with other reasonably available investment alternatives and justify why this particular product is suitable for the client's financial situation and investment objectives

In one enforcement case, Merrill Lynch was cited for Reg BI violations when it failed to adequately disclose conflicts of interest related to proprietary products. The firm had recommended these products without considering less costly alternatives, failing the care and conflict obligations mandated by Reg BI. This case underscores the importance of transparency and due diligence, emphasizing that brokers must not merely "check the box" but genuinely prioritize the client's best interests

The Know Your Customer (KYC) rule also plays a crucial role in ensuring suitable recommendations. Imagine a client approaches a broker to invest in high-yield bonds. The broker must first gather comprehensive information about the client's financial situation, risk tolerance, and investment goals. This includes understanding the client's income, net worth, investment experience, and liquidity needs. Only after obtaining and verifying this information can the broker make a suitable recommendation. For example, if the client is a retiree with a low-risk tolerance, recommending high-yield bonds without thorough consideration and documentation would violate the KYC rule

Suitability rules, governed by FINRA Rule 2111, require that any recommended investment strategy or transaction be suitable for the client based on the information obtained through KYC procedures. For instance, a broker recommending leveraged ETFs to a conservative investor would need to demonstrate that such a high-risk investment aligns with the investor's profile. If the broker fails to assess the client's risk tolerance and investment objectives adequately, this could lead to enforcement actions for suitability violations. An example of this is when a broker was disciplined for recommending speculative options strategies to clients without properly evaluating their suitability, leading to significant financial losses for the clients (FINRA, 2023).

These real-world examples demonstrate how critical it is for brokers to adhere to Reg BI, KYC, and Suitability rules

Ethical considerations in the financial industry

Discuss the importance of ethics in financial services

As we delve deeper into the ethical considerations in the financial industry, it's essential to grasp the significance of maintaining high ethical standards. Ethical behavior in financial services is not just about compliance with laws and regulations; it involves a commitment to honesty, transparency, integrity, and fairness. These principles are crucial for fostering trust and stability in financial markets, which ultimately benefits investors, clients, and the broader economy.

The importance of ethics in financial services can be highlighted through several high-profile cases that underscore the consequences of unethical behavior. Take, for example, the infamous Wells Fargo scandal, where employees created millions of fake accounts to meet aggressive sales targets. This unethical practice not only damaged the bank's reputation but also led to significant financial penalties and a loss of trust among consumers. This case illustrates how short-term profit motives can lead to long-term damage when ethical standards are compromised

Another prominent example is the collapse of Enron, which was once considered one of the most innovative companies in the U.S. Enron's executives engaged in widespread accounting fraud to hide the company's financial troubles and inflate its stock price. When the fraud was exposed, Enron filed for bankruptcy, leading to massive losses for shareholders and employees. The fallout from Enron's unethical practices led to the creation of the Sarbanes-Oxley Act, which imposed stricter regulatory requirements to enhance corporate accountability and prevent similar scandals

Ethics in finance also extends to the handling of insider information. Insider trading, where individuals use non-public information to gain an unfair advantage in the stock market, is illegal and unethical. For example, the case of Raj Rajaratnam, the Galleon Group's founder, highlights insider trading's severe consequences. Rajaratnam was convicted of securities fraud and conspiracy, receiving an 11-year prison sentence. This case underscored the importance of ethical behavior and the need for robust enforcement of insider trading laws to maintain market integrity .

Moreover, ethical considerations are crucial in the realm of financial advisory. Financial advisors must adhere to fiduciary standards, putting their clients' interests above their own. An advisor who recommends financial products primarily for personal gain, rather than the client's benefit, breaches ethical standards. For instance, advisors who push high-commission products without disclosing conflicts of interest are acting unethically. Clients rely on advisors for trustworthy guidance, and any breach of this trust can lead to significant financial harm and a loss of confidence in the advisory profession

Explain the consequences of unethical behavior

Understanding the severe consequences of unethical behavior in the financial industry is crucial for maintaining integrity and trust. The ramifications can be extensive, affecting individuals, organizations, and the broader economy.

One significant example is the case of Bernard Madoff, whose Ponzi scheme is perhaps the most infamous in financial history. Madoff's fraudulent investment firm promised and delivered unusually high and consistent returns, which attracted a significant number of investors. However, the firm was not actually investing the money, but rather paying returns to older investors using the capital from new investors. When the scheme collapsed in 2008, it resulted in losses estimated at around $65 billion. Madoff's actions led to his imprisonment for 150 years and highlighted the devastating impact of such unethical behavior on thousands of individuals, including charities and pension funds that trusted his firm

The financial crisis of 2007-2008 offers another stark example of the consequences of unethical behavior. Major financial institutions, driven by greed and short-term profit motives, engaged in reckless lending and investment practices. This included issuing subprime mortgages to unqualified borrowers and packaging these risky loans into complex securities sold to investors. The subsequent collapse of these financial products led to massive losses, a severe global recession, and the loss of millions of jobs and homes. This crisis underscored the far-reaching impact of unethical practices in finance and led to significant regulatory reforms, such as the Dodd-Frank Act, aimed at preventing future misconduct

Insider trading is another area where unethical behavior can have severe consequences. The case of Raj Rajaratnam, the founder of the Galleon Group, serves as a prominent example. Rajaratnam used non-public information to make profitable trades, gaining an unfair advantage in the stock market. This unethical practice not only resulted in financial penalties and a prison sentence for Rajaratnam but also damaged the integrity of financial markets. The case reinforced the importance of adhering to ethical standards and the severe repercussions of violating insider trading laws

Moreover, ethical breaches can also lead to reputational damage that is often irreparable. For instance, the Wells Fargo scandal, where employees created millions of unauthorized accounts to meet sales targets, resulted in substantial fines, a loss of customer trust, and a tarnished corporate image. This case demonstrated how unethical behavior, driven by aggressive corporate goals, can undermine a firm's reputation and long-term success

Customer account requirements and documentation

Detail the types of customer accounts and their specific requirements

Beyond these essential account types, it's important to be aware of specialized accounts that cater to specific financial needs, such as retirement accounts and custodial accounts. As we will discuss in Chapter 7, understanding these accounts is crucial for tailoring investment strategies to individual client needs.

Retirement accounts, like Individual Retirement Accounts (IRAs) and 401(k) plans, have unique rules and regulations regarding contributions, withdrawals, and tax treatment. For example, contributions to a Traditional IRA may be tax-deductible, while qualified withdrawals from a Roth IRA are tax-free. Custodial accounts, like Uniform Gifts to Minors Act (UGMA) and Uniform Transfers to Minors Act (UTMA) accounts, are designed to hold assets for minors until they reach the age of majority. These accounts have specific rules regarding who can control the assets and how they can be used.

The documentation required for these specialized accounts will typically include the same information as for individual accounts, along with additional forms specific to the type of account. For example, a 401(k) plan participant may need to complete beneficiary designation forms, while a custodial account will require information on the minor and the custodian.

Explain necessary documentation for account opening and maintenance

s we've discussed, different account types require specific documentation. For individual and joint accounts, you'll typically need each person's Social Security number (or Taxpayer Identification Number for non-U.S. residents), date of birth, and contact information. You'll also need employment details, which could include occupation, employer name and address, and length of employment. This is important not just for identification purposes, but also to comply with suitability regulations as we'll explore further in Chapter 7.

Remember the new account form we mentioned earlier? This is where the client outlines their financial goals and risk tolerance. This isn't just paperwork – it's a critical tool for you to understand your client's needs and ensure the recommendations you make are suitable for them. For example, a client nearing retirement may have different investment objectives than a young professional just starting their career.

For corporate accounts, you'll need a corporate resolution, a legal document that identifies the company and the individuals authorized to act on its behalf. You might also need a copy of the company's articles of incorporation and bylaws, along with recent financial statements to assess the company's financial health.

Trust accounts require a copy of the trust agreement, the legal document that establishes the trust and outlines its terms. You'll also need information on the trustee, the person or institution responsible for managing the trust assets, and the beneficiary, the person for whom the trust is established.

In addition to these basic requirements, you may need additional documentation depending on the specific circumstances of the client. For example, if the client is a politically exposed person (PEP), a term you'll encounter in Chapter 2, there may be additional due diligence requirements to meet anti-money laundering regulations.

It's also crucial to remember that the account opening process doesn't end with the initial documentation. Account maintenance is an ongoing process that requires regular updates to client information. This could include changes in employment status, financial situation, or investment objectives. For example, if a client experiences a significant life event like a marriage or the birth of a child, their investment goals may change. It's your responsibility as a registered representative to stay informed about these changes and ensure that the client's investment portfolio remains aligned with their needs.

The documentation required for account opening and maintenance is more than just a compliance exercise. It's a vital part of building a strong client relationship based on trust and understanding. By thoroughly understanding your client's financial situation and investment goals, you can provide personalized advice and recommendations that will help them achieve their long-term financial objectives.

Discuss privacy regulations and information security

Given the sensitive nature of the financial information collected during the account opening and maintenance process, privacy regulations and information security are of paramount importance. As we've discussed, maintaining accurate and up-to-date client information is not only crucial for compliance but also for providing suitable investment advice. But with this responsibility comes the obligation to safeguard this data with the utmost care.

In the United States, the Gramm-Leach-Bliley Act (GLBA), enacted in 1999, is the cornerstone of financial privacy regulation. GLBA requires financial institutions, including broker-dealers like those employing Series 7 license holders, to explain their information-sharing practices to their customers and to safeguard sensitive data.

The Federal Trade Commission (FTC) enforces the GLBA through its Safeguards Rule, which mandates that financial institutions develop a written information security plan that describes how they will protect client information. This plan must include measures for protecting data against unauthorized access, alteration, destruction, or disclosure. For example, firms might use encryption to protect data in transit and at rest, implement access controls to limit who can view sensitive information, and conduct regular security training for employees.

One notable example of the importance of information security is the Equifax data breach in 2017. In this incident, hackers exploited a vulnerability in Equifax's systems to gain access to the personal and financial data of nearly 148 million people. The breach had far-reaching consequences, including the theft of Social Security numbers, birth dates, and credit card information. It highlighted the need for robust information security measures in the financial industry.

Another critical aspect of privacy regulations is the requirement for firms to provide clients with a clear and conspicuous privacy notice that explains how their information will be collected, used, and shared. This notice must be provided to clients before any personal information is collected and annually thereafter.

As a registered representative, you have a responsibility to ensure that you are familiar with your firm's privacy policies and procedures. You must also take steps to protect client information from unauthorized access or disclosure. This includes using strong passwords, avoiding public Wi-Fi networks when accessing sensitive data, and reporting any suspected security breaches to your firm's compliance department.

Remember, privacy regulations and information security are not just about compliance; they are about protecting the trust that clients place in you and your firm. By upholding the highest standards of data security and privacy, you can demonstrate your commitment to ethical conduct and build strong, lasting relationships with your clients.

Anti-money laundering (AML) and know your customer (KYC) procedures

Explain the purpose and importance of AML and KYC regulations

As we delve deeper into customer account requirements and documentation, it's crucial to highlight the significance of Anti-Money Laundering (AML) and Know Your Customer (KYC) regulations. These regulations, interwoven with the information gathering process we've just discussed, form a robust framework to safeguard the integrity of the financial system.

Why are AML and KYC regulations so important? Their primary purpose is to prevent financial institutions from being exploited for illicit activities such as money laundering and terrorist financing. Money laundering, as you'll recall from Chapter 2, involves disguising the origins of illegally obtained funds to make them appear legitimate. This can have far-reaching consequences, including the funding of criminal enterprises, distortion of economic markets, and even the undermining of political stability.

KYC regulations require financial institutions to verify the identity of their clients and understand the nature of their financial activities. This involves collecting and verifying information such as names, addresses, dates of birth, and Social Security numbers. It may also involve obtaining additional information about the client's source of wealth and the intended use of the account.

AML regulations, on the other hand, focus on detecting and reporting suspicious activities that may indicate money laundering or other financial crimes. This involves monitoring transactions for red flags, such as large cash deposits, unusual wire transfers, or transactions with high-risk countries. Financial institutions are required to report any suspicious activity to the appropriate authorities, such as the Financial Crimes Enforcement Network (FinCEN) in the United States.

A notable example of the importance of AML regulations is the case of HSBC, which in 2012 was fined a record $1.9 billion for failing to adequately monitor transactions for suspicious activity. The bank was accused of facilitating money laundering by Mexican drug cartels and other criminal organizations. This case serves as a stark reminder of the consequences of non-compliance with AML regulations.

The implementation of AML and KYC regulations is not without its challenges. These regulations can be complex and costly to implement, and they may sometimes create friction for clients who may feel that their privacy is being invaded. However, the benefits of these regulations far outweigh the costs. By preventing financial crime, AML and KYC regulations protect the integrity of the financial system, safeguard investor assets, and promote economic stability.

In the next section, we'll take a closer look at the specific procedures involved in AML and KYC compliance, exploring the steps that financial institutions must take to verify client identities, monitor transactions, and report suspicious activity.

Provide step-by-step procedures for customer identification and verification

Now that we've established the "why" behind AML and KYC regulations, let's dive into the "how." The customer identification program (CIP), a core component of KYC, outlines a step-by-step procedure that financial institutions must follow to verify the identity of their clients.

First, upon account opening, clients are required to provide identifying information, as we've discussed earlier. This typically includes their full legal name, date of birth, residential address, and Social Security number. But it doesn't stop there. To ensure the information's accuracy, firms must verify this information against reliable independent sources.

This verification process can take several forms. One common method is documentary verification, where clients provide official documents such as a government-issued photo ID (like a driver's license or passport) and a proof of address (like a utility bill or bank statement). These documents are then compared against the information provided by the client to ensure consistency.

In addition to documentary verification, financial institutions may also use non-documentary methods to verify client identities. This can include checking information against credit bureaus, public databases, or commercially available databases. Some firms even use biometric verification, such as fingerprint or facial recognition, for added security.

But KYC is not just a one-time event. As we've discussed, ongoing monitoring of client activity is essential to detect any suspicious transactions that could indicate money laundering or other financial crimes. This involves keeping an eye on the volume and frequency of transactions, the types of products being traded, and the geographic locations involved.

For example, if a client suddenly starts making large cash deposits or wire transfers to high-risk countries, this could raise red flags and trigger further investigation. Firms may use automated transaction monitoring systems to scan for such red flags, but they also rely on the vigilance of their employees, including registered representatives like you, to identify any unusual activity.

If suspicious activity is detected, firms are required to file a Suspicious Activity Report (SAR) with FinCEN. SARs are a crucial tool in the fight against financial crime, as they provide valuable information to law enforcement agencies.

The CIP and ongoing monitoring processes may seem like a lot of work, but they are essential for maintaining the integrity of the financial system. By diligently following these procedures, you'll not only be fulfilling your regulatory obligations but also contributing to a safer and more secure financial environment for everyone. Remember, your role as a registered representative goes beyond simply selling financial products; it also involves safeguarding the interests of your clients and the broader financial community.

Discuss red flags for suspicious activity and reporting requirements

Beyond the initial CIP, your role as a registered representative in AML/KYC compliance extends to ongoing vigilance. As we've established, this involves actively monitoring client transactions and behaviors for red flags that could signal illicit activities like money laundering or terrorist financing.

But what exactly are these red flags? They're not always obvious, and they can vary depending on the client's profile and typical financial behavior. However, some common red flags include:

- **Large cash transactions:** Deposits or withdrawals of large sums of cash, especially if they are out of character for the client or if the client seems reluctant to explain the source of the funds. Remember, cash is often the preferred medium for illicit activities because it's difficult to trace.

- **Unusual wire transfers:** Transfers to or from high-risk countries, or transfers that have no apparent business or lawful purpose, can be a cause for concern. For example, if a client who typically invests in domestic stocks suddenly starts wiring money to offshore accounts, this could raise suspicions.

- **Structuring:** This involves breaking down a large transaction into smaller ones to avoid triggering reporting requirements. For example, a client might make multiple cash deposits of just under $10,000 each to avoid the bank's obligation to file a Currency Transaction Report (CTR).

- **Attempts to conceal ownership:** This could involve using shell companies, trusts, or other legal structures to obscure the true ownership of assets. As we discussed in Chapter 2, these structures can be used legitimately, but they can also be misused for illicit purposes.

- **Inconsistencies in information:** Discrepancies between the information provided by the client and the information obtained from independent sources can be a red flag. For example, if a client claims to be employed by a certain company, but a background check reveals no record of their employment, this could be a sign of identity theft or other fraudulent activity.

If you encounter any of these red flags, or if you have any other reason to suspect that a client may be involved in illicit activity, you have a legal and ethical obligation to report your suspicions to your firm's compliance department. In most cases, this will involve filing a Suspicious Activity Report (SAR) with FinCEN. SARs are confidential documents that are used by law enforcement agencies to investigate potential financial crimes.

Filing a SAR is not an accusation of guilt, nor does it necessarily mean that your client will be investigated or prosecuted. It simply means that you have observed activity that you believe warrants further scrutiny. By reporting your suspicions, you are contributing to the overall effort to combat financial crime and protect the integrity of the financial system.

Remember, as a registered representative, you are a gatekeeper for the financial industry. By being vigilant and proactive in identifying and reporting suspicious activity, you play a crucial role in preventing financial crime and protecting the interests of your clients and the broader community.

Summary and Review

In this section, we explored the various types of customer accounts and their specific documentation requirements. We discussed individual, joint, corporate, and trust accounts, as well as specialized accounts like retirement accounts and custodial accounts. We also emphasized the importance of privacy regulations and information security, particularly the Gramm-Leach-Bliley Act (GLBA) and the FTC's Safeguards Rule. Additionally, we delved into the significance of Anti-Money Laundering (AML) and Know Your Customer (KYC) regulations, highlighting the role of customer identification programs (CIPs), ongoing monitoring, and the reporting of suspicious activity.

Test Your Knowledge

1. What are the two main types of joint accounts, and how do they differ in terms of ownership and inheritance?

2. What additional documentation is typically required for corporate accounts compared to individual accounts?

3. What is the main purpose of a trust account, and who are the key parties involved?

4. What are some common red flags that may indicate suspicious activity in a client's account?

5. What is a Suspicious Activity Report (SAR), and when would you be required to file one?

Tips for Applying the Knowledge to Exam Questions

- **Understand the rationale:** Don't just memorize the requirements; understand why they are in place and how they protect investors and the financial system.

- **Pay attention to detail:** Exam questions may test your knowledge of specific document types or verification procedures.

- **Apply the concepts:** Be prepared to analyze scenarios and identify potential red flags for suspicious activity.

Real-World Examples and Case Studies

- **HSBC Case:** The HSBC case, where the bank was fined $1.9 billion for AML violations, highlights the importance of compliance with these regulations.

- **Equifax Data Breach:** The Equifax breach underscores the need for robust information security measures in the financial industry.

By mastering the concepts covered in this section, you'll be well-equipped to handle the customer account requirements you'll encounter in your career as a registered representative. Your diligence in these matters not only ensures compliance but also fosters trust and confidence among your clients, laying the foundation for long-lasting professional relationships.

Chapter 3: Equity Securities and Market Operations

In the vibrant world of finance, equity securities reign supreme, embodying the essence of ownership and opportunity. This chapter is your gateway to understanding the dynamics of these powerful financial instruments and the intricate markets where they are traded. You'll embark on a journey through the diverse landscape of stocks, from the fundamental characteristics of common and preferred shares to the intricacies of rights and warrants.

We'll delve into the bustling arenas of stock exchanges like the NYSE and NASDAQ, where fortunes are made and lost, and explore the alternative trading systems that operate beyond the traditional exchanges. You'll learn about the crucial roles played by market makers and specialists, the gatekeepers of liquidity and order in the markets.

Furthermore, we'll unravel the complexities of order types and execution strategies, equipping you with the knowledge to navigate the markets strategically. You'll gain insights into concepts like price improvement and best execution, ensuring you get the most favorable terms for your trades. We'll even touch upon the exhilarating world of short-term trading strategies like day trading and swing trading, where split-second decisions can yield significant gains.

Finally, we'll shed light on corporate actions, those pivotal events that can reshape a company's stock and impact investor portfolios. You'll learn about stock splits, reverse splits, and the intricacies of dividends, including ex-dividend dates and their effect on stock prices. We'll also explore the world of mergers, acquisitions, and tender offers, events that can trigger seismic shifts in the market landscape.

By the end of this chapter, you'll possess a comprehensive understanding of equity securities and market operations, empowering you to make informed investment decisions and navigate the complexities of the financial markets with confidence.

Learning Objectives

- Differentiate between common stock, preferred stock, rights, and warrants, and understand their unique characteristics.

- Compare and contrast the major stock exchanges (NYSE, NASDAQ) and alternative trading systems.

- Explain the roles of market makers and specialists in facilitating trading and maintaining market liquidity.

- Understand different order types (market, limit, stop) and their appropriate use in various trading scenarios.

- Grasp the concept of price improvement and the importance of best execution.

- Analyze the impact of corporate actions, such as stock splits, dividends, mergers, and acquisitions, on stock prices and investor holdings.

Key Terms and Concepts

- Common stock

- Preferred stock

- Rights

- Warrants

- Stock exchanges (NYSE, NASDAQ)

- Over-the-counter (OTC) markets

- Alternative trading systems (ATS)

- Market makers

- Specialists

- Order matching process

- Market orders

- Limit orders

- Stop orders

- Price improvement

- Best execution

- Day trading

- Swing trading

- Stock splits

- Reverse splits

- Dividends

- Ex-dividend date

- Mergers

- Acquisitions

- Tender offers

Brief overview of the importance of equity securities in the financial markets.

Building on our exploration of account types, documentation, and the critical AML/KYC regulations that ensure market integrity, we now turn our attention to the very heart of these financial transactions: equity securities. These instruments aren't mere abstract concepts; they represent real ownership stakes in companies, fueling economic growth and individual wealth creation.

Equity securities are the lifeblood of the financial markets, providing companies with the capital they need to innovate, expand, and create jobs. When you buy a share of Apple stock, you're not just making an investment; you're becoming a partial owner of one of the world's most innovative companies. Your investment dollars contribute to Apple's research and development efforts, its marketing campaigns, and its global expansion.

For investors, equity securities offer the potential for significant returns through capital appreciation and dividend payments. While the value of a stock can fluctuate based on market conditions and the company's performance, over the long term, the stock market has consistently outperformed other asset classes. For example, the S&P 500, a broad index of 500 large-cap U.S. companies, has delivered an average annual return of around 10% over the past century.

But equity securities are more than just investment vehicles; they are also barometers of economic health. Stock market indices like the Dow Jones Industrial Average and the NASDAQ Composite are closely watched indicators of investor sentiment and economic confidence. When these indices rise, it signals optimism about the future of the economy, while declines can indicate concerns about growth and stability.

Equity securities also play a crucial role in corporate governance. As shareholders, investors have the right to vote on important company decisions, such as electing board members and approving mergers and acquisitions. This gives investors a voice in how companies are run and ensures a degree of accountability.

In essence, equity securities are the engines that drive the modern economy. They provide companies with the fuel they need to grow and innovate, while offering investors the opportunity to share in their success. And by participating in the stock market, investors can not only grow their wealth but also contribute to the overall health and vitality of the economy.

Explanation of how equity securities represent ownership in a company and the potential for growth and income.

As we've established, equity securities are not merely financial instruments; they embody ownership. But what does that truly mean for investors? When you purchase a share of common stock, for example, you're essentially buying a tiny slice of the company's pie. You're not just an investor; you're a shareholder, a part-owner with a vested interest in the company's success.

This ownership stake comes with certain rights and privileges. As a shareholder, you have the right to vote on key company decisions, such as electing board members and approving mergers or acquisitions. You also have the right to receive a portion of the company's profits in the form of dividends, if the company chooses to distribute them.

1. www.numerade.com

But perhaps the most enticing aspect of owning equity securities is the potential for growth and income. When a company thrives, its stock price tends to rise, reflecting increased investor confidence and demand for its shares. If you purchased shares of Amazon in its early days, you'd have witnessed firsthand the power of equity growth. Amazon's stock price has skyrocketed over the years, turning early investors into millionaires.

Dividend payments are another way that equity securities can generate income. While not all companies pay dividends, those that do distribute a portion of their profits to shareholders on a regular basis, typically quarterly. Dividend-paying stocks can be an attractive option for income-seeking investors, providing a steady stream of cash flow.

However, it's important to remember that equity securities also carry risks. The stock market is inherently volatile, and stock prices can fluctuate significantly in response to economic news, company performance, and investor sentiment. There's no guarantee that a stock will go up in value, and it's possible to lose money on your investment.

For example, during the dot-com bubble of the late 1990s, many technology stocks soared to unsustainable heights, only to crash back down to earth when the bubble burst. Investors who bought in at the peak suffered significant losses.

Despite the risks, equity securities have historically been one of the most rewarding asset classes for long-term investors. By carefully researching companies and diversifying their portfolios, investors can mitigate risk and potentially achieve substantial returns over time.

In the following sections, we'll explore the different types of equity securities in more detail, examining their unique characteristics and how they fit into various investment strategies. Whether you're a seasoned investor or just starting out, understanding the nuances of equity securities is essential for making informed decisions and building a successful investment portfolio.

Introduction to the key concepts covered in this chapter, including different types of equity securities, stock markets, order types, and corporate actions.

Now that we've established the significance of equity securities in driving both corporate growth and individual wealth, let's unpack the key concepts that will guide us through this chapter. As aspiring financial professionals, mastering these concepts is not just about passing the Series 7 exam but also about building a solid foundation for a successful career in the securities industry.

First, we'll delve into the diverse world of equity securities. As we've discussed, equity represents ownership, but this ownership can take different forms. We'll explore the differences between **common stock** and **preferred stock**, understanding their distinct rights and privileges. We'll also examine **rights** and **warrants**, which are derivative securities that offer unique opportunities to investors and companies alike.

Next, we'll venture into the bustling **stock markets**, the arenas where these equity securities are traded. We'll focus on the major exchanges, like the **New York Stock Exchange (NYSE)** and the **NASDAQ**, which are home to some of the world's largest and most well-known companies. We'll also explore **over-the-counter (OTC)** markets and **alternative trading systems (ATS)**, where less liquid or smaller-cap stocks are often traded.

To understand how trades are executed in these markets, we'll examine the role of **market makers** and **specialists**, who provide liquidity and ensure orderly trading. We'll also delve into the **order matching process**, understanding how different types of orders, such as **market orders**, **limit orders**, and **stop orders**, are handled.

Understanding how to place and execute trades is essential for any investor, so we'll dedicate a significant portion of this chapter to exploring different **order types** and **execution strategies**. You'll learn when it's best to use a market order versus a limit order, and how stop orders can help you manage risk. We'll also touch upon advanced concepts like **price improvement** and **best execution**, ensuring that you're getting the best possible price for your trades.

Finally, we'll examine **corporate actions**, those significant events that can impact the value of your equity investments. We'll discuss **stock splits** and **reverse splits**, which can affect the number of shares you own and the price per share. We'll also explore **dividends**, the distributions of company profits to shareholders, and the significance of the **ex-dividend date**. And we'll delve into the world of **mergers, acquisitions, and tender offers**, understanding how these corporate maneuvers can create both opportunities and risks for investors.

By the end of this chapter, you'll have a comprehensive understanding of equity securities and market operations, empowering you to make informed investment decisions, navigate the complexities of the markets, and confidently advise your clients as a registered representative.

I. Types of Equity Securities and Their Characteristics

A. Common Stock

Definition of common stock and its significance as the most prevalent form of equity.

Now that we've set the stage for exploring the world of equity securities, let's begin by delving into the most fundamental and widespread type: common stock. Often referred to as the building blocks of the stock market, common stocks represent ownership shares in a corporation. When you purchase a share of common stock, you're essentially becoming a part-owner of that company, with a stake in its assets, profits, and future prospects.

Common stock is the most prevalent form of equity because it's the primary way that companies raise capital from the public. When a company goes public through an initial public offering (IPO), it issues shares of common stock to investors in exchange for capital. This capital can then be used to fund research and development, expand operations, pay down debt, or pursue other strategic initiatives.

For example, when Google went public in 2004, it raised over $1.6 billion by issuing shares of common stock. This influx of capital fueled Google's rapid growth and innovation, ultimately transforming it into one of the most valuable companies in the world.

But the significance of common stock goes beyond just raising capital for companies. It also provides investors with a stake in the company's future. If the company performs well, its stock price is likely to increase, allowing shareholders to profit from their investment. Additionally, many companies pay dividends to their common stockholders, providing a regular stream of income.

The performance of common stock can also reflect the overall health of the economy. Stock market indices, such as the S&P 500, are often used as benchmarks for economic performance. When these indices rise, it generally signals optimism about the economy, while declines can indicate concerns about future growth.

While common stock offers the potential for significant rewards, it's important to remember that it also carries risks. As we discussed earlier, the stock market can be volatile, and stock prices can fluctuate in response to various factors. It's crucial for investors to carefully research companies and diversify their portfolios to mitigate risk.

In the next sections, we will explore the specific rights and privileges associated with common stock ownership, such as voting rights and dividend rights. We will also discuss the role of common stock in various investment strategies and how to evaluate companies before investing in their stock.

Explanation of shareholder rights, including voting rights, dividend rights, and the right to residual assets.

This ownership stake in a company, represented by common stock, isn't just a symbolic gesture; it comes with tangible rights that empower shareholders to participate in the company's decision-making process and potentially reap financial rewards.

One of the most fundamental shareholder rights is the right to vote. Common stockholders typically have one vote per share, which they can exercise at the company's annual shareholder meeting or through proxy voting. This voting power allows shareholders to have a say in crucial matters such as electing the board of directors, approving mergers or acquisitions, and ratifying executive compensation plans. While individual shareholders may not have a significant impact on the outcome of these votes, collectively, they can influence the direction of the company. For instance, in 2017, shareholders of ExxonMobil voted in favor of a proposal requiring the company to disclose more information about the risks of climate change to its business, a landmark decision that demonstrated the growing power of shareholder activism.

Another important shareholder right is the right to receive dividends. When a company generates profits, it can choose to distribute a portion of those profits to shareholders in the form of dividends. The amount and frequency of dividend payments are determined by the company's board of directors and can vary significantly depending on the company's financial performance and dividend policy. For example, companies like Coca-Cola and Procter & Gamble have a long history of consistently paying and increasing dividends, making them attractive to income-seeking investors.

Finally, common stockholders have the right to residual assets. In the unfortunate event of a company's liquidation, after all debts and obligations have been paid, any remaining assets are distributed to shareholders. Common stockholders are last in line to receive these residual assets, behind bondholders and preferred stockholders. However, if the company is successful, the value of these residual assets can be substantial.

These rights – voting, dividends, and residual assets – collectively form the cornerstone of shareholder value. They empower investors to participate in the company's governance, share in its profits, and benefit from its long-term growth.

Understanding these rights is not only essential for passing the Series 7 exam but also for making informed investment decisions. As a registered representative, you'll need to be able to explain these rights to your clients and help them understand the potential benefits and risks of investing in common stock. By doing so, you'll empower them to make investment decisions that align with their financial goals and risk tolerance.

Examples of common stock investments and their role in diversified portfolios.

Now that we've established the rights inherent in common stock ownership, let's illustrate their real-world significance through examples of how these stocks fit into diversified investment portfolios.

Consider a hypothetical investor named Sarah. She's a young professional with a long time horizon and a moderate risk tolerance. Sarah is interested in growing her wealth over time, and she understands that common stocks can offer the potential for significant returns. However, she's also aware of the risks associated with investing in individual stocks, so she wants to diversify her portfolio to mitigate those risks.

To achieve this, Sarah decides to invest in a mix of common stocks from different sectors and industries. She includes shares of well-established companies like Apple, Microsoft, and Johnson & Johnson, which have a history of strong financial performance and consistent dividend payments. These blue-chip stocks provide a solid foundation for her portfolio, offering stability and income.

But Sarah also wants to add some growth potential to her portfolio. She invests in some smaller, faster-growing companies like Tesla and Square, which are disrupting their respective industries and have the potential for significant upside. These growth stocks add a layer of dynamism to her portfolio, although they also come with higher risk.

By diversifying her investments across different sectors and company sizes, Sarah is able to reduce her overall risk. If one sector or company experiences a downturn, the impact on her portfolio is likely to be limited by the performance of her other holdings.

Another investor, John, is nearing retirement and has a lower risk tolerance than Sarah. He's primarily interested in generating income to supplement his retirement savings. For John, dividend-paying stocks play a crucial role in his portfolio. He invests in companies with a history of paying consistent and growing dividends, such as utility companies, real estate investment trusts (REITs), and consumer staples companies.

John also allocates a portion of his portfolio to bonds, which are generally considered less risky than stocks. This mix of dividend-paying stocks and bonds provides him with a steady stream of income while also offering some potential for growth.

These are just a few examples of how common stocks can be used in diversified portfolios. The specific mix of stocks will vary depending on each investor's individual circumstances, risk tolerance, and investment goals. However, the principle of diversification remains constant. By spreading your investments across different sectors and companies, you can reduce your risk and increase your chances of achieving your financial objectives.

B. Preferred Stock
Definition of preferred stock and its unique features compared to common stock

Having explored the ins and outs of common stock, its inherent rights, and its potential role in diversified investment strategies, let's shift our focus to another key player in the equity landscape: preferred stock. While both common and preferred stock represent ownership in a company, preferred stock possesses unique characteristics that set it apart, offering a different risk-reward profile for investors.

Unlike common stock, which we've established as the most prevalent form of equity, preferred stock typically does not grant voting rights to shareholders. This might seem like a disadvantage, but it's often offset by other benefits that preferred stock offers. One such benefit is the priority in receiving dividends. Preferred stockholders are entitled to a fixed dividend payment, which is usually a percentage of the stock's par value or a specified dollar amount. This fixed dividend is paid out before any dividends are paid to common stockholders.

For instance, consider a company like Bank of America, which issues both common and preferred stock. If the company decides to distribute $1 million in dividends, the preferred stockholders will receive their fixed dividend payments first. Only after the preferred stockholders have been paid will the remaining funds be distributed to common stockholders. This priority in receiving dividends makes preferred stock appealing to income-seeking investors who value a steady stream of income.

Another distinguishing feature of preferred stock is its liquidation preference. In the event of a company's liquidation, preferred stockholders have priority over common stockholders in receiving their share of the company's assets. This means that if the company is forced to sell its assets to pay off its debts, preferred stockholders will be repaid the par value of their shares before common stockholders receive anything.

---

1. www.numerade.com

However, preferred stock is not without its drawbacks. Unlike common stock, which can appreciate significantly in value if the company performs well, preferred stock tends to have a more limited upside potential. Its value is often tied to its fixed dividend payment and the prevailing interest rates.

In essence, preferred stock occupies a unique position in the equity spectrum, offering a blend of features found in both stocks and bonds. It provides investors with a fixed income stream similar to bonds, while also offering the potential for capital appreciation like common stock, albeit to a more limited extent. Understanding the nuances of preferred stock is crucial for any financial professional, as it allows for tailored investment recommendations that cater to the specific needs and risk tolerances of diverse clients.

In the next sections, we will explore the different types of preferred stock in more detail, such as cumulative, participating, and convertible preferred stock. We'll also discuss the advantages and disadvantages of investing in preferred stock and how it can fit into various investment portfolios.

Explanation of different types of preferred stock, such as cumulative, participating, and convertible.

Delving deeper into the realm of preferred stock, we find that it isn't a monolithic entity. It's a diverse family of securities, each with unique attributes tailored to meet specific investor and issuer needs. Let's explore three prominent members of this family: cumulative, participating, and convertible preferred stock.

Cumulative Preferred Stock: This type of preferred stock offers a crucial advantage to investors: the right to accumulate unpaid dividends. If a company faces financial difficulties and cannot pay the scheduled dividend in a given period, those missed payments don't simply vanish. Instead, they accumulate and must be paid in full before any dividends can be paid to common stockholders.

For instance, imagine a company issued cumulative preferred stock with a $5 annual dividend. If the company skips two years of dividend payments, it owes preferred stockholders $15 per share (three years' worth of dividends) before it can distribute any profits to common stockholders. This feature provides a degree of protection to preferred stockholders, ensuring they receive their due even if the company faces temporary setbacks.

Participating Preferred Stock: Participating preferred stock offers the enticing possibility of additional dividends beyond the fixed rate. If the company's profits exceed a certain threshold, participating preferred stockholders may receive a share of the excess profits, alongside the common stockholders. This sharing arrangement can be a powerful incentive for investors, as it aligns their interests with the company's success.

Consider a scenario where a company with participating preferred stock experiences a windfall year. After paying the fixed dividend to preferred stockholders, the company may decide to distribute a portion of the remaining profits to both preferred and common stockholders. This bonus dividend for preferred stockholders can significantly boost their overall return on investment.

Convertible Preferred Stock: This unique type of preferred stock gives investors the best of both worlds: the stability of fixed dividends and the potential for growth through conversion into common stock. Convertible preferred stock can be converted into a predetermined number of common shares at the investor's discretion. This feature allows investors to lock in a steady income stream through dividends, while also having the option to participate in the company's growth if its common stock price appreciates.

Take the example of Tesla, which issued convertible preferred stock in 2014. Investors who purchased this stock received a fixed dividend payment, but they also had the option to convert their shares into common stock at a predetermined price. As Tesla's stock price soared in subsequent years, many investors exercised their conversion rights, reaping substantial gains.

Understanding these different types of preferred stock is crucial for tailoring investment recommendations to client needs. A risk-averse investor seeking stable income might be well-suited for cumulative preferred stock, while an investor seeking both income and growth potential might find participating or convertible preferred stock more appealing. Your ability to match the right type of preferred stock to the right investor is a testament to your expertise as a financial professional.

Discussion of preferred stock's fixed dividend payments and priority over common stock in liquidation.

Let's delve deeper into two of the most attractive features that distinguish preferred stock from its common counterpart: fixed dividend payments and priority in liquidation. These characteristics make preferred stock a unique hybrid, offering a blend of stability and potential upside, thus appealing to a specific subset of investors.

As we've noted, preferred stockholders are entitled to a fixed dividend payment, often stated as a percentage of the stock's par value or a specific dollar amount. This predictable income stream is a significant draw for investors seeking stability and consistent cash flow, particularly those nearing or in retirement. For example, a preferred stock with a par value of $100 and a 5% dividend rate would pay out a $5 dividend annually, regardless of the company's overall profitability. This is in stark contrast to common stock dividends, which can fluctuate or be suspended entirely based on the company's financial performance.

To illustrate this point, consider the case of AT&T, a well-established telecommunications company that issues both common and preferred stock. AT&T's preferred stockholders receive a consistent dividend payment, providing a reliable income source even when the company's earnings fluctuate or its common stock dividend is adjusted.

Furthermore, preferred stockholders have priority over common stockholders in the unfortunate event of a company's liquidation. If a company goes bankrupt and its assets are sold to repay debts, preferred stockholders are paid before common stockholders. This preferential treatment provides an added layer of security to preferred stock investments, making them less risky than common stock.

However, this priority also comes with a trade-off. Preferred stock typically doesn't offer the same growth potential as common stock. While common stock prices can soar if the company thrives, preferred stock prices tend to be more stable, reflecting their fixed dividend payments and lower risk profile.

Think of preferred stock as a bird in the hand versus the two in the bush that common stock represents. The bird in the hand, the fixed dividend, is a reliable source of income. The two in the bush, the potential for significant capital appreciation, are more elusive.

C. Rights and Warrants

Definition of rights and warrants as derivative securities.

Now that we've thoroughly explored common and preferred stock, let's turn our attention to another intriguing segment of the equity market: rights and warrants. While they might not be as widely known as their stock counterparts, rights and warrants are potent tools in the arsenal of both companies and investors.

To understand rights and warrants, we first need to introduce the concept of derivative securities. These financial instruments derive their value from an underlying asset, which in this case is the company's stock. In essence, rights and warrants are like side bets on the future performance of a company's stock.

Rights, also known as subscription rights, are issued by companies to their existing shareholders, granting them the privilege to purchase additional shares of the company's stock at a discounted price within a specified timeframe. This offering allows shareholders to maintain their proportionate ownership stake in the company if they choose to exercise their rights. For example, if a company issues rights to purchase one new share for every ten shares owned, a shareholder with 100 shares could purchase an additional ten shares at the discounted price.

Warrants, on the other hand, function similarly to rights but are typically issued to the public or as sweeteners in bond offerings. A warrant grants the holder the right, but not the obligation, to buy a company's stock at a predetermined price (the exercise price) before the warrant's expiration date. Warrants can be traded independently of the underlying stock, creating a separate market with its own pricing dynamics.

The allure of rights and warrants lies in their potential to amplify returns. If the underlying stock price rises above the exercise price, the holder of a right or warrant can purchase shares at a discount and immediately profit from the price difference. However, it's important to note that rights and warrants also carry risks. If the stock price doesn't rise above the exercise price before the expiration date, the right or warrant becomes worthless.

In essence, rights and warrants offer investors a leveraged way to participate in the potential upside of a company's stock. However, they also require careful consideration of the risks involved. Understanding these risks and rewards is crucial for any financial professional seeking to provide comprehensive investment advice to clients.

Explanation of how rights allow existing shareholders to purchase additional shares at a discounted price.

Rights, as we've noted, are a powerful tool in the hands of existing shareholders, providing them with the opportunity to bolster their ownership stake in a company. But how exactly do rights achieve this? Let's break down the mechanics of how rights allow for the purchase of additional shares at a discounted price.

When a company decides to issue rights, it essentially gives its existing shareholders the first dibs on buying newly issued shares. Each shareholder receives a certain number of rights, proportional to their existing shareholding. These rights are like golden tickets, granting access to a special offering where shares are sold at a price below the prevailing market price.

The discount offered on these shares is not arbitrary; it's a carefully calculated incentive designed to encourage shareholders to exercise their rights. This discount is typically expressed as a percentage below the market price, and it can vary depending on various factors, including the company's financial situation, the desired amount of capital to be raised, and market conditions.

Let's consider a hypothetical example. Imagine a company called XYZ Corporation, whose stock is currently trading at $50 per share. XYZ decides to issue rights to its shareholders, offering them the opportunity to purchase one new share for every five shares they currently own at a discounted price of $40 per share. A shareholder who owns 100 shares of XYZ would receive 20 rights, allowing them to purchase an additional 20 shares at the discounted price.

This discount not only allows shareholders to increase their ownership stake at a lower cost but also presents an opportunity for profit. If the market price of XYZ stock remains above $40 after the rights offering, the shareholder can immediately sell their newly acquired shares at a profit.

However, it's important to note that rights have a limited lifespan. They typically expire after a few weeks, and if shareholders don't exercise their rights within that timeframe, they lose the opportunity to purchase additional shares at the discounted price.

The issuance of rights can also impact the market price of a company's stock. Since rights effectively increase the number of outstanding shares, they can dilute the value of existing shares, leading to a potential decrease in the stock price. However, this dilution is often offset by the capital raised through the rights offering, which can be used to fund growth initiatives that ultimately benefit shareholders in the long run.

Rights offerings are a complex but powerful tool in corporate finance. By understanding their mechanics and implications, you'll be better equipped to advise your clients on whether to exercise their rights or sell them in the market, helping them make informed investment decisions that align with their financial goals.

Discussion of how warrants grant the right to buy shares at a specified price within a certain timeframe.

Now that we've distinguished rights from warrants, let's delve deeper into the unique mechanism of warrants. Unlike rights, which are typically offered to existing shareholders, warrants often cast a wider net, extending their allure to the general public or as enticements alongside bond offerings.

A warrant, in essence, acts as a golden ticket into a company's future. It grants the holder the right, but not the obligation, to purchase a specific number of the company's shares at a predetermined price — known as the exercise price or strike price — within a set timeframe. This timeframe, often spanning several years, gives warrant holders the flexibility to decide when, or if, they want to exercise their right.

Consider a scenario where a biotechnology company, BioTechCo, issues warrants with an exercise price of $20 per share and an expiration date five years in the future. If, during that five-year period, BioTechCo successfully develops a groundbreaking new drug and its stock price soars to $50 per share, the warrant holder can exercise their right to buy shares at the original $20 price, netting an immediate $30 profit per share.

This potential for substantial gains is what makes warrants so attractive to investors seeking leveraged returns. By investing a relatively small amount in a warrant, investors can gain exposure to a much larger number of shares, magnifying their potential profits.

However, it's crucial to remember that this potential for high reward comes with an equally high risk. If BioTechCo's drug development efforts falter and its stock price plummets, the warrant may never reach its exercise price, rendering it worthless at expiration. This "all or nothing" aspect of warrants makes them a high-risk, high-reward investment tool.

To illustrate this further, let's look at the case of Tesla. In 2014, Tesla issued warrants alongside a bond offering. These warrants gave investors the right to purchase Tesla shares at $314.20 per share before June 2021. As Tesla's stock price soared in the following years, these warrants became incredibly valuable, providing massive returns for those who exercised them. However, for those who held onto their warrants hoping for even higher prices, the expiration date loomed as a deadline, after which their warrants would lose all value if not exercised.

Understanding the dynamics of warrants, their potential for lucrative gains, and their inherent risks is crucial for guiding clients in making informed investment decisions. As a registered representative, your ability to explain these complexities in a clear and concise manner, while also tailoring your recommendations to each client's risk tolerance and financial goals, is a hallmark of your expertise.

Examples of how rights and warrants are used in corporate finance and investment strategies.

Building on our understanding of the mechanics of rights and warrants, let's explore how these versatile instruments are employed in the real world of corporate finance and investment strategies. Their applications are as diverse as the companies that issue them, each serving distinct purposes for both issuers and investors.

For companies, rights offerings can be a lifeline, injecting much-needed capital into their operations. In 2020, during the economic turmoil caused by the COVID-19 pandemic, many companies turned to rights offerings to shore up their finances. For example, Carnival Corporation, the world's largest cruise line operator, raised over $1 billion through a rights offering to weather the storm of suspended cruises and plummeting revenues. This influx of cash provided a critical buffer, allowing the company to stay afloat until travel restrictions eased and demand for cruises rebounded.

Warrants, as we've discussed, are often used as sweeteners in bond offerings. This was the case with Tesla in 2014, when the electric vehicle manufacturer included warrants in its bond offering to make it more attractive to investors. The warrants, with an exercise price of $314.20 per share, proved to be a lucrative investment for those who held on to them, as Tesla's stock price soared to over $3,000 per share in the following years.

From an investor's perspective, rights and warrants offer unique opportunities. For existing shareholders, rights can be a way to maintain their proportionate ownership in a company at a discounted price. In 2018, for instance, shareholders of AT&T were offered rights to purchase additional shares of the company's newly acquired subsidiary, WarnerMedia, at a discounted price. This allowed them to participate in the growth potential of WarnerMedia without having to buy shares on the open market.

Warrants, meanwhile, can be an attractive option for investors seeking leveraged exposure to a company's stock. In 2021, a wave of retail investors flocked to warrants of companies like GameStop and AMC Entertainment, fueling a surge in their stock prices. While many of these investors ultimately lost money due to the high-risk nature of warrants, some reaped substantial rewards as the stock prices briefly skyrocketed.

The use of rights and warrants isn't limited to established companies. Startups and smaller companies often use warrants to attract early-stage investors. By offering warrants alongside equity investments, these companies can provide an additional incentive for investors to take a chance on a young, unproven venture.

In essence, rights and warrants are versatile tools that can serve various purposes in the financial markets. They can provide companies with crucial capital, offer investors the chance to increase their ownership stake or gain leveraged exposure, and incentivize early-stage investment in promising startups.

II. Stock Markets, Exchanges, and Trading Mechanisms

A. Major Stock Exchanges (NYSE, NASDAQ)

Overview of the New York Stock Exchange (NYSE) and NASDAQ as leading stock exchanges.
Having explored the foundational types of equity securities, let's now step onto the grand stage where these instruments come to life: the stock markets. These bustling marketplaces are the beating heart of global finance, where buyers and sellers converge to trade ownership stakes in companies, fueling economic growth and shaping investment portfolios.

At the forefront of this vibrant ecosystem stand two titans: the New York Stock Exchange (NYSE) and the NASDAQ. These venerable institutions are not merely trading platforms; they are iconic symbols of capitalism, where fortunes are forged, and dreams are realized.

The NYSE, founded in 1792 under a buttonwood tree on Wall Street, is the oldest and largest stock exchange in the United States. It's renowned for its auction market structure, where designated market makers, known as specialists, facilitate trading by matching buy and sell orders and ensuring orderly markets. The NYSE is home to over 2,400 listed companies, boasting a combined market capitalization exceeding $25 trillion. Its iconic trading floor, with its chaotic symphony of shouts and hand signals, has been immortalized in countless films and TV shows, symbolizing the pulse of global finance.

The NASDAQ, established in 1971, is a relative newcomer compared to the NYSE, but it has quickly risen to prominence as the world's second-largest stock exchange by market capitalization. Unlike the NYSE's physical trading floor, NASDAQ operates as an electronic market, with multiple market makers competing to provide liquidity for each listed security. This dealer market structure fosters competition and efficiency, attracting a diverse array of companies, particularly those in the technology sector. Companies like Apple, Microsoft, Amazon, and Alphabet (Google's parent company) all call NASDAQ home.

Both the NYSE and NASDAQ have stringent listing requirements, ensuring that only companies that meet certain financial and governance standards can access these prestigious markets. These requirements serve to protect investors and maintain the integrity of the markets.

The NYSE and NASDAQ also differ in their trading hours and market focus. The NYSE's trading hours are typically 9:30 AM to 4:00 PM Eastern Time, while NASDAQ's extended hours allow for pre-market and after-hours trading. While both exchanges list a wide range of companies, NASDAQ has a reputation for being more tech-heavy, while the NYSE is known for its diverse mix of industries, including financials, industrials, and consumer goods.

Understanding the nuances of these two major exchanges is crucial for any investor or financial professional. The choice of where to list a company's stock can have significant implications for its visibility, liquidity, and valuation. As a registered representative, your knowledge of these exchanges will enable you to guide your clients toward the most suitable listing venue for their investment objectives.

In the next sections, we will explore the intricacies of over-the-counter (OTC) markets and alternative trading systems (ATS), as well as the role of market makers and specialists in facilitating trading and maintaining orderly markets.

Explanation of their listing requirements, trading hours, and market capitalization.

Now that we've introduced the New York Stock Exchange (NYSE) and the NASDAQ as the two titans of the U.S. equity market, let's dive into the specifics that set them apart, namely their listing requirements, trading hours, and market capitalization.

To gain entry into these prestigious clubs, companies must meet stringent criteria. The NYSE, known for its legacy and blue-chip reputation, has the most demanding requirements. A company seeking to list on the NYSE must have a minimum global market capitalization of $100 million, a minimum share price of $4, and a track record of profitability and strong corporate governance. The NASDAQ, while also selective, has slightly less stringent requirements, making it an attractive option for younger, high-growth companies. For instance, when Facebook went public in 2012, it chose to list on the NASDAQ, as its market capitalization and financial metrics met the exchange's criteria.

Trading hours on the NYSE and NASDAQ differ slightly. The NYSE traditionally operates from 9:30 AM to 4:00 PM Eastern Time, while the NASDAQ offers extended trading hours, with pre-market sessions starting as early as 4:00 AM and after-hours sessions continuing until 8:00 PM. These extended hours allow for greater flexibility and access for investors who can't trade during regular hours. This was particularly evident during the GameStop short squeeze in early 2021, where much of the trading activity occurred during after-hours sessions on platforms like Robinhood, which allow access to extended-hours trading.

Market capitalization, a concept we'll explore in more depth later in the book, is another key differentiator between the NYSE and NASDAQ. While both exchanges list a diverse array of companies, the NYSE tends to have a higher average market capitalization, reflecting its concentration of larger, more established companies. This is not surprising, given the NYSE's more stringent listing requirements. However, NASDAQ has been steadily increasing its market capitalization over the years, attracting larger tech companies like Apple and Microsoft, which now have market capitalizations exceeding $2 trillion.

These differences in listing requirements, trading hours, and market capitalization make the NYSE and NASDAQ complementary rather than competing marketplaces. Companies can choose the exchange that best aligns with their size, industry, and growth trajectory. For investors, both exchanges offer a wealth of opportunities, but understanding their unique characteristics is essential for making informed investment decisions. As a registered representative, you'll be able to leverage this knowledge to guide your clients toward the most suitable exchange for their investment goals and risk tolerance.

Comparison of the auction market structure of the NYSE and the dealer market structure of NASDAQ.

Beyond their individual characteristics, a key distinction between the NYSE and NASDAQ lies in their underlying market structures. These structures dictate how trades are executed, the role of market participants, and ultimately, the trading experience for investors.

The NYSE, as we've discussed, operates as an auction market. Picture this: a bustling trading floor filled with specialists, each assigned to a specific stock, shouting out bids and offers and matching buyers and sellers in a dynamic open outcry system. This auction-like environment promotes price discovery and transparency, as all bids and offers are visible to all market participants. The specialist, acting as an auctioneer, maintains an orderly market by matching orders and stepping in to buy or sell shares if there's an imbalance between supply and demand.

In contrast, the NASDAQ functions as a dealer market, also known as a market-maker system. Here, multiple market makers compete to provide liquidity for each listed stock. These market makers are broker-dealer firms that continuously quote prices at which they are willing to buy (bid) and sell (ask) shares. This competition among market makers helps to ensure tighter spreads between bid and ask prices, potentially leading to better execution for investors.

For example, if you want to buy shares of Apple, you might see quotes from several market makers on NASDAQ, each offering slightly different bid and ask prices. You can choose the market maker offering the best price, or your broker may automatically route your order to the market maker with the most competitive quote.

This decentralized structure of NASDAQ, with multiple market makers vying for your order, contrasts sharply with the NYSE's centralized auction model, where a single specialist manages the order flow for each stock.

The choice between these two market structures is not one of superiority, but rather of suitability. Each structure has its own strengths and weaknesses. The NYSE's auction market is praised for its transparency and price discovery, while NASDAQ's dealer market is lauded for its competitiveness and efficiency.

B. Over-the-Counter Markets and Alternative Trading Systems

Introduction to over-the-counter (OTC) markets and their role in trading unlisted securities.

While the NYSE and NASDAQ often steal the spotlight, the equity market landscape extends far beyond these well-known exchanges. A vast network of over-the-counter (OTC) markets and alternative trading systems (ATS) exists, providing avenues for trading securities not listed on traditional exchanges. These markets, often shrouded in a veil of mystery, play a crucial role in the financial ecosystem, offering unique opportunities and challenges for investors and traders alike.

Over-the-counter markets, as the name suggests, operate outside the confines of centralized exchanges. Instead of a physical trading floor or a single electronic platform, OTC markets consist of a decentralized network of broker-dealers who negotiate directly with each other to buy and sell securities. This decentralized structure allows for greater flexibility and access to a wider range of securities, including those that may not meet the stringent listing requirements of major exchanges.

One of the primary functions of OTC markets is to provide liquidity for unlisted securities. These securities, which may include stocks of smaller companies, bonds, derivatives, and even currencies, are not traded on traditional exchanges due to various reasons, such as low trading volume, lack of regulatory compliance, or simply a preference for private ownership. OTC markets offer a platform for these securities to be bought and sold, providing investors with access to a broader universe of investment opportunities.

For example, many penny stocks, which are stocks that trade for less than $5 per share, are exclusively traded on OTC markets. These stocks are often associated with smaller, less established companies, and they can be highly volatile and speculative. However, they also offer the potential for significant returns if the company succeeds.

The OTC Markets Group, a leading operator of OTC markets, provides a platform for trading over 12,000 securities across various tiers, including OTCQX, OTCQB, and Pink Open Market. Each tier has different reporting and disclosure requirements, offering investors a range of choices based on their risk tolerance and investment objectives.

OTC markets, while offering greater flexibility and access, also come with their own set of risks and challenges. The lack of centralized oversight and regulation can make OTC markets more susceptible to fraud and manipulation. Additionally, the lack of standardized pricing and reporting can make it difficult for investors to assess the true value of OTC securities.

Explanation of alternative trading systems (ATS), including electronic communication networks (ECNs) and dark pools.

As we move beyond the familiar territory of the NYSE and NASDAQ, we encounter a rapidly evolving landscape of alternative trading systems (ATS). These electronic platforms, distinct from traditional exchanges, have revolutionized the way securities are traded, offering new avenues for investors and traders to access the markets. Two prominent examples of ATS are electronic communication networks (ECNs) and dark pools.

ECNs, like bustling digital marketplaces, enable the direct trading of securities between market participants without the need for a traditional broker-dealer intermediary. This direct access fosters competition, potentially resulting in tighter spreads and faster execution for investors. Prominent ECNs like Archipelago and Instinet have played a crucial role in democratizing the markets, giving individual investors the tools to compete with institutional giants. For instance, during the 2021 GameStop frenzy, ECNs facilitated a significant portion of the trading volume, allowing retail investors to participate in the historic short squeeze.

Dark pools, on the other hand, operate in the shadows, away from the public eye. These private trading venues allow institutional investors to trade large blocks of shares anonymously, minimizing the market impact of their trades. This anonymity is particularly appealing to large institutional investors who want to avoid tipping their hand to the market or triggering adverse price movements. However, dark pools have also attracted scrutiny due to concerns about transparency and potential conflicts of interest. In 2014, Barclays was fined $150 million for misleading investors about the nature of its dark pool, highlighting the regulatory challenges posed by these opaque trading venues.

Both ECNs and dark pools represent a significant shift in the trading landscape. They offer increased competition, faster execution, and greater anonymity, respectively. However, as trading activity becomes dispersed across multiple venues, they also raise questions about market fragmentation and transparency.

Discussion of the advantages and disadvantages of OTC markets and ATS compared to traditional exchanges.

Having explored the intriguing realm of over-the-counter (OTC) markets and alternative trading systems (ATS), let's now weigh the advantages and disadvantages of these venues compared to traditional exchanges like the NYSE and NASDAQ. Each trading platform presents a unique set of pros and cons, making them suitable for different types of investors and securities.

OTC markets, as we've discussed, offer unparalleled flexibility. They provide a platform for trading a vast array of securities, including those not listed on traditional exchanges. This opens up a world of possibilities for investors seeking exposure to smaller companies, niche industries, or specific types of assets like bonds or derivatives. For instance, many micro-cap stocks, which have market capitalizations under $300 million, are exclusively traded OTC, providing early-stage investors with the potential for high growth but also carrying significant risk.

Furthermore, OTC markets can be more cost-effective than traditional exchanges, particularly for large institutional investors trading substantial volumes. The lack of exchange fees and the ability to negotiate prices directly with counterparties can result in significant cost savings.

However, OTC markets also come with their own set of drawbacks. The lack of centralized oversight and regulation can expose investors to greater risks of fraud and manipulation. Additionally, the lack of standardized pricing and reporting can make it difficult to assess the true value of securities, requiring investors to conduct thorough due diligence before investing. The illiquidity of some OTC securities can also make it difficult to buy or sell them at desired prices.

Alternative trading systems, such as ECNs and dark pools, offer distinct advantages over traditional exchanges. ECNs provide direct access to the markets, eliminating the need for intermediaries and potentially reducing transaction costs. This is particularly beneficial for active traders who value speed and efficiency. Dark pools, on the other hand, offer anonymity, which can be crucial for institutional investors executing large trades without impacting market prices.

However, ATS also have their shortcomings. The fragmentation of trading activity across multiple venues can lead to concerns about market transparency and price discovery. Dark pools, in particular, have been criticized for their lack of transparency and the potential for conflicts of interest between the operators of the dark pool and their clients. The rise of high-frequency trading (HFT), which often occurs on ATS, has also raised concerns about market manipulation and unfair advantages for certain market participants.

The choice between traditional exchanges, OTC markets, and ATS is not always clear-cut. Each platform serves a unique purpose and caters to different types of investors and securities. As a registered representative, it's crucial to understand the nuances of each venue to recommend the most suitable option for your clients. By weighing the advantages and disadvantages of each platform, you can help your clients achieve their investment goals while minimizing risk and maximizing returns. The world of equity markets is constantly evolving, with new trading venues and technologies emerging all the time. By staying informed about these developments, you can ensure that your clients have access to the most cutting-edge tools and strategies for achieving their financial objectives.

C. Market Makers, Specialists, and the Order Matching Process

Definition of market makers and specialists as key players in facilitating trading.

Now that we've contrasted the unique mechanisms of auction and dealer markets, let's shine a spotlight on the key players who keep these markets humming: market makers and specialists. These individuals and firms are the unsung heroes of the stock market, ensuring liquidity, facilitating trades, and maintaining orderly markets.

Market makers, as we've touched upon earlier, are the driving force behind the NASDAQ's dealer market. They are typically broker-dealer firms that quote both a bid price (the price they're willing to buy at) and an ask price (the price they're willing to sell at) for a particular security. By doing so, they create a market for the security, ensuring that buyers and sellers can always find a counterparty to trade with. This is crucial for maintaining liquidity, which is the ability to buy or sell a security quickly and easily without significantly impacting its price.

Specialists, on the other hand, are unique to the NYSE's auction market. Each specialist is assigned to a specific stock and is responsible for maintaining an orderly market for that stock. They do this by matching buy and sell orders, setting opening and closing prices, and stepping in to buy or sell shares from their own inventory if there's an imbalance between supply and demand.

In essence, both market makers and specialists play a vital role in facilitating trading and ensuring the smooth functioning of the markets. They provide liquidity, maintain fair and orderly markets, and help to prevent excessive price volatility.

Consider the role of Citadel Securities, a leading market maker on both the NYSE and NASDAQ. Citadel is responsible for providing liquidity for thousands of stocks, ensuring that there's always a buyer or seller available when an investor wants to trade. This is essential for maintaining investor confidence and ensuring that the markets function efficiently.

The specialist system on the NYSE has a long and storied history. In the early days of the exchange, specialists were individuals who stood in the trading crowd, shouting out bids and offers and matching buyers and sellers. Today, specialists are typically large financial firms with sophisticated trading algorithms, but their role remains the same: to maintain a fair and orderly market for their assigned stocks.

The order matching process, which is facilitated by both market makers and specialists, is the heart of how trades are executed. When you place an order to buy or sell a stock, your order is sent to the exchange, where it is matched with an order from another investor. The market maker or specialist ensures that the trade is executed at a fair price and in a timely manner.

Explanation of their role in providing liquidity and maintaining orderly markets.

Now that we've distinguished between the roles of market makers and specialists, let's delve deeper into their essential function: providing liquidity and maintaining orderly markets. These seemingly simple terms hold profound implications for the functioning of equity markets and the overall stability of the financial system.

Liquidity, as we've discussed, is the lifeblood of any market. It refers to the ease with which an asset can be bought or sold without causing drastic fluctuations in its price. In the context of the stock market, liquidity ensures that investors can readily buy or sell shares at a fair price, without having to wait extended periods for a matching order.

Market makers play a crucial role in providing this liquidity. By continuously quoting bid and ask prices, they create a market for a security, ensuring that there are always buyers and sellers available. This is particularly important for less actively traded stocks, which might otherwise face challenges in finding willing counterparties for trades. Consider a scenario where an investor wants to sell a large block of shares in a small-cap company. If there are no readily available buyers, the investor might have to lower their asking price significantly to entice a buyer, potentially incurring a substantial loss. However, with a market maker present, the investor can be assured of a buyer at a reasonable price, ensuring a smoother and more efficient transaction.

Specialists, in the context of the NYSE's auction market, also contribute to liquidity by acting as dealers of last resort. If there's a temporary imbalance between buy and sell orders, the specialist will step in and use their own inventory of shares to meet the excess demand or supply. This helps to maintain orderly markets by preventing sudden price spikes or drops due to imbalances in order flow.

Maintaining orderly markets goes beyond just providing liquidity. It involves ensuring that trading is fair and transparent, that prices reflect the true underlying value of securities, and that there's no manipulation or undue influence in the market. Market makers and specialists play a vital role in upholding these principles. They are bound by regulations to act in a fair and ethical manner, and they are monitored by exchange officials to ensure compliance.

The importance of liquidity and orderly markets was starkly highlighted during the Flash Crash of 2010. On May 6, 2010, the Dow Jones Industrial Average plunged nearly 1,000 points in a matter of minutes, causing widespread panic and disruption in the markets. While the exact cause of the crash remains a subject of debate, a lack of liquidity and a breakdown in the order matching process were identified as contributing factors. This event underscored the critical role that market makers and specialists play in maintaining the stability of the markets, especially during times of stress and volatility.

Detailed description of the order matching process, including the different types of orders (market, limit, stop) and how they are executed.

With a grasp of the roles market makers and specialists play in maintaining liquidity and order, we can now delve into the intricate dance of the order matching process. This process is the backbone of every stock market transaction, ensuring that buyers and sellers find each other and agree on a price. Let's break down this process, examining the different order types and how they interact in the market.

Imagine you've decided to invest in a company, let's say Tesla, and you place an order to buy 100 shares. This order, depending on its type, will be handled differently in the market.

If you place a **market order**, you're essentially instructing your broker to buy those 100 shares at the best available price immediately. This is the fastest way to execute a trade, but it comes with a caveat: you have no control over the exact price you pay. The market order will be filled at the current market price, which could be higher or lower than you anticipated, especially in a fast-moving market.

In contrast, a **limit order** gives you more control over the price. You set a specific price at which you're willing to buy or sell a stock. For example, you could place a limit order to buy Tesla at $700 per share. Your order will only be filled if the stock reaches that price or lower. While this gives you price protection, there's no guarantee that your order will be executed. If Tesla's stock price never drops to $700, your order will remain unfilled.

A **stop order** is a protective measure designed to limit losses or lock in profits. There are two types: stop-loss and stop-limit orders. A stop-loss order becomes a market order once the stock price reaches a specified "stop" price. For instance, if you bought Tesla at $750 and want to limit your loss, you could place a stop-loss order at $700. If the stock price falls to $700, your order will be triggered, and the shares will be sold at the prevailing market price, which could be lower than $700.

A stop-limit order, on the other hand, becomes a limit order once the stop price is reached. Using the same Tesla example, if you placed a stop-limit order at $700 with a limit price of $680, your order to sell at $680 or better will be activated once the stock price hits $700. However, if the stock price gaps down below $680, your order might not be filled.

The order matching process is the mechanism that brings these various order types together. On the NYSE, the specialist is responsible for matching buy and sell orders and ensuring that trades are executed at a fair price. On NASDAQ, multiple market makers compete to fill orders, with the most competitive bid or offer usually getting the trade.

The order matching process is a complex ballet of supply and demand, constantly adjusting to market conditions. By understanding how it works, and the different order types that drive it, you gain a significant advantage as an investor or trader. As a registered representative, you'll be able to explain these intricacies to your clients, helping them choose the right order type for their specific needs and objectives.

III. Order Types and Execution Strategies

A. Market Orders

Definition of market orders and their use for immediate execution at the prevailing market price.

Building upon our understanding of the market players and their roles, let's now turn our attention to the tactical side of trading – order types and execution strategies. Just as a carpenter wouldn't use a hammer for every job, a savvy investor or trader needs to know the right tool for the right situation. We'll begin with the most fundamental and straightforward order type: the market order.

A market order is the express lane of the stock market. It's a direct instruction to your broker to buy or sell a security at the best available current price. This emphasis on speed makes it an ideal choice when you need to enter or exit a position quickly, perhaps in response to breaking news or a sudden market movement. For example, if a pharmaceutical company announces a breakthrough drug approval and you want to buy shares before the price surges, a market order would be your go-to option.

The primary advantage of a market order is its virtually guaranteed execution. As long as there are willing sellers or buyers in the market, your order will be filled promptly. This speed is crucial in fast-moving markets, where hesitation can lead to missed opportunities or amplified losses.

However, this speed comes at a price – literally. The inherent drawback of market orders is their lack of price control. Since you're buying or selling at the prevailing market price, you're at the mercy of market fluctuations. In a volatile market, the price at which your order is filled could be significantly different from the price you saw when you placed the order. This phenomenon is known as slippage, and it can eat into your profits or exacerbate your losses.

To illustrate this, imagine you place a market order to buy 100 shares of Apple stock. At the time you place the order, the last traded price is $150 per share. However, by the time your order reaches the market and is filled, the price may have risen to $152 due to a sudden surge in buying activity. In this case, you'd end up paying $200 more than you initially anticipated, highlighting the potential downside of market orders in volatile conditions.

Therefore, while market orders offer the benefit of quick execution, they require careful consideration of market conditions and the potential for price fluctuations. As a registered representative, it's your responsibility to educate your clients about the risks and benefits of different order types, guiding them towards the most appropriate strategy for their specific needs and risk tolerance.

B. Limit Orders

Definition of limit orders and their use to buy or sell securities at a specified price or better.

Now that we've explored the express lane of the stock market - market orders - let's take a detour into a more nuanced route: limit orders. While market orders prioritize speed and guarantee execution, limit orders offer precision and control over the price at which you buy or sell.

Think of a limit order as setting a price target for your trade. If you want to buy shares of a company, but only if the price dips to a certain level, a limit order is your tool. Let's say you're interested in purchasing shares of Amazon, but you believe the current price is a bit too high. You could set a buy limit order at $3,000 per share, instructing your broker to only execute the trade if the price drops to that level or lower.

Similarly, if you're looking to sell a stock, you can use a limit order to set a minimum price at which you're willing to sell. For example, if you own shares of Tesla and want to lock in profits if the price reaches $900, you could place a sell limit order at that price. Your order will only be executed if the market price rises to $900 or higher.

The primary advantage of limit orders is price protection. They give you the power to set your desired entry or exit points, ensuring you don't overpay for a stock or sell it for less than you're willing to accept. This level of control can be particularly valuable in volatile markets, where prices can fluctuate rapidly.

However, this precision comes with a trade-off. Unlike market orders, which are virtually guaranteed to be executed, limit orders carry the risk of non-execution. If the market price doesn't reach your specified limit, your order will remain unfilled. This can be frustrating, especially if you miss out on a profitable trade because the price briefly touched your limit but didn't stay there long enough for your order to be filled.

Let's revisit our Amazon example. If you set a buy limit order at $3,000 and the stock price only dips to $3,001 before rebounding, your order won't be executed. You might miss out on a buying opportunity, as the price could continue to rise. Similarly, if you set a sell limit order for Tesla at $900, but the price peaks at $899 before retreating, your order won't be filled, and you might miss out on locking in profits.

The potential for non-execution is an inherent risk of limit orders. It's a balancing act between price control and the possibility of missed opportunities. As a registered representative, it's crucial to understand this dynamic and guide your clients towards the most suitable order type based on their individual needs and risk tolerances.

C. Stop Orders

Definition of stop orders and their use to limit losses or protect profits.

Having examined market and limit orders, let's now turn our attention to another indispensable tool in the trader's arsenal: stop orders. If market orders are the accelerator and limit orders the steering wheel, stop orders act as the brakes, providing a crucial safeguard against runaway losses or a means to lock in hard-earned profits.

In essence, a stop order is a conditional order that triggers a market or limit order once a specified price – known as the stop price – is reached. It's a proactive measure designed to automate your risk management strategy, ensuring you're not left holding the bag if the market turns against you.

Let's first dissect the **stop-loss order**, often a beginner investor's first line of defense. Imagine you've purchased shares of a promising tech startup, but the market sentiment sours and the stock price starts to slide. A stop-loss order acts as your safety net. You set a stop price below your purchase price, and if the stock falls to that level, the stop order is triggered, transforming into a market order to sell your shares at the prevailing market price. While you might incur a loss, the stop-loss helps to prevent further erosion of your capital if the stock continues its downward spiral.

For instance, let's say you bought shares of Netflix at $400, and you're worried about a potential market correction. You could place a stop-loss order at $380. If Netflix's share price falls to $380, your stop-loss is triggered, and your shares are sold at the best available price, which might be slightly below $380 depending on market conditions.

The **stop-limit order** adds a layer of precision to this protective mechanism. Instead of turning into a market order, the stop-limit order becomes a limit order once the stop price is triggered. This gives you more control over the selling price, but it also introduces the risk of non-execution. If the stock price gaps down below your limit price, your order might not be filled, potentially leaving you holding onto the shares as they continue to fall.

To illustrate this, let's revisit our Netflix example. If you place a stop-limit order with a stop price of $380 and a limit price of $375, your order to sell at $375 or better will be activated once the stock price hits $380. However, if the stock price plunges to $370, your order won't be filled, as there are no buyers willing to pay $375 or more.

Stop orders, both stop-loss and stop-limit, are essential risk management tools for any investor or trader. They offer a way to protect your profits and limit your losses, allowing you to navigate volatile markets with greater confidence. As a registered representative, it's crucial to educate your clients about the nuances of stop orders, empowering them to build resilient portfolios and weather market storms.

D. Price Improvement and Best Execution

Introduction to the concept of price improvement, where orders are executed at a price better than the quoted price.

As we navigate the intricacies of the various order types available to investors, it's important to highlight two critical concepts that directly impact the quality of trade executions: price improvement and best execution. These concepts, while often used interchangeably, represent distinct yet interconnected principles that safeguard investors' interests and promote fair and efficient markets.

Price improvement, in its essence, is a pleasant surprise for investors. It occurs when an order is executed at a price that's more favorable than the current best bid or offer (NBBO) at the time the order is routed. For instance, if you place a limit order to buy a stock at $50, but your broker manages to fill the order at $49.90, you've just experienced a 10-cent price improvement per share. While it might seem like a small amount, these savings can accumulate over time, especially for frequent traders or those executing large orders.

The ability to obtain price improvement is often touted by brokers as a key differentiator. However, it's important to understand that price improvement is not a guarantee. It depends on various factors, such as market conditions, the specific security being traded, and the broker's execution capabilities. Some brokers have access to sophisticated algorithms and trading platforms that allow them to scan multiple markets and identify hidden liquidity, potentially leading to price improvement opportunities.

Best execution, on the other hand, is a broader regulatory obligation that goes beyond just price improvement. It requires brokers to exercise reasonable diligence to obtain the most favorable terms for their clients' orders, considering factors such as price, speed, likelihood of execution, and settlement. In essence, best execution is about putting the client's interests first, ahead of the broker's own profits or convenience.

For example, if a client places a market order to buy a thinly traded stock, the broker has an obligation to route the order to the venue most likely to provide a timely and efficient execution, even if it means sacrificing a small amount of potential price improvement. Similarly, if a client places a large order that could impact the market price, the broker must take steps to minimize market impact and obtain the best possible price for the client.

The Financial Industry Regulatory Authority (FINRA) has established rules and guidelines to ensure that brokers adhere to their best execution obligations. These rules require brokers to disclose their order routing practices, conduct regular reviews of their execution quality, and take corrective action if any deficiencies are identified.

In 2019, for instance, FINRA fined several broker-dealers for best execution violations, including routing client orders to venues that resulted in inferior prices or delayed executions. These cases highlight the importance of regulatory oversight in ensuring that brokers act in their clients' best interests.

E. Day Trading and Swing Trading Strategies

Overview of day trading and swing trading as short-term trading strategies.

Having equipped ourselves with a comprehensive understanding of the different order types used in the equity markets, let's now shift gears to explore two distinct short-term trading strategies that rely heavily on these order types: day trading and swing trading. These strategies, while potentially lucrative, are not for the faint of heart and require discipline, skill, and a profound understanding of market dynamics.

Day trading, as the name suggests, involves buying and selling securities within the same trading day, aiming to profit from short-term price fluctuations. Day traders thrive on volatility, seeking to capitalize on rapid price movements by entering and exiting positions multiple times throughout the day. They often rely on technical analysis tools, such as charts, indicators, and patterns, to identify trading opportunities and time their entries and exits.

Swing trading, on the other hand, takes a slightly longer view, holding positions for a few days to a few weeks. Swing traders aim to capture price swings that occur within broader trends, utilizing both technical and fundamental analysis to identify potential trades. They are less concerned with minute-by-minute price movements and focus on capturing larger price waves.

Both day trading and swing trading offer the allure of significant short-term gains. The ability to leverage your capital through margin accounts and the potential to profit from both rising and falling markets can lead to substantial returns in a relatively short period. However, these strategies also carry significant risks.

The inherent volatility of short-term trading can lead to rapid losses if trades move against you. Moreover, the constant need to monitor the markets and make quick decisions can be mentally and emotionally taxing. Successful day and swing traders often spend countless hours honing their skills, developing trading plans, and practicing risk management techniques.

Technical analysis, which involves studying charts and historical price data to identify patterns and trends, is a cornerstone of both day trading and swing trading. Traders rely on indicators like moving averages, support and resistance levels, and candlestick patterns to make informed decisions about entry and exit points.

However, technical analysis is not a foolproof system. It requires interpretation and can be subject to bias. Experienced traders often combine technical analysis with fundamental analysis, which involves evaluating a company's financial health and prospects, to make more informed trading decisions.

Risk management is perhaps even more crucial in short-term trading than in long-term investing. The potential for rapid losses necessitates strict discipline in setting stop-loss orders and managing position sizes. Traders also need to be aware of the psychological aspects of trading, such as fear and greed, which can cloud judgment and lead to impulsive decisions.

IV. Corporate Actions and Their Impact on Securities

A. Stock Splits and Reverse Splits

Explanation of stock splits, where a company increases the number of outstanding shares and reduces the price per share proportionately.

Having built a solid foundation in the different types of equity securities and the mechanics of the market, we now move to the dynamic realm of corporate actions. These decisions, made by a company's board of directors, can significantly alter the landscape of its stock, influencing both its price and the number of shares outstanding. Let's start by dissecting one of the most common and investor-friendly corporate actions: the stock split.

A stock split is like slicing a pizza into more pieces. The pizza itself remains the same size, but now you have more slices to share. Similarly, in a stock split, a company increases the number of its outstanding shares, while proportionally reducing the price per share. The total value of the company, represented by its market capitalization, remains unchanged.

Let's imagine a company, GrowthTech Inc., whose stock is trading at $200 per share. The company announces a 2-for-1 stock split. This means that for every one share an investor owns, they will now own two shares. The price, however, is adjusted accordingly. Post-split, each share will be worth $100. If an investor owned 100 shares pre-split, valued at $20,000, they'll now own 200 shares, still valued at $20,000.

The primary reason companies opt for stock splits is to increase the liquidity of their shares. A lower share price can make the stock more accessible to a wider range of investors, potentially boosting trading volume and overall market interest. This was evident in the case of Apple, which has undergone several stock splits throughout its history. In 2020, Apple executed a 4-for-1 stock split, bringing its share price down from around $500 to around $125. This move made Apple shares more affordable for retail investors, contributing to a surge in trading volume and a continued upward trajectory for the stock price.

Another reason for stock splits is to signal confidence in the company's future prospects. A stock split is often seen as a positive sign by investors, indicating that the company's management believes its stock price will continue to rise. This can generate excitement and attract new investors, further driving up the stock price.

However, it's important to remember that a stock split, in and of itself, does not change the fundamental value of the company. The pizza analogy holds true: you have more slices, but the pizza's size remains the same. As a registered representative, it's crucial to educate your clients about this reality and help them understand that a stock split is not a guarantee of future gains. The company's underlying performance and market conditions will ultimately determine the stock's long-term trajectory.

Discussion of reverse splits, where a company reduces the number of outstanding shares and increases the price per share proportionately.

While stock splits are generally perceived as positive events, their lesser-known cousin, the reverse stock split, often carries a different connotation. If a stock split is akin to slicing a pizza into more pieces, a reverse stock split is the opposite – consolidating those slices back into a smaller, denser pie. In essence, a company reduces the number of its outstanding shares, simultaneously increasing the price per share proportionately.

Just as with a stock split, the company's overall value remains unchanged. If a company with 10 million shares trading at $1 per share executes a 1-for-10 reverse split, it will end up with 1 million shares trading at $10 per share. The market capitalization, calculated by multiplying the number of shares by the share price, remains constant at $10 million.

But why would a company choose to do a reverse stock split? Unlike stock splits, which often signal growth and confidence, reverse splits are often seen as a sign of distress. One of the primary motivations is to avoid delisting from a stock exchange. Many exchanges have minimum price requirements for listed stocks, and if a company's share price falls below this threshold for an extended period, it risks being delisted. A reverse split can artificially boost the share price, helping the company maintain its listing status.

For example, in 2020, Hertz Global Holdings, the car rental giant, faced delisting from the New York Stock Exchange after its share price plummeted due to the pandemic's impact on the travel industry. To avoid delisting, Hertz executed a 1-for-8 reverse split, consolidating its shares and raising its stock price above the minimum requirement.

Another reason for reverse splits is to improve the company's perception among investors. Penny stocks, which trade for less than $5 per share, often carry a stigma of being risky and speculative. A reverse split can elevate the share price, making the stock appear more "respectable" and potentially attracting institutional investors who may have restrictions on investing in low-priced stocks.

However, reverse splits are not a magic bullet for troubled companies. While they can temporarily boost the share price, they do not address the underlying issues that caused the stock price to decline in the first place. In fact, reverse splits are often seen as a red flag by investors, signaling potential financial difficulties or a lack of confidence in the company's future.

A classic example is Citigroup, which underwent a 1-for-10 reverse split in 2011 following the financial crisis. While the reverse split temporarily lifted Citigroup's stock price, it did little to alleviate concerns about the bank's long-term prospects. The stock continued to underperform for several years, highlighting the limitations of reverse splits as a solution to fundamental problems.

Examples of companies that have undergone stock splits or reverse splits and the impact on their stock prices.

As we've seen, the decision to split or reverse split a company's stock can be a strategic maneuver with far-reaching implications. Let's bring these theoretical concepts to life by examining some real-world examples of companies that have embarked on these corporate actions, and the subsequent ripples in their stock prices.

Stock splits, as we've established, are typically seen as a positive sign, reflecting a company's confidence in its growth prospects. A prime example is Apple, a company synonymous with innovation and market leadership. Over the years, Apple has split its stock five times, with the most recent being a 4-for-1 split in August 2020. Prior to this split, Apple shares were trading at nearly $500, making them less accessible to many retail investors. The split brought the price down to around $125, sparking a surge in buying activity and pushing the stock to new all-time highs in the following months.

Tesla, another high-flying tech company, has also embraced stock splits. In August 2020, just a few days after Apple's split, Tesla announced its own 5-for-1 split. This move, like Apple's, was aimed at making the stock more affordable for individual investors. Tesla's share price had been on a meteoric rise, and the split helped to broaden its investor base, contributing to further gains in the stock price.

On the other side of the coin, we have reverse stock splits, which, as we've discussed, are often associated with companies facing financial distress or struggling to maintain their listing status on major exchanges. A poignant example is Citigroup, a banking giant that was severely impacted by the 2008 financial crisis. In 2011, with its share price languishing below $5, Citigroup executed a 1-for-10 reverse split, artificially boosting its share price to around $45. While this move helped Citigroup avoid delisting, it did little to restore investor confidence. The stock continued to underperform for several years, a stark reminder that a reverse split is not a panacea for underlying problems.

Another example is AIG, the insurance conglomerate that received a massive government bailout during the financial crisis. In 2009, with its share price hovering near $1, AIG executed a 1-for-20 reverse split, consolidating its shares and raising the price to around $20. This move, while successful in keeping AIG listed on the NYSE, did not immediately translate into a sustained recovery for the stock. It took several years of restructuring and improved financial performance for AIG's stock to regain its footing.

B. Dividends

Definition of dividends as distributions of a company's earnings to shareholders.

Now that we've explored stock splits and reverse splits, let's shift our focus to another key aspect of corporate actions that holds immense significance for investors: dividends. While the potential for capital appreciation through stock price increases is undeniably attractive, dividends offer a more tangible and immediate reward for shareholders.

Essentially, dividends are a share of a company's profits that are distributed to shareholders, typically on a quarterly basis. Think of it as a company sharing a piece of the pie with its owners. The decision to pay dividends and the amount to be distributed is made by the company's board of directors, based on factors such as the company's profitability, cash flow, and growth prospects.

For investors, dividends can provide a steady stream of income, particularly those seeking stability and predictable cash flow, like retirees or those looking to build a passive income stream. Companies with a long history of consistent dividend payments, often referred to as "dividend aristocrats," are highly sought after by income-focused investors. For instance, Johnson & Johnson, a healthcare giant, has increased its dividend annually for over 50 years, making it a reliable source of income for generations of investors.

Dividends are not only beneficial for investors but also serve as a signal of a company's financial health and confidence in its future. A company that consistently pays dividends is generally perceived as financially stable and committed to rewarding its shareholders. This can attract investors and boost the company's stock price.

However, dividends are not without their complexities. The decision to pay dividends is a delicate balancing act for companies. On the one hand, paying dividends can attract investors and signal financial strength. On the other hand, it reduces the amount of cash available for reinvestment in the business, potentially hindering growth opportunities.

Furthermore, the tax treatment of dividends can vary depending on the investor's tax bracket and the type of account in which the dividends are received. In the United States, qualified dividends are taxed at a lower rate than ordinary income, making them more tax-efficient for investors.

Delving deeper into the multifaceted world of dividends, we find that they aren't just a simple distribution of cash. There are various flavors of dividends, each with its unique characteristics and implications for both the company and its shareholders. Let's explore three of the most common types: cash dividends, stock dividends, and property dividends.

Cash dividends, as the name suggests, are the most straightforward form of dividends. Companies distribute a portion of their profits directly to shareholders in the form of cash. This cash can be used by investors however they see fit – reinvesting in the company, purchasing other securities, or even covering personal expenses. For many investors, especially those seeking current income, cash dividends are a highly attractive feature.

Consider a company like AT&T, which we mentioned earlier as a reliable dividend payer. As of 2023, AT&T pays an annual dividend of $1.11 per share, providing shareholders with a steady stream of cash flow. This predictable income can be particularly appealing to retirees or those relying on their investments for living expenses.

Stock dividends, on the other hand, involve the distribution of additional shares of the company's stock to existing shareholders. Instead of receiving cash, shareholders receive more shares, usually in proportion to their existing holdings. For example, a company might declare a 10% stock dividend, meaning that for every 10 shares an investor owns, they will receive one additional share.

While stock dividends don't provide immediate cash flow like cash dividends, they can still benefit investors in several ways. First, they increase the number of shares an investor owns, potentially increasing their overall stake in the company. Second, if the company's stock price continues to rise, the additional shares can lead to increased capital gains in the future. However, it's important to note that stock dividends can also dilute the value of existing shares, as the company's earnings are now spread across a larger number of shares.

Finally, property dividends involve the distribution of assets other than cash or the company's own stock. These assets could include physical goods, real estate, or even shares of another company's stock. While property dividends are less common than cash or stock dividends, they can offer unique benefits to shareholders. For instance, a company with a large real estate portfolio might distribute shares in a real estate investment trust (REIT) as a property dividend, providing shareholders with exposure to a new asset class.

While the prospect of receiving a dividend payout can be enticing, it's not as simple as merely owning a stock. The timing of your purchase, relative to a crucial date known as the ex-dividend date, determines your eligibility for the next dividend distribution.

The ex-dividend date, often shortened to "ex-date," marks a critical cut-off point for dividend eligibility. It typically falls two business days before the record date, which is the date on which the company identifies its shareholders for the purpose of distributing dividends. To be eligible for the dividend, you must own the stock before the market opens on the ex-dividend date. If you purchase the stock on or after the ex-dividend date, you'll miss out on the upcoming dividend, even if you hold the stock on the record date.

To understand this better, let's say a company, Tech Innovators Inc., declares a dividend with a record date of August 15th. The ex-dividend date would then be August 13th. If you buy Tech Innovators stock on or before August 12th, you'll be entitled to the dividend. However, if you buy the stock on August 13th or later, the seller of the shares will receive the dividend, not you.

The reason for this seemingly arbitrary rule lies in the settlement process for stock trades. It typically takes two business days for a trade to settle, meaning that the ownership of the shares is officially transferred from the seller to the buyer. To ensure that the dividend is paid to the rightful owner, the ex-dividend date is set two days before the record date.

The ex-dividend date also has an interesting effect on the stock price. On the ex-dividend date, the stock price is typically adjusted downward by the amount of the dividend. This reflects the fact that the company's assets have been reduced by the amount of cash paid out as dividends. For example, if Tech Innovators' stock is trading at $50 per share and the company declares a $1 dividend, the stock price is likely to drop to $49 on the ex-dividend date.

This price adjustment is important to understand, as it can impact your investment strategy. If you're buying a stock just before the ex-dividend date solely to capture the dividend, you might end up losing money if the price drop on the ex-dividend date exceeds the dividend amount.

C. Mergers, Acquisitions, and Tender Offers

Overview of mergers and acquisitions (M&A) as corporate actions that involve the combination of two or more companies.

Having examined the impact of stock splits and dividends on the dynamics of equity securities, let's shift our focus to the transformative corporate actions of mergers, acquisitions, and tender offers. These events, where companies combine or acquire each other, can reshape entire industries, creating both opportunities and challenges for investors and employees alike.

Mergers and acquisitions (M&A) are strategic maneuvers that involve the consolidation of two or more companies into a single entity. In a merger, two companies of roughly equal size agree to combine, forming a new entity with a new name and shared ownership. A classic example is the 1998 merger of Exxon and Mobil, two oil giants that joined forces to create ExxonMobil, the largest publicly traded oil and gas company in the world.

An acquisition, on the other hand, occurs when one company buys another, typically with the acquiring company being the larger of the two. The acquired company may continue to operate as a subsidiary or be fully integrated into the acquiring company. A notable recent example is Microsoft's acquisition of Activision Blizzard, a leading video game publisher, in 2022 for a staggering $68.7 billion. This acquisition expands Microsoft's gaming empire and strengthens its position in the rapidly growing gaming industry.

Both mergers and acquisitions can be driven by a variety of factors, including the desire to expand market share, gain access to new technologies or products, achieve economies of scale, or simply eliminate a competitor. The impact of these transactions on shareholders can be significant. In some cases, shareholders of the acquired company receive a premium for their shares, leading to immediate gains. In other cases, the merger or acquisition may create long-term value for shareholders of both companies by combining their strengths and resources.

However, M&A deals are not always smooth sailing. They can face regulatory scrutiny, cultural clashes, and integration challenges. For instance, the proposed merger between AT&T and Time Warner in 2017 faced opposition from the U.S. Department of Justice, which argued that the merger would harm competition and lead to higher prices for consumers. The merger was eventually approved after a lengthy legal battle, but it highlights the potential hurdles that M&A deals can encounter.

Explanation of tender offers, where a company offers to buy shares from existing shareholders at a premium.

While mergers and acquisitions often involve negotiations between company boards and executives, tender offers take the battle for corporate control directly to the shareholders. In essence, a tender offer is a public invitation from one company (the acquirer) to the shareholders of another company (the target) to tender, or sell, their shares at a specified price within a certain timeframe.

This specified price is typically set at a premium to the current market price, incentivizing shareholders to sell. It's a strategic maneuver that can be employed in both friendly and hostile takeover attempts. In a friendly takeover, the target company's board supports the acquisition and recommends that shareholders accept the tender offer. In a hostile takeover, the acquirer bypasses the target's board and appeals directly to shareholders, hoping to gain enough control to oust the existing management.

A classic example of a hostile takeover via a tender offer is Oracle's acquisition of PeopleSoft in 2004. Oracle, a software giant, launched a tender offer for PeopleSoft's shares at a significant premium to the market price. PeopleSoft's board initially resisted the offer, but after a protracted battle lasting over a year, Oracle ultimately succeeded in acquiring PeopleSoft.

Tender offers can create a whirlwind of activity in the market. The target company's stock price often surges in response to the offer, as investors anticipate the potential premium. However, there's no guarantee that the deal will go through. The acquirer may set conditions, such as acquiring a certain percentage of shares, for the tender offer to be successful. If these conditions are not met, the offer may be withdrawn, and the stock price could plummet back to its pre-offer level.

For shareholders, a tender offer presents a unique opportunity and a complex decision. On the one hand, the premium offered can be tempting, especially if the shareholder is sitting on unrealized gains. On the other hand, if the shareholder believes in the long-term prospects of the target company, they might choose to hold onto their shares, hoping for a higher offer or a successful defense by the target's management.

The complexities surrounding tender offers underscore the importance of informed decision-making. As a registered representative, you'll play a crucial role in guiding your clients through these situations. By providing them with objective information about the tender offer, analyzing the potential risks and rewards, and helping them assess the offer in the context of their overall investment goals, you can empower them to make the best possible decision for their financial well-being. Whether it's accepting the offer, holding onto the shares, or exploring alternative options, your guidance can make all the difference in navigating this high-stakes corporate chess game.

Discussion of the potential impact of M&A and tender offers on shareholders and the financial markets.

Having examined the mechanics of mergers, acquisitions, and tender offers, let's explore the potential ripples they can create, not only within the companies involved but also across the broader financial markets and among shareholders, both large and small.

For shareholders of the target company, a successful M&A deal or tender offer can bring windfall profits. The acquiring company typically offers a premium over the current market price to entice shareholders to sell their shares. This was the case in 2018 when Disney acquired 21st Century Fox. Fox shareholders received a 39% premium over the stock's pre-announcement price, translating into significant gains for those who tendered their shares.

However, for shareholders of the acquiring company, the impact can be less clear-cut. While the acquisition may lead to long-term growth and synergies, it can also result in short-term volatility and uncertainty. The acquiring company may incur significant debt to finance the deal, which can impact its financial health and future profitability. Additionally, integrating two companies can be challenging, leading to disruptions in operations and potential cultural clashes. The 2016 merger between AT&T and Time Warner, for example, while creating a media and telecom giant, faced initial skepticism from investors who questioned the strategic rationale and potential integration challenges.

The financial markets, too, can react dramatically to M&A news. The announcement of a deal can send the target company's stock soaring, while the acquirer's stock might experience a temporary dip due to concerns about the cost and complexities of the transaction. The broader market may also be affected, especially if the deal involves large, influential companies in key sectors. For instance, the 2018 merger between CVS Health and Aetna, two healthcare giants, sparked a broader rally in the healthcare sector, as investors anticipated further consolidation and potential benefits from the combined entity.

Beyond the immediate financial impact, M&A and tender offers can have far-reaching consequences for employees, customers, and the competitive landscape. Job cuts, changes in product offerings, and shifts in market dynamics are all potential outcomes of these corporate maneuvers. The 2016 merger between Dell and EMC, for instance, led to significant job losses and restructuring within the newly formed company, as it sought to eliminate redundancies and streamline operations.

the impact of M&A and tender offers is multifaceted, affecting various stakeholders and the overall financial ecosystem. As a registered representative, it's your responsibility to navigate these complexities with your clients, providing them with objective information and guidance to make informed decisions. Whether it's analyzing the terms of a tender offer, assessing the potential impact of a merger on a client's portfolio, or simply explaining the broader implications of these corporate actions, your expertise can empower your clients to make the most of these opportunities and challenges in the ever-evolving world of equity securities.

Conclusion

In this chapter, we've embarked on a journey through the dynamic world of equity securities and market operations, exploring the various types of stocks, the intricate mechanisms of exchanges and trading systems, and the transformative power of corporate actions. We've witnessed how common stock, with its inherent rights and growth potential, forms the bedrock of investment portfolios, while preferred stock offers a unique blend of stability and income. We've ventured into the world of rights and warrants, discovering their leveraged potential and inherent risks.

We've also navigated the bustling arenas of the NYSE and NASDAQ, understanding their distinct market structures and the vital roles played by market makers and specialists. We've mastered the art of placing and executing orders, choosing the right tools for different market scenarios. And we've witnessed the far-reaching impact of corporate actions, from stock splits and dividends to mergers, acquisitions, and tender offers, shaping the landscape of the equity markets and influencing investor portfolios.

By mastering these concepts, you've not only equipped yourself to excel on the Series 7 exam but also laid a solid foundation for a successful career in the financial industry. As a registered representative, your ability to understand and explain these complex concepts to your clients will be invaluable. You'll be able to guide them through the intricacies of the markets, help them make informed investment decisions, and ultimately, empower them to achieve their financial goals.

Test Your Knowledge

1. What are the key differences between common stock and preferred stock?

2. Explain the difference between a market order and a limit order.

3. What is the purpose of a stop-loss order, and how does it differ from a stop-limit order?

4. What are some common red flags that may indicate suspicious activity in a client's account?

5. Explain the difference between a stock split and a reverse stock split, and their potential impact on shareholders.

Summary and Review

This chapter provided a comprehensive overview of equity securities and market operations. We covered the following key topics:

- Types of equity securities: common stock, preferred stock, rights, and warrants

- Stock markets and exchanges: NYSE, NASDAQ, OTC markets, and ATS

- Market participants: market makers and specialists

- Order types and execution strategies: market orders, limit orders, stop orders, price improvement, and best execution

- Corporate actions: stock splits, reverse splits, dividends, mergers, acquisitions, and tender offers

Tips for Applying the Knowledge to Exam Questions

- Focus on understanding the underlying concepts and their practical applications.

- Pay attention to the specific details of each topic, such as the different types of preferred stock or the various order types.

- Practice applying your knowledge to real-world scenarios and case studies.

Real-World Examples and Case Studies

- Apple and Tesla stock splits

- Citigroup and AIG reverse splits

- Microsoft's acquisition of Activision Blizzard

- AT&T's acquisition of Time Warner

- The Flash Crash of 2010

By reviewing these key concepts and examples, you'll be well-prepared to tackle the equity securities and market operations section of the Series 7 exam. Remember, the knowledge you gain in this chapter will not only help you pass the exam but also serve as a valuable foundation for your career in the financial industry.

Chapter 4: Debt Securities and Interest Rate Calculations

In this chapter, we embark on a journey into the realm of debt securities, where investors lend money to corporations, governments, and municipalities in exchange for regular interest payments and the return of principal at maturity. This world is filled with its own set of intricacies, from understanding the different types of debt securities to navigating the complex interplay between bond prices, yields, and interest rate risk.

You'll gain a comprehensive understanding of the debt market landscape, distinguishing between corporate bonds issued by companies to fund their operations, government bonds backed by the full faith and credit of a nation, and municipal bonds used to finance public projects. We'll delve into the specific characteristics of Treasury securities, including bills, notes, and bonds, and explore the unique features of agency securities issued by government-sponsored entities.

Beyond merely identifying the types of debt securities, you'll equip yourself with the tools to analyze their pricing, calculate yields, and assess the impact of interest rate fluctuations. You'll learn how to calculate key metrics like current yield and yield to maturity, empowering you to make informed investment decisions based on your clients' financial goals and risk tolerance.

We'll also unravel the mysteries of the yield curve, understanding its different shapes and their implications for the economy. You'll discover how the yield curve can serve as a powerful predictor of economic growth and recessions, aiding in making strategic investment choices.

Finally, we'll explore the secondary market for debt securities, where bonds are traded after their initial issuance. You'll gain insights into the factors that influence bond liquidity and pricing, as well as the crucial role of bond ratings in assessing creditworthiness and marketability.

By the end of this chapter, you'll possess a solid grasp of debt securities, their characteristics, and the forces that shape their prices and yields. This knowledge will enable you to confidently navigate the bond market, providing sound advice to your clients and building diversified portfolios that balance risk and reward.

I. Types of Debt Securities

Corporate Bonds

Transitioning from the world of equities where ownership is the cornerstone, we now delve into the realm of debt securities, where the relationship between issuer and investor transforms into that of borrower and lender. Within this realm, corporate bonds stand out as a powerful instrument for companies seeking capital and investors seeking stable income.

Corporate bonds are essentially IOUs issued by companies to raise funds for various purposes, such as expanding operations, launching new products, or refinancing existing debt. When an investor purchases a corporate bond, they are effectively lending money to the company. In return, the company promises to pay the investor periodic interest payments, known as coupon payments, and to repay the principal amount, also known as the face value or par value, at maturity.

The terms of a corporate bond, including its maturity date, coupon rate, and credit rating, are outlined in a legal document called an indenture. The coupon rate determines the amount of interest the investor will receive, typically expressed as a percentage of the bond's par value. For example, a $1,000 bond with a 5% coupon rate will pay $50 in interest annually. The maturity date signifies when the bond reaches its full term and the principal is repaid to the investor.

One of the most critical aspects of corporate bonds is their credit rating. Independent rating agencies like Standard & Poor's and Moody's assess the creditworthiness of the issuer, assigning a rating that reflects the perceived risk of default. Higher-rated bonds, such as those with AAA or AA ratings, are considered safer investments, offering lower interest rates. Lower-rated bonds, often referred to as "junk bonds," carry higher default risk and therefore offer higher yields to compensate investors for the increased risk.

For instance, consider a bond issued by a well-established company like Apple, which enjoys a high credit rating. This bond is likely to offer a lower coupon rate than a bond issued by a struggling startup with a lower credit rating. The Apple bond is perceived as a safer investment, while the startup bond carries greater risk of default but also offers the potential for higher returns.

Corporate bonds provide investors with several advantages, including regular income through coupon payments, relative safety compared to stocks, and diversification benefits for portfolios. However, they also come with risks, such as credit risk (the risk that the issuer may default on its payments), interest rate risk (the risk that rising interest rates will decrease the bond's value), and liquidity risk (the risk that the bond may be difficult to sell at a fair price).

Understanding these characteristics, risks, and rewards is essential for any financial professional seeking to navigate the corporate bond market effectively.

Government Bonds

Shifting our gaze from the corporate landscape, we now explore the realm of government bonds, a cornerstone of the fixed-income market, offering investors a unique blend of stability and income.

When a government, be it federal, state, or local, needs to raise funds for infrastructure projects, social programs, or even to cover budget deficits, it turns to the bond market. By issuing government bonds, the government is essentially borrowing money from investors, promising to pay them back with interest over a specified period. This interest, often referred to as the "coupon," provides a predictable income stream for bondholders, making government bonds particularly attractive to risk-averse investors seeking stability.

Unlike corporate bonds, where the creditworthiness of the issuer can vary significantly, government bonds issued by stable and developed economies are generally considered to be among the safest investments in the world. This is because they are backed by the full faith and credit of the issuing government, which has the power to tax its citizens and print currency to meet its debt obligations. As a result, government bonds typically offer lower interest rates than corporate bonds, reflecting their lower perceived risk of default.

A prime example of a government bond is the U.S. Treasury bond, issued by the U.S. federal government. These bonds are considered to be virtually risk-free, as the U.S. government has never defaulted on its debt obligations. As such, they are often used as a benchmark for pricing other fixed-income securities. During times of economic uncertainty, investors often flock to U.S. Treasuries as a safe haven, driving their prices up and yields down.

However, even government bonds are not entirely risk-free. While the risk of default is minimal for bonds issued by developed countries, they are still subject to interest rate risk. As we'll discuss later in this chapter, when interest rates rise, the value of existing bonds tends to fall. This can lead to capital losses for investors who sell their bonds before maturity.

Moreover, the yield on government bonds can vary depending on the maturity date. Longer-term bonds typically offer higher yields than shorter-term bonds, reflecting the increased uncertainty and risk associated with longer holding periods. This relationship between bond yields and maturity dates is visualized in the yield curve, a powerful tool for analyzing economic trends and forecasting future interest rate movements.

Municipal Bonds

Now that we've explored the sturdy world of government bonds, let's turn our attention to another unique segment of the debt market: municipal bonds, or "munis" as they're colloquially known. Issued by state and local governments, these bonds play a crucial role in financing public projects and offer distinct advantages for certain investors.

When a city needs to build a new school, or a state wants to upgrade its highways, they often turn to the bond market for financing. By issuing municipal bonds, these entities borrow money from investors, promising to repay the principal with interest over time. This interest, like with other bonds, provides a regular income stream for bondholders. However, munis have a special allure: their interest payments are generally exempt from federal income tax, and sometimes even state and local taxes, depending on where the investor resides and the bond's origin.

This tax advantage makes munis particularly attractive to high-net-worth individuals in high tax brackets. For example, a California resident in the top tax bracket who invests in a California municipal bond effectively earns a higher after-tax return compared to a taxable corporate bond with the same interest rate. This tax efficiency can be a significant factor in investment decisions, especially for those seeking to maximize their after-tax income.

However, municipal bonds are not without their complexities. They come in two primary flavors: general obligation bonds and revenue bonds. General obligation bonds are backed by the full faith and credit of the issuing municipality, meaning they are supported by the issuer's taxing power. This makes them generally considered safer than revenue bonds, which are backed by the revenue generated from a specific project, such as a toll road or a water treatment plant.

The safety of municipal bonds isn't absolute, though. There's always a risk that the issuer may face financial difficulties and default on its payments. The 1975 default of New York City on its municipal bonds serves as a stark reminder that even government entities can face fiscal challenges. Credit rating agencies play a vital role in assessing the creditworthiness of municipal bond issuers, helping investors gauge the risk associated with their investments.

Treasury Securities (Bills, Notes, Bonds)

From the broad landscape of government bonds, we now zoom in on a specific and crucial segment: Treasury securities. Issued by the U.S. Department of the Treasury, these debt instruments are widely regarded as among the safest investments in the world, backed by the full faith and credit of the U.S. government. Let's unpack the three primary types: Treasury bills, Treasury notes, and Treasury bonds.

Treasury bills, or T-bills, are short-term securities with maturities ranging from a few days to one year. They are unique in that they don't pay periodic interest like traditional bonds. Instead, they are issued at a discount to their face value and mature at par. The difference between the purchase price and the face value represents the investor's interest. For instance, if you buy a $10,000 T-bill for $9,800, you'll receive $10,000 at maturity, earning $200 in interest. T-bills are highly liquid and often used by investors seeking a safe place to park their cash for short periods.

Treasury notes, or T-notes, have intermediate maturities, ranging from two to ten years. Unlike T-bills, T-notes pay semi-annual interest payments based on a fixed coupon rate. For example, a 10-year T-note with a 3% coupon rate and a face value of $1,000 would pay $15 in interest every six months. T-notes offer a balance of income and relative safety, making them suitable for investors seeking a steady stream of income without taking on excessive risk.

Treasury bonds, or T-bonds, are the long-distance runners of the Treasury family, with maturities of 20 or 30 years. Like T-notes, they pay semi-annual interest based on a fixed coupon rate. T-bonds can be an attractive option for investors seeking to lock in long-term yields and hedge against inflation. However, they also carry greater interest rate risk than T-bills or T-notes, as their prices can fluctuate more significantly in response to changes in interest rates.

The yields on Treasury securities are closely watched indicators of market sentiment and economic expectations. When investors perceive increased risk in the market, they often flock to Treasuries as a safe haven, driving their prices up and yields down. This phenomenon was vividly illustrated during the 2008 financial crisis, when the yield on the 10-year Treasury note plunged to historic lows as investors sought refuge from the turmoil in the stock market.

Agency Securities

Now that we've established the bedrock of safety and stability represented by U.S. Treasury securities, let's turn our attention to another vital segment of the debt market: agency securities. These securities, while not directly issued by the U.S. Treasury, are closely tied to the government and play a crucial role in supporting specific sectors of the economy.

Agency securities are issued by two types of entities: federal government agencies and government-sponsored enterprises (GSEs). Federal government agencies, such as the Government National Mortgage Association (Ginnie Mae), are part of the U.S. government and their securities are backed by the full faith and credit of the U.S. government, just like Treasury securities. GSEs, on the other hand, are privately owned corporations with a public purpose, such as providing liquidity to the mortgage market. Prominent GSEs include the Federal National Mortgage Association (Fannie Mae) and the Federal Home Loan Mortgage Corporation (Freddie Mac).

While GSE securities are not explicitly backed by the U.S. government, they are implicitly backed, meaning the government is highly likely to intervene if they face financial difficulties. This implicit backing stems from the critical role that GSEs play in the housing market and the broader economy. During the 2008 financial crisis, for instance, the U.S. government took control of Fannie Mae and Freddie Mac to prevent their collapse and stabilize the housing market.

Agency securities offer several advantages to investors. First, they typically provide higher yields than Treasury securities with comparable maturities, reflecting their slightly higher perceived risk. Second, they are considered relatively safe investments due to their implicit or explicit government backing. Third, they offer diversification benefits, as their performance may be less correlated with the broader stock market than corporate bonds.

For example, an investor seeking a higher yield than a 10-year Treasury note might consider a 10-year agency bond issued by Fannie Mae or Freddie Mac. While the agency bond carries a slightly higher risk, it also offers the potential for higher returns.

However, it's important to note that agency securities are not without risks. While the risk of default is generally low, it's not zero. The financial crisis of 2008 served as a reminder that even GSEs can face challenges that require government intervention. Furthermore, like all fixed-income securities, agency securities are subject to interest rate risk. If interest rates rise, the value of existing agency bonds can decline, potentially leading to capital losses for investors who sell before maturity.

II. Bond Pricing, Yield Calculations, and Interest Rate Risk

Inverse relationship between bond prices and interest rates

Having explored the diverse array of debt securities available in the market, let's now turn our attention to the fascinating and often counterintuitive relationship between bond prices and interest rates. This inverse relationship lies at the heart of bond market dynamics, influencing investment decisions and creating opportunities for both gains and losses.

The central tenet of this relationship is this: as interest rates rise, bond prices fall, and vice versa. This might seem puzzling at first, but it makes perfect sense when we consider the mechanics of bond pricing. Remember that a bond is essentially a loan, with the issuer paying periodic interest to the bondholder until maturity, when the principal is repaid. The coupon rate, or interest rate, on a bond is fixed at the time of issuance.

Now, imagine you own a bond issued a few years ago with a 5% coupon rate. If market interest rates suddenly rise to 6%, new bonds being issued will offer this higher rate. Your existing bond, with its 5% coupon, becomes less attractive to investors. To compensate for the lower interest rate, the market price of your bond will decrease until its yield aligns with the prevailing market rate. This is why rising interest rates cause bond prices to fall.

Conversely, if interest rates decline, your 5% bond becomes more valuable. New bonds issued will offer lower rates, making your existing bond with its higher coupon more desirable. As a result, the market price of your bond will increase until its yield matches the lower market rate.

This inverse relationship between bond prices and interest rates is a fundamental principle of bond investing. It highlights the importance of interest rate risk, which is the potential for an investor to experience losses due to changes in interest rates. For instance, during the 1970s and early 1980s, when the Federal Reserve aggressively raised interest rates to combat inflation, bond investors experienced significant losses as bond prices plummeted.

Yield calculations (current yield, yield to maturity)

Having established the inverse relationship between bond prices and interest rates, let's now equip ourselves with the tools to measure a bond's return. This brings us to the realm of yield calculations, where two key metrics take center stage: current yield and yield to maturity (YTM). These metrics, though seemingly similar, provide distinct perspectives on a bond's profitability, allowing investors to make informed decisions based on their individual needs and investment horizons.

Current yield offers a snapshot of a bond's annual return based on its current market price. It's calculated by dividing the bond's annual interest payment (coupon payment) by its current market price. For example, if a bond with a 5% coupon rate and a par value of $1,000 is currently trading at $950, its current yield would be 5.26% ($50 / $950). This metric is useful for quickly comparing the income potential of different bonds, especially for investors primarily concerned with generating current income.

However, current yield doesn't tell the whole story. It doesn't take into account the potential gain or loss an investor might experience if they hold the bond until maturity. This is where yield to maturity (YTM) comes in.

YTM represents the total return an investor can expect to earn if they hold the bond until it matures, assuming all coupon payments are reinvested at the same rate. It factors in not only the coupon payments but also the difference between the purchase price and the par value received at maturity. Calculating YTM can be complex, often requiring the use of financial calculators or spreadsheet functions. However, understanding its significance is crucial for making informed investment decisions.

To illustrate the difference between current yield and YTM, let's consider a bond with a 5% coupon rate, a par value of $1,000, and five years remaining until maturity. If the bond is currently trading at a discount for $900, its current yield would be 5.56% ($50 / $900). However, its YTM would be higher, as it also accounts for the $100 gain the investor will realize at maturity.

The choice between focusing on current yield or YTM depends on the investor's objectives. An investor primarily seeking current income might prioritize bonds with high current yields. However, an investor with a longer time horizon might be more interested in YTM, as it reflects the total return potential of the bond over its remaining life.

Duration and convexity

While the inverse relationship between bond prices and interest rates sets the stage for understanding bond market dynamics, the concepts of duration and convexity add layers of nuance and precision to our understanding of how bond prices react to shifts in interest rates. These concepts are crucial for managing interest rate risk, a key consideration for any investor venturing into the fixed-income arena.

Duration, often referred to as the "weighted average time to maturity," measures a bond's sensitivity to changes in interest rates. It's a complex calculation that considers not only the bond's maturity date but also its coupon rate and yield to maturity. A bond with a higher duration will experience a larger price change in response to a given interest rate movement than a bond with a lower duration.

Think of duration as a bond's "elasticity." A high-duration bond is like a rubber band that stretches significantly when pulled, while a low-duration bond is like a stiff spring that barely moves. For example, a 30-year Treasury bond with a low coupon rate will have a much higher duration than a 2-year Treasury note with a similar coupon rate. If interest rates rise by 1%, the 30-year bond's price will decline more sharply than the 2-year note's price.

But duration, while useful, has its limitations. It assumes a linear relationship between bond prices and interest rates, which isn't always the case. This is where convexity comes into play.

Convexity measures the curvature in the relationship between bond prices and interest rates. It accounts for the fact that the price change of a bond is not perfectly linear, but rather exhibits a slight curve. A bond with positive convexity will experience larger price increases when interest rates fall and smaller price decreases when interest rates rise compared to a bond with the same duration but lower convexity.

To illustrate this, let's compare two hypothetical bonds with the same duration but different levels of convexity. If interest rates decline by 1%, the bond with higher convexity will see a larger price increase than the bond with lower convexity, even though their durations are the same. This is because the higher convexity bond captures the additional "curve" in the price-yield relationship.

Duration and convexity are invaluable tools for managing interest rate risk. By understanding these concepts, you can assess the potential impact of interest rate movements on your bond portfolio and make informed decisions about buying or selling bonds. For example, if you anticipate rising interest rates, you might choose to shorten the duration of your bond portfolio to minimize potential losses. Conversely, if you expect interest rates to fall, you might favor bonds with longer durations and higher convexity to maximize potential gains.

III. The Yield Curve and Its Economic Implications

Normal, inverted, and flat yield curves

Having equipped ourselves with the tools to measure bond yields, let's now turn our attention to a powerful visual representation that encapsulates the interplay between bond yields and their maturities: the yield curve. This seemingly simple graph, plotting the yields of bonds with different maturities, holds a wealth of information about the market's expectations for future interest rates and economic growth. It's a compass that can guide investors and policymakers alike, offering insights into the health of the economy and potential risks on the horizon.

In its most common form, the yield curve exhibits an upward slope, often referred to as a "normal" yield curve. This shape reflects the expectation that longer-term bonds will offer higher yields than shorter-term bonds. This makes intuitive sense, as investors typically demand higher compensation for tying up their money for longer periods, facing the uncertainty and potential risks that come with a longer time horizon. A normal yield curve signals a healthy economy, with investors anticipating growth and moderate inflation in the future.

However, the yield curve is not always upward sloping. Sometimes, it can become flat or even inverted. A flat yield curve occurs when there is little difference in yields between short-term and long-term bonds. This can indicate uncertainty about the future direction of the economy, with investors unsure whether to expect growth or a slowdown.

An inverted yield curve, on the other hand, is a more ominous sign. It occurs when short-term yields are higher than long-term yields, suggesting that investors anticipate economic weakness and potential rate cuts in the future. An inverted yield curve has historically been a reliable predictor of recessions. In fact, every recession in the U.S. since 1955 has been preceded by an inverted yield curve.

For instance, in 2019, the yield curve briefly inverted, with the yield on the 10-year Treasury note falling below the yield on the 2-year Treasury note. This inversion sparked widespread concerns about a potential recession, and indeed, the U.S. economy entered a recession in 2020, triggered in part by the COVID-19 pandemic.

Yield curve as an economic indicator

Having dissected the various shapes a yield curve can take—normal, flat, or inverted—we arrive at the crux of its significance: its role as a powerful economic indicator. The yield curve isn't just a static graph; it's a dynamic reflection of the market's collective expectations about the future of the economy, interest rates, and inflation.

Essentially, the yield curve functions as a crystal ball, offering a glimpse into the future. Its slope, whether steep, flat, or inverted, can reveal a great deal about where the economy might be headed. For example, a steep yield curve, where long-term yields are significantly higher than short-term yields, often suggests that investors anticipate robust economic growth and potential inflationary pressures. This expectation stems from the belief that central banks will need to raise interest rates in the future to curb inflation, pushing up yields on longer-term bonds.

Conversely, a flat or inverted yield curve signals a different narrative. A flat curve, with minimal difference between short-term and long-term yields, implies uncertainty about the economic outlook. Investors are hesitant to commit to longer-term bonds, fearing that economic growth may stall or that central banks may be forced to cut interest rates to stimulate the economy.

An inverted yield curve, as we've discussed, is often seen as a harbinger of recession. The inversion signals that investors are so concerned about future economic weakness that they are willing to accept lower yields on longer-term bonds in exchange for the perceived safety of locking in their investments for a longer duration. This phenomenon is driven by the expectation that central banks will eventually lower interest rates to combat an economic slowdown, making existing long-term bonds with higher coupons more valuable.

The predictive power of the yield curve has been validated by numerous studies and historical data. The Federal Reserve Bank of New York, for instance, has developed a model that uses the slope of the yield curve to calculate the probability of a recession in the United States twelve months ahead. This model has a track record of accurately predicting recessions, including the 2008 financial crisis and the 2020 COVID-19 recession.

However, the yield curve is not an infallible predictor. It's a complex tool influenced by a multitude of factors, including monetary policy, inflation expectations, global economic conditions, and investor sentiment. While an inverted yield curve has historically been a reliable recession indicator, it's not a guarantee. Other factors, such as geopolitical events or unforeseen shocks, can also trigger economic downturns.

Despite its limitations, the yield curve remains a valuable tool for understanding the market's collective wisdom and making informed investment decisions. As a registered representative, your ability to interpret the yield curve and explain its implications to your clients will demonstrate your expertise and enhance your credibility. By leveraging the insights gleaned from this powerful indicator, you can help your clients navigate the complexities of the bond market, make strategic investment choices, and position their portfolios for long-term success.

Historical examples of yield curve changes

The yield curve's ability to foreshadow economic shifts is not merely theoretical; it's etched in the annals of financial history. Let's journey back in time to examine a few key instances where dramatic yield curve changes presaged pivotal economic events, shaping investment strategies and impacting the lives of millions.

In the lead-up to the Great Recession of 2008, the yield curve flashed a warning sign that few heeded. In 2006, the curve inverted, with short-term yields surpassing long-term yields, a classic indicator of an impending economic downturn. This inversion, driven by the Federal Reserve's aggressive interest rate hikes to combat inflation, signaled that investors were increasingly worried about the future. Unfortunately, these concerns proved prescient. The housing bubble burst, triggering a domino effect that toppled financial institutions and plunged the global economy into its worst recession since the Great Depression.

Fast forward to 2019, and the yield curve once again inverted, sparking fears of another recession. This time, the inversion was driven by a confluence of factors, including slowing global growth, trade tensions, and concerns about the Federal Reserve's monetary policy.

While the economy did eventually enter a recession in 2020, this time triggered by the COVID-19 pandemic, the yield curve's inversion served as a stark reminder of its predictive power.

But the yield curve doesn't only signal recessions. It can also herald periods of economic expansion and prosperity. In the early 1990s, as the U.S. economy emerged from a recession, the yield curve steepened dramatically, with long-term yields rising significantly above short-term yields. This steepening reflected growing optimism about the economic recovery, as investors anticipated increased borrowing and spending, leading to higher interest rates in the future. The subsequent years saw a period of robust economic growth, with low unemployment and rising stock prices.

Similarly, in the aftermath of the 2008 financial crisis, as the Federal Reserve embarked on a series of quantitative easing programs to stimulate the economy, the yield curve steepened again. This signaled that investors were gaining confidence in the recovery and anticipating a gradual normalization of interest rates. The ensuing years saw a prolonged bull market in stocks and a steady decline in unemployment, validating the yield curve's positive outlook.

These historical examples illustrate the profound impact that yield curve changes can have on the economy and investment landscape.

IV. Debt Securities on the Secondary Market

Trading of bonds after initial issuance

Now that we've established the foundational knowledge of various debt securities, their yields, and the interplay with interest rates, let's explore the dynamic ecosystem where these securities change hands after their initial debut - the secondary bond market. Understanding this arena is vital for both investors and financial professionals alike, as it offers opportunities to capitalize on changing market conditions, manage risk, and achieve investment objectives.

The secondary bond market is the bustling bazaar where previously issued bonds are bought and sold between investors. It's a realm of continuous trading, where bond prices fluctuate based on a myriad of factors, from interest rate movements to credit rating changes, economic news, and even geopolitical developments.

Unlike the primary market, where bonds are initially issued by corporations, governments, or municipalities to raise capital, the secondary market serves as a platform for investors to trade existing bonds. This dynamic marketplace ensures liquidity for bondholders, allowing them to sell their bonds before maturity if needed, without having to wait for the issuer to repay the principal. It also provides opportunities for new investors to enter the bond market and purchase bonds that align with their investment goals and risk tolerances.

Consider a scenario where an investor purchased a 10-year corporate bond a few years ago. If their financial circumstances change or they anticipate a rise in interest rates, they can sell their bond in the secondary market. The price they receive for the bond will depend on its current yield relative to prevailing market interest rates. If interest rates have risen since the bond was issued, the bond's price will likely be lower than its par value. Conversely, if interest rates have fallen, the bond's price will likely be higher than its par value.

The secondary bond market operates through a network of broker-dealers who act as intermediaries between buyers and sellers. These broker-dealers may maintain inventories of bonds, providing liquidity and ensuring that trades can be executed quickly and efficiently. They also play a crucial role in disseminating information about bond prices and market conditions, helping investors make informed decisions.

The trading of bonds in the secondary market is not limited to individual investors. Institutional investors, such as pension funds, insurance companies, and mutual funds, are also active participants in this market. Their large trades can significantly impact bond prices and market liquidity.

Factors affecting bond liquidity and pricing

As bonds change hands in the bustling secondary market, their prices and liquidity are in constant flux, responding to a symphony of economic, market, and issuer-specific factors. Understanding these dynamics is not just academic; it's at the heart of successful bond investing, allowing you to navigate the complexities of the market and make informed decisions on behalf of your clients.

Let's start with interest rates, the conductor of the bond market orchestra. As we've already discussed, there's an inverse relationship between bond prices and interest rates. When prevailing interest rates rise, newly issued bonds offer higher yields, making existing bonds with lower coupon rates less attractive. To compensate for this, their prices fall, adjusting their yields to be competitive in the market. This impact is amplified for bonds with longer maturities, as their prices are more sensitive to interest rate changes due to their longer duration.

Credit quality, another key factor, plays a starring role in bond pricing. The creditworthiness of the issuer, as reflected in their bond rating, influences the perceived risk of default. Highly rated bonds, issued by financially stable entities, are seen as less risky and thus command lower yields, translating to higher prices. Conversely, lower-rated or "junk" bonds, with higher default risk, must offer higher yields to entice investors, resulting in lower prices. For example, a bond issued by a blue-chip company like Microsoft will typically trade at a higher price and lower yield than a bond issued by a struggling company with a less favorable credit rating.

Market demand also plays a significant role in bond pricing. The more buyers there are for a particular bond, the higher its price will tend to be. Conversely, if there are few buyers and many sellers, the price will be pressured downwards. This supply-demand dynamic is influenced by various factors, including economic conditions, investor sentiment, and the availability of alternative investments. During the 2020 pandemic, for instance, investors flocked to safe-haven assets like U.S. Treasury bonds, driving their prices up and yields down, reflecting the increased demand for these securities.

Bond liquidity, or the ease with which a bond can be bought or sold, is intertwined with these factors and further influences its pricing. Highly liquid bonds, with active trading and ample buyers and sellers, tend to have tighter bid-ask spreads and more stable prices. Less liquid bonds, typically those issued by smaller companies or with unique features, may experience wider spreads and greater price volatility.

Factors like the maturity date, call features, and the overall economic climate can also impact a bond's liquidity and pricing. For example, bonds with shorter maturities tend to be more liquid than longer-term bonds, as they are less sensitive to interest rate changes. Callable bonds, which give the issuer the right to redeem the bond before maturity, may be less liquid as investors face the risk of having their investment cut short.

Role of bond ratings and their impact

Having examined the dynamic forces that influence bond prices and liquidity, let's shine a spotlight on a critical factor that underpins investor confidence and shapes bond valuations: bond ratings. These seemingly simple letter grades, assigned by independent credit rating agencies, carry immense weight in the bond market, acting as a compass for investors navigating the vast sea of fixed-income securities.

Bond ratings, issued by agencies like Standard & Poor's, Moody's, and Fitch, essentially gauge the issuer's creditworthiness and ability to meet debt obligations in a timely manner. Think of them as a report card for borrowers, with ratings ranging from AAA (highest quality) to D (in default). These ratings aren't just abstract assessments; they have a tangible impact on bond yields and investor demand.

Bonds with high ratings, often referred to as "investment-grade" bonds, are perceived as having a low risk of default. Investors are more confident in their ability to receive timely interest payments and the return of their principal at maturity. As a result, these bonds command lower yields, reflecting their lower perceived risk.

On the other hand, bonds with lower ratings, often called "junk bonds" or "high-yield bonds," carry a higher perceived risk of default. Investors demand higher yields to compensate for this increased risk, pushing down the prices of these bonds.

The impact of bond ratings on the market is profound. A downgrade in a company's bond rating can send shockwaves through the market, causing its bond prices to plummet and its borrowing costs to soar. For example, in 2011, Standard & Poor's downgraded the United States' sovereign credit rating from AAA to AA+, citing concerns about the country's fiscal outlook. This downgrade, while controversial, sent ripples through the global financial markets, triggering a sell-off in U.S. Treasuries and raising concerns about the stability of the U.S. economy.

Conversely, an upgrade in a company's bond rating can boost investor confidence, leading to higher bond prices and lower borrowing costs. This can be particularly beneficial for companies seeking to refinance their debt or raise additional capital at favorable rates.

The role of bond ratings extends beyond just influencing prices and yields. They also impact the liquidity and marketability of bonds. Highly rated bonds tend to be more liquid, meaning they can be easily bought or sold in the secondary market. This is because they are more widely held by institutional investors and have a broader appeal due to their lower perceived risk. Lower-rated bonds, on the other hand, can be less liquid, making them more difficult to trade and potentially resulting in wider bid-ask spreads.

Chapter Summary and Review:

In this chapter, we delved into the complexities of debt securities, unraveling their various types, the factors that influence their pricing, and their role in the broader financial landscape. We started by distinguishing between corporate bonds, government bonds, municipal bonds, Treasury securities, and agency securities, highlighting their unique characteristics and risk-reward profiles.

We then explored the inverse relationship between bond prices and interest rates, understanding how changes in interest rates impact bond valuations. We also equipped ourselves with the tools to calculate key yield metrics, such as current yield and yield to maturity, enabling us to assess the return potential of different bonds. We further deepened our understanding by examining the concepts of duration and convexity, which measure a bond's sensitivity to interest rate changes and provide a more nuanced perspective on interest rate risk.

Next, we ventured into the realm of the yield curve, uncovering its various shapes and their implications for the economy. We saw how a normal yield curve signals a healthy economy, while an inverted curve can be a harbinger of recession. We also explored historical examples of yield curve changes, reinforcing its predictive power and its significance in shaping investment strategies.

Finally, we navigated the secondary bond market, where previously issued bonds are traded between investors. We examined the factors influencing bond liquidity and pricing, from interest rate movements to credit ratings and market demand. We also highlighted the crucial role of bond ratings in assessing creditworthiness and shaping investor perceptions.

Key Terms and Concepts:

- Corporate bonds
- Government bonds
- Municipal bonds
- Treasury securities (bills, notes, bonds)
- Agency securities
- Coupon rate
- Maturity date
- Yield to maturity (YTM)
- Current yield
- Interest rate risk
- Duration
- Convexity
- Yield curve
- Normal yield curve
- Inverted yield curve
- Flat yield curve
- Bond ratings
- Liquidity
- Marketability

Test Your Knowledge:

1. What is the key difference between a corporate bond and a government bond?

2. How does a change in interest rates affect the price of a bond?

3. What is the difference between current yield and yield to maturity?

4. Explain the concept of duration and its significance in bond investing.

5. What does an inverted yield curve indicate about the economic outlook?

Tips for Applying the Knowledge to Exam Questions:

- **Understand the fundamentals:** Grasp the basic principles of bond pricing, yields, and interest rate risk.

- **Know the different types of bonds:** Be able to distinguish between corporate, government, municipal, Treasury, and agency securities.

- **Calculate yields:** Practice calculating current yield and yield to maturity.

- **Interpret the yield curve:** Understand the implications of different yield curve shapes for the economy.

- **Analyze credit risk:** Be able to assess the creditworthiness of bond issuers based on their ratings.

Real-World Examples and Case Studies

- The 2008 financial crisis and its impact on bond yields

- The U.S. credit rating downgrade in 2011

- The yield curve inversion in 2019 and the subsequent recession

By mastering the concepts covered in this chapter, you'll be well-equipped to navigate the complexities of the bond market, make informed investment decisions, and provide sound advice to your clients. Your understanding of debt securities, their yields, and the interplay with economic factors will empower you to build diversified portfolios that balance risk and reward, paving the way for long-term financial success.

Chapter 5: Beyond the Basics: Exploring Packaged Products and Alternative Investments

Having navigated the world of stocks and bonds, we now embark on a journey into a realm of diversified and sophisticated investment vehicles: packaged products and alternative investments. This chapter will broaden your horizons beyond the traditional securities we've explored thus far, opening doors to strategies that can enhance portfolio diversification, potentially boost returns, and cater to specific investor needs.

We'll begin by delving into the world of mutual funds, those baskets of securities that offer instant diversification and professional management. You'll understand the various types of mutual funds, from equity and bond funds to balanced and money market funds, and grasp their distinct risk-reward profiles. We'll also explore the operational differences between open-end and closed-end funds, providing you with the knowledge to recommend the most suitable structures to your clients. Finally, we'll touch upon the regulatory considerations surrounding mutual funds, ensuring you're well-versed in prospectus requirements and the calculation of Net Asset Value (NAV), a critical metric for evaluating fund performance.

Next, we'll step into the realm of exchange-traded funds (ETFs), the modern cousins of mutual funds that trade like stocks on exchanges. You'll discover the structural advantages of ETFs, such as their intraday tradability and potential tax efficiency, and explore the diverse array of ETF offerings, from broad market index ETFs to sector-specific and leveraged ETFs. We'll also shed light on unit investment trusts (UITs), a less common but still relevant type of packaged product with its own unique features and applications.

Venturing further into alternative investments, we'll explore the world of real estate investment trusts (REITs), which provide exposure to the real estate market without the need for direct property ownership. You'll learn about the different types of REITs, their tax implications, and their potential role in diversifying portfolios. We'll also touch upon direct participation programs (DPPs), a more specialized type of investment that offers direct ownership in real estate or other ventures but comes with its own set of risks and rewards.

Finally, we'll conclude our exploration with a glimpse into the exclusive world of hedge funds and private equity. You'll gain a basic understanding of hedge fund strategies, the concept of accredited investors, and the regulatory considerations surrounding these sophisticated investment vehicles. We'll also briefly touch upon private equity, its role in financing companies and generating potential high returns, and the challenges and limitations associated with these types of investments.

By the end of this chapter, you'll possess a broader perspective on the investment landscape, armed with knowledge about various packaged products and alternative investments. This will empower you to craft more nuanced and diversified portfolios for your clients, catering to their unique needs and risk appetites. Whether it's pursuing growth through equity mutual funds, seeking stable income through bond ETFs, or exploring alternative investments for diversification, you'll be equipped to navigate this expansive universe with confidence and expertise.

I. Mutual Funds

Types (equity, bond, balanced, money market)

Having explored the vast landscape of individual securities, from stocks and bonds to options and warrants, we now shift our focus to the realm of packaged products, where these individual instruments are bundled together to create diversified investment solutions. Our first stop on this journey is the world of mutual funds, a popular and accessible way for investors to gain exposure to a broad range of securities with the added benefit of professional management.

Mutual funds are, in essence, investment pools where numerous investors combine their money to purchase a diversified portfolio of securities. This pooling structure allows investors to access a wider array of investments than they could typically afford individually. Furthermore, these funds are managed by professional portfolio managers, who utilize their expertise and research capabilities to select securities that align with the fund's investment objectives.

Within the vast universe of mutual funds, we encounter a spectrum of options, each catering to distinct risk tolerances and investment goals. Equity funds, for example, primarily invest in stocks, offering the potential for long-term growth but also carrying higher risk compared to other fund types. Bond funds, on the other hand, focus on fixed-income securities like government and corporate bonds, providing a steadier stream of income but with generally lower potential for capital appreciation.

For investors seeking a balanced approach, balanced funds offer a mix of stocks and bonds, striking a middle ground between growth and income. The allocation between stocks and bonds can vary depending on the fund's specific objectives, ranging from conservative to aggressive.

Money market funds, meanwhile, invest in short-term debt instruments like Treasury bills and commercial paper, prioritizing safety and liquidity. They offer minimal returns but are considered among the safest investment options, suitable for parking cash for short periods or for investors with a low-risk appetite.

The choice of mutual fund type depends largely on the investor's financial goals, risk tolerance, and time horizon. A young investor with a long time horizon might favor equity funds for their growth potential, while a retiree seeking stable income might opt for bond or money market funds.

Beyond these primary types, there's a plethora of specialized mutual funds catering to niche interests or specific sectors. These include sector funds focused on industries like technology or healthcare, international funds investing in foreign companies, and socially responsible funds that prioritize environmental, social, and governance (ESG) factors.

The mutual fund landscape is a dynamic and ever-evolving space, offering investors a wide range of options to achieve their financial objectives. By understanding the different types of mutual funds and their distinct characteristics, you'll be equipped to guide your clients toward the most suitable investments, creating portfolios that balance risk and reward and pave the way for long-term financial success.

Fund structures (open-end, closed-end)

Having explored the diverse landscape of mutual fund types, let's now turn our attention to the structural underpinnings of these investment vehicles: open-end and closed-end funds.

While both structures provide access to professionally managed portfolios, they differ significantly in how they operate, their liquidity profiles, and their potential impact on investors.

Open-end funds, as we've discussed, are like an ever-expanding balloon. They continuously issue and redeem shares based on investor demand. When an investor wants to buy shares of an open-end fund, the fund simply creates new shares and sells them at the current net asset value (NAV), which is the value of the fund's assets minus its liabilities divided by the number of shares outstanding. Similarly, when an investor wants to sell their shares, the fund redeems them at NAV. This flexibility and liquidity are key advantages of open-end funds, as investors can easily enter or exit the fund based on their individual needs and market conditions.

For example, consider the Vanguard 500 Index Fund, one of the largest and most popular mutual funds in the world. This open-end fund tracks the performance of the S&P 500 index, offering investors broad exposure to the U.S. large-cap stock market. Investors can buy or sell shares of this fund at any time, providing them with the flexibility to adjust their portfolios as needed.

Closed-end funds, on the other hand, operate more like traditional stocks. They issue a fixed number of shares through an initial public offering (IPO), and these shares are then traded on a stock exchange like any other listed security. The price of a closed-end fund's shares is determined by supply and demand in the market and can deviate from the fund's NAV. This can create opportunities for investors to buy shares at a discount to NAV or sell them at a premium, potentially enhancing their returns.

The Gabelli Equity Trust, for instance, is a closed-end fund that invests in a concentrated portfolio of undervalued stocks. Its shares trade on the NYSE, and their price can fluctuate based on market sentiment, regardless of the fund's underlying NAV.

However, closed-end funds also have their drawbacks. Their fixed number of shares can lead to less liquidity compared to open-end funds, as buying or selling shares depends on finding a willing counterparty in the market. Additionally, the potential for shares to trade at a discount or premium to NAV adds an element of complexity to valuation and can create opportunities for arbitrage.

Regulatory considerations (prospectus, NAV)

Now that we've established the distinction between open-end and closed-end mutual funds, it's time to navigate the regulatory landscape that governs these investment vehicles. While mutual funds offer numerous benefits to investors, they also operate within a complex regulatory framework designed to protect investors and ensure fair and transparent practices. Two key components of this framework are the prospectus and the calculation of Net Asset Value (NAV).

The prospectus serves as a comprehensive guide to a mutual fund, providing essential information about its investment objectives, strategies, risks, fees, and historical performance. It's a crucial document that empowers investors to make informed decisions, akin to a product's user manual. The Securities Act of 1933 mandates that mutual funds provide a prospectus to potential investors before they invest. This ensures transparency and enables investors to assess whether the fund aligns with their financial goals and risk tolerance.

The prospectus must be updated annually and whenever material changes occur in the fund's operations. For example, if a fund changes its investment strategy or its management team, it must disclose these changes in an updated prospectus. The Securities and Exchange

Commission (SEC) plays a vital role in overseeing the accuracy and completeness of mutual fund prospectuses, ensuring they meet stringent disclosure requirements.

Net Asset Value (NAV), as we've discussed earlier, is the per-share value of a mutual fund, calculated by subtracting its liabilities from its assets and dividing by the number of shares outstanding. NAV is typically calculated at the end of each trading day, reflecting the closing market prices of the securities held in the fund's portfolio. This daily calculation ensures transparency and allows investors to track the fund's performance over time.

The accuracy and reliability of NAV calculations are critical, as they directly impact the price at which investors buy or sell mutual fund shares. The Investment Company Act of 1940 establishes strict guidelines for NAV calculations, requiring funds to use fair value pricing for their securities and to account for any accrued expenses or income. The SEC closely monitors these calculations to prevent any fraudulent or misleading practices.

In 2003, several mutual fund companies were embroiled in a scandal involving late trading and market timing, practices that allowed favored investors to profit at the expense of ordinary shareholders. These scandals, which exposed flaws in NAV calculation and trading practices, led to significant regulatory reforms and increased scrutiny of mutual fund operations.

II. Exchange-Traded Funds (ETFs) and Unit Investment Trusts (UITs)

ETF structure & benefits vs. mutual funds

Having gained a firm grasp of mutual funds—those baskets of securities professionally managed for diversification—we now venture into a close relative that has taken the investment world by storm: Exchange-Traded Funds, or ETFs. While they share the core concept of pooling assets to invest in a diversified portfolio, ETFs offer a distinct set of structural advantages that set them apart from traditional mutual funds.

At their core, ETFs are similar to mutual funds in that they represent a collection of securities, such as stocks, bonds, or commodities. However, the key distinction lies in how they're traded. ETFs are listed on stock exchanges and trade throughout the day just like individual stocks. This intraday tradability provides investors with greater flexibility and control compared to mutual funds, which are priced and traded only once at the end of each trading day based on their net asset value (NAV).

Let's imagine an investor who believes that the technology sector is poised for a surge. With an ETF that tracks a technology index, such as the Invesco QQQ Trust, which mirrors the performance of the Nasdaq-100 Index, the investor can quickly and easily buy shares during the trading day, capitalizing on real-time market movements. In contrast, if they were to invest in a technology mutual fund, they'd have to wait until the end of the day to purchase shares at the calculated NAV, potentially missing out on intraday price movements.

This intraday tradability also enables the use of various trading strategies with ETFs, such as limit orders, stop orders, and even options, providing investors with greater precision and control over their trades.

Another advantage of ETFs lies in their potential tax efficiency. Due to their unique creation and redemption process, ETFs generally experience lower capital gains distributions compared to mutual funds, resulting in potential tax savings for investors, particularly those in taxable accounts. This tax advantage can make a significant difference in long-term investment returns, especially for those in higher tax brackets.

Furthermore, ETFs often boast lower expense ratios than their mutual fund counterparts. This is partly due to their passive management style, where most ETFs track a specific index rather than relying on active stock picking by a portfolio manager. Lower expense ratios translate into higher net returns for investors, as less of their investment is eaten up by fees.

The combination of intraday tradability, potential tax efficiency, and lower expense ratios has made ETFs a popular choice for investors seeking a cost-effective and flexible way to gain diversified market exposure. Whether you're a long-term investor looking to build a core portfolio or an active trader seeking to capitalize on short-term market movements, ETFs offer a versatile tool to meet your investment needs.

ETF types (index, sector, leveraged)

As the popularity of Exchange-Traded Funds (ETFs) has exploded in recent years, so too has the diversity of available options. Beyond the simple tracking of broad market indices, ETFs now cater to a wide array of investment strategies and risk appetites. Let's delve into three key types of ETFs that showcase this variety: index ETFs, sector ETFs, and leveraged ETFs.

Index ETFs, as we discussed earlier, aim to replicate the performance of a specific market index, such as the S&P 500 or the Nasdaq-100. These funds offer investors broad market exposure, providing a cost-effective way to participate in the overall performance of a particular market segment. For instance, the SPDR S&P 500 ETF (SPY), one of the oldest and largest ETFs, tracks the S&P 500 index, allowing investors to essentially "own" a slice of the 500 largest U.S. companies.

Sector ETFs, as their name suggests, focus on specific sectors of the economy, such as technology, healthcare, or energy. These funds offer a way for investors to gain targeted exposure to industries they believe are poised for growth or to hedge their portfolios against specific sector risks. The Energy Select Sector SPDR Fund (XLE), for example, tracks the energy sector of the S&P 500, allowing investors to participate in the performance of oil and gas companies, renewable energy firms, and other energy-related businesses.

Leveraged ETFs, the risk-takers of the ETF world, aim to amplify the returns of an underlying index or benchmark, typically by a factor of two or three. This leverage is achieved through the use of derivatives, such as futures contracts or swaps, which magnify the fund's exposure to market movements. While leveraged ETFs can offer the potential for significant gains in a short period, they also carry heightened risk, as losses are magnified as well. The ProShares UltraPro QQQ (TQQQ), for instance, seeks to provide three times the daily return of the Nasdaq-100 Index. While this can lead to impressive gains when the tech sector is booming, it can also result in steep losses during market downturns.

Understanding these different types of ETFs is crucial for tailoring investment recommendations to client needs. Index ETFs provide a cost-effective way to gain broad market exposure, while sector ETFs offer a targeted approach for those seeking to capitalize on specific industry trends. Leveraged ETFs, on the other hand, are suitable only for sophisticated investors who understand and are comfortable with the risks involved.

UIT features & role in portfolios

Now that we've contrasted the dynamic nature of ETFs with the more traditional structure of mutual funds, let's turn our attention to another member of the packaged product family, one that offers a unique blend of stability and simplicity: Unit Investment Trusts, or UITs.

UITs are like time capsules of investments, holding a fixed portfolio of securities, typically bonds or stocks, for a predetermined period, known as the trust's life. Unlike mutual funds and ETFs, where the portfolio manager can actively buy and sell securities, a UIT maintains a static portfolio throughout its life. This "buy and hold" strategy can be appealing to investors who seek a predictable investment with minimal turnover and associated transaction costs.

The structure of a UIT is straightforward. A sponsor, typically a broker-dealer, selects a basket of securities that align with the trust's stated investment objective. The trust then issues a fixed number of units, each representing a fractional ownership interest in the underlying portfolio. These units are sold to investors, who hold them until the trust matures.

At maturity, the underlying securities are liquidated, and the proceeds are distributed to the unit holders. This pre-determined lifespan can be appealing to investors with specific time horizons, such as those planning for retirement or saving for a child's education. For example, a UIT with a maturity date of 2030 could be an attractive option for an investor looking to accumulate funds for their child's college expenses.

UITs offer several benefits that make them an attractive addition to certain portfolios. Their fixed portfolio and buy-and-hold strategy provide predictability and transparency. Investors know exactly what they are buying and when they can expect to receive their principal back. Additionally, UITs often have lower expense ratios than actively managed mutual funds, as there's no need for ongoing portfolio management.

However, UITs also have their drawbacks. Their static nature can be a disadvantage in volatile markets, as the portfolio manager cannot adjust the holdings in response to changing conditions. Furthermore, UITs generally have limited secondary market trading, meaning investors may face challenges in selling their units before maturity if needed.

A historical example of a UIT is the Lehman Brothers Aggregate Bond Index Fund, which was a popular UIT in the early 2000s. This fund held a diversified portfolio of investment-grade bonds and offered investors exposure to the U.S. bond market with a fixed maturity date. However, the collapse of Lehman Brothers in 2008 and the subsequent financial crisis highlighted the risks associated with UITs, as investors in the Lehman Brothers fund faced significant losses due to the decline in bond values.

UITs occupy a unique niche in the investment landscape, offering a blend of stability, predictability, and potential tax efficiency. They can be a valuable addition to portfolios for investors seeking fixed-income exposure with a defined time horizon. However, their lack of flexibility and limited secondary market liquidity should be carefully considered before investing.

III. Real Estate Investment Trusts (REITs) and Direct Participation Programs (DPPs)

REIT structure & types (equity, mortgage, hybrid)

Having explored the liquid and accessible world of mutual funds and ETFs, let's now shift gears and delve into the real estate sector, a tangible asset class that has long captivated investors with its potential for steady income and long-term appreciation. But direct real estate ownership, with its complexities and substantial capital requirements, is often out of reach for many investors. This is where Real Estate Investment Trusts (REITs) step in, offering a bridge between the stock market and the brick-and-mortar world of property ownership.

REITs are companies that own, operate, or finance income-generating real estate across a spectrum of property sectors, from sprawling shopping malls and towering office buildings to sprawling apartment complexes and specialized properties like data centers and cell towers. By pooling capital from multiple investors, REITs provide a way to participate in the real estate market without the need for direct property ownership. They trade like stocks on major exchanges, offering liquidity and accessibility to a wide range of investors.

Just like there's a variety of properties in the real estate market, there's also a diversity of REITs, each with its unique focus and risk-reward profile. Equity REITs, the most common type, own and operate income-producing real estate. Their revenue streams primarily come from rental income, making them akin to landlords on a grand scale. Simon Property Group, a prominent equity REIT, owns and manages a vast portfolio of shopping malls and outlet centers, generating revenue from tenant leases and property management fees.

Mortgage REITs, on the other hand, don't own physical properties; they finance them. These REITs generate income by lending money to real estate owners and operators through mortgages or by purchasing mortgage-backed securities (MBS). Their profits hinge on the difference between the interest they earn on their investments and the interest they pay on their borrowings, a delicate balance influenced by interest rate movements and the creditworthiness of their borrowers. Annaly Capital Management, a leading mortgage REIT, invests primarily in agency MBS, which are backed by government agencies like Fannie Mae and Freddie Mac, offering relative stability but also vulnerability to interest rate fluctuations.

Hybrid REITs, as their name implies, combine elements of both equity and mortgage REITs. They invest in both physical properties and mortgages, offering a diversified approach to real estate investing. This hybrid model aims to balance the steady income potential of equity REITs with the interest rate sensitivity of mortgage REITs. However, hybrid REITs have become less common in recent years, as most REITs now focus exclusively on either equity or mortgage investments.

REIT tax implications & benefits

As we navigate the realm of Real Estate Investment Trusts (REITs), it's crucial to recognize the unique tax implications they present. While REITs offer an attractive avenue to participate in the real estate market without the burdens of direct property ownership, their tax treatment requires careful consideration, as it can significantly impact an investor's overall returns.

One of the most notable features of REITs is their pass-through taxation structure. Unlike traditional corporations, which are subject to double taxation (once at the corporate level and again at the individual level when dividends are distributed), REITs are generally not taxed at the corporate level as long as they meet certain requirements. These requirements include distributing at least 90% of their taxable income to shareholders in the form of dividends.

This pass-through structure shifts the tax burden primarily to the shareholders. REIT dividends, unlike qualified dividends from common stocks, are typically taxed as ordinary income at the investor's marginal tax rate. This can be a significant consideration for investors in high tax brackets. For example, an investor in the 37% tax bracket would pay a substantial portion of their REIT dividends in taxes, reducing their net return.

However, there are also potential tax benefits associated with REITs. One such benefit is the deduction for qualified business income (QBI), which allows eligible REIT investors to deduct up to 20% of their REIT dividend income, effectively reducing their taxable income. This deduction is available for tax years 2018 through 2025 and can significantly enhance the after-tax returns of REIT investments.

Furthermore, certain REIT dividends may qualify for a lower tax rate if they are considered "capital gain dividends" or "return of capital" distributions. Capital gain dividends are distributions of the REIT's capital gains, which are taxed at the long-term capital gains rate, which is generally lower than the ordinary income tax rate. Return of capital distributions, on the other hand, are not taxed immediately but rather reduce the investor's cost basis in the REIT shares, potentially resulting in lower capital gains taxes when the shares are sold.

It's important to note that the tax treatment of REITs can be complex and varies depending on the investor's and the REIT's specific circumstances. Factors such as the holding period of the REIT shares, the type of REIT, and the composition of the REIT's distributions can all influence the tax implications.

DPP types & risk/reward profiles

Having explored the ins and outs of REITs, which offer a liquid and accessible way to tap into the real estate market, we now turn our attention to Direct Participation Programs (DPPs). These unique investment vehicles offer the allure of direct ownership in various ventures, but they come with their own set of complexities and risk-reward considerations that require careful evaluation.

DPPs are essentially partnerships that allow investors to directly participate in the profits and losses of a business venture. Unlike REITs, which provide indirect ownership through shares traded on exchanges, DPPs offer a more hands-on approach, with investors becoming limited partners in the underlying business. This direct participation can be enticing, as it offers the potential for higher returns compared to more traditional investments. However, it also comes with greater risks and complexities.

DPPs encompass a wide range of ventures, spanning industries such as real estate, oil and gas, equipment leasing, and even agriculture. Each type of DPP has its own distinct risk-reward profile, requiring investors to carefully consider their investment objectives and risk tolerance before venturing into this territory.

Real estate limited partnerships (RELPs), for example, allow investors to pool their money to invest in commercial or residential real estate projects. These partnerships offer the potential for attractive returns through rental income, property appreciation, and tax benefits. However, they are also subject to risks such as property vacancies, declining property values, and potential management issues.

Oil and gas limited partnerships provide investors with the opportunity to participate in the exploration and production of oil and gas reserves. These partnerships can offer high potential returns if successful wells are drilled, but they also carry significant risks, including dry holes, volatile commodity prices, and environmental concerns.

Equipment leasing programs involve investing in equipment, such as airplanes or medical devices, which is then leased to businesses. These programs can provide a steady stream of income through lease payments, but they are also subject to risks such as equipment obsolescence, default by lessees, and changing economic conditions.

Agricultural and livestock partnerships offer investors the chance to participate in farming or livestock operations. These partnerships can benefit from rising food prices and increasing global demand, but they are also exposed to weather-related risks, disease outbreaks, and market fluctuations.

The risk-reward profile of DPPs is largely driven by the nature of the underlying venture. High-risk ventures, such as oil and gas exploration or early-stage technology companies, offer the potential for substantial gains but also carry a high probability of loss. Lower-risk ventures, such as real estate or equipment leasing, offer more predictable income streams but with limited upside potential.

Furthermore, DPPs are generally illiquid investments, meaning that investors may find it difficult to sell their interests before the partnership's termination. This lack of liquidity can be a significant drawback, especially for investors who may need to access their funds unexpectedly.

IV. Hedge Funds and Private Equity Basics

Hedge fund structure & strategies

Having journeyed through the realm of packaged products that offer a degree of diversification and professional management, we now delve into the enigmatic and often exclusive world of alternative investments, where hedge funds reign supreme. These investment vehicles, known for their complex strategies and high-risk, high-reward profiles, cater to a select group of sophisticated investors seeking to outperform traditional markets.

Hedge funds, in essence, are private investment partnerships that pool capital from accredited investors and employ a wide range of strategies to generate returns. Unlike mutual funds, which are subject to strict regulations and limitations on their investment activities, hedge funds operate with greater flexibility, allowing them to pursue a broader spectrum of investment opportunities and strategies.

This flexibility is evident in the diverse strategies employed by hedge funds. Some funds specialize in long-short equity strategies, where they take both long and short positions in stocks, aiming to profit from both rising and falling markets. Others focus on event-driven strategies, such as merger arbitrage, where they capitalize on price discrepancies that arise during corporate events like mergers and acquisitions. There are also global macro funds that make bets on macroeconomic trends, such as interest rate movements or currency fluctuations, and quantitative funds that rely on complex algorithms and mathematical models to identify trading opportunities.

This diversity of strategies is both a strength and a weakness of hedge funds. On the one hand, it allows them to adapt to changing market conditions and potentially generate returns in both bull and bear markets. On the other hand, it also makes them more complex and difficult to understand for the average investor.

The structure of a hedge fund typically involves a general partner, who manages the fund's investments, and limited partners, who provide the capital. The general partner receives a management fee, usually a percentage of the fund's assets under management, and a performance fee, typically a percentage of the profits generated by the fund. This "two and twenty" fee structure, while controversial, incentivizes hedge fund managers to generate high returns for their investors.

However, access to hedge funds is restricted to accredited investors, who meet certain income and net worth requirements. This exclusivity is intended to protect less sophisticated investors from the complexities and risks associated with hedge fund strategies. For example, the minimum investment for many hedge funds is $1 million or more, making them out of reach for the average retail investor.

Despite their exclusivity and complexity, hedge funds play a significant role in the financial markets. They provide liquidity, contribute to price discovery, and can act as a counterbalance to traditional investment strategies. For instance, during the 2008 financial crisis, some hedge funds profited by betting against the housing market, highlighting their potential to generate returns even in challenging market conditions.

Given the complex nature and higher risks often associated with hedge funds, the Securities and Exchange Commission (SEC) has established stringent requirements to determine who qualifies as an "accredited investor," and thus who can invest in these exclusive vehicles. These requirements, designed to safeguard less sophisticated investors, create a clear demarcation between those deemed financially capable of handling such investments and those who are not.

The criteria for accredited investor status hinge primarily on two factors: income and net worth. An individual can qualify if they've earned an annual income exceeding $200,000 (or $300,000 jointly with a spouse) in each of the two most recent years, with a reasonable expectation of maintaining the same or a higher income in the current year. This income threshold serves as a proxy for financial sophistication, suggesting that individuals meeting this criterion have the capacity to withstand potential losses in high-risk investments.

Alternatively, an individual can also qualify based on net worth. If their net worth, either individually or jointly with a spouse, exceeds $1 million, excluding the value of their primary residence, they are considered accredited. This net worth threshold implies a certain level of financial stability and the ability to absorb potential investment losses.

It's important to note that these are not the only paths to accredited investor status. The SEC also recognizes certain entities as accredited investors, such as banks, insurance companies, registered investment companies, and certain types of trusts. Additionally, individuals holding specific professional certifications, such as Series 7, Series 65, or Series 82 licenses, also qualify.

These stringent requirements are not merely bureaucratic hurdles; they serve a vital purpose in protecting investors. Hedge funds often employ complex strategies involving leverage, derivatives, and illiquid assets, which can amplify both gains and losses. By limiting access to accredited investors, the SEC aims to ensure that those participating in these ventures have the financial means and sophistication to understand and bear the associated risks.

For instance, imagine a young professional with a modest income and limited investment experience. While they might be tempted by the allure of potential high returns offered by a hedge fund, they may not fully comprehend the complex strategies employed or the potential for substantial losses. The accredited investor requirements serve to shield such individuals from investments that might be unsuitable for their financial situation and risk tolerance.

Private equity overview & role in portfolios

Having ventured into the complex realm of hedge funds, we now turn our attention to another prominent player in the alternative investment arena: private equity. While both hedge funds and private equity cater to a select group of accredited investors, they differ significantly in their structures, strategies, and roles within investment portfolios.

Private equity, in essence, involves investing in privately held companies, or taking public companies private, with the goal of actively managing and improving their operations to generate significant returns. Unlike hedge funds, which often employ complex trading strategies across various asset classes, private equity firms typically take a longer-term, hands-on approach to their investments. They often acquire majority stakes in companies, allowing them to influence strategic decisions and operational improvements.

The private equity landscape is vast and varied, encompassing various strategies and investment stages. Venture capital, a prominent subset of private equity, focuses on investing in early-stage, high-growth companies with innovative technologies or disruptive business models. Prominent venture capital firms like Sequoia Capital and Andreessen Horowitz have backed some of the most successful companies of our time, including Apple, Google, and Facebook.

Buyout firms, another major player in private equity, target more mature companies, often taking them private through leveraged buyouts (LBOs). These transactions involve using a significant amount of debt to finance the acquisition, with the goal of improving the company's operations and selling it at a profit in the future. Blackstone Group and KKR are among the leading buyout firms, known for their successful acquisitions and transformations of companies like Hilton Hotels and Toys "R" Us.

Private equity investments offer the potential for high returns, driven by the active management and operational improvements implemented by the private equity firms. However, they also come with substantial risks and limitations.

One of the primary risks is illiquidity. Private equity investments are not publicly traded, meaning investors cannot easily sell their stakes. This lock-up period can last several years, making private equity unsuitable for investors who may need to access their funds in the short term. Furthermore, private equity investments often involve a high degree of leverage, amplifying both gains and losses.

The exclusive nature of private equity, accessible only to accredited investors, is another crucial factor. These high minimum investment requirements can limit access for many individuals, making private equity a realm predominantly occupied by institutional investors and high-net-worth individuals.

Despite these limitations, private equity plays a significant role in the portfolios of institutional investors and wealthy individuals. It offers the potential for diversification beyond traditional public markets and the opportunity to participate in the growth and transformation of privately held companies.

Chapter Summary and Review

This chapter broadened our investment horizons beyond individual securities, venturing into the realm of packaged products and alternative investments. We started by exploring mutual funds, understanding their diverse types, structures, and the regulatory framework that governs them. We then turned our attention to exchange-traded funds (ETFs), highlighting their structural advantages over mutual funds, including intraday tradability, potential tax efficiency, and lower expense ratios. We also examined unit investment trusts (UITs), which offer a fixed portfolio and a predetermined lifespan, providing predictability and stability for investors.

Next, we explored the real estate sector, focusing on real estate investment trusts (REITs) as a way to access this market without direct property ownership. We discussed the various types of REITs, including equity, mortgage, and hybrid REITs, and their distinct risk-reward profiles. We also delved into the tax implications of REIT investments, considering the pass-through taxation structure, the qualified business income (QBI) deduction, and the potential for capital gain or return of capital distributions.

Finally, we ventured into the exclusive world of alternative investments, examining the complex strategies and high-risk, high-reward profiles of hedge funds. We also discussed the criteria for accredited investors, who are eligible to invest in these sophisticated vehicles, and briefly explored private equity, its various strategies, and its role in portfolio diversification.

Key Terms and Concepts

- Mutual funds (equity, bond, balanced, money market)
- Open-end and closed-end funds
- Net Asset Value (NAV)
- Exchange-traded funds (ETFs)
- Index ETFs
- Sector ETFs
- Leveraged ETFs
- Unit Investment Trusts (UITs)
- Real Estate Investment Trusts (REITs)
- Equity REITs
- Mortgage REITs
- Hybrid REITs
- Direct Participation Programs (DPPs)
- Hedge funds
- Accredited investors
- Private equity

Test Your Knowledge

1. What are the key differences between open-end and closed-end mutual funds?
2. How do ETFs differ from mutual funds in terms of trading and tax efficiency?
3. Explain the pass-through taxation structure of REITs and its implications for investors.
4. What are the main criteria for qualifying as an accredited investor?
5. What are some common strategies employed by hedge funds?

Tips for Applying the Knowledge to Exam Questions

- Understand the unique characteristics of each packaged product and alternative investment.
- Focus on the risk-reward profiles and suitability considerations for different investor types.
- Be familiar with regulatory requirements, such as prospectus disclosures and accredited investor criteria.
- Practice analyzing scenarios and selecting appropriate investment vehicles based on client needs.

Real-World Examples and Case Studies

- Vanguard 500 Index Fund (VFINX) as an example of a popular open-end mutual fund

- SPDR S&P 500 ETF (SPY) as an example of a widely traded index ETF

- Simon Property Group (SPG) as an example of an equity REIT

- Annaly Capital Management (NLY) as an example of a mortgage REIT

- Blackstone Group and KKR as examples of leading private equity firms

By mastering the concepts and examples presented in this chapter, you'll gain a comprehensive understanding of packaged products and alternative investments, empowering you to make informed investment recommendations and build diversified portfolios that cater to the unique needs and risk tolerances of your clients.

Chapter 6: Mastering Options: Strategies, Calculations, and Regulations

Buckle up, because we're about to enter the exhilarating world of options! In this chapter, we'll unravel the complexities of these versatile financial derivatives, empowering you to understand their mechanics, harness their potential, and navigate the regulatory landscape with confidence.

Think of options as tools that provide you with the right, but not the obligation, to buy or sell a specific security at a predetermined price within a set timeframe. This flexibility opens up a world of opportunities for investors and traders, allowing them to hedge their portfolios, generate income, or speculate on market movements.

We'll start by laying the foundation with the fundamental concepts and terminology of options, explaining calls, puts, strike prices, expiration dates, and the intrinsic and time value components of option pricing. You'll gain a clear understanding of how options derive their value from underlying securities and how various factors influence their pricing.

Then, we'll delve into both basic and advanced options strategies, equipping you with a diverse toolkit to manage risk and pursue profit opportunities. From covered calls and protective puts to more complex strategies like spreads, straddles, and strangles, you'll learn how to apply these tools effectively in different market scenarios.

Next, we'll explore the fascinating world of options pricing and risk assessment. We'll introduce you to the Black-Scholes model, a cornerstone of options pricing theory, and break down its key components. We'll also demystify the "Greeks" – delta, gamma, theta, and vega – those enigmatic measures that quantify the sensitivity of option prices to various factors. Armed with this knowledge, you'll be able to assess and manage the risks associated with options positions, ensuring you're prepared for potential market fluctuations.

Finally, we'll navigate the regulatory landscape surrounding options trading. You'll become familiar with the rules and regulations set forth by FINRA and the Options Clearing

Corporation (OCC), including suitability requirements and disclosure obligations. By understanding these guidelines, you'll be able to conduct options transactions in a compliant and ethical manner, protecting both your clients and your professional reputation.

By the end of this chapter, you'll have a comprehensive understanding of options, their strategies, pricing, and regulations. This knowledge will empower you to make informed investment decisions, navigate the complexities of options trading, and provide expert guidance to your clients as a registered representative. Whether you're seeking to hedge your portfolio, generate income, or capitalize on market movements, options offer a world of possibilities, and this chapter will equip you with the tools to navigate it successfully.

I. Fundamental Options Concepts

Calls, puts, strike prices, expiration dates

As we step into the intricate world of options, let's first demystify its core components, the fundamental building blocks that empower you to navigate this sophisticated landscape. Understanding calls, puts, strike prices, and expiration dates is not just theoretical knowledge; it's the bedrock upon which you'll build your expertise as a financial professional, enabling you to confidently advise clients and make informed investment decisions.

Think of options as contracts that grant you specific rights, but not obligations, regarding a particular stock or other underlying asset. The two primary types of options, calls and puts, represent contrasting perspectives on the market's direction. A **call option** gives you the right to buy a stock at a certain price (the strike price) by a certain time (the expiration date). It's essentially a bet that the stock price will rise above the strike price before the option expires.

For example, imagine you're optimistic about Apple's future and believe its stock price will increase. You could buy a call option with a strike price of $180 that expires in three months. If Apple's stock price climbs to $200 before the expiration date, you can exercise your option, buying the stock at the discounted strike price of $180 and immediately reaping a $20 profit per share.

A **put option**, in contrast, gives you the right to sell a stock at a certain price (the strike price) by a certain time (the expiration date). It's a bet that the stock price will fall below the strike price before the option expires. Let's say you're concerned about a potential market downturn and want to protect your investment in Tesla. You could buy a put option with a strike price of $800 that expires in six months. If Tesla's stock price drops to $750 before the expiration date, you can exercise your option, selling the stock at the higher strike price of $800, thereby mitigating your losses.

The strike price is the pivotal point around which an option's value revolves. It's the price at which you have the right to buy (call) or sell (put) the underlying stock. The relationship between the strike price and the current market price determines whether an option is "in the money," "at the money," or "out of the money," a concept we'll explore in more detail later.

The expiration date marks the deadline for exercising your option. If you don't exercise your option before it expires, it becomes worthless, and you lose the premium you paid to purchase it. Therefore, timing is a critical consideration in options trading. You need to assess not only the direction of the stock price but also the timeframe within which you expect the price movement to occur.

By understanding these core components of options—calls, puts, strike prices, and expiration dates—you lay the groundwork for navigating the complex world of options trading. Whether you're seeking to hedge your portfolio, generate income, or speculate on market movements, these fundamental concepts will empower you to make informed decisions and utilize options strategically to achieve your investment objectives.

Options as derivatives & relation to underlying securities

Now that we've established the core components of calls, puts, strike prices, and expiration dates, let's delve a bit deeper into the nature of options. These financial instruments, with their seemingly straightforward buy or sell rights, belong to a broader category known as derivatives.

Derivatives, in essence, are contracts whose value is derived from an underlying asset, such as a stock, bond, commodity, or even an index. Think of them as financial side bets, their fate intertwined with the performance of their underlying asset. Options, as contracts that give you the right to buy or sell an underlying stock, fit squarely within this definition.

This connection between options and their underlying securities is fundamental to understanding their behavior and pricing. The value of an option is intimately tied to the price movements of the underlying stock. If the stock price rises, a call option on that stock becomes more valuable, as the right to buy the stock at a lower strike price becomes more attractive. Conversely, a put option on that same stock would decrease in value, as the right to sell the stock at a higher strike price becomes less appealing.

Let's consider a simple example. Imagine you buy a call option on Amazon stock with a strike price of $3,500. If Amazon's stock price rises to $3,800 before the option expires, your call option gains value, as you now have the right to buy shares at a $300 discount to the market price. You could exercise the option, buy the shares at $3,500, and immediately sell them in the market for $3,800, pocketing a tidy profit.

On the other hand, if Amazon's stock price drops to $3,200, your call option loses value. The right to buy shares at $3,500 is no longer attractive when you can buy them for less in the open market. In this scenario, your call option might expire worthless, and you'd lose the premium you paid to buy it.

This dynamic relationship between options and their underlying securities is what makes them such powerful tools for investors and traders. By understanding how option prices react to changes in the underlying stock's price, you can utilize options to hedge your portfolio against potential losses, generate income through premium collection, or speculate on market movements with leveraged positions.

Remember, the Series 7 exam will rigorously test your comprehension of these fundamental concepts. You'll need to be able to analyze option scenarios and determine how changes in the underlying security's price will affect the value of calls and puts. By mastering these foundational principles, you'll be well-equipped to navigate the complexities of the options market and make informed investment decisions that align with your client's needs and risk tolerance.

Options pricing factors (intrinsic value, time value)

Having grasped the foundational concepts of calls, puts, strike prices, and expiration dates, as well as the derivative nature of options, we now turn our attention to the fascinating world of options pricing. Understanding how options are valued is not only intellectually stimulating but also critical for making informed investment decisions and assessing risk. Let's break down the two primary components that contribute to an option's price: intrinsic value and time value.

Intrinsic value represents the inherent worth of an option if it were exercised immediately. For call options, intrinsic value is calculated as the difference between the current market price of the underlying stock and the strike price, but only if the market price is higher than the strike price. If the market price is lower, the call option has no intrinsic value. Conversely, for put options, intrinsic value is the difference between the strike price and the market price, but only if the market price is lower than the strike price. If the market price is higher, the put option has no intrinsic value.

To put it simply, intrinsic value reflects the potential profit you could realize by exercising the option right now. Let's say you own a call option on Microsoft stock with a strike price of $300, and the current market price is $320. Your call option has an intrinsic value of $20 per share because you could exercise the option, buy Microsoft shares at $300, and immediately sell them in the market for $320, pocketing a $20 profit.

However, options rarely trade at their intrinsic value alone. There's an additional component that adds to their price: time value. Time value reflects the possibility that the option's intrinsic value could increase before it expires. The more time remaining until expiration, the higher the time value, as there's more opportunity for the underlying stock price to move in a favorable direction.

Think of time value as the "hope" premium embedded in an option's price. Even if an option is currently out-of-the-money (meaning its strike price is unfavorable compared to the market price), it still has some value due to the chance that it could become in-the-money before it expires. This time value decays as the expiration date approaches, eventually reaching zero at expiration. This phenomenon, known as time decay, is a crucial concept in options trading and risk management.

Imagine you buy a call option on Tesla with a strike price of $1,000 that expires in one year. Even if Tesla's stock price is currently below $1,000, the option will still have some value due to the possibility that the price could rise above the strike price within the next year. However, as the expiration date draws closer, the time value of the option will gradually decline, even if the stock price remains unchanged.

II. Options Strategies

Basic strategies (covered calls, protective puts, married puts)

With the foundational concepts of options firmly in place, we now embark on a journey into the realm of options strategies. These strategies, akin to a seasoned chess player's repertoire of moves, offer a multitude of ways to leverage options for profit, protection, or income generation. Let's start by examining three basic yet powerful strategies that every aspiring financial professional should understand: covered calls, protective puts, and married puts.

Covered calls are often regarded as the gateway into the world of options trading due to their relative simplicity and the potential to generate income from existing stock holdings. The strategy involves owning shares of a stock and simultaneously selling call options on those shares. By selling the call options, you essentially give the buyer the right to purchase your shares at the strike price before the expiration date. In return, you receive a premium, which is yours to keep regardless of whether the option is exercised.

Imagine you own 100 shares of Coca-Cola and decide to implement a covered call strategy. You sell one call option with a strike price of $60 that expires in one month. In exchange for this right, you receive a premium of $2 per share, or $200 total. Now, if Coca-Cola's stock price stays below $60 by the expiration date, the option expires worthless, and you keep the $200 premium as profit, in addition to any dividends paid on your Coca-Cola shares. However, if the stock price rises above $60, the option buyer is likely to exercise their right, and you'll be obligated to sell your shares at $60, potentially missing out on further upside.

Protective puts, on the other hand, are like an insurance policy for your stock holdings. If you own shares of a stock and are concerned about a potential market decline, you can buy a put option on those shares. This gives you the right to sell your shares at the strike price, even if the market price falls below that level. The premium you pay for the put option acts as the insurance premium, protecting you from potential losses.

For example, if you own shares of Tesla and are worried about a market correction, you could buy a put option with a strike price of $800. If Tesla's stock price drops to $700, your put option allows you to sell your shares at the higher strike price of $800, limiting your loss to the difference between your purchase price and the strike price, plus the premium paid for the put.

A married put is essentially a combination of buying a stock and simultaneously buying a put option on that same stock. It's like buying a car and purchasing an auto insurance policy at the same time. The put option provides downside protection, limiting your potential loss if the stock price falls. However, it also caps your potential profit, as you've paid a premium for the put option.

These three basic options strategies—covered calls, protective puts, and married puts—are foundational building blocks for more complex strategies that we'll explore later. Understanding these basic strategies, their risk-reward profiles, and their suitability for different market scenarios is essential for any financial professional seeking to navigate the options market successfully. As you progress through this chapter, you'll gain the knowledge and confidence to apply these strategies in a real-world context, helping your clients achieve their investment objectives while managing risk effectively.

Advanced strategies (spreads, straddles, strangles)

Having mastered the foundational options strategies of covered calls, protective puts, and married puts, we now ascend to the realm of advanced tactics. Here, the interplay of multiple options contracts creates intricate strategies with nuanced risk-reward profiles. Spreads, straddles, and strangles are just a glimpse into the diverse landscape of advanced options strategies, each tailored to specific market outlooks and investor objectives.

Let's begin with spreads, which involve the simultaneous buying and selling of options of the same type (calls or puts) on the same underlying security, but with different strike prices or expiration dates. Think of a spread as a calculated bet on the magnitude of a stock's price movement. For instance, a bull call spread involves buying a call option with a lower strike price and selling a call option with a higher strike price. This strategy profits if the stock price rises moderately, but the profit is capped at the difference between the strike prices minus the net premium paid.

Next, we encounter straddles, a strategy that embraces volatility. A long straddle involves buying both a call and a put option on the same stock with the same strike price and expiration date. This strategy thrives on significant price swings, regardless of direction. If the stock price makes a substantial move either up or down, one of the options will become profitable, offsetting the cost of the other option and generating a net gain. Imagine a biotech company awaiting FDA approval for a new drug. A straddle on this company's stock could be profitable if the stock price surges on approval or plummets on rejection.

Finally, we explore strangles, a strategy similar to straddles but with a twist. A long strangle involves buying a call option with a higher strike price and a put option with a lower strike price, both on the same stock with the same expiration date. This strategy, like a straddle, benefits from significant price volatility, but it requires a larger price move to be profitable, as the options are initially out-of-the-money. A strangle might be employed on a stock expected to experience a significant price swing after an earnings announcement, with the direction of the move uncertain.

These advanced strategies, while potentially lucrative, are not without risks. They involve multiple option contracts, increasing complexity and potential losses if the market moves against your expectations. As a registered representative, it's crucial to have a deep understanding of these strategies, their risk-reward profiles, and their suitability for different market conditions.

The Series 7 exam will test your knowledge of these advanced options strategies, often through scenario-based questions that require you to analyze a client's situation and recommend the most appropriate course of action. By mastering these complex strategies, you'll demonstrate your ability to navigate the intricacies of the options market and provide sophisticated investment advice to your clients. Remember, with great power comes great responsibility, and your expertise in options can be a valuable asset in helping your clients achieve their financial goals while managing risk effectively.

Examples of strategy application

Let's now put these strategies into motion, breathing life into the concepts of covered calls, protective puts, and married puts with tangible examples of how they might be applied in real-world scenarios. These illustrations will solidify your understanding and better prepare you for the practical applications you'll encounter on the Series 7 exam and in your future career.

Imagine Sarah, a seasoned investor, holds a significant position in Apple stock, which is currently trading at $175 per share. She's moderately bullish on Apple's prospects but is also open to generating additional income from her holdings. A covered call strategy fits this scenario perfectly. Sarah could sell a call option with a strike price of $180 that expires in one month. In exchange, she receives a premium, let's say $3 per share. Now, if Apple's stock price stays below $180 by expiration, Sarah keeps the premium, effectively boosting her return on the stock. Even if the stock price rises above $180, she's still obligated to sell her shares at that price, locking in a profit. However, she'll miss out on any further upside potential beyond $180.

Now, let's consider David, a cautious investor who recently purchased shares of Tesla at $850. While he's optimistic about Tesla's long-term growth, he's also wary of the stock's volatility and wants to protect his investment from potential downside risk. A protective put strategy aligns perfectly with David's concerns. He could buy a put option with a strike price of $800 that expires in six months. This put option acts as an insurance policy, guaranteeing him the right to sell his shares at $800, even if the market price plummets. If Tesla's stock price remains above $800, the put option will expire worthless, and David's only cost will be the premium he paid for the option. However, if the stock price falls below $800, the put option will gain value, offsetting his losses on the stock.

Finally, let's meet Emily, a new investor who's excited about the potential of Amazon but is also nervous about the risks associated with the stock market. She wants to participate in Amazon's growth but also wants to limit her downside risk. A married put strategy could be the solution for Emily. She could buy shares of Amazon and simultaneously purchase a put option on those shares with a strike price slightly below the current market price. This combination provides her with the upside potential of owning Amazon stock, while the put option acts as a safety net, limiting her potential losses if the stock price declines.

These examples illustrate how covered calls, protective puts, and married puts can be strategically employed in various investment scenarios. The Series 7 exam might present you with similar situations, asking you to identify the most appropriate strategy based on a client's investment objectives and risk tolerance. By understanding the practical applications of these strategies and their potential outcomes, you'll be well-equipped to navigate the complexities of the options market and provide sound advice to your clients.

III. Options Pricing & Risk Assessment

Black-Scholes model & components

Having laid the groundwork with the essential building blocks of options and explored various strategies for their application, we now delve into the intricate mechanics of options pricing. Here, we encounter a cornerstone of financial mathematics, the Black-Scholes model, a Nobel Prize-winning formula that revolutionized the way options are valued.

At its heart, the Black-Scholes model is a mathematical equation that attempts to calculate the theoretical fair value of an option. It's a complex formula, but understanding its key components provides valuable insights into the factors that drive option prices, enabling you to make more informed investment decisions and assess the risk associated with options positions.

The model takes into account several key variables that influence an option's price. First, there's the current price of the underlying stock. Intuitively, the higher the stock price, the more valuable a call option becomes, as the right to buy the stock at a lower strike price becomes more attractive. Similarly, the lower the stock price, the more valuable a put option becomes, as the right to sell the stock at a higher strike price becomes more appealing.

Next, there's the strike price, which we've already established as the predetermined price at which the option can be exercised. The relationship between the strike price and the current market price is crucial in determining an option's intrinsic value.

Time to expiration, or the time remaining until the option expires, also plays a pivotal role. As we've discussed, time value represents the possibility that an option's intrinsic value could change before expiration. The longer the time to expiration, the greater the uncertainty and the higher the time value component of the option's price.

Volatility, a measure of how much the stock price is expected to fluctuate, is another critical factor. Higher volatility translates to a greater probability of the stock price reaching the strike price, increasing the option's value. Think of it this way: a stock that's prone to wild price swings offers more potential for an option to become profitable, hence the higher price.

Finally, the risk-free interest rate and dividends, if any, paid by the underlying stock are also incorporated into the model. The risk-free interest rate reflects the time value of money, while dividends can impact the stock price and, consequently, the option's value.

While the Black-Scholes model is a powerful tool, it's important to remember that it's based on certain assumptions that may not always hold true in the real world. For example, the model assumes that stock prices follow a log-normal distribution and that volatility remains constant over the option's life, which may not always be the case. Nevertheless, the Black-Scholes model provides a valuable framework for understanding the factors that influence options pricing and serves as a benchmark for evaluating option premiums.

As you prepare for the Series 7 exam, you'll encounter questions that test your comprehension of the Black-Scholes model and its components. By mastering these concepts, you'll be able to confidently analyze options, assess their fair value, and make informed investment recommendations to your clients.

Greeks (delta, gamma, theta, vega) & significance

Beyond the foundational elements of options pricing—intrinsic value and time value—lies a realm of deeper analysis and risk management guided by the "Greeks." These metrics, named after Greek letters, provide a sophisticated understanding of how an option's price will react to changes in various factors. Think of them as the vital signs of an option, offering insights into its sensitivity to market movements and the passage of time.

Delta, perhaps the most well-known of the Greeks, measures the rate of change of an option's price relative to a change in the price of its underlying security. It tells us how much the option's price is expected to move for every $1 change in the stock price. A delta of 0.5, for instance, implies that if the stock price increases by $1, the option's price is expected to increase by $0.50. Delta values for call options range from 0 to 1, while put options have delta values from -1 to 0.

Gamma, the second derivative of an option's price with respect to the underlying asset's price, measures the rate of change of delta itself. In essence, gamma tells us how much delta will change as the stock price moves. A high gamma indicates that delta will change rapidly, making the option more sensitive to price swings in the underlying stock. This can be both a blessing and a curse, leading to amplified gains or losses depending on the direction of the price movement.

Theta, often referred to as time decay, measures the rate at which an option's value erodes as time passes. It's the ticking clock of the options world, reminding us that options have a finite lifespan. All else being equal, an option's price will decrease each day as it approaches its expiration date. Theta is typically expressed as a negative number, representing the daily decline in the option's value.

Vega, the final Greek we'll explore here, gauges an option's sensitivity to changes in implied volatility. Implied volatility, a concept we've discussed earlier, reflects the market's expectation of future price fluctuations in the underlying security. A higher implied volatility indicates greater uncertainty and translates to a higher option premium. Vega tells us how much the option's price is expected to change for a 1% change in implied volatility.

Understanding the Greeks is essential for assessing and managing the risks associated with options positions. By knowing how an option's price will respond to changes in the underlying stock's price, time decay, and volatility, you can make more informed decisions about buying, selling, or holding options.

For instance, if you're long a call option with a high delta and gamma, you're essentially betting on a significant upward movement in the stock price. However, you're also exposed to amplified losses if the price moves against you. Conversely, if you're short a put option with a low delta and gamma, you're expecting the stock price to remain stable or rise slightly. While your potential profit is limited to the premium received, your downside risk is also relatively low.

The Series 7 exam will undoubtedly test your understanding of the Greeks. You may be asked to analyze option scenarios and determine how changes in various factors will impact their prices. By mastering these concepts, you'll be well-prepared to navigate the complexities of the options market, make informed investment decisions, and confidently advise your clients on options strategies tailored to their specific needs and risk tolerances. Remember, the Greeks are not just theoretical constructs; they are practical tools that can help you unlock the full potential of options while managing their inherent risks.

Risk assessment & management examples

Understanding the "Greeks" — delta, gamma, theta, and vega — isn't merely an exercise in theoretical finance; it's the cornerstone of effective risk assessment and management in the dynamic world of options trading. Let's bring these concepts to life with a few illustrative examples that showcase their practical implications, bridging the gap between theory and real-world application.

Imagine you hold a portfolio of blue-chip stocks and decide to implement a covered call strategy to generate additional income. You sell call options on some of your holdings, collecting premiums while retaining ownership of the underlying shares. In this scenario, delta becomes your compass, indicating how much your portfolio value will change for every $1 move in the underlying stock prices. If the delta of your written calls is high, say 0.8, your portfolio will be highly sensitive to upward movements in the stock prices, potentially limiting your upside potential but also providing significant downside protection.

Now, let's say you're concerned about a potential market correction and decide to purchase put options on a broad market index ETF like SPY as a hedge. In this case, vega becomes your key metric. It tells you how much the value of your put options will change in response to fluctuations in implied volatility, which tends to spike during market downturns. If vega is high, your put options will act as a powerful shock absorber, increasing in value as market volatility rises and offsetting potential losses in your stock portfolio.

Time decay, represented by theta, is an ever-present force in the options market. It's the silent erosion of an option's value as time passes, a reminder that options are wasting assets with a finite lifespan. Understanding theta is crucial for managing short option positions, such as covered calls or cash-secured puts. If you've sold a call option with a high theta, you're essentially racing against the clock, hoping the stock price remains below the strike price before the option expires and its time value decays to zero.

Finally, gamma, the rate of change of delta, adds another layer of complexity to risk assessment. A high gamma implies that your option's delta will change rapidly as the stock price moves. This can be beneficial if the price moves in your favor, amplifying your gains. However, it can also be detrimental if the price moves against you, accelerating your losses.

Consider a scenario where you're long a call option on a volatile stock like Tesla. If the stock price makes a sudden upward move, the high gamma of your call option will cause its delta to increase rapidly, magnifying your gains. However, if the stock price reverses course and plummets, the high gamma will work against you, accelerating your losses.

These examples highlight how the Greeks serve as powerful tools for assessing and managing risk in options trading. By understanding their significance and interpreting their values, you can gain valuable insights into the potential behavior of your options positions under different market scenarios. The Series 7 exam will challenge you to apply these concepts to various situations, requiring you to analyze the impact of the Greeks on different option strategies and make informed decisions based on your risk tolerance and investment objectives. By mastering these analytical tools, you'll elevate your understanding of options trading and be well-prepared to navigate the complexities of this dynamic market.

IV. Regulatory Considerations

FINRA & OCC regulations

Now that we've explored the mechanics and strategies behind options trading, let's pivot towards the regulatory landscape that governs this complex yet dynamic market. As aspiring financial professionals, understanding the rules and obligations set forth by regulatory bodies like the Financial Industry Regulatory Authority (FINRA) and the Options Clearing Corporation (OCC) is not just about compliance—it's about upholding ethical standards, protecting investors, and ensuring the integrity of the options market.

FINRA, as the primary self-regulatory organization for the U.S. securities industry, plays a crucial role in overseeing options trading. Its rules and regulations are designed to promote just and equitable principles of trade, prevent fraudulent and manipulative practices, and protect investors. For instance, FINRA Rule 2360 sets forth comprehensive guidelines for options trading, covering everything from account approval procedures and suitability requirements to position limits and margin requirements.

The OCC, on the other hand, is the world's largest equity derivatives clearing organization. Its primary function is to clear and settle transactions in the options market, ensuring that trades are executed smoothly and efficiently. The OCC also plays a vital role in managing risk by acting as a guarantor for all trades, ensuring that obligations are met even if one party defaults.

One key regulatory requirement for options trading is the account approval process. Before a client can trade options, their account must be approved by their brokerage firm, which involves assessing their financial situation, investment objectives, and risk tolerance. This process ensures that clients are suitable for options trading and understand the associated risks. Failure to obtain proper account approval can result in regulatory violations and potential penalties for both the broker and the firm.

Suitability is another critical consideration in options trading. FINRA Rule 2360 requires that options recommendations be suitable for the customer based on their financial situation and investment objectives. This means that brokers must carefully assess each client's risk tolerance and investment experience before recommending any options strategies. For example, recommending a complex, high-risk strategy like a naked call to a conservative, risk-averse investor would be a clear violation of suitability requirements.

Disclosure is also paramount in the options market. Investors must receive a copy of the Options Disclosure Document (ODD), which explains the characteristics and risks of standardized options, before their account can be approved for options trading. Furthermore, brokers must provide ongoing disclosures about the risks associated with specific options strategies and transactions.

In 2021, FINRA fined Robinhood Financial $70 million for various regulatory violations, including misleading communications and options-related supervisory failures. This case highlights the importance of adherence to regulatory guidelines and the potential consequences of non-compliance.

By understanding the roles of FINRA and the OCC, and by adhering to their rules and regulations, you'll not only protect yourself and your firm from regulatory scrutiny but also demonstrate your commitment to ethical conduct and investor protection. This will enhance your credibility as a financial professional and build trust with your clients, paving the way for long-lasting and successful relationships in the dynamic world of options trading.

Suitability requirements for options investors

Building on our exploration of the regulatory framework surrounding options trading, let's zero in on a crucial aspect that every registered representative must grasp: suitability requirements for options investors. This principle, embedded in FINRA Rule 2111, is not merely a regulatory checkbox; it's an ethical imperative that ensures options recommendations align with an investor's unique financial situation, investment objectives, and risk tolerance.

Essentially, suitability mandates that any options transaction recommended to a client must be appropriate and fitting, given their individual circumstances. This means that before even broaching the topic of options, you must conduct a thorough assessment of your client's financial profile.

This assessment involves a deep dive into their income, net worth, investment experience, risk tolerance, and investment objectives. For example, recommending highly leveraged options strategies to a retiree heavily reliant on investment income would be a glaring violation of suitability, as the potential losses could jeopardize their financial security.

But suitability goes beyond just financial metrics; it's also about understanding your client's emotional capacity for risk. Some investors are naturally more risk-averse and might be uncomfortable with the potential volatility associated with options. Others might be more aggressive and willing to accept higher risks in pursuit of greater returns. As a registered representative, it's your duty to gauge your client's emotional response to risk and ensure that any options recommendations are aligned with their comfort level.

Furthermore, the complexity of options strategies must be considered. Certain strategies, like spreads and strangles, involve multiple option contracts and intricate risk-reward profiles. Recommending such strategies to a novice investor who lacks the knowledge and experience to understand their nuances would be a clear violation of suitability.

A classic example of a suitability violation is the case of a broker who recommended highly leveraged options trades to an elderly client with limited investment experience and a conservative risk profile. The client incurred significant losses, leading to regulatory action against the broker and their firm. This case serves as a stark reminder of the importance of suitability and the potential consequences of disregarding it.

The Series 7 exam will rigorously test your understanding of suitability requirements. You'll be presented with various scenarios involving hypothetical clients, and you'll need to assess whether specific options recommendations are suitable based on the client's financial profile and investment objectives. By mastering this concept, you'll demonstrate not only your knowledge of the regulations but also your commitment to ethical conduct and investor protection. Remember, suitability is not just a rule; it's a guiding principle that fosters trust, builds lasting relationships, and ensures that your clients' investments are aligned with their individual needs and aspirations.

Required disclosures & documentation

As we round out our exploration of the regulatory landscape that governs options trading, let's shine a light on the essential element of transparency: required disclosures and documentation. This isn't just about bureaucratic paperwork; it's about empowering investors with the knowledge they need to make informed decisions in a complex and potentially risky market.

Foremost among the required disclosures is the Options Disclosure Document (ODD), aptly titled "Characteristics and Risks of Standardized Options." This document, mandated by the SEC and published by the OCC, serves as a comprehensive primer on options trading, detailing everything from basic terminology to the intricacies of various strategies and the potential risks involved. Before a client's account can be approved for options trading, they must receive a copy of the ODD and acknowledge its receipt. This ensures that investors are equipped with the fundamental knowledge to navigate the options market, even if they choose not to delve into advanced strategies.

Beyond the ODD, brokers are obligated to provide additional disclosures tailored to the specific options transactions their clients engage in. These disclosures typically include information on the risks associated with the particular strategy, the potential profit and loss scenarios, and the impact of various market factors on the option's value. For instance, if a client is considering selling a covered call, the broker must disclose the potential upside gain (the premium received) as well as the potential downside risk (missing out on further stock price appreciation if the option is exercised).

Documentation is another vital component of options trading compliance. Every options trade must be accompanied by an options agreement, which outlines the terms of the trade, including the underlying security, the strike price, the expiration date, and the premium paid or received. This document serves as a record of the transaction and provides evidence of the client's understanding and acceptance of the risks involved.

Moreover, brokers must maintain meticulous records of all options-related communications with clients, including emails, phone calls, and even in-person meetings. These records serve as a valuable audit trail, demonstrating that the broker has fulfilled their suitability and disclosure obligations.

In 2020, the SEC charged a broker-dealer with failing to maintain adequate documentation of its options communications with clients. The firm was fined and ordered to implement remedial measures to ensure future compliance. This case underscores the importance of diligent record-keeping and the potential consequences of failing to meet regulatory requirements.

expect questions that probe your understanding of these required disclosures and documentation. You'll need to demonstrate your knowledge of the ODD, the specific disclosures associated with various options strategies, and the importance of maintaining accurate records. By mastering these regulatory aspects of options trading, you'll not only ensure compliance but also establish yourself as a trustworthy and ethical financial professional, dedicated to serving your clients' best interests.

Chapter 6: Summary and Review

This chapter delved into the intricate world of options, mastering its fundamental concepts, exploring diverse strategies, unraveling pricing models, and navigating the regulatory landscape. We defined calls and puts, strike prices, and expiration dates, establishing the basic building blocks of options trading. We then explored the concept of options as derivatives, their inherent relationship with underlying securities, and the dual forces of intrinsic value and time value that shape their prices.

Next, we ventured into the realm of options strategies, starting with the foundational covered calls, protective puts, and married puts, and progressing to more advanced tactics like spreads, straddles, and strangles. Through illustrative examples, we demonstrated how these strategies can be applied in real-world scenarios to generate income, hedge portfolios, or capitalize on market volatility.

We also embarked on a journey into the quantitative side of options, introducing the Black-Scholes model and its key components, including the enigmatic "Greeks"—delta, gamma, theta, and vega. By understanding these metrics, we gained insights into an option's sensitivity to various market factors, enabling us to assess and manage risk effectively.

Finally, we navigated the regulatory landscape of options trading, exploring the rules and obligations set forth by FINRA and the OCC, focusing on suitability requirements and disclosure obligations. We emphasized the importance of ethical conduct and investor protection, highlighting the potential consequences of non-compliance.

Test Your Knowledge:

1. What is the difference between a call option and a put option?

2. How does a change in the underlying stock's price affect the value of a call option versus a put option?

3. Explain the concept of intrinsic value and time value in options pricing.

4. What are the four "Greeks," and what do they measure?

5. What are the suitability requirements for recommending options to clients?

Tips for Applying the Knowledge to Exam Questions

- Focus on understanding the core concepts and their practical applications.

- Practice calculating intrinsic value and time value for different option scenarios.

- Familiarize yourself with the Greeks and their impact on option prices.

- Analyze case studies and scenarios to identify suitable options strategies for different investor profiles.

- Review FINRA and OCC regulations to ensure compliance and ethical conduct.

Real-World Examples and Case Studies

- Apple and Tesla stock options for illustrating covered calls and protective puts.

- The 2021 GameStop short squeeze and the role of options in driving market volatility.

- The Robinhood regulatory fines for highlighting the importance of compliance and investor protection.

By mastering the concepts and examples covered in this chapter, you'll be well-equipped to navigate the complexities of the options market, make informed investment decisions, and provide expert guidance to your clients. Remember, options are powerful tools that can enhance your investment arsenal, but they also require a deep understanding of their mechanics, risks, and regulatory framework. With diligence and practice, you'll be able to harness the potential of options while safeguarding your clients' interests and upholding the highest standards of ethical conduct.

Chapter 7: Customer Accounts and Investment Strategies

Chapter 7: Tailoring Success: Customer Accounts and Investment Strategies

Having explored the vast and intricate world of securities – from equities and options to the diverse landscape of fixed-income instruments – we now arrive at a pivotal juncture: aligning these investment vehicles with the unique needs and aspirations of your clients. This chapter delves into the heart of client-centric financial advising, focusing on understanding their financial goals, assessing their risk tolerance, and crafting investment strategies that pave the way for their long-term success.

We'll begin by navigating the diverse landscape of customer accounts, from individual and joint accounts to specialized accounts catering to corporations, trusts, retirement savers, and even minors. Understanding the nuances of these accounts is crucial for ensuring compliance, facilitating seamless transactions, and tailoring investment recommendations to each client's specific circumstances.

Next, we'll embark on the critical task of assessing your clients' investment objectives and risk tolerance. This involves more than just crunching numbers; it's about understanding their dreams, fears, and aspirations. We'll explore a range of tools and questionnaires designed to gauge risk tolerance, and discuss how to align investment strategies with these individual profiles.

From there, we'll delve into the principles of portfolio management and asset allocation, building on the concepts of diversification and risk management we've touched on in previous chapters. We'll introduce you to modern portfolio theory and the efficient frontier, powerful tools that can help you construct portfolios that optimize returns for a given level of risk. We'll also discuss the art of rebalancing, ensuring that your clients' portfolios remain aligned with their evolving goals and market conditions.

Finally, we'll address the often-overlooked yet critical aspect of tax considerations in investment planning. You'll learn about the tax treatment of capital gains, dividends, and interest income, and discover strategies to minimize tax liabilities and maximize after-tax returns. We'll also explore the concept of tax-loss harvesting, a powerful tool for turning market losses into tax advantages.

By the end of this chapter, you'll possess the knowledge and skills to build strong and lasting client relationships based on personalized investment strategies. You'll understand how to tailor investment recommendations to individual needs, balance risk and reward, and navigate the complexities of the financial markets with confidence and expertise. Whether your clients are seeking growth, income, or capital preservation, you'll be equipped to guide them toward financial success.

I. Types of Customer Accounts

Individual Accounts

Now that we've established the critical link between understanding client needs and constructing suitable portfolios, let's delve into the first and most common type of account you'll encounter as a registered representative: the individual account. These accounts, as their name suggests, are designed for a single person to manage their investments and financial assets.

Think of an individual account as a personal vault, tailored to hold and grow the wealth of a single person. It's the simplest and most straightforward type of account, granting the account owner complete control over their investments and the authority to make all decisions regarding the account's activity. For instance, a young professional looking to start investing for retirement might open an individual brokerage account to purchase stocks, bonds, or mutual funds, while a seasoned investor might use it to execute more complex options strategies.

Opening an individual account typically requires providing personal identification information such as your name, address, Social Security number, and date of birth. This is in line with the Know Your Customer (KYC) regulations discussed earlier, ensuring that financial institutions can verify the identity of their clients and prevent illicit activities such as money laundering. Additionally, to comply with suitability obligations, you'll need to gather information about the individual's financial situation, investment experience, risk tolerance, and investment objectives. This information helps you, as a registered representative, make recommendations that are appropriate for the client's specific needs and circumstances.

The versatility of individual accounts makes them suitable for a wide range of investors. Whether someone is just starting their investment journey or is a seasoned pro, an individual account offers the flexibility and control needed to implement their chosen investment strategies.

Furthermore, individual accounts can be tailored to specific investment goals. For instance, a young investor saving for a down payment on a house might opt for a taxable brokerage account, allowing for easy access to funds when needed. In contrast, someone nearing retirement might prefer a tax-advantaged individual retirement account (IRA) to accumulate savings for their golden years.

It's important to remember that while individual accounts offer autonomy and control, they also come with sole responsibility. The account owner is solely liable for any gains or losses incurred in the account. This underscores the importance of diversification and risk management, principles we will discuss in more detail later in this chapter.

Joint Accounts

Moving beyond the realm of individual accounts, we now encounter a common yet multifaceted account type: the joint account. As its name implies, a joint account involves two or more individuals sharing ownership and control over a single account. This shared ownership model can be a convenient and effective way for couples, families, or business partners to manage their finances collectively. However, it's important to remember that with shared control comes shared responsibility, and it's essential to fully understand the nuances of joint accounts before recommending them to your clients.

As a registered representative, it's crucial to recognize that the suitability of a joint account hinges heavily on the relationship between the parties involved. When I first started in the financial industry, I vividly recall a case where a well-intentioned son opened a joint account with his elderly mother to assist her with bill payments and financial management. However, the lack of clear communication and understanding about the account's purpose led to misunderstandings and disputes, ultimately straining their relationship. This experience underscored the importance of thoroughly discussing the implications of joint accounts with clients and ensuring all parties are on the same page regarding its purpose, access, and control.

The most common type of joint account is the **Joint Tenants with Rights of Survivorship (JTWROS)** account. In this structure, each account holder has equal ownership and control over the assets, and upon the death of one owner, their share automatically passes to the surviving owner(s). This feature can simplify estate planning and avoid probate, making it a popular choice for married couples or close family members.

Another common type is the **Tenants in Common (TIC)** account. Here, each account holder owns a specific percentage of the assets, which can be equal or unequal depending on their contributions. Upon the death of one owner, their share passes to their estate, not automatically to the surviving owner(s). TIC accounts can be useful for business partners or individuals who want to maintain separate ownership of their assets within a shared account.

Opening a joint account typically requires the same documentation as an individual account, but for each account holder. This includes providing identification, verifying their information, and assessing their risk tolerance and investment objectives. It's crucial to remember that suitability applies to all account holders, and the recommended investments must be appropriate for each individual's financial situation and goals.

Joint accounts offer several advantages, such as simplified bill payment, convenient access to funds for all account holders, and potential estate planning benefits. However, they also come with potential drawbacks. Shared control can lead to disputes, especially if there's a lack of communication or trust between the parties. Additionally, creditors of one account holder may be able to access the joint account's assets, potentially impacting the other owners.

Corporate Accounts

Moving from the personal to the professional, our next stop on the tour of client account types is the corporate account. As a future registered representative, understanding the specificities of these accounts is crucial, as businesses, both large and small, are significant players in the financial markets.

Corporate accounts are established by businesses to manage their investments and financial transactions. They provide a structured framework for companies to trade securities, access capital markets, and manage their cash flows. While the basic principles of account opening and suitability still apply, as we've discussed earlier, corporate accounts come with their own set of documentation requirements and considerations.

Imagine a tech startup, let's call it "InnovateX," that has recently received a round of venture capital funding. They need a secure and efficient way to manage this capital, invest in growth opportunities, and potentially access public markets in the future. A corporate brokerage account would be an ideal solution, offering them the necessary tools and services to achieve these goals.

To open a corporate account, businesses typically need to provide their Employer Identification Number (EIN), equivalent to an individual's Social Security number, along with articles of incorporation, bylaws, and a corporate resolution authorizing the opening of the account and designating individuals with trading authority. This documentation ensures legal compliance and establishes a clear chain of command for managing the account's activities.

The suitability assessment for corporate accounts also differs from that of individual accounts. Instead of focusing on an individual's risk tolerance and investment objectives, you'll need to consider the company's financial health, industry outlook, and strategic goals. For example, a well-established company with a strong balance sheet and consistent cash flow might be comfortable with a more aggressive investment strategy compared to a startup with limited resources and uncertain prospects.

Moreover, corporate accounts often have unique tax considerations. Corporate income is subject to taxation, and investment gains or losses can impact a company's overall tax liability. As a registered representative, you'll need to be mindful of these tax implications and advise your clients accordingly.

One crucial aspect of corporate accounts is the potential for multiple authorized traders. This introduces an added layer of complexity, requiring clear communication and internal controls to ensure that trades are executed in line with the company's investment policy and risk tolerance. A real-world example of the potential pitfalls of multiple authorized traders is the case of a rogue trader who caused billions of dollars in losses for his employer, a major European bank, by engaging in unauthorized and risky trades. This incident highlights the importance of strong internal controls and oversight in corporate accounts.

Trust Accounts

Moving on from accounts designed for individuals and corporations, we delve into the unique world of trust accounts. As a financial advisor, understanding these accounts is essential, as they serve a distinct purpose in wealth preservation, estate planning, and managing assets for beneficiaries who may not be equipped to do so themselves.

A trust account is not simply another type of investment account; it's a legal entity that holds and manages assets on behalf of a beneficiary or beneficiaries. Think of it as a financial guardian, ensuring that assets are used according to the grantor's (the person who establishes the trust) wishes and that the beneficiaries are taken care of.

There are several types of trust accounts, each serving unique purposes. A revocable trust, also known as a living trust, is created during the grantor's lifetime and can be modified or revoked at their discretion. This type of trust can be a useful tool for managing assets during incapacity and avoiding probate, the often lengthy and costly legal process of distributing assets after death.

Irrevocable trusts, on the other hand, are generally unchangeable once established. They offer greater asset protection and potential tax benefits, as the assets are no longer considered part of the grantor's estate. However, the grantor gives up control over the assets once they are transferred to the trust.

A charitable remainder trust (CRT) is a specific type of irrevocable trust that allows the grantor to receive income from the trust during their lifetime, with the remaining assets going to a designated charity upon their death. This type of trust can provide both income and tax benefits for the grantor, while also supporting their philanthropic goals.

The documentation required for a trust account includes a copy of the trust agreement, which outlines the terms of the trust, including the beneficiaries, the trustee (the person or entity responsible for managing the trust), and the distribution instructions. Additionally, information on the grantor and beneficiaries, such as their Social Security numbers and dates of birth, is also necessary.

Opening and managing a trust account requires a thorough understanding of trust law and fiduciary responsibilities. The trustee has a legal obligation to act in the best interests of the beneficiaries, make prudent investment decisions and adhere to the terms of the trust agreement.

Remember, on the Series 7 exam, you may encounter scenarios involving trust accounts. Understanding the different types of trusts, their purposes, and their unique features is crucial for answering these questions correctly. Additionally, as a registered representative, you may work with clients with trust accounts or considering establishing one. Your knowledge of trust accounts will enable you to provide valuable guidance and ensure that these accounts are managed effectively to meet the grantor's intentions and the beneficiaries' needs.

Retirement Accounts (Traditional IRA, Roth IRA, 401(k), etc.)

Transitioning from accounts designed for general investing and saving, we now step into the realm of retirement accounts. These specialized accounts offer unique tax advantages and incentives to encourage individuals to save for their golden years. As a registered representative, understanding the intricacies of these accounts, their eligibility criteria, contribution limits, and withdrawal rules is not just crucial for the Series 7 exam but also for guiding your clients towards a secure and comfortable retirement.

We'll start with Individual Retirement Accounts (IRAs), the cornerstones of retirement planning for many Americans. The Traditional IRA allows individuals to make pre-tax contributions, reducing their taxable income in the current year. The earnings within the account grow tax-deferred, meaning you won't owe taxes on them until you start making withdrawals in retirement. However, there are limits to how much you can contribute each year, and early withdrawals before age 59 ½ are generally subject to a 10% penalty, in addition to income taxes.

The Roth IRA, on the other hand, offers a different set of tax advantages. Contributions to a Roth IRA are made with after-tax dollars, so there's no upfront tax deduction. However, the earnings within the account grow tax-free, and qualified withdrawals in retirement are completely tax-free. This can be a significant advantage for individuals who expect to be in a higher tax bracket in retirement. Eligibility for Roth IRAs is based on income limits, which can change annually.

Beyond IRAs, employer-sponsored retirement plans, such as 401(k) plans, offer another avenue for retirement savings. These plans allow employees to contribute a portion of their pre-tax salary, often with matching contributions from their employer. Like Traditional IRAs,

401(k) contributions and earnings grow tax-deferred, and withdrawals are subject to income tax in retirement. The contribution limits for 401(k) plans are generally higher than those for IRAs, providing an opportunity for individuals to supercharge their retirement savings.

Other types of retirement accounts exist, each with its unique features and eligibility requirements. Simplified Employee Pension (SEP) IRAs and Savings Incentive Match Plan for Employees (SIMPLE) IRAs are options for small businesses and self-employed individuals. 403(b) plans are available to employees of certain tax-exempt organizations, such as schools and hospitals.

The Series 7 exam will test your knowledge of these accounts extensively, presenting scenarios where you'll need to recommend suitable retirement plans based on client profiles and investment objectives.

Moreover, in your career as a registered representative, you'll be guiding individuals and families in their retirement planning journey, helping them choose the right accounts, make informed investment decisions, and ultimately secure a comfortable and fulfilling retirement. By staying informed about the ever-changing landscape of retirement accounts and their tax implications, you can provide invaluable guidance to your clients, empowering them to build a solid foundation for their financial future.

Custodial Accounts (UGMA/UTMA)

Now that we've explored retirement accounts, which help individuals plan for their financial futures, let's turn our attention to another unique account type designed with the future in mind: Custodial Accounts. These accounts, established under either the Uniform Gifts to Minors Act (UGMA) or the Uniform Transfers to Minors Act (UTMA), offer a straightforward way for adults to set aside assets for minors, providing a financial head start for their education, future endeavors, or general well-being.

Custodial accounts function under the stewardship of an adult custodian, often a parent or guardian, who manages the account's assets on behalf of the minor beneficiary. These accounts can hold a variety of investments, including stocks, bonds, mutual funds, and even certain types of real estate, depending on whether it's a UGMA or UTMA account. Think of them as a financial gift that keeps on giving, potentially growing in value over time and providing the beneficiary with a significant nest egg upon reaching adulthood.

One of the appealing aspects of custodial accounts is their simplicity. Unlike trusts, which can involve complex legal structures and ongoing administrative costs, custodial accounts are relatively easy to establish and manage. They also offer flexibility, with the custodian having discretion over investment choices and the ability to make withdrawals for the benefit of the minor. For example, a grandparent might open a custodial account for their grandchild, investing in a diversified portfolio of stocks and bonds, and then use the funds to pay for college tuition or a first car when the grandchild reaches adulthood.

However, it's important to understand that custodial accounts come with certain limitations and tax implications. Once assets are transferred to a custodial account, they become the property of the minor and cannot be revoked. The custodian has a fiduciary duty to manage the assets prudently, but the minor gains full control of the account upon reaching the age of majority, which varies by state but is typically 18 or 21.

Moreover, the tax treatment of custodial accounts can be complex. While a portion of the minor's investment income may be tax-free, any income exceeding certain thresholds is taxed at the parent's marginal tax rate, potentially negating some of the tax benefits. It's crucial to understand these tax implications and how they might affect the overall investment strategy for the custodial account.

In the context of the Series 7 exam, you'll need to be well-versed in the specifics of UGMA and UTMA accounts, including their eligibility requirements, contribution limits, investment options, and tax implications. You may encounter questions that test your ability to recommend suitable custodial accounts for different client scenarios, considering factors such as the minor's age, financial needs, and the custodian's investment objectives.

By mastering the intricacies of custodial accounts, you'll be equipped to provide valuable guidance to your clients, helping them make informed decisions about securing their loved ones' financial futures. Remember, these accounts are not just about saving money; they're about investing in the next generation and providing them with the tools to achieve their dreams.

II. Investment Objectives & Risk Tolerance Assessment

Investment objectives (growth, income, capital preservation)

With a firm understanding of the various account types at your disposal, let's turn our attention to the cornerstone of personalized financial advice: understanding your client's investment objectives. Just as a skilled tailor crafts a garment to fit the wearer's unique measurements, a successful financial advisor constructs an investment strategy that aligns perfectly with their client's specific goals.

Three primary investment objectives often guide client discussions: growth, income, and capital preservation. Each objective represents a distinct financial aspiration, and recognizing these nuances is key to crafting portfolios that truly resonate with your clients' needs.

Growth-oriented investors seek to maximize their portfolio's value over time. They're willing to embrace some level of risk in pursuit of potentially higher returns, often favoring investments in stocks, growth-oriented mutual funds, or even emerging market securities. A young professional, for example, with a long investment horizon and a desire to build wealth for the future, might prioritize growth as their primary objective.

Income-focused investors, in contrast, prioritize generating a steady stream of cash flow from their investments. They're often drawn to dividend-paying stocks, bond funds, or real estate investment trusts (REITs) that provide regular distributions. This objective is particularly common among retirees or individuals seeking to supplement their income.

Capital preservation, as the name implies, focuses on protecting the value of the initial investment. Investors with this objective prioritize safety and stability, often favoring low-risk investments like U.S. Treasury securities, high-quality bonds, or money market funds. This objective might be suitable for an individual nearing retirement who wants to safeguard their nest egg and avoid significant losses.

However, investment objectives are rarely mutually exclusive. Many investors seek a balance between growth, income, and capital preservation, depending on their age, financial situation, and risk tolerance. A middle-aged investor, for instance, might allocate a portion of their portfolio to growth-oriented investments to build wealth for the future, while also holding income-generating assets to supplement their current income and capital preservation investments to protect against market downturns.

The Series 7 exam will challenge you to understand these investment objectives and identify suitable investment strategies for various client scenarios.

You might be presented with a case study of a client with specific financial goals and risk tolerance, and you'll need to recommend appropriate investments based on their objectives. By mastering the concepts of growth, income, and capital preservation, you'll be equipped to tailor investment solutions that truly resonate with your clients' aspirations and help them achieve their financial dreams. Remember, understanding your clients' objectives is the first step towards building a successful and enduring financial partnership.

Tools & questionnaires for risk tolerance assessment

Having identified the primary investment objectives of growth, income, and capital preservation, we now embark on the crucial task of assessing your clients' risk tolerance. This isn't simply a matter of asking, "How much risk are you comfortable with?" It requires a more nuanced approach, employing tools and questionnaires designed to delve deeper into their financial psyche and uncover their true capacity for risk.

Risk tolerance questionnaires are widely used in the financial industry to gauge an individual's willingness and ability to withstand market volatility and potential investment losses. These questionnaires typically consist of a series of questions that probe the investor's financial situation, investment experience, and emotional response to market fluctuations.

For instance, a questionnaire might ask investors to choose between hypothetical investment scenarios, such as a guaranteed 5% return versus a 50% chance of a 10% return or a 50% chance of a 0% return. Their answers reveal their preferences for risk and reward, providing valuable insights into their risk tolerance.

Another approach to assessing risk tolerance is through scenario analysis. This involves presenting clients with hypothetical market downturns and observing their reactions. A client who panics at the thought of a 20% market decline might have a lower risk tolerance than someone who remains calm and sees it as a buying opportunity.

It's important to remember that risk tolerance is not static; it can evolve over time based on life events, financial circumstances, and market experiences. A young investor with a long time horizon might have a higher risk tolerance than someone nearing retirement who relies on their investments for income. Similarly, a client who experienced significant losses during the 2008 financial crisis might have a lower risk tolerance now compared to before the crisis.

Beyond questionnaires and scenario analysis, there are other tools that can aid in assessing risk tolerance. Investment personality quizzes can provide insights into a client's behavioral tendencies and their approach to investing. These quizzes often use metaphors or analogies to gauge a client's comfort level with risk. For example, a client who identifies with a cautious tortoise might have a lower risk tolerance than someone who sees themselves as a daring eagle.

As you prepare for the Series 7 exam, you'll encounter questions that require you to assess a client's risk tolerance based on their financial profile and responses to hypothetical scenarios. By understanding the various tools and questionnaires used for risk tolerance assessment, you'll be well-equipped to answer these questions and demonstrate your ability to tailor investment recommendations to individual client needs.

Remember, risk tolerance assessment is an ongoing process. Revisiting this assessment periodically and adjusting your clients' portfolios as their circumstances and risk tolerance evolve is crucial. By striking the right balance between risk and reward, you can help your clients achieve their financial goals while ensuring their peace of mind.

Aligning strategies with goals & risk profiles

Once you have a solid understanding of your client's investment objectives and their risk tolerance, the next crucial step is to align these two aspects to craft a tailored investment strategy. It's akin to a navigator charting a course – the destination represents the client's objectives, and the risk tolerance serves as the compass guiding the journey. This alignment ensures that the chosen path is not only directed towards the desired goals but also navigates within the client's comfort zone, fostering a sense of security and confidence throughout the investment journey.

For a growth-oriented investor with a high risk tolerance, for example, a portfolio heavily tilted towards equities, particularly those of emerging growth companies or specific sectors poised for expansion, might be appropriate. Think of a young professional investing in technology stocks or a venture capital fund, aiming to ride the wave of innovation and achieve significant capital appreciation over the long term. However, this strategy would be ill-suited for a retiree seeking stable income and capital preservation. Their portfolio would likely lean more towards dividend-paying stocks, high-quality bonds, and other fixed-income securities that generate predictable cash flow and minimize downside risk.

It's also crucial to recognize that risk tolerance and investment objectives can change over time. A client who starts their investment journey with an aggressive growth mindset might become more conservative as they approach retirement or experience significant life events like starting a family. Regularly revisiting these assessments and adjusting investment strategies accordingly is vital to maintain alignment and ensure that portfolios remain suitable for evolving needs.

Furthermore, aligning strategies with goals and risk profiles goes beyond simply choosing the right asset classes. It also involves considering factors such as liquidity needs, time horizon, and tax implications. For instance, a client with a short-term investment goal, such as saving for a down payment on a house, might prioritize liquidity over high potential returns, opting for investments that can be easily converted to cash without significant losses.

On the Series 7 exam, you'll likely encounter scenarios where you'll need to evaluate a client's investment profile and recommend suitable strategies. These questions aim to test your ability to apply your knowledge of investment objectives and risk tolerance assessment to real-world situations. By mastering these concepts and practicing their application, you'll not only excel on the exam but also develop the critical skills needed to provide personalized and effective financial advice to your clients.

Remember, the ultimate goal is to create portfolios that empower your clients to achieve their financial dreams while minimizing unnecessary risks. By aligning investment strategies with their individual goals and risk tolerances, you'll build lasting relationships based on trust, confidence, and shared success.

III. Portfolio Management Principles & Asset Allocation

Modern portfolio theory & efficient frontier

With a firm understanding of our clients' investment objectives and risk tolerance, we can now step into the fascinating realm of portfolio management, where the art and science of investing converge. The cornerstone of modern portfolio management is Modern Portfolio Theory (MPT), a revolutionary framework that emphasizes the power of diversification and the pursuit of optimal risk-adjusted returns. Central to MPT is the concept of the efficient frontier, a graphical representation that illustrates the optimal balance between risk and reward.

Imagine a vast landscape of investment opportunities, each with its own potential return and associated risk. MPT posits that by combining different asset classes in a portfolio, investors can achieve a higher level of return for a given level of risk, or conversely, a lower level of risk for a given level of return. This is the essence of diversification, a principle we've touched upon throughout this book. By spreading your investments across various asset classes that don't move in lockstep, you can reduce the overall risk of your portfolio without necessarily sacrificing returns.

The efficient frontier takes this concept a step further. It's a curve that plots various portfolios based on their expected return and risk, as measured by standard deviation. The portfolios that lie on the efficient frontier are considered optimal, as they offer the highest possible return for a given level of risk or the lowest possible risk for a given level of return. Any portfolio that lies below the efficient frontier is suboptimal, meaning it's either taking on too much risk for the return it's generating or not generating enough return for the risk it's taking.

For example, consider a simple portfolio consisting of just two assets: stocks and bonds. Stocks generally offer higher potential returns but also come with higher volatility, while bonds provide stability but with lower returns. By combining these two asset classes in different proportions, you can create a range of portfolios with varying levels of risk and return. The efficient frontier shows you the optimal combinations of stocks and bonds that maximize return for each level of risk.

This powerful concept has significant implications for investment strategies. A risk-averse investor might choose a portfolio that lies on the left side of the efficient frontier, emphasizing capital preservation and accepting lower returns. A more aggressive investor, on the other hand, might opt for a portfolio on the right side of the frontier, seeking higher returns but also accepting higher volatility.

In the context of the Series 7 exam, expect to encounter questions that test your understanding of MPT and the efficient frontier. You may be asked to identify optimal portfolios based on given risk and return data or to analyze the impact of adding or removing assets from a portfolio on its risk-return profile. By mastering these concepts, you'll demonstrate your ability to construct efficient portfolios that align with your clients' investment objectives and risk tolerance.

Remember, MPT and the efficient frontier are not just theoretical constructs; they are practical tools that can guide you in building diversified and optimized portfolios for your clients. By understanding the interplay between risk and return, you can help your clients achieve their financial goals while minimizing unnecessary risk, solidifying your role as a trusted and knowledgeable financial advisor.

Diversification strategies

Now that we've established the framework of modern portfolio theory and the quest for optimal portfolios on the efficient frontier, let's explore the practical implementation of this theory through diversification strategies. As you know, diversification is not simply about owning a multitude of assets; it's about strategically allocating investments across various asset classes that respond differently to market forces. This balanced approach aims to reduce overall portfolio risk, smoothing out the inevitable ups and downs of the market and enhancing long-term returns.

Think of diversification as assembling a well-rounded team. You wouldn't want a basketball team composed entirely of centers, nor a baseball team filled solely with pitchers. Similarly, a well-diversified portfolio isn't just about owning many stocks; it's about owning stocks from different sectors, bonds with varying maturities, and potentially other asset classes like real estate or commodities.

One common diversification strategy involves allocating investments across different asset classes, such as stocks, bonds, and cash. The classic 60/40 portfolio, for example, allocates

60% to stocks for growth potential and 40% to bonds for stability and income. This balanced approach aims to capture the upside of the stock market while mitigating downside risk through the inclusion of fixed-income securities.

Diversification can also be achieved within asset classes. For example, within the stock portion of your portfolio, you could invest in a mix of large-cap, mid-cap, and small-cap stocks, as well as companies from different sectors and geographic regions. This reduces the impact of any single company or sector's poor performance on your overall portfolio.

Another layer of diversification involves considering different investment styles. You could blend value stocks, which are considered undervalued by the market, with growth stocks, which are expected to experience rapid earnings growth. This mix of styles aims to capture different market phases and reduce the risk of being overly exposed to a single investment approach.

Beyond traditional asset classes, alternative investments, such as real estate, commodities, or hedge funds, can further enhance diversification. These assets often have low correlations with traditional stocks and bonds, meaning they may move independently of the broader market, providing additional risk mitigation benefits.

A classic example of the power of diversification is the performance of the S&P 500 index during the dot-com bubble of the late 1990s. While technology stocks soared to unprecedented heights, other market sectors lagged. Investors who were heavily concentrated in tech stocks experienced significant losses when the bubble burst, while those with more diversified portfolios were better able to weather the storm.

In the Series 7 exam context, expect to encounter questions that assess your understanding of diversification strategies. You may be asked to identify suitable asset allocations for clients with different risk tolerances and investment objectives. You might also be challenged to analyze the impact of adding or removing specific assets from a portfolio on its overall risk and diversification level.

Rebalancing techniques & implementation

Having crafted a well-diversified portfolio that aligns with your client's risk tolerance and investment goals, you might think your job is done. However, the ever-shifting tides of the market require ongoing attention, which brings us to the essential practice of portfolio rebalancing.

Imagine your portfolio as a meticulously balanced scale, with different asset classes representing the weights on each side. Over time, as some investments outperform others, this balance can shift. Rebalancing is the process of bringing the portfolio back to its original allocation, ensuring that your client's desired risk-reward balance is maintained.

Without rebalancing, a portfolio can drift from its intended allocation, potentially exposing the investor to unintended risks. For example, let's say a client's portfolio started with a 60/40 allocation to stocks and bonds. After a strong bull market, the stock portion might grow to 70% or even 80%, increasing the portfolio's overall risk exposure. If a market correction occurs, the investor could face larger losses than they are comfortable with.

Rebalancing techniques can vary, but two common approaches are calendar rebalancing and percentage-of-portfolio rebalancing. Calendar rebalancing involves reviewing the portfolio at predetermined intervals, such as quarterly or annually, and adjusting the holdings to bring them back in line with the original allocation. This systematic approach ensures regular maintenance of the desired risk profile.

Percentage-of-portfolio rebalancing, on the other hand, triggers adjustments when a particular asset class deviates from its target allocation by a certain percentage, often 5% or 10%. This method allows for more flexibility and can be useful in volatile markets, where frequent adjustments may be needed to maintain balance.

The implementation of rebalancing can involve selling a portion of overweighted assets and using the proceeds to purchase underweighted assets. It's crucial to consider tax implications during this process, as selling appreciated securities can trigger capital gains taxes. However, rebalancing can also present opportunities for tax-loss harvesting, where losses on certain investments can be used to offset gains elsewhere, potentially reducing tax liabilities.

Consider a scenario where a client's portfolio has become overweight in technology stocks due to their strong performance. To rebalance, you might recommend selling some of these stocks and using the proceeds to purchase bonds or other asset classes underweighted in the portfolio. This reduces the concentration risk and brings the portfolio back to its intended risk profile.

In the Series 7 exam, you'll likely encounter questions that assess your understanding of rebalancing techniques and their implementation. You may be presented with scenarios where a client's portfolio has drifted from its target allocation, and you'll need to recommend appropriate rebalancing actions. By mastering these concepts and understanding their practical applications, you'll demonstrate your ability to proactively manage client portfolios and ensure they remain aligned with their long-term financial goals.

IV. Tax Considerations in Investment Planning

Capital gains, dividends, & interest income taxation

Now that we've explored a wide range of investment vehicles, it's time to tackle a crucial aspect that can significantly impact your clients' net returns: taxes. While the allure of investment gains is undeniable, understanding the tax implications of those gains is essential for crafting effective and efficient financial plans. Let's delve into the tax treatment of three primary sources of investment income: capital gains, dividends, and interest income.

Capital gains, as you'll recall from our earlier discussions on equity securities, arise when you sell an investment for more than its purchase price. These gains are subject to capital gains tax, the rate of which depends on how long you held the investment. Short-term capital gains, realized on assets held for one year or less, are taxed as ordinary income at your marginal tax rate. Long-term capital gains, on the other hand, realized on assets held for more than one year, are taxed at a preferential rate, currently 0%, 15%, or 20% depending on your income level.

For example, if you bought shares of Apple at $100 and sold them a year later for $150, your $50 gain would be considered a long-term capital gain and taxed at the applicable rate. However, if you sold those shares after only six months, the gain would be considered short-term and taxed as ordinary income. Understanding these distinctions is vital for making tax-efficient investment decisions.

Dividends, as we've explored in the context of stocks and REITs, are distributions of a company's profits to shareholders. The tax treatment of dividends depends on their classification as qualified or non-qualified. Qualified dividends, which meet certain holding period requirements, are taxed at the same preferential rates as long-term capital gains. Non-qualified dividends, on the other hand, are taxed as ordinary income. This distinction underscores the importance of understanding the tax implications of different dividend-paying investments.

Finally, interest income, earned from investments like bonds and savings accounts, is generally taxed as ordinary income at your marginal tax rate. However, there are exceptions. Interest earned on municipal bonds, for instance, is often exempt from federal income tax, and sometimes even state and local taxes, making them attractive to investors in high tax brackets.

In the context of the Series 7 exam, you'll encounter questions that test your knowledge of these tax implications. You may be asked to calculate the tax liability on various investment gains or to recommend suitable investments based on a client's tax situation. By mastering these concepts, you'll be well-prepared to navigate the complexities of tax-efficient investing and help your clients minimize their tax burden while maximizing their after-tax returns.

Remember, tax considerations are an integral part of investment planning. By understanding the tax treatment of capital gains, dividends, and interest income, you can help your clients make informed decisions that align with their financial goals and optimize their tax efficiency. This expertise will not only showcase your comprehensive knowledge of the financial markets but also solidify your position as a trusted advisor, capable of guiding your clients towards long-term financial success.

Tax-efficient investing strategies

Understanding the tax implications of various investment incomes is only half the battle. Now, armed with this knowledge, let's explore how we can strategically maneuver within the tax code to optimize our clients' after-tax returns. This is where tax-efficient investing strategies come into play, offering a powerful arsenal of techniques to minimize tax liabilities and enhance long-term financial outcomes.

A cornerstone of tax-efficient investing is the strategic use of tax-advantaged accounts. As we've previously discussed, retirement accounts like Traditional IRAs and 401(k)s offer tax-deferred growth, allowing investments to compound over time without immediate tax implications. Similarly, Roth IRAs and Roth 401(k)s, while funded with after-tax dollars, offer tax-free withdrawals in retirement, a significant advantage for those anticipating higher tax rates in their golden years.

But tax-efficient investing goes beyond just retirement accounts. Consider the holding period for investments. As we've learned, long-term capital gains, realized on assets held for more than a year, are taxed at a lower rate than short-term gains. Therefore, adopting a buy-and-hold strategy, where investments are held for the long term, can be a powerful tax-minimization tool.

For instance, if you purchase shares of a promising growth company and hold them for several years, allowing them to appreciate significantly, you'll benefit from the lower long-term capital gains tax rate when you eventually sell. In contrast, frequent trading, even if profitable, can generate short-term capital gains that are taxed at your ordinary income rate, potentially eroding your net returns.

Another tax-efficient strategy involves asset location, which refers to strategically placing investments in different types of accounts to optimize their tax treatment. For example, high-dividend stocks or actively managed mutual funds, which tend to generate higher taxable distributions, might be better suited for tax-advantaged accounts like IRAs, where those distributions can grow tax-deferred. Meanwhile, tax-efficient investments, such as index funds or municipal bonds, can be held in taxable accounts, where their tax advantages can be fully utilized.

Tax-loss harvesting is another powerful tool in the tax-efficient investor's toolkit. It involves selling investments that have declined in value to realize losses, which can then be used to offset capital gains elsewhere in your portfolio. This strategy can help reduce your tax liability in the current year, potentially freeing up more capital for reinvestment. However, it's important to be mindful of the wash-sale rule, which prohibits repurchasing the same or substantially identical security within 30 days of selling it at a loss.

Tax-loss harvesting & benefits

While the pursuit of investment gains is a core objective, savvy investors and their advisors understand that the tax implications of those gains can significantly impact their net returns. It's here that the strategic technique of tax-loss harvesting emerges as a valuable tool for mitigating tax liabilities and potentially enhancing portfolio performance.

Tax-loss harvesting, in essence, is the practice of selling securities that have experienced a loss in order to offset capital gains realized from the sale of other profitable investments. This strategic maneuver allows investors to reduce their tax burden in the current year, potentially freeing up capital for reinvestment and ultimately boosting their long-term returns.

Let's imagine a scenario where an investor, let's call her Sarah, holds shares of Company A, which have declined in value since her initial purchase. Meanwhile, she also owns shares of Company B, which have appreciated significantly. Sarah is considering selling her shares of Company B to lock in her gains, but she's hesitant due to the potential capital gains tax implications. This is where tax-loss harvesting comes in.

By selling her shares of Company A at a loss, Sarah can generate a capital loss that can be used to offset the capital gains from the sale of Company B shares. If the loss on Company A exceeds the gain on Company B, she can even use up to $3,000 of the excess loss to offset ordinary income, further reducing her tax liability.

The benefits of tax-loss harvesting extend beyond just immediate tax savings. By strategically selling losing positions and reinvesting the proceeds, investors can potentially improve their portfolio's overall performance. For example, Sarah could use the proceeds from the sale of Company A shares to purchase shares of a similar company with better growth prospects, effectively upgrading her portfolio while also reaping tax benefits.

It's important to note that tax-loss harvesting is not a one-size-fits-all strategy. It requires careful consideration of various factors, including the investor's tax bracket, investment horizon, and overall financial goals. Furthermore, the wash-sale rule, which prohibits repurchasing the same or substantially identical security within 30 days of selling it at a loss, must be carefully navigated to avoid negating the tax benefits.

Chapter 7:Summary and Review

In this chapter, we delved into the heart of client-centric financial advising, focusing on understanding their unique needs and crafting personalized investment strategies. We began by navigating the diverse landscape of customer accounts, from individual and joint accounts to specialized accounts catering to corporations, trusts, retirement savers, and minors. We emphasized the importance of understanding the unique features and requirements of each account type to ensure compliance and tailor recommendations effectively.

Next, we embarked on the critical task of assessing client investment objectives and risk tolerance, utilizing tools and questionnaires to gain insights into their financial aspirations and comfort levels with market volatility. We explored the three primary investment objectives—growth, income, and capital preservation—and discussed the importance of aligning investment strategies with these objectives and individual risk profiles.

We then ventured into the principles of portfolio management and asset allocation, building upon the foundation of modern portfolio theory and the efficient frontier. We examined diversification strategies, emphasizing the importance of spreading investments across various asset classes and styles to reduce risk and enhance returns. We also discussed the practice of rebalancing, ensuring that portfolios remain aligned with target allocations and risk profiles over time.

Finally, we addressed the crucial aspect of tax considerations in investment planning. We explored the tax treatment of capital gains, dividends, and interest income, highlighting the benefits of tax-advantaged accounts and long-term investing. We also discussed tax-loss harvesting as a strategic tool for offsetting gains and minimizing tax liabilities.

Test Your Knowledge:

1. What are the key differences between individual and joint accounts?

2. Explain the three primary investment objectives: growth, income, and capital preservation.

3. How can risk tolerance questionnaires and scenario analysis help in assessing a client's risk tolerance?

4. What is the efficient frontier, and how does it relate to portfolio construction?

5. What are the tax implications of capital gains, dividends, and interest income?

Tips for Applying the Knowledge to Exam Questions:

- **Understand account types:** Be able to differentiate between various account types and their suitability for different client situations.

- **Assess risk tolerance:** Practice using questionnaires and scenario analysis to gauge risk tolerance.

- **Apply MPT:** Understand how to construct portfolios that lie on the efficient frontier.

- **Implement diversification:** Recognize the importance of diversifying across asset classes, styles, and sectors.

- **Consider tax implications:** Factor in the tax treatment of different investments when making recommendations.

Chapter 8: Mastering Municipal Bonds: A Deep Dive into the Tax-Advantaged World

In this chapter, we explore municipal bonds, a unique corner of the fixed-income market that holds a special allure for investors seeking tax-efficient income. These bonds, issued by state and local governments, play a vital role in financing public projects while offering distinct advantages that set them apart from other debt securities. We'll delve into their intricate characteristics, explore their regulatory framework, and understand their role in crafting balanced and tax-efficient portfolios.

You'll gain a comprehensive understanding of the different types of municipal bonds, from general obligation bonds backed by the full faith and credit of the issuer to revenue bonds tied to specific projects. We'll also examine specialized bonds like industrial development bonds and private activity bonds, each with its own unique features and considerations. Additionally, we'll unravel the concept of bond insurance and how it can impact the perceived risk and pricing of municipal bonds.

We'll then navigate the issuance process and regulatory framework governing municipal bonds, exploring the role of underwriters, the Municipal Securities Rulemaking Board (MSRB), and the critical disclosure requirements that ensure transparency and investor protection. You'll gain insights into the lifecycle of a municipal bond, from its initial offering to its eventual maturity or call.

Next, we'll delve into the enticing world of tax-exempt income, a key benefit of municipal bond investments. You'll learn how this tax advantage can significantly enhance after-tax returns for certain investors and how to assess its impact based on individual tax situations. We'll also address the complexities of the Alternative Minimum Tax (AMT) and how it can affect the tax treatment of municipal bonds. Furthermore, we'll explore state-specific tax implications, highlighting the nuances that can arise when investing in bonds issued by different states or localities.

Finally, we'll confront municipal bonds' inherent risks and suitability considerations. You'll learn about credit, interest rate, and liquidity risks and how to assess these factors when evaluating municipal bond investments. We'll also discuss call provisions, understanding their potential impact on investor returns and strategies for managing call risk. By the chapter's conclusion, you'll be equipped to analyze the suitability of municipal bonds for different client profiles, considering their investment objectives, risk tolerance, and tax situations.

Through this in-depth exploration, you'll emerge with a profound understanding of municipal securities, empowering you to make informed investment recommendations and construct portfolios that leverage the unique benefits of this asset class. Whether your clients are seeking tax-efficient income, diversification, or exposure to specific public projects, your municipal bonds expertise will be invaluable in guiding them toward their financial goals.

I. Types & Characteristics

General Obligation vs. Revenue Bonds

As we journey further into the world of municipal bonds, it's essential to distinguish between its two primary categories: General Obligation (GO) bonds and Revenue bonds. Each type has its own unique characteristics, backing, and risk profile, understanding which is crucial for both the Series 7 exam and your future career as a financial advisor.

General Obligation bonds, as the name suggests, are backed by the "full faith and credit" of the issuing municipality. This essentially means they are supported by the issuer's unlimited taxing power. If the municipality faces a shortfall in revenue to pay the bond's interest or principal, it can raise taxes to meet its obligations. This backing provides a strong sense of security for investors, making GO bonds generally less risky than other types of municipal bonds. Think of them as a promise secured by the government's ability to generate revenue through taxation.

Revenue bonds, in contrast, are not backed by the full taxing power of the issuer. Instead, they are supported by the revenue generated from a specific project or enterprise, such as a toll road, a water treatment plant, or an airport. This revenue stream serves as the primary source of funds to pay the bond's interest and principal. While this can create a direct link between the project's success and the bond's performance, it also introduces an element of risk. If the project fails to generate sufficient revenue, the bondholders may face delayed or even missed payments.

Let's imagine two scenarios to illustrate this difference. A city issues GO bonds to finance the construction of a new school. Even if the school's enrollment falls short of projections, the city can still raise taxes to ensure bondholders receive their promised payments. On the other hand, if the same city issues revenue bonds to build a new stadium, the bond's repayment depends solely on the revenue generated by the stadium, such as ticket sales, concessions, and events. If attendance is low, the bondholders may face financial difficulties.

This fundamental difference in backing leads to variations in credit risk and yield. GO bonds, with their stronger backing, typically carry lower interest rates compared to revenue bonds, reflecting their lower perceived risk. Revenue bonds, on the other hand, often offer higher yields to compensate investors for the additional risk associated with the project's revenue stream.

Special Types (industrial development, private activity)

While general obligation and revenue bonds form the bedrock of the municipal bond market, several specialized types exist to cater to unique financing needs and policy objectives. Among these are industrial development bonds (IDBs) and private activity bonds (PABs), each with distinct characteristics and implications for investors.

Industrial development bonds, or IDBs, are a tool municipalities employ to stimulate economic growth and job creation. They are issued to finance the construction or acquisition of facilities used by private businesses. For example, a city might issue IDBs to help a manufacturing company build a new factory or expand an existing one. The key feature of IDBs is that the interest on them is taxable at the federal level, unlike traditional municipal bonds. However, they often offer higher yields than comparable taxable bonds due to their unique structure and the potential economic benefits they generate for the community. This makes them an attractive option for investors seeking higher yields while still supporting local development initiatives.

Private activity bonds (PABs), on the other hand, are issued by municipalities on behalf of private entities, such as non-profit organizations or corporations, to finance projects that serve a public purpose. These projects might include affordable housing, hospitals, airports, or even sports stadiums. While PABs offer tax-exempt interest, they are subject to certain restrictions and limitations, including volume caps and alternative minimum tax (AMT) considerations, which we will explore in more detail later in this chapter. A classic example of a PAB is the bond issued to finance the construction of the Barclays Center in Brooklyn, New York, home to the NBA's Brooklyn Nets. While the stadium is owned by a private entity, its construction was deemed to serve a public purpose, justifying the issuance of tax-exempt PABs.

Both IDBs and PABs highlight the versatility of municipal bonds as a financing tool, enabling municipalities to support economic development and public projects while offering investors unique investment opportunities. However, their specialized nature and potential tax implications require careful consideration and analysis.

Bond Insurance & its impact

Now that we've explored the different flavors of municipal bonds, let's turn our attention to an additional layer of security that can bolster investor confidence and even enhance a bond's marketability: bond insurance. Think of it as an extra safety net for bondholders, a promise from a third-party insurer to step in and make timely payments of interest and principal in the unlikely event that the issuer defaults.

Bond insurance is essentially a financial guarantee provided by insurance companies specializing in this niche market. These insurers, with their own strong financial standing and credit ratings, essentially "wrap" the municipal bond, transferring the credit risk from the issuer to themselves. This can be particularly appealing for investors seeking an added layer of security, especially for bonds issued by smaller or less financially robust municipalities.

The impact of bond insurance on municipal securities is multifaceted. First and foremost, it enhances the credit quality of the bond. Since the bond's rating is now based on the insurer's creditworthiness, rather than the issuer's, it can lead to a higher rating and a lower perceived risk of default. This, in turn, can translate into lower interest rates for the issuer, reducing their borrowing costs and potentially saving taxpayers' money.

For investors, bond insurance provides peace of mind. It ensures that even if the issuer faces financial difficulties, their investment is protected. This can be especially valuable during times of economic uncertainty or for bonds with longer maturities, where the risk of default may be higher. Furthermore, insured bonds tend to be more liquid in the secondary market, as their perceived safety attracts a wider pool of buyers.

However, bond insurance is not without its costs. Issuers must pay a premium to the insurer for this guarantee, which can add to the overall cost of borrowing. For investors, insured bonds may offer slightly lower yields compared to uninsured bonds with similar credit ratings, reflecting the reduced risk of default.

The financial crisis of 2008 had a significant impact on the bond insurance industry. Several major insurers, including Ambac and MBIA, faced financial difficulties due to their exposure to mortgage-backed securities, leading to downgrades in their credit ratings. This, in turn, reduced the value of the insurance they provided and impacted the marketability of insured bonds. As a result, the demand for bond insurance declined, and many issuers opted to issue uninsured bonds to avoid the additional cost of insurance premiums.

However, the bond insurance market has been gradually recovering in recent years, with new players entering the market and renewed interest from issuers and investors seeking greater security in an uncertain economic climate. As a registered representative, it's essential to stay informed about the evolving landscape of bond insurance and its impact on municipal securities. Your ability to assess the value of bond insurance for different clients and incorporate it into your investment recommendations will demonstrate your expertise and commitment to risk management.

II. Issuance & Regulation

Underwriting Process

Having dissected the various types of municipal bonds, let's turn our attention to the intricate process that brings them to life: underwriting. This critical stage, where municipalities partner with financial intermediaries to access the capital markets, involves a series of carefully orchestrated steps designed to ensure the successful issuance and distribution of these bonds.

Think of the underwriting process as a relay race, with the baton passing from the municipality to the underwriter and finally to the investors. It all begins when a municipality identifies a need for funding, such as building a new school or upgrading its infrastructure. They then assemble a team of financial advisors, bond counsel, and underwriters to guide them through the issuance process.

The underwriter, typically a large investment bank or a syndicate of firms, acts as a bridge between the municipality and the investors. They purchase the bonds from the issuer at a negotiated price and then resell them to the public at a slightly higher price, earning the difference as their compensation. This process ensures that the municipality receives the funds they need upfront, while investors gain access to a new investment opportunity.

The underwriting process typically involves several key stages. First, the municipality prepares an official statement, a comprehensive disclosure document that provides detailed information about the issuer, the purpose of the bond offering, the source of repayment, and any associated risks. This document, similar to a prospectus for a stock offering, is essential for investors to make informed decisions.

Next, the underwriter conducts a thorough due diligence process, assessing the municipality's financial health, creditworthiness, and the feasibility of the project being financed. This analysis helps the underwriter determine the appropriate pricing and interest rate for the bonds, ensuring they are attractive to investors while also meeting the issuer's needs.

Once the due diligence is complete and the official statement is finalized, the underwriter begins marketing the bonds to potential investors. This may involve roadshows, presentations, and direct communication with institutional and retail investors. The underwriter's goal is to generate enough demand for the bonds to ensure a successful sale.

Finally, the bonds are priced and sold to investors. The price is determined by the underwriter based on market conditions, investor demand, and the credit quality of the issuer. Once the sale is complete, the municipality receives the proceeds, and the bonds begin trading in the secondary market.

Understanding the underwriting process is crucial for the Series 7 exam and your future career. You may be asked to identify the different parties involved in the process, their roles and responsibilities, or the steps involved in bringing a municipal bond to market. Additionally, as a registered representative, you may be involved in selling newly issued municipal bonds to your clients. Your knowledge of the underwriting process will enable you to explain the offering to your clients confidently, address their questions, and help them make informed investment decisions.

While the underwriting process brings municipal bonds to the market, it's the Municipal Securities Rulemaking Board (MSRB) that ensures the integrity and transparency of this vital sector. Established by Congress in 1975, the MSRB plays a critical role in safeguarding the municipal bond market, setting the rules of engagement for those involved in its issuance and trading.

The MSRB, an independent self-regulatory organization, writes the rules governing the activities of broker-dealers, municipal advisors, and other market participants. These rules cover a vast array of topics, from ethical standards and professional conduct to pricing and disclosure requirements. Think of the MSRB as the referee, ensuring that all players follow the rules and that the game is played fairly.

One of the MSRB's key functions is to promote price transparency in the municipal bond market. It operates the Electronic Municipal Market Access (EMMA) system, a centralized repository of official statements, trade data, and other key information related to municipal securities. EMMA provides investors with free and easy access to critical data, empowering them to make informed decisions.

For instance, if an investor is considering purchasing a municipal bond issued by the City of Los Angeles, they can access EMMA to view the bond's official statement, which outlines the details of the offering, the city's financial condition, and the risks associated with the investment. This transparency helps level the playing field, allowing individual investors to make informed decisions comparable to those of large institutional investors.

The MSRB also plays a crucial role in establishing professional qualifications and standards for individuals engaged in the municipal securities business. It administers the Series 52 Municipal Securities Representative Qualification Examination (Series 52 Exam) and the Series 50 Municipal Advisor Representative Qualification Examination (Series 50 Exam), ensuring that those who work in this sector possess the necessary knowledge and expertise.

Furthermore, the MSRB develops educational materials and resources for investors, issuers, and market professionals, promoting understanding and best practices in the municipal securities industry. Its website offers a wealth of information on various topics, from bond basics to regulatory updates, helping individuals navigate the complexities of this market.

The MSRB's oversight and rulemaking authority is critical for maintaining the integrity and efficiency of the municipal bond market. By setting clear standards of conduct, promoting transparency, and ensuring that market participants are qualified and informed, the MSRB helps to foster trust and confidence in this vital segment of the fixed-income market.

As you prepare for the Series 7 exam, expect questions that assess your understanding of the MSRB's role and its various rules and regulations. You might be asked to identify specific MSRB rules governing municipal securities professionals or to explain the importance of disclosure and transparency in the market. By mastering this knowledge, you'll not only excel on the exam but also demonstrate your commitment to ethical conduct and investor protection, key attributes of a successful financial advisor in the municipal bond market.

Disclosure & Continuing Obligations

As we've navigated the complexities of municipal bond issuance, from the underwriter's role to the MSRB's regulatory oversight, it becomes evident that transparency is paramount in this market. To foster investor confidence and ensure fair trading practices, issuers of municipal securities are bound by a series of disclosure requirements and continuing obligations that extend far beyond the initial bond offering.

At the heart of these disclosure requirements is the Official Statement (OS), a comprehensive document that serves as the investor's primary source of information about the bond. Think of it as the bond's autobiography, detailing its purpose, structure, risks, and the financial health of the issuer. This document, prepared by the issuer with the assistance of their bond counsel, must be provided to potential investors before they make a purchase. It covers a range of topics, from the project being financed and the source of repayment to the issuer's financial statements, debt levels, and any pending litigation that could affect their ability to repay the bond.

However, the issuer's responsibility doesn't end with the issuance of the OS. They are also subject to continuing disclosure obligations, requiring them to provide updated information to the market on an ongoing basis. This includes annual financial reports, audited financial statements, and notices of any material events that could impact the bond's value or the issuer's ability to repay its debt. For example, if a city experiences a significant decline in tax revenues that could jeopardize its ability to make bond payments, it's obligated to disclose this information to the market promptly.

These continuing disclosures are not just a matter of courtesy; they are mandated by the Securities and Exchange Commission (SEC) Rule 15c2-12. This rule requires underwriters to ensure that issuers have entered into a written agreement to provide ongoing disclosures to the MSRB's Electronic Municipal Market Access (EMMA) system. EMMA serves as a centralized repository for these disclosures, making them readily accessible to investors and the public.

The importance of disclosure and continuing obligations was highlighted in a 2013 SEC case involving the City of Harrisburg, Pennsylvania. The city failed to disclose its deteriorating financial condition and mounting debt obligations to investors, leading to significant losses when it eventually defaulted on its bonds. The SEC charged the city with securities fraud, emphasizing the critical need for issuers to provide accurate and timely information to the market.

As a registered representative, understanding these disclosure requirements and continuing obligations is vital for protecting your clients and ensuring they make informed investment decisions. You should be familiar with the contents of an official statement, know how to access continuing disclosures on EMMA, and be able to interpret this information to assess the creditworthiness of the issuer and the risks associated with the bond.

Remember, the municipal bond market relies heavily on transparency and trust. By upholding the highest standards of disclosure and ensuring your clients have access to all material information, you can help them navigate this market with confidence and build lasting relationships based on integrity and sound financial advice.

III. Tax Implications

Tax-exempt status & benefits

As we navigate the intricacies of the municipal bond market, one of its most alluring features comes into sharp focus: the potential for tax-exempt income. This unique characteristic, enshrined in the U.S. tax code, can significantly enhance the after-tax returns for investors, particularly those in higher tax brackets. Let's delve deeper into this tax advantage and understand how it can be leveraged to achieve optimal investment outcomes.

The tax-exempt status of municipal bonds means that the interest income they generate is generally exempt from federal income tax. This exemption stems from the principle of reciprocal immunity, which prevents the federal government from taxing the interest on state and local government obligations. This can translate into significant savings for investors, especially those in higher tax brackets who would otherwise face a hefty tax bill on their interest income.

Imagine two investors, Emily and John, both considering investing in a bond. Emily, in the 35% tax bracket, is drawn to a California municipal bond yielding 4%. John, in the 12% tax bracket, is eyeing a corporate bond yielding 5%. At first glance, John's corporate bond seems more attractive with its higher yield. However, after factoring in taxes, Emily's municipal bond actually provides a higher after-tax return. This is because her interest income is tax-exempt, while John's interest income is subject to federal income tax.

The tax benefits of municipal bonds can be even more pronounced for investors residing in states with high income tax rates. In many cases, the interest on municipal bonds issued within the investor's state of residence is also exempt from state and local income taxes. This "double" or even "triple" tax exemption can significantly boost the after-tax yield for these investors.

However, it's important to remember that not all municipal bonds offer tax-exempt interest. Certain types of municipal bonds, such as private activity bonds (PABs) or bonds issued to finance non-essential projects, may be subject to the alternative minimum tax (AMT), which we will explore in more detail in the next section. Additionally, the tax-exempt status of municipal bonds doesn't apply to capital gains realized from selling the bonds at a profit.

Alternative Minimum Tax (AMT)

While the tax-exempt status of municipal bonds is a significant allure, it's essential to be aware of a potential hurdle that could impact their attractiveness for certain investors: the Alternative Minimum Tax (AMT). This parallel tax system, enacted in 1969 to ensure that high-income individuals pay their fair share, operates alongside the regular income tax system, requiring some taxpayers to calculate their tax liability under both systems and pay the higher of the two.

The AMT operates by disallowing certain deductions and exemptions that are normally permitted under the regular tax code. This broader tax base can potentially capture income that would otherwise escape taxation, ensuring that wealthy individuals do not unfairly benefit from loopholes and deductions. However, this can also impact the tax-exempt status of certain municipal bonds, particularly private activity bonds (PABs), which we discussed earlier.

PABs, issued to finance projects for private entities like airports or sports stadiums, often offer higher yields than traditional municipal bonds due to their potential AMT exposure. If an investor subject to the AMT holds a PAB, the interest income from that bond may become taxable under the AMT calculation, negating some or all of the tax benefits.

Let's imagine an investor named Sarah, who is in the top tax bracket and subject to the AMT. She's considering two bonds: a general obligation bond yielding 3% and a PAB yielding 4%. While the PAB's higher yield is initially tempting, Sarah needs to carefully evaluate whether the potential AMT liability would outweigh the tax benefits. If the interest from the PAB becomes taxable under the AMT, its after-tax yield might be lower than that of the GO bond, making it a less attractive investment.

This complexity surrounding the AMT and its potential impact on municipal bond investments is something you'll encounter on the Series 7 exam. You might be presented with scenarios where clients are considering PABs and need to assess their suitability based on their AMT liability. Your understanding of the AMT and its implications will be crucial for providing accurate and informed advice.

Beyond the exam, in your professional practice, you'll encounter clients with diverse tax situations. Some might be subject to the AMT, while others might not. Your ability to navigate these complexities, explain the potential impact of the AMT on municipal bond investments, and tailor your recommendations accordingly will showcase your expertise and earn your clients' trust. Remember, tax-efficient investing is not just about maximizing returns; it's also about minimizing unnecessary tax liabilities and helping your clients achieve their financial goals in the most optimal way possible.

State-specific tax implications

While the allure of federal tax-exempt income from municipal bonds is undeniable, we must now navigate the nuanced waters of state-specific tax implications. As you prepare for the Series 7 exam, and later, when advising clients, it's vital to recognize that the tax treatment of municipal bonds can vary significantly depending on the investor's state of residence and the bond's issuing state.

The general rule of thumb is that interest earned on municipal bonds issued within an investor's home state is typically exempt from both federal and state income taxes. This "double tax exemption" can significantly enhance the after-tax yield for investors residing in high-tax states like California or New York. However, if an investor ventures beyond their state borders and purchases bonds issued by another state, their home state may impose its own income tax on the interest earned. This can erode some of the tax advantages and impact the overall attractiveness of the investment.

Imagine a scenario where an investor living in California is considering two municipal bonds: one issued by the state of California and another issued by the state of New York. Both bonds offer a 4% yield. While the California bond would be exempt from both federal and California state income tax, the New York bond's interest would likely be subject to California state income tax, potentially reducing its after-tax yield.

Therefore, it's crucial to carefully consider the state-specific tax implications before recommending municipal bonds to clients. You'll need to be familiar with the tax laws of your clients' states of residence, as well as the tax treatment of bonds issued by different states. This will enable you to assess the true after-tax yield of each investment and make recommendations that align with your clients' tax optimization goals.

Furthermore, some states offer additional tax benefits for certain types of municipal bonds, such as those issued to finance specific projects or those targeted towards specific investor groups. It's essential to stay informed about these nuances and leverage them to create tax-efficient portfolios for your clients.

The Series 7 exam will undoubtedly test your knowledge of state-specific tax implications for municipal bonds. You might be presented with scenarios involving investors residing in different states and asked to calculate the after-tax yield of various bond options. By mastering this complex aspect of municipal bond investing, you'll showcase your expertise and ability to provide your clients comprehensive and tailored financial advice.

Chapter 9: Navigating the Frontiers: Complex Products and Emerging Markets

Having established a solid foundation in traditional securities and investment strategies, we now venture beyond the familiar, into the exciting and often uncharted territories of complex products and emerging markets. This chapter will expand your investment horizons, introducing you to sophisticated financial instruments and burgeoning global opportunities that can add a new dimension to your clients' portfolios.

We'll begin by delving into the world of structured products, those intricate creations that blend various securities and derivatives to offer tailored risk-return profiles. You'll learn about principal-protected notes that offer downside protection, reverse convertibles that provide enhanced income potential, and other innovative structures designed to meet specific investor needs. We'll also explore the risk factors associated with these products, ensuring you're equipped to make informed recommendations to your clients.

Next, we'll embark on a journey into the rapidly evolving realm of cryptocurrency and blockchain technology. You'll gain a foundational understanding of the blockchain, the decentralized ledger system that underpins cryptocurrencies, and explore the characteristics of major cryptocurrencies like Bitcoin and Ethereum. We'll also navigate cryptocurrency investments' evolving regulatory landscape, ensuring you stay compliant while advising clients on this emerging asset class.

Then, we'll broaden our horizons to encompass international markets, where American Depositary Receipts (ADRs) offer a gateway for U.S. investors to access foreign companies. You'll learn how ADRs work, their benefits, and the potential risks of international investing, including currency exchange fluctuations and geopolitical events.

Finally, we'll underscore the importance of suitability and disclosure when dealing with complex products. You'll understand the heightened standards of care required for these investments and the necessity of providing clear and comprehensive disclosures to clients. We'll also offer best practices for explaining these intricate products in an informative and engaging way, empowering your clients to make informed decisions.

By the end of this chapter, you'll possess a broader perspective on the investment landscape, armed with the knowledge to navigate the complexities of structured products, cryptocurrencies, and international markets. You'll be able to identify potential opportunities for your clients, while also diligently assessing and managing the associated risks. This expertise will set you apart as a financial advisor, capable of crafting sophisticated and diversified portfolios that meet the evolving needs of today's investors.

I. Structured Products

Types (principal-protected notes, reverse convertibles)

Now that we've established the foundation for understanding packaged products and alternative investments, let's delve into the fascinating realm of structured products. These sophisticated financial instruments, often crafted by combining various securities and derivatives, offer investors tailored risk-return profiles to match their specific needs and market outlooks. Within this intricate tapestry of structured products, two prominent players stand out: principal-protected notes and reverse convertibles.

Principal-protected notes, often abbreviated as PPNs, offer a unique blend of potential upside and downside protection. They typically combine a zero-coupon bond, which guarantees the return of principal at maturity, with an option or other derivative that provides exposure to the performance of an underlying asset, such as a stock index or a basket of stocks. In essence, PPNs offer investors the opportunity to participate in potential market gains while safeguarding their initial investment.

For example, imagine a PPN linked to the performance of the S&P 500 index with a maturity of five years. If the index rises over that period, the investor receives a portion of the gains, often capped at a predetermined percentage. However, even if the index declines, the investor is still guaranteed to receive their initial investment back at maturity. This downside protection can be particularly appealing to risk-averse investors who want to participate in the market's upside potential while limiting their potential losses.

Reverse convertibles, on the other hand, offer a different kind of appeal, namely enhanced income potential. These structured products typically consist of a high-yielding bond coupled with a short-term option on an underlying stock. The investor receives attractive coupon payments, often significantly higher than those of traditional bonds, but at a cost. If the underlying stock price falls below a certain level (the "knock-in" level) before maturity, the investor may be obligated to purchase shares of the stock at a predetermined price, potentially incurring a loss if the stock price has declined significantly.

Let's consider an example: an investor buys a reverse convertible linked to Apple stock with a one-year maturity and a 10% coupon rate. The knock-in level is set at 80% of the initial stock price. If Apple's stock price remains above this level throughout the year, the investor receives their principal back plus the 10% coupon payment. However, if the stock price falls below the knock-in level, the investor may be forced to buy Apple shares at a price that's now higher than the market price, potentially resulting in a loss.

Both principal-protected notes and reverse convertibles offer unique risk-reward profiles that cater to specific investor needs. PPNs provide a sense of security with their principal protection feature, while reverse convertibles offer the allure of high yields but with the potential downside of forced stock ownership.

As a registered representative preparing for the Series 7 exam, you'll encounter questions that test your understanding of these complex products. You'll need to be able to explain their features, risks, and potential benefits to clients and determine their suitability based on individual investment objectives and risk tolerance. Remember, structured products can be valuable tools for diversification and risk management, but they require careful analysis and clear communication to ensure they align with your clients' financial goals and expectations.

Risk factors

While structured products can offer enticing combinations of potential return and risk mitigation, it's imperative to remember that they are not without their complexities and potential pitfalls. A thorough understanding of the risk factors inherent in these products is essential for both aspiring financial professionals and seasoned investors alike.

Credit risk, as we've discussed in the context of bonds, also looms large in the world of structured products. These products are typically issued by banks or other financial institutions, and their ability to meet their obligations depends on the issuer's financial strength and creditworthiness. If the issuer defaults, investors could face significant losses, potentially even losing their entire principal investment. The 2008 financial crisis serves as a stark reminder of this risk, as the collapse of Lehman Brothers left many investors holding worthless structured products issued by the bank.

Market risk is another key consideration. Structured products are often linked to the performance of underlying assets, such as stocks, indices, or commodities. If these underlying assets perform poorly, the structured product's return could be significantly impacted, even if the principal is protected. For example, a principal-protected note linked to the S&P 500 index might offer limited upside potential if the index remains relatively flat over the investment period, even though the principal is guaranteed at maturity.

Liquidity risk is also a factor, particularly for less actively traded structured products. Unlike stocks or exchange-traded funds (ETFs), which can be easily bought and sold on the open market, some structured products may have limited secondary market trading, making it difficult for investors to exit their positions if needed. This lack of liquidity can be particularly problematic in times of market stress or if the investor needs to access their funds unexpectedly.

Complexity is another hallmark of structured products. Their intricate structures and embedded derivatives can be challenging to understand, even for seasoned investors. This lack of transparency can make it difficult to accurately assess the risks and potential rewards of these products. Moreover, the fees and commissions associated with structured products can be high, further eroding their potential returns.

Finally, it's important to be aware of the potential for conflicts of interest in the structured product market. The issuer of a structured product is typically also the seller, creating a potential conflict between their interests and those of the investor. As a registered representative, it's your duty to carefully evaluate the terms of any structured product, understand its risks, and ensure that it aligns with your client's investment objectives and risk tolerance.

The Series 7 exam will undoubtedly test your knowledge of these risk factors. You might be presented with scenarios involving structured products and asked to identify the potential risks faced by investors. By mastering these concepts, you'll be equipped to make informed recommendations to your clients, balancing the potential rewards of structured products with their inherent complexities and risks.

Regulatory considerations & disclosure requirements

While structured products offer enticing opportunities for investors seeking tailored risk-return profiles, they also operate within a stringent regulatory framework designed to protect investors and ensure fair practices. These regulations, enforced by bodies such as the Financial Industry Regulatory Authority (FINRA) and the Securities and Exchange Commission (SEC), mandate specific disclosure requirements and impose heightened suitability standards on those recommending these complex products.

FINRA, as we've discussed, has established a comprehensive set of rules governing the sale of complex products, including structured products. These rules emphasize the importance of suitability, requiring registered representatives to conduct a thorough assessment of their clients' financial situation, investment objectives, and risk tolerance before recommending any structured product.

Furthermore, FINRA mandates that brokers provide clear and comprehensive disclosures to clients regarding the features, risks, and costs associated with structured products. These disclosures must be tailored to the specific product being offered and presented in a manner that is easily understandable to the client. For example, if a client is considering a principal-protected note, the broker must explain the mechanics of the note, the potential return scenarios, and the risks associated with the underlying asset and the issuer's creditworthiness.

The SEC also plays a crucial role in regulating structured products. It requires issuers to file registration statements and prospectuses with the SEC, providing detailed information about the product's terms, risks, and fees. The SEC reviews these documents to ensure they meet stringent disclosure requirements and are not misleading to investors.

In recent years, there has been increased scrutiny of structured products by regulators, particularly in the wake of the 2008 financial crisis, where many investors suffered significant losses due to complex and opaque structured products. The SEC has taken several actions to enhance transparency and investor protection in this market. For instance, in 2014, the SEC adopted new rules requiring greater disclosure of the costs and risks associated with structured notes.

As a registered representative, understanding these regulatory considerations and disclosure requirements is paramount. You'll be responsible for ensuring that your clients receive all necessary information about structured products and that any recommendations you make are suitable for their individual needs and risk tolerance. Failure to comply with these regulations can result in disciplinary action from FINRA or the SEC, including fines, suspensions, or even revocation of your license.

II. Cryptocurrency & Blockchain Technology

Basic blockchain explanation

Now, as we shift gears from the world of structured products, let's dive headfirst into the disruptive and rapidly evolving domain of cryptocurrency and blockchain technology. While the regulatory landscape is still catching up with the innovations in this space, a foundational understanding of blockchain technology is crucial for any forward-thinking financial professional. It's the backbone upon which the entire cryptocurrency ecosystem is built, and its potential applications extend far beyond just digital currencies.

In its essence, blockchain technology is a decentralized, distributed ledger system that records transactions across a network of computers. Imagine a traditional ledger, like a checkbook register, where transactions are recorded sequentially. Now, picture this ledger being replicated and shared across numerous computers, with each computer verifying and updating the ledger independently. This distributed nature eliminates the need for a central authority or intermediary, making the system resistant to censorship and manipulation.

Each transaction on the blockchain is bundled into a "block," which is then linked to the previous block using cryptographic hashes, creating an immutable chain of records. This immutability ensures that once a transaction is recorded on the blockchain, it cannot be altered or deleted, creating a high level of trust and transparency.

To illustrate this, imagine a simple transaction where Alice sends Bob one Bitcoin. This transaction is broadcast to the network, where it is verified by multiple computers and added to a block. This block is then linked to the previous block, creating a permanent and unalterable record of the transaction. Even if one computer in the network were to be compromised, the other computers would maintain the integrity of the ledger, preventing any fraudulent activity.

The blockchain's decentralized and immutable nature has far-reaching implications beyond just cryptocurrencies. It has the potential to revolutionize various industries, from supply chain management and healthcare to voting systems and identity verification. For example, Walmart is using blockchain technology to track the provenance of its food products, ensuring transparency and safety throughout the supply chain. Similarly, governments are exploring the use of blockchain for secure and tamper-proof voting systems.

While the Series 7 exam currently focuses primarily on traditional securities, the growing prominence of cryptocurrencies and blockchain technology suggests that future iterations of the exam might include questions related to these topics. Understanding the basics of blockchain technology, its underlying principles, and its potential applications will not only enhance your overall financial knowledge but also prepare you for the evolving landscape of the investment world.

Major cryptocurrencies & characteristics

With the foundational concept of blockchain in mind, let's delve into the vibrant and ever-evolving world of cryptocurrencies. Within this digital ecosystem, a multitude of coins and tokens exist, each with its unique characteristics and purpose. However, a few major players stand out, leading the charge in terms of market capitalization, adoption, and technological innovation.

Bitcoin, the original and most well-known cryptocurrency, launched in 2009 by the enigmatic Satoshi Nakamoto, remains the undisputed king of the crypto world. It's a decentralized digital currency that operates on a peer-to-peer network, enabling secure and transparent transactions without the need for intermediaries like banks. Bitcoin's scarcity, with a capped supply of 21 million coins, and its increasing acceptance as a form of payment and store of value, have contributed to its meteoric rise in price over the years. However, its price volatility and energy-intensive mining process remain key challenges.

Ethereum, launched in 2015, is more than just a digital currency; it's a programmable blockchain platform that enables the creation of decentralized applications (dApps) and smart contracts. This versatility has propelled Ethereum to the second-largest cryptocurrency by market capitalization, fostering a thriving ecosystem of decentralized finance (DeFi) applications, non-fungible tokens (NFTs), and other innovative use cases. Ethereum's recent transition to a proof-of-stake consensus mechanism, known as "The Merge," significantly reduced its energy consumption and paved the way for further scalability and innovation.

Tether, or USDT, is a stablecoin pegged to the value of the U.S. dollar. It aims to provide stability and minimize volatility in the often-turbulent crypto market. Tether is widely used as a trading pair on cryptocurrency exchanges, allowing traders to quickly move in and out of positions without converting back to fiat currency. However, its lack of transparency and concerns about its reserves have also attracted regulatory scrutiny.

Beyond these giants, a plethora of other cryptocurrencies exists, each with its unique features and use cases. Solana, for example, is a high-performance blockchain known for its fast transaction speeds and low fees, making it a popular choice for decentralized applications and gaming. Cardano, on the other hand, focuses on sustainability and scalability, utilizing a proof-of-stake consensus mechanism and a layered architecture to enable secure and efficient transactions.

Understanding the characteristics of major cryptocurrencies is crucial for navigating this dynamic and evolving market. As a registered representative, you may encounter clients interested in adding cryptocurrencies to their portfolios. It's your responsibility to educate them about the risks and potential rewards, ensuring that any recommendations align with their investment objectives and risk tolerance.

While the Series 7 exam doesn't currently delve deep into specific cryptocurrencies, your knowledge of their characteristics and the underlying blockchain technology can demonstrate your commitment to staying ahead of the curve and understanding the evolving landscape of the financial markets.

Regulatory stance on crypto investments

As we navigate the exciting and rapidly evolving world of cryptocurrencies, it's crucial to recognize the complex and often uncertain regulatory landscape that surrounds them. Unlike traditional securities like stocks and bonds, which operate within a well-established regulatory framework, cryptocurrencies exist in a somewhat nebulous zone, where different agencies and jurisdictions grapple with how to classify and regulate these digital assets.

In the United States, the regulatory stance on crypto investments is a patchwork of evolving rules and interpretations. The Securities and Exchange Commission (SEC) has asserted its authority over certain cryptocurrencies, classifying them as securities if they meet the criteria of an "investment contract" under the Howey Test. This means that initial coin offerings (ICOs) and certain token sales may be subject to SEC registration and disclosure requirements, akin to traditional securities offerings.

The Commodity Futures Trading Commission (CFTC), on the other hand, views some cryptocurrencies, particularly Bitcoin and Ether, as commodities, similar to gold or oil. This classification places them under the CFTC's regulatory purview, which includes overseeing derivatives markets and enforcing anti-fraud and manipulation provisions.

The Internal Revenue Service (IRS), meanwhile, treats cryptocurrencies as property for tax purposes. This means that any gains or losses from buying and selling cryptocurrencies are subject to capital gains taxes, just like gains or losses from selling stocks or real estate.

This fragmented regulatory landscape can create challenges for both investors and financial professionals. The lack of a unified regulatory framework can lead to uncertainty and confusion, making it difficult to navigate the legal and compliance aspects of cryptocurrency investments.

Moreover, the SEC's approach of "regulation by enforcement" has led to high-profile lawsuits against cryptocurrency exchanges and projects, such as the ongoing legal battle between the SEC and Ripple Labs over the classification of XRP as a security. These enforcement actions underscore the importance of staying informed about regulatory developments and ensuring that any recommendations or transactions involving cryptocurrencies are compliant with applicable laws and regulations.

Despite the regulatory uncertainties, cryptocurrencies have gained significant traction in recent years, with institutional investors and major corporations increasingly embracing these digital assets. The launch of Bitcoin futures ETFs in 2021 marked a significant milestone in the mainstream acceptance of cryptocurrencies, providing investors with a regulated way to gain exposure to Bitcoin's price movements.

As a registered representative preparing for the Series 7 exam, it's essential to be aware of the evolving regulatory landscape surrounding cryptocurrencies. While the exam may not delve deep into the specifics of crypto regulations, understanding the general regulatory stance and the potential risks and challenges associated with these investments is crucial.

Remember, the cryptocurrency market is still in its nascent stages, and its regulatory framework is likely to continue evolving. By staying informed about these developments and exercising due diligence when advising clients on crypto investments, you can navigate this exciting new frontier responsibly and ethically, safeguarding your clients' interests and upholding the integrity of the financial industry.

III. International Markets & ADRs

How ADRs work & benefits for U.S. investors

Now that we've explored the regulatory challenges and opportunities surrounding cryptocurrencies, let's shift our focus to another exciting dimension of the investment world: international markets. As the global economy becomes increasingly interconnected, the allure of investing in companies beyond U.S. borders has grown significantly. However, navigating foreign markets can be complex and daunting, with different currencies, trading regulations, and settlement processes. Here, American Depositary Receipts (ADRs) step in, offering a bridge between U.S. investors and foreign companies, facilitating access to global opportunities without the complexities of direct overseas investment.

So, how do ADRs work? It all starts with a U.S. bank, known as a depositary bank, purchasing a block of shares of a foreign company in its home market. These shares are then held in custody by the bank, which issues ADRs representing ownership in the foreign company's stock. Each ADR typically represents a specific number of underlying shares, allowing investors to buy and sell ADRs on U.S. stock exchanges just like any other domestic security. For example, one ADR of the popular Chinese e-commerce giant Alibaba represents eight ordinary shares of the company.

ADRs offer a myriad of benefits for U.S. investors. First and foremost, they provide a convenient and accessible way to invest in foreign companies without the complexities and costs of directly accessing foreign markets. This allows investors to diversify their portfolios geographically, tapping into growth opportunities in emerging markets or accessing unique industries and sectors not readily available in the U.S.

Additionally, ADRs are denominated in U.S. dollars, eliminating the need for currency conversions and simplifying the investment process. They also pay dividends in U.S. dollars, providing a steady stream of income for investors. Furthermore, ADRs are subject to U.S. securities regulations, offering investors a degree of familiarity and protection.

For instance, an American investor interested in the growth potential of the Indian technology sector might consider investing in the Infosys ADR, which represents shares of Infosys Limited, a leading Indian IT company listed on the NYSE. This allows the investor to gain exposure to the Indian market without having to navigate the complexities of trading on the Indian stock exchange or dealing with currency conversions.

As you prepare for the Series 7 exam, you'll encounter questions that test your understanding of ADRs and their benefits for U.S. investors. You might be asked to identify the advantages of ADRs compared to direct foreign stock ownership or to explain how ADRs facilitate access to international markets. By mastering these concepts, you'll demonstrate your knowledge of global investment opportunities and your ability to guide clients towards diversified portfolios that encompass both domestic and international securities. Remember, in today's interconnected world, the ability to navigate international markets is a valuable asset for any financial professional seeking to provide comprehensive investment advice to their clients.

Risks of international investing

While ADRs provide a bridge to global investment opportunities, it's imperative to remember that venturing into international markets introduces a new layer of complexity and risk. As we navigate this terrain, let's shed light on the potential pitfalls that investors must be aware of, ensuring they make informed decisions that align with their risk tolerance and financial goals.

One of the most prominent risks of international investing is currency risk. The value of foreign currencies can fluctuate significantly against the U.S. dollar, impacting the returns of investments denominated in those currencies. Imagine an American investor purchasing shares of a German company through an ADR. If the euro depreciates against the dollar, the investor's return in dollar terms will be reduced, even if the underlying stock price remains stable. Conversely, if the euro appreciates, the investor's return will be amplified. This currency risk underscores the importance of considering exchange rate fluctuations when evaluating international investments.

Another key risk is political and economic instability. Emerging markets, while offering potential for high growth, can also be prone to political unrest, economic turmoil, and regulatory changes that can adversely affect investment values. For example, a sudden change in government or a currency crisis in a developing country could lead to a sharp decline in the value of its stock market, impacting the returns of any investments tied to that market.

Differences in accounting and reporting standards can also pose challenges for international investors. Companies in different countries may adhere to varying accounting practices, making it difficult to compare financial statements and assess the true value of their securities. This lack of transparency can increase the risk of fraud or misrepresentation, requiring investors to conduct thorough due diligence before investing in foreign companies.

Liquidity risk is another consideration. While ADRs of large, well-known companies tend to be relatively liquid, those of smaller or less-established companies may be less so. This can make it difficult to buy or sell these securities at desired prices, especially during times of market stress.

Furthermore, geopolitical events and global economic trends can impact international investments. Trade tensions, tariffs, or even armed conflicts can create uncertainty and volatility in global markets, affecting the performance of international investments.

For instance, during the U.S.-China trade war in 2018 and 2019, the Chinese stock market experienced significant declines due to concerns about the impact of tariffs on Chinese exports and economic growth. Investors holding ADRs of Chinese companies felt the impact of these geopolitical tensions firsthand.

Currency exchange considerations

While navigating the waters of international investments can open doors to exciting opportunities, it's imperative to remember that currency exchange rates play a critical role in the final outcome. As the world's economies ebb and flow, the relative values of currencies shift, creating an additional layer of complexity and potential risk for investors venturing beyond domestic borders. Understanding these currency exchange considerations is crucial for making informed investment decisions and maximizing returns in the global marketplace.

Think of currency exchange rates as a constantly fluctuating bridge between different economies. When you invest in a foreign company, you're not only betting on the company's performance but also on the relative strength of its home currency against the U.S. dollar. If the foreign currency appreciates, your investment gains value in dollar terms, even if the underlying asset's price remains unchanged. Conversely, if the foreign currency depreciates, your investment loses value, potentially offsetting any gains from the asset itself.

Let's illustrate this with a simple example. Suppose an American investor buys shares of a Japanese company on the Tokyo Stock Exchange. At the time of purchase, the exchange rate is 100 Japanese yen to 1 U.S. dollar. If the Japanese stock price rises by 10%, but the yen depreciates by 5% against the dollar during the same period, the investor's overall return in dollar terms will be diminished. This highlights the importance of considering currency fluctuations when evaluating international investments.

For investors seeking to mitigate currency risk, various hedging strategies are available. One common approach is to use currency forwards or futures contracts to lock in a specific exchange rate for a future transaction. This can help protect against adverse currency movements and provide greater certainty in investment returns. However, hedging also comes with costs and complexities, and it may not be suitable for all investors.

Understanding currency exchange considerations is not just about risk management; it's also about identifying potential opportunities. A weakening dollar, for instance, can boost the returns of international investments for U.S. investors, as their dollar-denominated gains are amplified when converted back from a stronger foreign currency.

In the Series 7 exam, you'll encounter questions that test your understanding of currency exchange risks and their impact on international investments. You might be asked to calculate the return on a foreign investment considering both the asset's price movement and the change in exchange rates. By mastering these concepts, you'll be equipped to navigate the complexities of the global marketplace and provide your clients with sophisticated and comprehensive investment advice.

Chapter 9: Summary and Review

This chapter explored beyond the traditional realms of stocks and bonds, delving into the sophisticated and rapidly evolving world of complex products and emerging markets. We began by dissecting the intricacies of structured products and meticulously crafted financial instruments that combine various securities and derivatives to offer tailored risk-return profiles. We examined principal-protected notes, which provide a safety net for investors seeking downside protection, and reverse convertibles, which offer enhanced income potential but with the caveat of potential forced stock ownership.

Next, we ventured into the groundbreaking world of cryptocurrencies and blockchain technology. We demystified the blockchain, the decentralized ledger system that underpins cryptocurrencies and explored the characteristics of major players like Bitcoin and Ethereum. We also navigated the complex and evolving regulatory landscape surrounding crypto investments, emphasizing the importance of compliance and investor protection.

We then broadened our horizons to encompass international markets, where American Depositary Receipts (ADRs) act as a bridge for U.S. investors seeking exposure to foreign companies. We elucidated the mechanics of ADRs, their benefits for investors, and the inherent risks of international investing, including currency exchange fluctuations, political instability, and varying accounting standards.

Finally, we underscored the critical importance of suitability and disclosure when dealing with complex products. We highlighted the heightened standards of care required for these investments and the necessity of providing clear and comprehensive disclosures to clients. We also offered best practices for explaining these intricate products in a way that empowers investors to make informed decisions.

Test Your Knowledge:

1. What are the key differences between principal-protected notes and reverse convertibles?

2. Explain the basic concept of blockchain technology and its potential applications beyond cryptocurrencies.

3. What are the advantages and disadvantages of investing in American Depositary Receipts (ADRs)?

4. What are some of the risks associated with international investing?

5. Why is suitability particularly important when recommending complex products to clients?

Tips for Applying the Knowledge to Exam Questions:

- **Understand the structures:** Be able to differentiate between various complex products and their underlying components.

- **Assess risk-reward profiles:** Analyze the potential risks and rewards associated with each product and strategy.

- **Stay current on regulations:** Keep abreast of evolving regulations governing cryptocurrencies and other complex investments.

- **Prioritize suitability:** Always consider the client's financial situation, investment objectives, and risk tolerance when recommending complex products.

- **Communicate clearly:** Explain complex products in a way that's easily understandable to clients, ensuring informed decision-making.

Chapter 10: Decoding the Market: Economic Factors and Securities Analysis

In this chapter, we move beyond the mechanics of individual securities and portfolios, venturing into the broader forces that shape the financial landscape. We'll explore the intricate relationship between economic indicators and the performance of securities markets, providing you with the tools to interpret economic data and anticipate its impact on various asset classes.

We'll delve into the contrasting worlds of fundamental and technical analysis, two distinct approaches to evaluating securities and making investment decisions. You'll learn about key ratios and metrics used in fundamental analysis, such as price-to-earnings ratios and debt-to-equity ratios, and discover how to dissect financial statements to assess a company's financial health and prospects. We'll also explore the world of technical analysis, deciphering chart patterns, trend lines, and other visual cues that can help identify trading opportunities.

Moreover, we'll navigate the complex landscape of market trends and cyclical factors, understanding how economic cycles and broader industry trends can influence investment decisions. You'll gain insights into the difference between secular and cyclical trends and discover strategies for adapting your investment approach to varying market conditions.

By the end of this chapter, you'll possess a deeper understanding of the macroeconomic forces that shape the financial markets and the analytical tools used to evaluate securities. This knowledge will empower you to make more informed investment decisions, anticipate market trends, and provide sophisticated and comprehensive advice to your clients. Whether you're a seasoned professional or just starting your journey in the financial industry, the insights gained in this chapter will prove invaluable in navigating the complexities of the market and achieving long-term success.

I. Economic Indicators & Market Impact

Key indicators (GDP, inflation, unemployment)

Now that we've established the significance of understanding broader economic forces in shaping investment decisions, let's turn our attention to the key economic indicators that serve as the pulse of the market. These indicators, like vital signs for a patient, provide valuable insights into the health and trajectory of the economy, influencing investor sentiment and ultimately driving the performance of various asset classes.

Gross Domestic Product (GDP), often dubbed the "king of economic indicators," measures the total value of goods and services produced within a country's borders over a specific period. It serves as a barometer of economic activity, with higher GDP growth generally signaling a robust and expanding economy, while declining GDP can indicate a recession or economic contraction. Investors closely monitor GDP figures, as they directly impact corporate profits, consumer spending, and overall market sentiment.

For example, during the COVID-19 pandemic in 2020, the U.S. GDP experienced a sharp decline due to lockdowns and business closures. This contraction reverberated through the markets, causing stock prices to plummet as investors anticipated lower corporate earnings and reduced consumer spending.

Inflation, the persistent rise in the general price level of goods and services, is another key indicator that investors and policymakers watch closely. Moderate inflation is generally considered a sign of a healthy economy, as it suggests demand is outpacing supply, leading to price increases. However, high or runaway inflation can erode purchasing power, decrease consumer confidence, and create uncertainty in the markets. Central banks, like the Federal Reserve in the United States, employ various tools, such as interest rate adjustments and open market operations, to manage inflation and maintain price stability.

The unemployment rate, which measures the percentage of the labor force that is actively seeking employment but unable to find a job, also plays a pivotal role in assessing the health of the economy. A low unemployment rate indicates a strong labor market, with ample job opportunities and rising wages, which can boost consumer spending and overall economic growth. Conversely, a high unemployment rate signifies economic weakness and potential social unrest, which can dampen investor sentiment and lead to market downturns.

The interplay between these key economic indicators – GDP, inflation, and unemployment – is complex and dynamic. For instance, strong GDP growth often leads to lower unemployment rates, but it can also fuel inflationary pressures if demand outstrips supply. Central banks, therefore, must carefully balance their efforts to promote economic growth with the need to maintain price stability.

As you prepare for the Series 7 exam, expect questions that assess your understanding of these key indicators and their impact on the markets. You might be asked to analyze how changes in GDP, inflation, or unemployment rates could affect the performance of different asset classes, such as stocks, bonds, or commodities. By mastering this knowledge, you'll not only excel on the exam but also be able to make more informed investment decisions and provide valuable insights to your clients.

Impact on different asset classes (stocks, bonds, etc.)

Understanding the significance of GDP, inflation, and unemployment is vital, but the true mastery lies in comprehending how their fluctuations send ripples across the vast ocean of asset classes. Each asset class, from the dynamic world of stocks to the more stable realm of bonds, reacts uniquely to economic shifts, creating a complex web of interdependencies that savvy investors must navigate.

Let's begin with stocks, the quintessential growth-oriented asset class. A robust GDP, fueled by increased consumer spending and business investment, typically bodes well for stocks. Companies see their profits rise, leading to increased investor confidence and a surge in stock prices. However, rising inflation can dampen this enthusiasm, as it erodes consumer purchasing power and increases input costs for businesses. The Federal Reserve's response to inflation, often through interest rate hikes, can also negatively impact stocks, as higher borrowing costs can weigh on corporate profitability and dampen investor sentiment.

Bonds, the stalwarts of stability and income, have a more intricate relationship with economic indicators. As we've explored previously, bond prices and interest rates move in opposite directions. Therefore, a rise in inflation or expectations of future economic growth, which can lead to higher interest rates, tends to push bond prices down. Conversely, a slowing economy or fears of recession, which might prompt central banks to lower interest rates, can boost bond prices. This dynamic interplay between bonds and economic indicators underscores the importance of understanding the yield curve and its predictive power.

Commodities, such as gold, oil, and agricultural products, can also react strongly to economic shifts. Rising inflation, for instance, can drive up the prices of commodities, as investors seek tangible assets to hedge against the erosion of their purchasing power. Similarly, a booming global economy, with increased demand for raw materials and energy, can lead to a surge in commodity prices. However, a global recession or a slowdown in major economies can dampen demand for commodities, causing their prices to fall.

Real estate, another popular asset class, is also influenced by economic indicators. Low interest rates can make it cheaper to borrow money for mortgages, fueling demand for housing and driving up property values. Strong economic growth and low unemployment rates can also boost the real estate market, as more people have the financial means to purchase homes or invest in commercial properties. However, a recession or rising interest rates can lead to a decline in real estate values, as affordability decreases and demand weakens.

Leading, lagging, & coincident indicators

Now that we've established the influence of key economic indicators on various asset classes, let's delve deeper into the timing of their movements, which introduces the concepts of leading, lagging, and coincident indicators. Understanding this temporal dimension is key to anticipating market trends and making informed investment decisions.

Think of these indicators as a three-act play, each act providing clues about the economy's performance. Leading indicators, like the first act, offer a glimpse into the future, signaling potential turning points in the business cycle before they become apparent in other economic data. Examples include the stock market, building permits, and consumer confidence surveys. A rising stock market, for instance, often precedes a period of economic expansion, as investors anticipate future growth and profitability.

Lagging indicators, akin to the third act, confirm trends that have already taken place, providing valuable validation but limited predictive power. These indicators include unemployment rates and corporate profits. A rising unemployment rate, for instance, typically lags behind an economic downturn, reflecting the delayed impact of reduced business activity on the labor market.

Coincident indicators, as the name suggests, move in tandem with the overall economy, providing a real-time snapshot of its current state. These indicators include industrial production, personal income, and retail sales. They are useful for confirming whether the economy is currently expanding or contracting and at what pace.

The interplay between these three types of indicators creates a dynamic picture of the economic landscape. For example, a surge in building permits (leading indicator) might suggest an upcoming increase in construction activity and economic growth. This could then be corroborated by a rise in industrial production (coincident indicator) and eventually lead to a decline in the unemployment rate (lagging indicator).

As a registered representative, recognizing these patterns and understanding the temporal relationships between different economic indicators can give you an edge in anticipating market movements and advising your clients accordingly. For instance, if you observe a decline in leading indicators, such as a drop in consumer confidence or a slowdown in manufacturing activity, you might recommend adjusting your clients' portfolios to include more defensive assets like bonds or high-quality dividend stocks.

The Series 7 exam will likely test your understanding of these indicator types. You might be presented with a list of economic indicators and asked to classify them as leading, lagging, or coincident. Or, you might be given a scenario where certain indicators are moving in a particular direction and asked to predict the likely impact on the overall economy or specific asset classes. By mastering this knowledge, you'll demonstrate your ability to interpret economic data, anticipate market trends, and provide strategic investment advice to your clients, even in the face of economic uncertainty.

II. Fundamental vs. Technical Analysis

Key ratios & metrics in fundamental analysis

Having surveyed the broader economic landscape, let's now focus on the microscope and scalpel of securities analysis. We're about to delve into the contrasting worlds of fundamental and technical analysis, two distinct yet complementary approaches that equip investors with the tools to dissect and evaluate securities.

Fundamental analysis, the bedrock of value investing, centers on scrutinizing a company's financial health and intrinsic worth. Think of it as peering under the hood of a car to assess its engine, transmission, and overall condition. In the investment realm, this involves dissecting financial statements, analyzing industry trends, and evaluating management quality to determine if a security is trading at a discount or premium to its intrinsic value.

Key ratios and metrics lie at the core of fundamental analysis. The Price-to-Earnings (P/E) ratio, for instance, compares a company's stock price to its earnings per share, offering a glimpse into its valuation relative to its profitability. A high P/E ratio might suggest that the market is optimistic about the company's future growth prospects, while a low P/E ratio could indicate that the stock is undervalued.

The Debt-to-Equity (D/E) ratio, another crucial metric, measures a company's financial leverage, comparing its total debt to its shareholders' equity. A high D/E ratio suggests that the company relies heavily on debt financing, which can amplify its risk profile. A low D/E ratio, on the other hand, indicates a more conservative capital structure.

Other essential ratios and metrics include the return on equity (ROE), which gauges a company's profitability relative to its shareholders' equity, and the current ratio, which assesses its short-term liquidity, or its ability to meet its near-term obligations.

Fundamental analysts also pay close attention to qualitative factors, such as the quality of a company's management team, its competitive landscape, and its industry outlook. For instance, a company with a visionary CEO and a strong track record of innovation might be viewed more favorably than a company with a history of poor management and declining market share.

Common technical analysis tools & chart patterns

In stark contrast to fundamental analysis, which focuses on the intrinsic value of a security based on financial and economic factors, technical analysis takes a different approach. It studies historical price and volume data, seeking to identify patterns and trends that can predict future price movements. Think of it as reading the tea leaves of the market, where past price action is believed to hold clues about future direction.

Technical analysts rely on a wide range of tools and chart patterns to gain insights into market sentiment and potential turning points. One of the most widely used tools is the moving average, which smooths out price data over a specified period, helping to identify trends and filter out noise. A simple moving average (SMA), for instance, calculates the average price over a set number of periods, while an exponential moving average (EMA) gives more weight to recent prices, making it more responsive to current trends.

Another popular tool is the Relative Strength Index (RSI), a momentum oscillator that measures the magnitude of recent price changes to evaluate overbought or oversold conditions in the market. An RSI above 70 typically suggests that a stock is overbought and due for a pullback, while an RSI below 30 might indicate an oversold condition and a potential buying opportunity.

Chart patterns, formed by the price action of a security over time, also play a pivotal role in technical analysis. These patterns, such as head and shoulders, double tops and bottoms, and triangles, are believed to represent recurring investor psychology and can be used to predict potential trend reversals or continuations.

For instance, a head and shoulders pattern, characterized by three peaks with the middle peak being the highest, is often seen as a bearish reversal signal, suggesting that an uptrend is likely to reverse into a downtrend. Conversely, a bullish flag pattern, formed by a brief consolidation period within an uptrend, often signals a continuation of the upward momentum.

The Series 7 exam will often challenge you to interpret charts and identify various technical indicators and patterns. You may be presented with a chart of a stock's price history and asked to identify the prevailing trend, potential support and resistance levels, or likely future price movements based on technical analysis principles. Therefore, familiarizing yourself with common technical analysis tools and chart patterns is essential for success on the exam.

While technical analysis can be a powerful tool for identifying trading opportunities and timing market entries and exits, it's crucial to remember that it's not infallible. It's based on the assumption that historical price patterns will repeat themselves, which is not always the case. Experienced traders often combine technical and fundamental analysis, utilizing quantitative and qualitative factors to make informed investment decisions. By mastering fundamental and technical analysis tools, you'll be equipped to navigate the complexities of the market and provide comprehensive and nuanced advice to your clients.

Pros & cons of each approach

Having explored the contrasting philosophies of fundamental and technical analysis, let's now weigh their strengths and weaknesses, recognizing that each approach offers unique insights into the market's mysteries. As a financial professional preparing for the Series 7 exam, a nuanced understanding of these pros and cons will equip you to make informed investment decisions and recommend suitable strategies to your clients.

Fundamental analysis, with its focus on a company's financial health and intrinsic value, can be a powerful tool for identifying long-term investment opportunities. By carefully analyzing financial statements, evaluating management quality, and understanding industry trends, fundamental analysts seek to uncover hidden gems – companies whose true value is not yet reflected in their stock prices.

The legendary investor Warren Buffett, often dubbed the "Oracle of Omaha," is a staunch advocate of fundamental analysis. His investment philosophy, centered on identifying undervalued companies with strong competitive advantages, has yielded extraordinary returns over decades, inspiring countless investors to follow in his footsteps.

However, fundamental analysis is not without its drawbacks. It requires a deep understanding of accounting principles, industry dynamics, and economic trends. This can be time-consuming and challenging, especially for those new to investing. Furthermore, even the most meticulous fundamental analysis cannot predict the future with absolute certainty. Market sentiment, unexpected events, and even irrational exuberance can lead to stock prices deviating from their intrinsic values, creating opportunities for both gains and losses.

Technical analysis, with its emphasis on historical price and volume data, offers a different perspective. By identifying patterns and trends in charts, technical analysts aim to predict future price movements and time their entries and exits accordingly. This approach can be particularly appealing to short-term traders who seek to capitalize on market momentum and volatility.

Jesse Livermore, a legendary trader from the early 20th century, is often credited with pioneering many of the technical analysis techniques still used today. His ability to read charts and anticipate market turns earned him both fame and fortune, demonstrating the potential power of technical analysis.

However, technical analysis also has its limitations. Its reliance on historical data assumes that past patterns will repeat themselves, which is not always guaranteed. Moreover, the interpretation of charts and patterns can be subjective, leading to different conclusions among analysts. Furthermore, technical analysis alone may not provide a complete picture of a security's value, ignoring fundamental factors that could impact its long-term prospects.

In the context of the Series 7 exam, you'll encounter questions that test your understanding of both fundamental and technical analysis. You may be presented with financial statements and asked to calculate ratios or interpret their significance. You might also be given charts and asked to identify patterns or predict future price movements. By mastering both approaches, you'll demonstrate your comprehensive understanding of securities analysis and your ability to apply different tools to evaluate investment opportunities.

Remember, neither fundamental nor technical analysis is a silver bullet. They are complementary approaches, each with its strengths and weaknesses. A well-rounded investor or financial advisor combines both perspectives, using fundamental analysis to assess a company's intrinsic value and technical analysis to gauge market sentiment and timing. By leveraging the strengths of both approaches, you can make more informed investment decisions, manage risk effectively, and help your clients achieve their financial goals.

III. Financial Statement Analysis

Reading & interpreting financial statements

Having explored both the big-picture economic view and the intricacies of market analysis techniques, it's time to roll up our sleeves and delve into the heart of fundamental analysis: deciphering the language of financial statements. These documents, the balance sheet, income statement, and cash flow statement, are the lifeblood of a company, narrating its financial story and offering invaluable insights into its health, performance, and prospects.

Think of financial statements as a company's autobiography, chronicling its assets, liabilities, revenues, expenses, and cash flows. Understanding how to read and interpret these statements is akin to learning a new language, unlocking a treasure trove of information that can guide your investment decisions.

The balance sheet, a snapshot of a company's financial position at a specific point in time, reveals its assets, liabilities, and shareholders' equity. It's like a financial selfie, showcasing what the company owns, what it owes, and what's left for its shareholders. For example, a healthy balance sheet might show a strong cash position, manageable debt levels, and a growing equity base, signaling financial stability and potential for future growth.

The income statement, in contrast, tracks a company's revenues and expenses over a specific period, culminating in its net income or loss. It's like a profit and loss ledger, revealing how much the company earned, how much it spent, and the resulting bottom line. A company with consistently growing revenues and expanding profit margins is generally seen as a more attractive investment than one with stagnant or declining earnings.

The cash flow statement, the final piece of the puzzle, illustrates how cash flows in and out of a company during a specific period. It's like a financial river, showing the sources and uses of cash, and highlighting the company's ability to generate cash from its operations, investments, and financing activities. A company with strong operating cash flow is generally viewed as financially healthy and capable of sustaining its operations and growth initiatives.

However, reading financial statements is more than just recognizing the numbers. It's about interpreting them in context, understanding the relationships between different line items, and identifying trends over time. For instance, a company with a high debt-to-equity ratio might raise concerns about its financial leverage and its ability to weather economic downturns. On the other hand, a company with a consistently high return on equity (ROE) might signal efficient management and strong profitability.

In the Series 7 exam, you'll encounter questions requiring you to analyze financial statements and interpret key ratios and metrics. You might be presented with a company's balance sheet and asked to calculate its current or debt-to-equity ratio. Or, you might be given an income statement and asked to determine the company's profit margin or its earnings per share. By mastering the art of reading and interpreting financial statements, you'll not only excel on the exam but also gain a valuable skill that will serve you well throughout your career as a financial professional.

Key financial ratios & significance

Having learned to read and interpret financial statements, we now shift our focus to extracting meaningful insights from these documents through the lens of key financial ratios. These ratios, calculated from the raw data within the balance sheet, income statement, and cash flow statement, act as powerful diagnostic tools, allowing investors and analysts to assess a company's financial health, profitability, efficiency, and overall attractiveness as an investment.

One of the most fundamental ratios is the **current ratio**, which measures a company's short-term liquidity, or its ability to meet its near-term obligations. It's calculated by dividing current assets by current liabilities. A current ratio greater than 1 indicates that the company has more current assets than current liabilities, suggesting a healthy liquidity position. A current ratio below 1, however, might raise concerns about the company's ability to pay its bills on time.

Another critical liquidity ratio is the **quick ratio**, also known as the acid-test ratio. It's a more stringent measure of liquidity, excluding inventory from current assets, as inventory might not be easily convertible to cash. The quick ratio is particularly relevant for companies in industries with slow-moving inventory or those facing potential supply chain disruptions.

Moving on to profitability ratios, the **gross profit margin** measures the percentage of revenue that remains after deducting the cost of goods sold. It reveals how efficiently a company manages its production costs and pricing strategies. A higher gross profit margin generally indicates greater profitability and pricing power. For example, a software company with a high gross profit margin might have more room to invest in research and development or expand its market share compared to a retailer with a lower gross profit margin facing intense price competition.

The **net profit margin**, on the other hand, measures the percentage of revenue that translates into net income after accounting for all expenses, including taxes and interest. It reflects the company's overall profitability and efficiency in managing its operations. A rising net profit margin is generally a positive sign, indicating improved cost control or increased sales volume.

The **return on equity (ROE)**, a key indicator of shareholder value creation, measures the company's profitability relative to its shareholders' equity. It's calculated by dividing net income by shareholders' equity. A high ROE indicates that the company is effectively utilizing its equity capital to generate profits, a desirable trait for investors seeking long-term growth.

Leverage ratios, such as the **debt-to-equity ratio**, provide insights into a company's capital structure and its reliance on debt financing. A high debt-to-equity ratio suggests that the company is using a significant amount of debt to finance its operations, which can amplify its risk profile. A lower ratio indicates a more conservative approach to capital structure, potentially reducing financial risk but also limiting potential returns.

These are just a few examples of the numerous financial ratios used in fundamental analysis. The Series 7 exam will test your ability to calculate and interpret these ratios, understand their significance, and apply them in various investment scenarios. By mastering these analytical tools, you'll be equipped to assess the financial health and prospects of companies, identify undervalued or overvalued securities, and make informed investment recommendations that align with your client's risk tolerance and financial goals.

Industry-specific considerations

As we navigate the realm of financial statement analysis, armed with an understanding of key ratios and their implications, we must recognize that a one-size-fits-all approach doesn't always suffice. Just as a doctor wouldn't prescribe the same treatment for every patient, a financial analyst must tailor their evaluation to the specific industry in which a company operates. Different industries have distinct dynamics, risks, and success factors, and these nuances must be considered when interpreting financial statements and making investment decisions.

Let's delve into a few illustrative examples. In the technology sector, where innovation and intellectual property reign supreme, a company's research and development (R&D)

expenditure is a crucial metric to track. A company like Alphabet, Google's parent company, invests heavily in R&D, reflecting its commitment to pushing the boundaries of technology and staying ahead of the curve. This high R&D spending, while impacting short-term profitability, can be a sign of future growth potential, a key consideration for investors evaluating tech companies.

In contrast, in the utility sector, where stability and regulated returns are the norm, metrics like debt levels and interest coverage ratios take center stage. Utilities often rely on debt financing to fund their infrastructure investments, and their ability to service that debt, as reflected in their interest coverage ratio, is a key indicator of financial health. For example, a utility company with a high debt-to-equity ratio but a strong interest coverage ratio might still be considered a safe investment, as its stable cash flows can comfortably cover its debt obligations.

In the retail industry, inventory turnover is a crucial metric to monitor. This ratio measures how quickly a company sells its inventory, reflecting its operational efficiency and sales performance. A high inventory turnover suggests that the company is effectively managing its inventory and generating sales, while a low turnover might indicate sluggish sales or excess inventory, potentially leading to markdowns and lower profitability.

For instance, a fast-fashion retailer like Zara, known for its rapid inventory turnover, can quickly adapt to changing trends and minimize the risk of holding outdated merchandise. In contrast, a luxury retailer with a slower inventory turnover might face challenges in clearing out unsold inventory, potentially impacting its margins.

These examples highlight just a few of the industry-specific considerations that can impact financial statement analysis. The energy sector's reliance on commodity prices, the pharmaceutical industry's dependence on research and development pipelines, and the cyclical nature of the automotive industry are just a few more examples of how industry dynamics can shape financial performance and investment considerations.

As you prepare for the Series 7 exam, be ready to apply your knowledge of financial ratios and interpret financial statements in the context of different industries. You might encounter questions that ask you to identify the most relevant ratios for a particular sector or to evaluate a company's performance relative to its industry peers. By mastering this skill, you'll demonstrate your ability to conduct nuanced and insightful financial analysis, a crucial competency for any aspiring financial professional. Remember, understanding each industry's unique characteristics is key to unlocking the full potential of financial statement analysis and making sound investment recommendations tailored to your clients' needs and risk tolerances.

Chapter 10: Summary and Review

In this chapter, we expanded our understanding of the financial landscape, venturing beyond individual securities and portfolios to explore the broader economic forces and analytical tools that drive market behavior. We began by examining key economic indicators such as GDP, inflation, and unemployment, and how their fluctuations can impact various asset classes. We also differentiated between leading, lagging, and coincident indicators, providing a temporal framework for understanding and anticipating economic trends.

Next, we delved into the contrasting worlds of fundamental and technical analysis, two distinct approaches to evaluating securities. We explored key ratios and metrics used in fundamental analysis, such as price-to-earnings ratios and debt-to-equity ratios, and learned how to interpret financial statements to assess a company's financial health and prospects. We also ventured into the realm of technical analysis, deciphering chart patterns, trend lines, and other visual cues that can help identify trading opportunities.

We also navigated the complexities of market trends and cyclical factors, understanding how economic cycles and broader industry trends can influence investment decisions. We differentiated between secular and cyclical trends and explored strategies for adapting investment approaches to varying market conditions. Finally, we emphasized the importance of industry-specific considerations in financial analysis, recognizing that different sectors have unique dynamics and key metrics that must be carefully evaluated.

Test Your Knowledge:

1. What are the three primary types of economic indicators, and how do they differ in terms of their timing and relationship to the business cycle?

2. Explain the difference between fundamental analysis and technical analysis, and provide examples of tools and techniques used in each approach.

3. What are some key financial ratios used to evaluate a company's liquidity, profitability, and leverage?

4. How can the understanding of business cycles and industry trends inform investment decision-making?

5. Why is it important to consider industry-specific factors when conducting financial analysis?

Tips for Applying the Knowledge to Exam Questions:

- Be prepared to interpret economic data and understand its impact on different asset classes.

- Know how to calculate and interpret key financial ratios.

- Be able to identify common chart patterns and technical indicators.

- Understand the difference between secular and cyclical trends and their implications for investing.

- Recognize the importance of industry-specific analysis when evaluating

Chapter 11: Mastering Exam Techniques and Calculations

Chapter 11: Sharpening Your Edge: Mastering Exam Techniques and Calculations

You've diligently absorbed the vast knowledge of securities, regulations, and investment strategies, but now it's time to hone your skills for the ultimate test: the Series 7 exam. This chapter is your training ground, where we'll equip you with the tactics and techniques to conquer the exam with confidence and precision.

Consider this your final push before the big game. We'll delve into strategies for tackling the various question types you'll encounter, from deciphering multiple-choice questions to mastering intricate calculations and analyzing complex scenarios. You'll learn time management techniques to ensure you're pacing yourself effectively and avoid getting bogged down on challenging questions.

We'll then provide a comprehensive arsenal of key formulas and calculation shortcuts, empowering you to swiftly and accurately solve numerical problems, a crucial component of the exam. You'll also discover mental math tricks and learn how to identify and avoid common calculation errors, saving valuable time and boosting your accuracy.

Finally, we'll put your skills to the test with a variety of practice problems covering all major exam topics. These problems, accompanied by step-by-step solutions and alternative approaches, will solidify your understanding and build your confidence. Think of it as a dress rehearsal, allowing you to fine-tune your performance and identify areas for further review.

By the end of this chapter, you'll be more than just knowledgeable; you'll be exam-ready. You'll have the strategies, techniques, and practice needed to approach the Series 7 exam with a calm and focused mindset, maximizing your chances of success. Remember, this exam is not just a hurdle to overcome; it's a gateway to a rewarding career in the financial industry. Let's sharpen your edge and ensure you cross that threshold with flying colors.

Strategies for approaching different question types

As you prepare to face the Series 7 exam, consider this chapter your tactical playbook. We'll dissect the various question types you'll encounter, equipping you with the strategies and mental agility needed to conquer each one efficiently and accurately. Time is of the essence on this exam, so we'll delve into time management techniques tailored to each question type, ensuring you allocate your precious minutes wisely. Additionally, we'll shine a spotlight on common pitfalls that can trip up even the most prepared test-takers, arming you with the foresight to avoid these traps and boost your overall performance.

Multiple-choice questions, the bread and butter of the Series 7 exam, can be deceptively challenging. Don't fall into the trap of rushing through them. Take a moment to carefully read the question and all answer choices before making your selection. Look out for keywords and qualifiers, such as "except" or "not," which can drastically alter the meaning of a question. If you're unsure, use the process of elimination to narrow down the possibilities. Remember, sometimes the best answer is the one that's most true, even if it's not perfectly ideal.

Calculation-based questions demand a different approach. Here, your mastery of formulas and mental math skills will be put to the test. Don't get bogged down in complex calculations; often, there are shortcuts and estimation techniques that can lead you to the correct answer efficiently. Remember those key formulas we covered in earlier chapters? Now's the time to put them into practice. For example, if a question asks you to calculate the current yield of a bond, recall the formula: Annual Interest Payment / Current Market Price.

Scenario-based questions can be the most daunting, as they often involve complex situations and multiple variables. Take a deep breath and break down the scenario into its core components. Identify the key facts, the relevant rules and regulations, and the potential courses of action. Then, apply your knowledge and critical thinking skills to select the most appropriate answer. These questions often mirror real-world situations you'll encounter as a registered representative, so consider them valuable practice for your future career.

Time management is your ally in conquering the Series 7 exam. Allocate your time strategically based on the weight and complexity of each question type. Don't spend too much time on a single question, especially if you're unsure of the answer. Flag it for review and move on. Remember, every question carries equal weight, so it's better to answer several easier questions than to get stuck on a single difficult one.

As you practice, be mindful of common pitfalls that can derail your progress. Rushing through questions, second-guessing yourself, and failing to read carefully can all lead to unnecessary errors. Develop a disciplined approach, focus on one question at a time, and trust your instincts. Remember, you've put in the hard work and preparation; now it's time to showcase your knowledge and skills.

By mastering these exam techniques and honing your calculation skills, you'll be well-prepared to tackle the Series 7 exam with confidence and achieve the success you deserve. Remember, this exam is not just a test of knowledge; it's a testament to your dedication, perseverance, and commitment to excellence in the financial industry.

Time management during the exam

With the conceptual foundation of the Series 7 exam laid, let's shift gears into a tactical approach to conquering it - mastering time management during the actual test. The Series 7 is notorious for its breadth and depth of knowledge, but beyond knowing the material, it's about applying it strategically within the ticking clock.

First and foremost, let's allocate your time wisely. The exam comprises 125 scored questions and 10 additional, unscored questions, all to be completed within a 3 hour and 45-minute window. A quick calculation tells us you have roughly 1.8 minutes per question. However, a strategic breakdown is crucial. As the exam's content areas vary in complexity, we shouldn't treat each question equally.

For instance, straightforward questions about basic securities definitions or regulatory concepts might require less time than intricate calculations involving options pricing or complex bond yields. Allocate more time for the weightier topics like equity and debt securities, options strategies, and investment company products, while budgeting less for areas like account opening procedures or regulatory bodies.

This allocation isn't set in stone; it's a dynamic guide to adapt as you move through the exam. The key is to be mindful of the clock without succumbing to its pressure. If you find yourself spending too much time on a particular question, don't hesitate to flag it for review and move on. Remember, every question carries equal weight, and it's better to secure points on questions you're confident about than to dwell on one that might derail your momentum.

Pacing yourself effectively is crucial. Don't rush through the initial questions, thinking you'll have ample time later. Maintain a steady rhythm, and if you're ahead of schedule, use the extra time to review flagged questions or double-check your answers. Conversely, if you're falling behind, don't panic. Strategically prioritize questions based on your strengths and the topic's weight, aiming to maximize your potential score.

Inevitably, you'll encounter difficult or confusing questions. The key here is not to get stuck. Take a deep breath, analyze the question, and eliminate any obviously incorrect answers. If you're still unsure, make an educated guess and move on. Don't let a single question consume a disproportionate amount of time and energy.

Remember, the Series 7 exam is not just about knowing the material; it's about applying it effectively under pressure. By mastering time management techniques and developing a strategic approach to different question types, you'll be well-equipped to navigate the exam with confidence and achieve the success you've been diligently working towards.

Key formulas and calculation shortcuts

Now that we've established the foundational concepts and analytical frameworks for deciphering the market, it's time to sharpen our quantitative skills. The Series 7 exam isn't just about theoretical knowledge; it's also about applying that knowledge to solve real-world problems and make informed investment decisions. In this section, we'll provide you with a comprehensive list of essential formulas, illuminate mental math techniques to expedite your calculations, and identify common errors to help you avoid costly mistakes on exam day.

Consider this your mathematical toolkit, carefully curated to equip you with the formulas and techniques you'll need to navigate the quantitative challenges of the Series 7 exam. From calculating bond yields and accrued interest to determining option premiums and stock valuations, these formulas are your keys to unlocking the numerical mysteries of the financial world.

Let's start with some of the most crucial formulas you'll encounter. The **current yield** of a bond, as we've discussed, is calculated by dividing the annual interest payment by the bond's current market price. The **yield to maturity (YTM)**, a more comprehensive measure of a bond's return, requires a more complex calculation, often involving financial calculators or spreadsheet functions. However, understanding the relationship between YTM and a bond's coupon rate, maturity, and market price is essential for making informed investment decisions.

In the realm of options, the **Black-Scholes model** reigns supreme. While the full formula is complex, understanding its key components, such as the underlying stock price, strike price, time to expiration, volatility, and risk-free interest rate, will enable you to grasp the factors that influence option premiums.

When it comes to stock valuation, the **price-to-earnings (P/E) ratio** is a fundamental metric that compares a company's stock price to its earnings per share. It offers a quick and easy way to gauge a company's valuation relative to its peers and the broader market. A high P/E ratio might suggest that the market is optimistic about the company's future growth prospects, while a low P/E ratio could indicate undervaluation.

But memorizing formulas is only half the battle. The Series 7 exam is a timed test, and you'll need to be able to perform calculations quickly and accurately. This is where mental math techniques can come in handy. For instance, knowing how to quickly calculate percentages, convert fractions to decimals, and estimate square roots can save you valuable time and reduce the risk of errors.

Furthermore, it's important to be mindful of common calculation errors that can trip up even the most seasoned test-takers. These include misinterpreting the question, using the wrong formula, inputting incorrect values into your calculator, or simply making careless mistakes. Double-checking your work and using estimation techniques to verify your answers can help you avoid these pitfalls.

As you progress through this chapter, we'll provide you with a comprehensive list of essential formulas, mental math tips, and strategies for avoiding common calculation errors. We'll also offer a variety of practice problems and solutions, allowing you to hone your skills and build confidence. Remember, practice makes perfect, and the more you practice applying these formulas and techniques, the more comfortable and efficient you'll become on exam day.

Practice problems with step-by-step solutions

Now that you're equipped with a robust set of formulas and calculation shortcuts, it's time to put your knowledge into practice. The Series 7 exam isn't simply a test of memorization; it demands the ability to apply these concepts to real-world scenarios and solve problems efficiently. To hone your skills and boost your confidence, let's dive into a collection of practice problems covering the gamut of exam topics, each accompanied by detailed step-by-step solutions and, where applicable, alternative solution methods.

These practice problems are more than just numerical exercises; they're your training ground for mastering the analytical thinking required to excel on the Series 7 exam. Consider them a dress rehearsal for the main event, allowing you to identify your strengths and weaknesses and fine-tune your approach before the big day.

We'll start with problems related to equity securities, challenging you to calculate dividend yields, price-to-earnings ratios, and the impact of stock splits on shareholder positions. Then, we'll venture into the bond market, testing your ability to calculate current yield, yield to maturity, accrued interest, and the impact of interest rate changes on bond prices.

Next, we'll tackle the world of options, asking you to determine the intrinsic and time value of calls and puts, calculate option premiums using the Black-Scholes model, and assess the risk associated with various options strategies using the Greeks. We'll also explore margin requirements and the potential profit and loss scenarios for different option positions.

Moving on to packaged products and alternative investments, we'll challenge you to calculate the net asset value (NAV) of mutual funds, understand the creation and redemption process of ETFs, and evaluate the suitability of various investment vehicles for different client profiles.

Finally, we'll integrate your knowledge of economic indicators and market analysis techniques by presenting scenarios where you'll need to interpret economic data, analyze financial statements, and make informed investment recommendations based on market trends and client objectives.

Each practice problem will be accompanied by a detailed solution, walking you through each step of the calculation or analysis process. We'll also highlight potential pitfalls and common mistakes to help you avoid them. Where applicable, we'll provide alternative solution methods, allowing you to choose the approach that best suits your problem-solving style.

Remember, the key to success on the Series 7 exam is not just knowing the formulas, but understanding how to apply them in a variety of scenarios. These practice problems will help you build that critical thinking and problem-solving skills, ensuring that you're well-prepared to tackle any challenge the exam throws your way.

Chapter 12: Emotional Preparation and Test-Taking Psychology

Managing test anxiety and building confidence

Now that you're equipped with a robust set of formulas and calculation shortcuts, it's time to put your knowledge into practice. The Series 7 exam isn't simply a test of memorization; it demands the ability to apply these concepts to real-world scenarios and solve problems efficiently. To hone your skills and boost your confidence, let's dive into a collection of practice problems covering the gamut of exam topics, each accompanied by detailed step-by-step solutions and, where applicable, alternative solution methods.

These practice problems are more than just numerical exercises; they're your training ground for mastering the analytical thinking required to excel on the Series 7 exam. Consider them a dress rehearsal for the main event, allowing you to identify your strengths and weaknesses and fine-tune your approach before the big day.

We'll start with problems related to equity securities, challenging you to calculate dividend yields, price-to-earnings ratios, and the impact of stock splits on shareholder positions. Then, we'll venture into the bond market, testing your ability to calculate current yield, yield to maturity, accrued interest, and the impact of interest rate changes on bond prices.

Next, we'll tackle the world of options, asking you to determine the intrinsic and time value of calls and puts, calculate option premiums using the Black-Scholes model, and assess the risk associated with various options strategies using the Greeks. We'll also explore margin requirements and the potential profit and loss scenarios for different option positions.

Moving on to packaged products and alternative investments, we'll challenge you to calculate the net asset value (NAV) of mutual funds, understand the creation and redemption process of ETFs, and evaluate the suitability of various investment vehicles for different client profiles.

Finally, we'll integrate your knowledge of economic indicators and market analysis techniques by presenting scenarios where you'll need to interpret economic data, analyze financial statements, and make informed investment recommendations based on market trends and client objectives.

Each practice problem will be accompanied by a detailed solution, walking you through each step of the calculation or analysis process. We'll also highlight potential pitfalls and common mistakes to help you avoid them. Where applicable, we'll provide alternative solution methods, allowing you to choose the approach that best suits your problem-solving style.

Remember, the key to success on the Series 7 exam is not just knowing the formulas, but understanding how to apply them in a variety of scenarios. These practice problems will help you build that critical thinking and problem-solving skills, ensuring that you're well-prepared to tackle any challenge the exam throws your way.

Concentration and memory enhancement techniques

Having equipped yourself with the formulas and analytical tools necessary for success on the Series 7 exam, let's now turn our attention to sharpening your cognitive abilities for optimal retention and recall. This journey isn't just about cramming information; it's about harnessing the power of your brain to absorb, process, and retrieve vast amounts of complex financial knowledge. We'll delve into evidence-based study techniques like spaced repetition and active recall, explore strategies to maintain laser-sharp focus during those marathon study sessions, and even uncover some clever mnemonics tailored to the unique content of the Series 7 exam.

Spaced repetition, a technique rooted in cognitive science, involves reviewing information at increasing intervals, gradually expanding the time between each review as you master the material. Think of it as building a sturdy mental scaffolding, reinforcing connections over time rather than hastily constructing a flimsy structure that's prone to collapse. For example, instead of cramming all your options strategies review into one marathon session, you could spread it out over several days or weeks, revisiting the material at increasingly longer intervals. This allows your brain to consolidate the information and strengthen neural pathways, leading to more durable and long-lasting memory.

Active recall, the practice of actively retrieving information from memory without the aid of cues or prompts, is another powerful technique for enhancing retention. It's like flexing a muscle, forcing your brain to work harder and strengthening the neural connections associated with the information. Flashcards, practice quizzes, and teaching the material to someone else are all effective methods for implementing active recall. For instance, after studying bond pricing, try to recall the formula for calculating yield to maturity without looking at your notes. This active retrieval process solidifies your understanding and prepares you for the rigors of the exam.

Maintaining focus during long study sessions can be a challenge, but it's crucial for effective learning. Techniques like the Pomodoro method, which involves breaking study sessions into focused intervals with short breaks, can help combat mental fatigue and improve concentration. Creating a distraction-free environment, setting clear goals for each study session, and incorporating mindfulness or meditation practices can further enhance your focus and productivity.

Finally, let's explore the power of mnemonics, those memory aids that leverage creative associations and wordplay to make complex information more memorable. The Series 7 exam, with its abundance of rules, regulations, and acronyms, is ripe for mnemonic devices. For example, to remember the suitability obligations under FINRA Rule 2111, you could use the acronym "CAR": **C**ustomer, **A**ccount, **R**isks. This simple mnemonic provides a quick and easy way to recall the key factors to consider when evaluating the suitability of investment recommendations.

By incorporating these evidence-based study techniques into your exam preparation, you'll be well on your way to conquering the Series 7. Remember, this exam is not just a test of knowledge; it's also a test of your ability to focus, retain information, and apply it effectively under pressure. By harnessing the power of your brain and utilizing these proven techniques, you'll be equipped to not only pass the exam but also build a solid foundation for a successful career in the financial industry.

Motivation strategies and goal setting

As you embark on the challenging but rewarding journey towards conquering the Series 7 exam, motivation and goal-setting become your steadfast companions. The path to success is paved with dedication and perseverance, but even the most driven individuals can encounter moments of doubt or struggle with the sheer volume of material to master. Fear not, for in this section, we'll unveil a treasure trove of motivation strategies and goal-setting techniques to keep you on track, engaged, and ultimately, victorious.

The cornerstone of effective goal-setting lies in the SMART framework. Your goals should be **Specific**, outlining precisely what you want to achieve. Instead of a vague goal like "study more," a specific goal could be "complete two practice exams this week." **Measurable** goals allow you to track your progress and celebrate milestones along the way. For example, "increase my average practice exam score by 5% each week" provides a tangible metric to gauge your improvement. **Achievable** goals are realistic and attainable, given your available time and resources. Setting an ambitious goal like "memorize the entire textbook in one week" might set you up for disappointment and demotivation. Instead, break down the material into manageable chunks and set achievable targets for each study session.

Relevant goals align with your broader objectives. Remind yourself why you're pursuing the Series 7 license and how it will impact your career aspirations. This connection to your deeper purpose can be a powerful motivator when the going gets tough. **Time-bound** goals create a sense of urgency and accountability. Instead of a vague goal like "pass the Series 7 exam," a time-bound goal would be "pass the Series 7 exam within three months." This deadline provides focus and helps you create a structured study plan.

But setting SMART goals is just the beginning. Tracking your progress is equally essential. Maintain a study log or use a progress tracker app to monitor your achievements, celebrate milestones, and identify areas that need more attention. Visualizing your progress can be a powerful motivator, reminding you of how far you've come and fueling your desire to reach the finish line.

Maintaining motivation over extended study periods can be a challenge, but it's crucial for success. Celebrate small victories along the way, reward yourself for reaching milestones, and find ways to make the learning process enjoyable. Join a study group, find a mentor, or connect with other aspiring financial professionals to share your experiences and support each other.

Procrastination and study fatigue are common hurdles on the path to exam success. To overcome these challenges, break down your study sessions into smaller, more manageable chunks. Set realistic deadlines and use time management techniques like the Pomodoro method to stay focused and productive. Remember, consistency is key. Even dedicating 30 minutes a day to studying can yield significant progress over time.

Most importantly, don't be afraid to seek help if you're struggling. Reach out to your study group, mentor, or a trusted friend or family member for support. Remember, you're not alone in this journey, and there are resources available to help you succeed.

By setting SMART goals, tracking your progress, maintaining motivation, and overcoming procrastination, you'll be well-equipped to conquer the Series 7 exam. Remember, this journey is not just about passing an exam; it's about unlocking a world of opportunities in the financial industry. Embrace the challenge, stay focused, and let your determination guide you to success.

Exam day preparation and success strategies

As you approach the culmination of your Series 7 exam preparation, the focus shifts from knowledge acquisition to exam-day readiness. This is where preparation meets execution, and a well-structured approach can significantly impact your performance. Think of it as a marathon runner meticulously planning their race strategy, hydrating the day before, and visualizing their success. Let's craft your exam day checklist and outline strategies to maintain focus during the exam, as well as provide guidance for post-exam reflection and next steps.

The day before the exam, resist the urge to cram. Instead, focus on light review, revisiting key concepts, formulas, and practice problems. Ensure you have a good night's sleep and a nutritious breakfast the morning of the exam. Pack your essentials: a valid photo ID, your FINRA exam admission ticket, a calculator (pre-approved by FINRA), and any permitted comfort items like earplugs or a sweater. Arrive at the testing center early to allow for check-in procedures and to acclimate to the environment.

During the exam, maintaining focus is crucial. Start with a quick scan of the entire exam to gauge its length and difficulty. Begin with questions you're confident about, marking those that require more thought for later review. Avoid dwelling on a single question for too long; remember, every question carries the same weight. If you're unsure, make an educated guess and move on. You can always revisit flagged questions later if time permits.

Time management is key. Keep an eye on the clock and pace yourself accordingly. If you find yourself falling behind, adjust your strategy and focus on answering the questions you know well. Don't be afraid to skip difficult questions initially and return to them later with a fresh perspective.

Post-exam, take a moment to decompress and reflect on your experience. Regardless of the outcome, acknowledge the effort you've put into your preparation. If you pass, celebrate your achievement and begin planning your next steps in your financial career. If you don't pass, don't despair. Review your score report, identify areas for improvement, and develop a plan for retaking the exam. Remember, many successful financial professionals have faced setbacks along the way. Persistence and resilience are key traits in this industry.

Regardless of the immediate outcome, the Series 7 exam is a valuable learning experience. The knowledge and skills you've acquired will serve you well throughout your career, even if you don't pursue a traditional financial advisor role. The exam's emphasis on securities, regulations, and ethical conduct provides a strong foundation for various career paths in the financial industry.

Remember, the Series 7 exam is not just a test of your knowledge but also of your ability to perform under pressure and apply your skills strategically. By preparing diligently, maintaining focus, and approaching the exam with a positive mindset, you'll be well on your way to achieving your goal and embarking on a fulfilling career in finance.

Chapter 13: 500 Practice Questions and Answers

1. Straightforward Question:

Q1. Which of the following securities is exempt from registration under the Securities Act of 1933?

- A. Treasury bonds

- B. Corporate bonds

- C. Municipal bonds

- D. Common stock

2. Complex Scenario-Based Question:

Q2. An investor wishes to protect their investment in a volatile market. Which of the following strategies would be most appropriate?

- A. Short selling

- B. Buying call options

- C. Writing covered calls

- D. Buying put options

3. Regulatory Question:

Q3. Under the USA PATRIOT Act, which of the following is true regarding customer identification programs (CIPs) for broker-dealers?

- A. Broker-dealers must verify the identity of all customers regardless of risk.

- B. Broker-dealers must establish procedures for verifying the identity of customers within a reasonable time before or after account opening.

- C. Broker-dealers are exempt from CIP requirements for certain types of customers.

- D. Broker-dealers are required to report suspicious activity but not verify customer identities.

4. Taxation Question:

Q4. A client is considering investing in municipal bonds. Which of the following is an advantage of investing in municipal bonds?

- A. Interest income is exempt from federal income tax.

- B. Interest income is fully taxable at the federal level.

- C. Capital gains are taxed at a higher rate than other investments.

- D. Dividends are taxed at a lower rate than other investments.

5. Ethics and Professional Responsibility Question:

Q5. A financial advisor learns that a client plans to engage in insider trading. What is the advisor's ethical responsibility?

- A. Report the client to the SEC.

- B. Convince the client not to engage in insider trading.

- C. Ignore the situation to maintain client confidentiality.

- D. Advise the client on how to execute the trade discreetly.

6. Investment Strategies Question:

Q6. Which of the following investment strategies is most appropriate for a conservative investor seeking steady income?

- A. Investing in high-yield junk bonds

- B. Investing in a diversified portfolio of blue-chip stocks

- C. Investing in municipal bonds

- D. Investing in speculative technology stocks

7. Options Question:

Q7. An investor buys a call option with a strike price of $50. The option premium is $2. What is the breakeven point for this investment?

- A. $48

- B. $50

- C. $52

- D. $54

8. Regulatory Environment Question:

Q8. Under Regulation T, what is the initial margin requirement for purchasing securities on margin?

- A. 25%

- B. 50%

- C. 75%

- D. 100%

9. Market Structure Question:

Q9. Which of the following best describes a "market order"?

- A. An order to buy or sell a stock at a specific price

- B. An order to buy or sell a stock immediately at the best available price

- C. An order to buy or sell a stock at the closing price of the day

- D. An order to buy or sell a stock only if the price reaches a certain level

10. Economic Factors Question:

Q10. Which of the following is typically a leading economic indicator?

- A. Gross Domestic Product (GDP)

- B. Unemployment Rate

- C. Stock Market Performance

- D. Consumer Price Index (CPI)

11. Fixed Income Securities Question:

Q11. Which of the following best describes the primary risk associated with long-term bonds?

- A. Credit risk

- B. Liquidity risk

- C. Interest rate risk

- D. Reinvestment risk

12. Mutual Funds Question:

Q12. An investor is interested in a mutual fund that aims to achieve high growth. Which type of mutual fund should they consider?

- A. Money market fund

- B. Growth fund

- C. Income fund

- D. Balanced fund

13. Retirement Accounts Question:

Q13. Which of the following is a feature of a Roth IRA?

- A. Contributions are tax-deductible

- B. Qualified distributions are tax-free

- C. Required minimum distributions (RMDs) begin at age 72

- D. Contributions can only be made with pre-tax dollars

14. Trading Practices Question:

  Q14. What is the primary function of a market maker?

  - A. To facilitate the trading of large blocks of stock

  - B. To provide liquidity by buying and selling securities

  - C. To set the initial public offering (IPO) price

  - D. To ensure fair trading practices on the exchange

15. Securities Analysis Question:

  Q15. An analyst is using the price-to-earnings (P/E) ratio to evaluate a stock. What does a high P/E ratio generally indicate?

  - A. The stock is undervalued

  - B. The stock is overvalued

  - C. Investors expect high future growth

  - D. The company has high dividend payouts

16. Equity Securities Question:

  Q16. What is the primary benefit of owning preferred stock over common stock?

  - A. Higher potential for capital appreciation

  - B. Priority in dividend payments

  - C. Voting rights in the company's annual meetings

  - D. Lower risk of loss in the case of company bankruptcy

17. Debt Instruments Question:

  Q17. Which of the following bonds would likely have the highest yield?

  - A. U.S. Treasury bond

  - B. Municipal bond

  - C. Investment-grade corporate bond

  - D. High-yield corporate bond

18. Margin Accounts Question:

Q18. In a margin account, what is the maintenance margin requirement set by FINRA?

- A. 15%

- B. 25%

- C. 30%

- D. 50%

19. Retirement Plans Question:

Q19. Which of the following is a characteristic of a 401(k) plan?

- A. Contributions are made with after-tax dollars

- B. Contributions are tax-deductible

- C. Distributions are tax-free

- D. Contributions are limited to employees of non-profit organizations

20. Corporate Actions Question:

Q20. If a company declares a 2-for-1 stock split, what happens to the price of the stock and the number of shares outstanding?

- A. The stock price doubles, and the number of shares outstanding remains the same

- B. The stock price remains the same, and the number of shares outstanding doubles

- C. The stock price halves, and the number of shares outstanding doubles

- D. The stock price remains the same, and the number of shares outstanding remains the same

Q21. Which of the following is an advantage of investing in an ETF compared to a mutual fund?

- A. ETFs typically have higher management fees

- B. ETFs can be traded throughout the trading day

- C. ETFs do not offer diversification

- D. ETFs require a minimum investment

Q22. An investor writes a covered call on a stock they own. Which of the following is true?

- A. The investor can potentially benefit from a decline in the stock's price

- B. The investor's potential profit is unlimited

- C. The investor receives a premium from selling the call

- D. The investor is obligated to buy more shares if the call is exercised

Q23. What is the primary tax advantage of investing in municipal bonds?

- A. Interest income is exempt from federal income tax

- B. Capital gains are tax-free

- C. Dividends are tax-free

- D. Interest income is taxed at a lower rate than other income

Q24. What is the main purpose of a stop-loss order?

- A. To guarantee a purchase price

- B. To limit a loss on a stock position

- C. To maximize profit on a stock position

- D. To secure a dividend payment

Q25. What is a key difference between a closed-end fund and an open-end mutual fund?

- A. Closed-end funds issue new shares continuously

- B. Open-end mutual funds have a fixed number of shares

- C. Closed-end funds trade on an exchange

- D. Open-end mutual funds are not redeemable by the issuer

Q26. Which of the following municipal bonds is backed by the full faith and credit of the issuing municipality?

- A. Revenue bonds

- B. General obligation bonds

- C. Industrial development bonds

- D. Special assessment bonds

Q27. Which of the following types of risk cannot be eliminated through diversification?

- A. Market risk

- B. Credit risk

- C. Liquidity risk

- D. Company-specific risk

Q28. A company has declared a cash dividend of $0.50 per share. If an investor owns 200 shares, what will be the total dividend payment received by the investor?

- A. $50

- B. $100

- C. $200

- D. $250

Q29. At what age can an individual start taking penalty-free withdrawals from a traditional IRA?

- A. 55

- B. 59 1/2

- C. 62

- D. 65

Q30. Which of the following best describes a no-load mutual fund?

- A. It does not charge a sales commission or load

- B. It does not charge any fees

- C. It charges a front-end load

- D. It charges a back-end load

Q31. If a bond with a face value of $1,000 is currently trading at $950 and has an annual coupon rate of 5%, what is the bond's current yield?

- A. 4.74%

- B. 5.00%

- C. 5.26%

- D. 5.50%

Q32. Which of the following financial statements provides a snapshot of a company's financial position at a specific point in time?

- A. Income Statement

- B. Statement of Cash Flows

- C. Statement of Shareholders' Equity

- D. Balance Sheet

Q33. What is "duration" in the context of bond investing?

- A. The length of time until the bond matures

- B. A measure of a bond's sensitivity to interest rate changes

- C. The amount of time interest payments are received

- D. The time required to recover the bond's purchase price

Q34. An investor purchases a stock for $100 per share and sells it for $120 per share. If the stock paid a $2 dividend per share, what is the total return on the investment?

- A. 20%

- B. 22%

- C. 24%

- D. 30%

Q35. An advisor is aware that a client's investment portfolio contains several high-risk securities that are not suitable for the client's risk tolerance. What is the advisor's primary ethical responsibility?

- A. To suggest selling all high-risk securities immediately

- B. To disclose the risks involved and recommend adjustments to the portfolio

- C. To ignore the client's risk tolerance if the securities are performing well

- D. To focus on the potential for high returns rather than the risks

Q36. If a company's stock price is $80 and it pays an annual dividend of $4 per share, what is the dividend yield?

- A. 4.00%

- B. 4.50%

- C. 5.00%

- D. 5.50%

Q37. What does the term "beta" measure in the context of stock investing?

- A. The stock's historical volatility compared to the market

- B. The stock's dividend yield

- C. The stock's earnings per share

- D. The stock's price-to-earnings ratio

Q38. If an investor wants to hedge against a decline in the price of a stock they own, which of the following strategies would be appropriate?

- A. Buying a call option

- B. Writing a put option

- C. Buying a put option

- D. Selling short

Q39. An investor purchases a $1,000 face value bond with a 6% coupon rate, paying $950 for it. What is the bond's yield to maturity if held to maturity and assuming no other costs?

- A. 5.00%

- B. 6.00%

- C. 6.32%

- D. 6.67%

Q40. What is the primary objective of a bond issuer when conducting a callable bond issuance?

- A. To provide investors with guaranteed returns

- B. To reduce the interest expense if rates decline

- C. To lock in a higher interest rate for the issuer

- D. To increase the marketability of the bond

Q41. An investor buys a bond with a face value of $1,000, a coupon rate of 4%, and a maturity of 10 years. If the bond is currently trading at $950, what is the bond's current yield?

- A. 4.00%

- B. 4.21%

- C. 4.44%

- D. 4.74%

Q42. What is the primary purpose of a defensive stock in an investment portfolio?

- A. To maximize capital gains

- B. To provide a high dividend yield

- C. To offer stability during economic downturns

- D. To enhance portfolio diversification

Q43. An investor holds a long position in a stock and writes (sells) a call option on the same stock. What type of strategy is this?

- A. Covered call

- B. Naked call

- C. Protective put

- D. Straddle

Q44. In the context of mutual funds, what does the term "net asset value (NAV)" refer to?

- A. The market price of a fund's shares

- B. The total assets minus the total liabilities of the fund

- C. The average annual return of the fund

- D. The value of the fund's securities at the time of purchase

Q45. What happens to the price of a bond if market interest rates increase?

- A. The price of the bond increases

- B. The price of the bond remains unchanged

- C. The price of the bond decreases

- D. The bond's yield becomes less predictable

Q46. An investor purchases a stock for $50 per share and sells it later for $60 per share. If the stock paid a $2 dividend per share, what is the total return on the investment?

- A. 20%

- B. 22%

- C. 24%

- D. 26%

Q47. If a company issues a new bond with a higher coupon rate than its existing bonds, what is likely to happen to the price of the existing bonds?

- A. The price of existing bonds will increase

- B. The price of existing bonds will decrease

- C. The price of existing bonds will remain unchanged

- D. The price of existing bonds will become less volatile

Q48. What does the term "equity" refer to in the context of a company's balance sheet?

- A. The company's total liabilities

- B. The difference between total assets and total liabilities

- C. The total amount of cash on hand

- D. The company's total revenue

Q49. If a company announces a 5% stock dividend, how does this affect the stock's price and the number of shares outstanding?

- A. The stock price increases and the number of shares decreases

- B. The stock price decreases and the number of shares increases

- C. The stock price remains the same and the number of shares decreases

- D. The stock price remains the same and the number of shares increases

Q50. What is the primary purpose of using a bond's call feature?

- A. To allow the bondholder to sell the bond back to the issuer at a specified price

- B. To enable the issuer to redeem the bond before maturity if interest rates decline

- C. To increase the bond's yield to maturity

- D. To guarantee the bondholder a minimum return

Q51. An investor buys a bond with a face value of $1,000 and a coupon rate of 7%. If the bond is currently trading at $1,050, what is the bond's current yield?

- A. 6.67%

- B. 7.00%

- C. 7.50%

- D. 8.00%

Q52. Which type of order allows an investor to buy or sell a security at the best available price immediately?

- A. Market order

- B. Limit order

- C. Stop order

- D. Fill-or-kill order

Q53. In the context of portfolio management, what does "rebalancing" refer to?

- A. Adjusting the investment strategy based on market conditions

- B. Buying and selling securities to maintain the desired asset allocation

- C. Changing the risk profile of the portfolio

- D. Increasing the portfolio's overall return

Q54. What is the main difference between a traditional IRA and a Roth IRA regarding tax treatment?

- A. Traditional IRA contributions are tax-deductible, while Roth IRA contributions are not

- B. Roth IRA distributions are taxable, while traditional IRA distributions are not

- C. Traditional IRA contributions are made with after-tax dollars, while Roth IRA contributions are made with pre-tax dollars

- D. Traditional IRA earnings grow tax-free, while Roth IRA earnings are taxed

Q55. An investor is concerned about inflation eroding the value of their fixed-income investments. Which of the following types of bonds would best protect against inflation?

- A. Zero-coupon bonds

- B. Callable bonds

- C. Inflation-protected securities

- D. Convertible bonds

Q56. If a company's stock is trading at $80 and an investor wants to purchase it with a limit order at $75, what will happen if the stock price never reaches $75?

- A. The order will be executed at the market price

- B. The order will be filled at the current price of $80

- C. The order will remain unfilled

- D. The order will automatically convert to a market order

Q57. What is the primary advantage of investing in a mutual fund over individual securities?

- A. Mutual funds guarantee a return on investment

- B. Mutual funds offer professional management and diversification

- C. Mutual funds provide tax-free returns

- D. Mutual funds have higher fees compared to individual securities

Q58. An investor has a portfolio consisting of 60% stocks and 40% bonds. If the stock portion increases in value and now represents 70% of the portfolio, what action might the investor take to restore the original asset allocation?

- A. Sell bonds and buy more stocks

- B. Sell stocks and buy more bonds

- C. Sell both stocks and bonds proportionally

- D. Increase cash holdings to rebalance

Q59. Which of the following investments is typically considered the most speculative?

- A. U.S. Treasury bonds

- B. Blue-chip stocks

- C. High-yield bonds

- D. Certificates of deposit

Q60. What is the purpose of a "stop-limit order" in trading?

- A. To execute a trade at the best available price once the stop price is reached

- B. To trigger a market order once the stop price is reached

- C. To execute a trade only within a specified price range after the stop price is reached

- D. To cancel a trade if the stock price moves beyond a certain limit

Q61. An investor holds a bond with a 5% coupon rate, a face value of $1,000, and a maturity of 15 years. If the bond is currently priced at $950, what is the bond's yield to maturity (YTM)?

- A. 4.95%

- B. 5.00%

- C. 5.26%

- D. 5.50%

Q62. Which type of mutual fund is designed to invest in a specific sector or industry, such as technology or healthcare?

- A. Index fund

- B. Sector fund

- C. Balanced fund

- D. Money market fund

Q63. What is a "margin call" in the context of margin trading?

- A. A request for additional collateral when the value of the margin account falls below a certain level

- B. A notice that a margin loan has been fully repaid

- C. An offer to increase the investment position at the current margin rate

- D. A statement that the investor has reached the maximum allowable margin

Q64. Which of the following types of orders guarantees the execution of a trade but not the price?

- A. Limit order

- B. Market order

- C. Stop order

- D. All-or-nothing order

Q65. An investor purchases 100 shares of a stock at $50 per share and sells a call option with a strike price of $55. If the stock rises to $60 and the call option is exercised, what is the investor's profit per share?

- A. $5

- B. $10

- C. $15

- D. $20

Q66. If an investor buys a bond at a premium (i.e., above its face value), which of the following will be true about the bond's yield to maturity (YTM) compared to its coupon rate?

- A. YTM will be higher than the coupon rate

- B. YTM will be lower than the coupon rate

- C. YTM will be equal to the coupon rate

- D. YTM will be zero

Q67. An investor is considering buying a stock with a beta of 1.5. How does this beta value affect the stock's risk relative to the market?

- A. The stock is less risky than the market

- B. The stock has the same risk level as the market

- C. The stock is more risky than the market

- D. The stock is risk-free

Q68. Which type of investment is typically considered the safest and least volatile?

- A. Common stocks

- B. High-yield bonds

- C. U.S. Treasury bills

- D. Real estate investment trusts (REITs)

Q69. What does a "debit spread" mean in options trading?

- A. A strategy where the trader buys and sells options with the same expiration date and strike price

- B. A strategy where the trader buys one option and sells another option with a different strike price or expiration date, resulting in a net debit

- C. A strategy where the trader only sells options

- D. A strategy involving no net cost

Q70. What is the main purpose of a "cover letter" in a new issue of municipal securities?

- A. To disclose any conflicts of interest in the underwriting process

- B. To provide detailed information about the use of proceeds and the issuing authority's financial condition

- C. To offer a summary of the bond's credit rating

- D. To confirm the legal validity of the issue

Q71. What is the primary purpose of an "index fund" in investment?

- A. To outperform the market

- B. To track the performance of a specific market index

- C. To invest in a diversified portfolio of individual stocks

- D. To minimize investment risk

Q72. If an investor buys a put option on a stock, what is the investor hoping for in terms of the stock's price movement?

- A. For the stock price to increase

- B. For the stock price to decrease

- C. For the stock price to remain unchanged

- D. For the stock price volatility to increase

Q73. Which financial statement shows a company's revenues, expenses, and net income over a specific period of time?

- A. Balance Sheet

- B. Statement of Cash Flows

- C. Income Statement

- D. Statement of Shareholders' Equity

Q74. What is the primary advantage of investing in dividend-paying stocks?

- A. Potential for high capital gains

- B. Guaranteed return on investment

- C. Ability to reinvest dividends for compounded growth

- D. Lower risk compared to non-dividend stocks

Q75. How does a company's debt-to-equity ratio (D/E ratio) affect its financial risk?

- A. A higher D/E ratio indicates lower financial risk

- B. A lower D/E ratio indicates higher financial risk

- C. D/E ratio does not impact financial risk

- D. D/E ratio measures profitability, not risk

Q76. Which of the following best describes the term "liquidity" in the context of financial markets?

- A. The ease with which an asset can be converted into cash without affecting its market price

- B. The interest rate at which banks lend to each other overnight

- C. The overall level of activity in the stock market

- D. The amount of cash a company has on hand

Q77. What is the primary function of a stock exchange?

- A. To determine the intrinsic value of stocks

- B. To facilitate the buying and selling of securities

- C. To guarantee a profit for investors

- D. To provide financial advice to investors

Q78. If an investor expects interest rates to rise, which type of bond would likely be most negatively affected?

- A. Short-term bonds

- B. Long-term bonds

- C. Municipal bonds

- D. Inflation-protected bonds

Q79. What is the primary advantage of a Roth IRA over a traditional IRA?

- A. Contributions are tax-deductible

- B. Distributions are tax-free if certain conditions are met

- C. Higher annual contribution limits

- D. Ability to invest in a wider range of assets

Q80. Which of the following best describes a "bull market"?

- A. A market in which prices are falling

- B. A market characterized by rising prices and investor optimism

- C. A market with low trading volumes and high volatility

- D. A market where bonds outperform stocks

Q81. Which of the following investment strategies involves selecting stocks that are undervalued by the market?

- A. Growth investing

- B. Value investing

- C. Momentum investing

- D. Income investing

Q82. An investor buys a stock for $40 per share and sells it for $50 per share. If the stock paid a $1 dividend during the holding period, what is the investor's total return?

- A. 20%

- B. 22.5%

- C. 25%

- D. 27.5%

Q83. What is a key characteristic of "preferred stock"?

- A. It usually has voting rights

- B. It has a fixed dividend and priority over common stock in dividend payments

- C. It typically offers higher growth potential than common stock

- D. It is exempt from taxes

Q84. Which type of bond is backed by the credit and taxing power of the issuing municipality?

- A. Corporate bond

- B. Revenue bond

- C. General obligation bond

- D. Convertible bond

Q85. What is the purpose of the Securities Investor Protection Corporation (SIPC)?

- A. To insure investors against losses in the stock market

- B. To protect customers if a brokerage firm fails

- C. To regulate trading activities on major stock exchanges

- D. To provide financial advice to investors

Q86. If an investor holds a diversified portfolio of 20 different stocks, what is the primary benefit they are seeking?

- A. Higher returns

- B. Reduced transaction costs

- C. Lower overall risk

- D. Guaranteed dividends

Q87. Which of the following best describes "short selling"?

- A. Buying a security with the expectation that its price will increase

- B. Selling a security you do not own, with the intention of buying it back at a lower price

- C. Holding a security for a long period to earn dividends

- D. Selling a security at a profit after holding it for more than a year

Q88. What is the "ex-dividend date"?

- A. The date by which a stock must be purchased to receive the next dividend

- B. The date the company declares a dividend

- C. The date the dividend is paid to shareholders

- D. The date the company records its list of shareholders eligible for the dividend

Q89. An investor wants to know the internal rate of return (IRR) of a potential investment. What does IRR represent?

- A. The discount rate that makes the net present value (NPV) of all cash flows from the investment zero

- B. The future value of the investment's cash flows

- C. The annual return expected from the investment

- D. The rate at which the investment will double in value

Q90. Which of the following best explains "dollar-cost averaging"?

- A. Investing a fixed amount of money at regular intervals regardless of the market price

- B. Buying a large number of shares when prices are low and fewer shares when prices are high

- C. Selling off investments incrementally to minimize loss

- D. Adjusting investment amounts based on market conditions

Q91. What is the primary advantage of a mutual fund over individual stock investing?

- A. Higher potential returns

- B. Diversification and professional management

- C. Lower risk of loss

- D. Guaranteed dividends

Q92. What is a "call option"?

- A. An option to buy a stock at a specific price before the expiration date

- B. An option to sell a stock at a specific price before the expiration date

- C. An obligation to buy a stock at a specific price before the expiration date

- D. An obligation to sell a stock at a specific price before the expiration date

Q93. Which of the following best describes "market capitalization"?

- A. The total value of a company's outstanding shares of stock

- B. The amount of capital a company has raised through stock issuance

- C. The market value of a company's assets

- D. The price per share of a company's stock

Q94. What is the primary purpose of a bond rating?

- A. To predict the future price of the bond

- B. To evaluate the creditworthiness of the bond issuer

- C. To determine the bond's interest rate

- D. To assess the liquidity of the bond

Q95. An investor holds a convertible bond. What is a unique feature of this type of bond?

- A. It pays interest only at maturity

- B. It can be converted into a predetermined number of shares of the issuing company's stock

- C. It guarantees a higher interest rate than non-convertible bonds

- D. It is backed by a pool of mortgages

Q96. What does the term "alpha" measure in investment performance evaluation?

- A. The overall return of a portfolio relative to a benchmark

- B. The consistency of returns over time

- C. The volatility of a portfolio

- D. The excess return of a portfolio compared to its expected return given its level of risk

Q97. What is the primary role of a financial advisor?

- A. To guarantee investment returns

- B. To provide legal advice

- C. To assist clients in managing their finances and investments

- D. To sell financial products

Q98. Which of the following is a key characteristic of a 401(k) retirement plan?

- A. Contributions are tax-deductible

- B. Withdrawals before age 59½ may incur penalties

- C. Contributions are matched by the employer

- D. Withdrawals are tax-free

Q99. In finance, what does the term "beta" measure?

- A. The total return of an investment

- B. The risk of an investment relative to the market

- C. The dividend yield of an investment

- D. The liquidity of an investment

Q100. Which of the following best describes the term "fiduciary duty" in finance?

- A. The duty of financial advisors to maximize profits for clients

- B. The duty of financial institutions to disclose all risks to clients

- C. The duty of financial professionals to act in the best interest of their clients

- D. The duty of financial regulators to monitor market activities

Answers

1. Explanation for Q1:

- Correct Answer: A. Treasury bonds are exempt from registration under the Securities Act of 1933 as they are issued by the federal government.

- Incorrect Answers: B, C, and D are incorrect because corporate bonds, municipal bonds, and common stock are subject to registration under the Securities Act of 1933 unless an exemption applies.

2. Explanation for Q2:

- Correct Answer: D. Buying put options allows the investor to protect their investment by establishing a floor for potential losses.

- Incorrect Answers: A, B, and C are strategies that involve varying degrees of risk and may not necessarily protect the investor's investment in a volatile market.

3. Explanation for Q3:

- Correct Answer: B. Broker-dealers must establish procedures for verifying the identity of customers within a reasonable time before or after account opening under the USA PATRIOT Act.

- Incorrect Answers: A, C, and D are incorrect because broker-dealers must verify the identity of customers subject to certain risk-based procedures and are generally not exempt from CIP requirements.

4. Explanation for Q4:

- Correct Answer: A. Interest income from municipal bonds is generally exempt from federal income tax, providing a tax advantage.

- Incorrect Answers: B, C, and D are incorrect because interest income from municipal bonds is tax-exempt at the federal level, and capital gains and dividends are taxed differently depending on the investment.

5. Explanation for Q5:

- Correct Answer: A. Financial advisors have an ethical responsibility to report illegal activities such as insider trading to the appropriate regulatory authorities.

- Incorrect Answers: B, C, and D are incorrect because they do not align with ethical standards that require reporting illegal activities.

6. Explanation for Q6:

- Correct Answer: C. Municipal bonds are generally considered safe investments and provide steady income, which is suitable for a conservative investor.

- Incorrect Answers: A involves high risk; B, while relatively safe, does not guarantee steady income; and D is speculative and not suitable for a conservative investor.

7. Explanation for Q7:

- Correct Answer: C. The breakeven point for a call option is the strike price plus the premium paid, so $50 + $2 = $52.

- Incorrect Answers: A is incorrect as it subtracts the premium; B does not account for the premium; D adds an incorrect amount.

8. Explanation for Q8:

- Correct Answer: B. Regulation T, set by the Federal Reserve Board, requires an initial margin of 50% for purchasing securities on margin.

- Incorrect Answers: A, C, and D are incorrect as they do not reflect the 50% requirement set by Regulation T.

9. Explanation for Q9:

- Correct Answer: B. A market order is an order to buy or sell a stock immediately at the best available price.

- Incorrect Answers: A describes a limit order; C does not specify the immediate execution characteristic of a market order; D describes a stop order.

10. Explanation for Q10:

- Correct Answer: C. Stock market performance is considered a leading economic indicator as it can predict future economic activity.

- Incorrect Answers: A, B, and D are lagging or coincident indicators that reflect economic conditions after they have occurred.

11. Explanation for Q11:

- Correct Answer: C. Interest rate risk is the primary risk for long-term bonds because their prices are more sensitive to changes in interest rates.

- Incorrect Answers: A and B are risks but not the primary concern for long-term bonds; D affects short-term investments more than long-term bonds.

12. Explanation for Q12:

- Correct Answer: B. Growth funds invest in stocks that are expected to grow at an above-average rate compared to other companies, aiming for high capital appreciation.

- Incorrect Answers: A focuses on low-risk, short-term investments; C focuses on generating income; D balances growth and income.

13. Explanation for Q13:

- Correct Answer: B. Qualified distributions from a Roth IRA are tax-free if certain conditions are met.

- Incorrect Answers: A and D are features of traditional IRAs; C applies to traditional IRAs, not Roth IRAs.

14. Explanation for Q14:

- Correct Answer: B. Market makers provide liquidity by continuously buying and selling securities at publicly quoted prices.

- Incorrect Answers: A and C are not primary functions of a market maker; D is the role of regulatory bodies and the exchange itself.

15. Explanation for Q15:

- Correct Answer: C. A high P/E ratio typically indicates that investors expect high future growth from the company.

- Incorrect Answers: A indicates the opposite; B can sometimes be true but is not the primary implication; D is not related to the P/E ratio.

16. Explanation for Q16:

- Correct Answer: B. Preferred stockholders have priority over common stockholders in receiving dividends.

- Incorrect Answers: A is typically true for common stock; C is a right of common stockholders; D is incorrect because preferred stockholders do have a higher claim on assets in bankruptcy but are still behind debt holders.

17. Explanation for Q17:

- Correct Answer: D. High-yield corporate bonds (also known as junk bonds) have higher yields to compensate for higher credit risk.

- Incorrect Answers: A, B, and C generally have lower yields due to lower risk compared to high-yield corporate bonds.

18. Explanation for Q18:

- Correct Answer: B. FINRA requires a minimum maintenance margin of 25% for a margin account.

- Incorrect Answers: A, C, and D do not reflect the correct minimum maintenance margin requirement set by FINRA.

19. Explanation for Q19:

- Correct Answer: B. Contributions to a 401(k) plan are typically made with pre-tax dollars and are tax-deductible.

- Incorrect Answers: A is incorrect because contributions are made with pre-tax dollars; C is incorrect because distributions are taxed as ordinary income; D applies to 403(b) plans, not 401(k) plans.

20. Explanation for Q20:

- Correct Answer: C. In a 2-for-1 stock split, the stock price is halved, and the number of shares outstanding doubles.

- Incorrect Answers: A, B, and D do not correctly describe the effects of a 2-for-1 stock split.

Explanation for Q21:

- Correct Answer: B. ETFs can be traded throughout the trading day at market prices, unlike mutual funds which are priced at the end of the trading day.

- Incorrect Answers: A is incorrect because ETFs usually have lower management fees; C is incorrect because ETFs often offer diversification; D is incorrect because ETFs do not typically require a minimum investment.

Explanation for Q22:

- Correct Answer: C. The investor receives a premium for writing (selling) the call option.

- Incorrect Answers: A is incorrect because the investor is still exposed to downside risk in the stock; B is incorrect because the profit is limited to the premium received and the difference between the stock price and the strike price; D is incorrect because the writer of a call option is obligated to sell shares if the option is exercised.

Explanation for Q23:

- Correct Answer: A. Interest income from municipal bonds is generally exempt from federal income tax, and may also be exempt from state and local taxes if the investor resides in the state of issuance.

- Incorrect Answers: B is incorrect because capital gains on municipal bonds are subject to tax; C is incorrect because municipal bonds do not pay dividends; D is incorrect because interest income from municipal bonds is not taxed, rather than being taxed at a lower rate.

Explanation for Q24:

- Correct Answer: B. A stop-loss order is designed to limit an investor's loss on a stock position by selling the stock when it reaches a certain price.

- Incorrect Answers: A is incorrect because a stop-loss order does not guarantee a purchase price; C is incorrect because it is aimed at limiting losses, not maximizing profits; D is incorrect because it does not relate to dividend payments.

Explanation for Q25:

- Correct Answer: C. Closed-end funds trade on an exchange like stocks, and their share prices fluctuate based on supply and demand.

- Incorrect Answers: A is incorrect because closed-end funds do not issue new shares continuously; B is incorrect because open-end mutual funds issue and redeem shares continuously; D is incorrect because open-end mutual funds are redeemable by the issuer at the NAV.

Explanation for Q26:

- Correct Answer: B. General obligation bonds are backed by the full faith and credit of the issuing municipality, which typically means they are supported by the issuer's taxing power.

- Incorrect Answers: A are backed by revenues from specific projects; C are backed by lease payments made by a private company; D are backed by assessments on the beneficiaries of specific improvements.

Explanation for Q27:

- Correct Answer: A. Market risk (also known as systematic risk) affects the entire market and cannot be eliminated through diversification.

- Incorrect Answers: B, C, and D are incorrect because these types of risks can be mitigated through diversification.

Explanation for Q28:

- Correct Answer: B. The total dividend payment would be $0.50 per share x 200 shares = $100.

- Incorrect Answers: A is incorrect because it assumes 100 shares; C is incorrect because it assumes $1 per share; D is incorrect because it miscalculates the dividend payment.

Explanation for Q29:

- Correct Answer: B. Withdrawals from a traditional IRA can be taken penalty-free starting at age 59 1/2.

- Incorrect Answers: A, C, and D are incorrect as they do not match the correct age for penalty-free withdrawals.

Explanation for Q30:

- Correct Answer: A. A no-load mutual fund does not charge a sales commission or load, allowing investors to purchase and sell shares without paying additional fees.

- Incorrect Answers: B is incorrect because no-load funds still charge management fees and other expenses; C and D are incorrect as they describe mutual funds that charge sales loads either at purchase or redemption.

Explanation for Q31:

- Correct Answer: C. Current yield is calculated as the annual coupon payment divided by the current market price. For this bond: $50 (annual coupon) / $950 (current price) = 5.26%.

- Incorrect Answers: A underestimates the current yield; B is the coupon rate, not the current yield; D overestimates the current yield.

Explanation for Q32:

- Correct Answer: D. The Balance Sheet provides a snapshot of a company's assets, liabilities, and shareholders' equity at a specific point in time.

- Incorrect Answers: A shows revenues and expenses over a period of time; B details cash inflows and outflows; C shows changes in equity over a period.

Explanation for Q33:

- Correct Answer: B. Duration measures a bond's sensitivity to changes in interest rates, reflecting the average time to receive the bond's cash flows.

- Incorrect Answers: A describes bond maturity; C is not a standard measure of risk; D is not related to duration.

Explanation for Q34:

- Correct Answer: C. Total return includes both capital gains and dividends: ($120 - $100 + $2) / $100 = 22%.

- Incorrect Answers: A only accounts for capital gain; B underestimates the total return; D overestimates the total return.

Explanation for Q35:

- Correct Answer: B. The advisor must disclose the risks and recommend adjustments to align with the client's risk tolerance and investment objectives.

- Incorrect Answers: A may not be appropriate without considering the client's overall strategy; C and D do not adhere to ethical standards of managing risk and suitability.

Explanation for Q36:

- Correct Answer: C. Dividend yield is calculated as the annual dividend divided by the stock price. For this stock: $4 / $80 = 5.00%.

- Incorrect Answers: A, B, and D are incorrect calculations of the dividend yield based on the given data.

Explanation for Q37:

- Correct Answer: A. Beta measures the stock's volatility relative to the market; a beta of 1 indicates that the stock moves with the market.

- Incorrect Answers: B, C, and D are not related to beta but rather to other aspects of stock performance and valuation.

Explanation for Q38:

- Correct Answer: C. Buying a put option provides the investor with the right to sell the stock at a specified price, which can protect against a price decline.

- Incorrect Answers: A is a strategy for potential gains if the stock price increases; B involves obligations rather than protection; D involves betting against the stock, which is different from hedging.

Explanation for Q39:

- Correct Answer: C. Yield to maturity considers the bond's annual interest payments relative to its purchase price, with adjustments for the face value. Here: [($60 annual interest + ($1,000 - $950) / Years to maturity) / $950] = approximately 6.32%.

- Incorrect Answers: A, B, and D are incorrect as they do not accurately calculate the yield to maturity given the bond's price and interest rate.

Explanation for Q40:

- Correct Answer: B. Callable bonds allow the issuer to redeem the bonds before maturity if interest rates decline, thus reducing the issuer's interest expense.

- Incorrect Answers: A, C, and D do not align with the primary purpose of a callable bond, which is to provide flexibility in managing interest expenses.

Explanation for Q41:

- Correct Answer: B. Current yield is calculated as the annual coupon payment divided by the current market price. Here: ($40 annual coupon / $950 current price) = 4.21%.

- Incorrect Answers: A reflects the coupon rate, not the current yield; C and D are incorrect calculations based on the given price.

Explanation for Q42:

- Correct Answer: C. Defensive stocks are designed to provide stability and consistent performance during economic downturns.

- Incorrect Answers: A and B are not primary characteristics of defensive stocks; D is true for many stocks but is not the main purpose of defensive stocks.

Explanation for Q43:

- Correct Answer: A. Writing a call option on a stock the investor already owns is known as a covered call strategy, used to generate additional income.

- Incorrect Answers: B involves selling call options without owning the underlying stock; C involves buying a put option for protection; D involves holding both a call and put option with the same strike price and expiration.

Explanation for Q44:

- Correct Answer: B. NAV is calculated as the total assets of the fund minus the total liabilities, divided by the number of outstanding shares.

- Incorrect Answers: A refers to the trading price of the fund's shares; C is not related to NAV; D describes the value at purchase, not the current NAV.

Explanation for Q45:

- Correct Answer: C. When market interest rates increase, the price of existing bonds generally decreases to align with the new higher rates.

- Incorrect Answers: A and B are incorrect because bond prices move inversely to interest rate changes; D is incorrect as yield predictability is not directly affected by interest rate changes.

Explanation for Q46:

- Correct Answer: C. Total return includes both capital gains and dividends: [($60 - $50 + $2) / $50] x 100% = 24%.

- Incorrect Answers: A underestimates the total return; B is incorrect as it doesn't include the dividend; D overestimates the return.

Explanation for Q47:

- Correct Answer: B. The price of existing bonds will generally decrease when new bonds with higher coupon rates are issued, as they offer higher yields.

- Incorrect Answers: A and C are incorrect as the price of existing bonds typically falls; D is not directly related to the coupon rate of new bonds.

Explanation for Q48:

- Correct Answer: B. Equity represents the difference between total assets and total liabilities, and reflects the owners' residual interest in the company.

- Incorrect Answers: A describes liabilities; C is not related to equity; D describes revenue, not equity.

Explanation for Q49:

- Correct Answer: D. A stock dividend increases the number of shares outstanding but does not change the total value of the investment; the stock price adjusts accordingly.

- Incorrect Answers: A and B are incorrect as the stock price decreases, not increases; C is incorrect as the number of shares increases.

Explanation for Q50:

- Correct Answer: B. The call feature allows the issuer to redeem the bond before maturity, often to refinance at lower interest rates if rates decline.

- Incorrect Answers: A describes a put feature, not a call feature; C and D do not align with the purpose of a call feature.

Explanation for Q51:

- Correct Answer: A. Current yield is calculated as the annual coupon payment divided by the current market price. Here: ($70 annual coupon / $1,050 current price) = 6.67%.

- Incorrect Answers: B reflects the coupon rate, not the current yield; C and D are incorrect calculations based on the given price.

Explanation for Q52:

- Correct Answer: A. A market order executes immediately at the best available price.

- Incorrect Answers: B specifies a price limit; C is used to trigger a market order when a specific price is reached; D is a specific order type that must be filled immediately or canceled.

Explanation for Q53:

- Correct Answer: B. Rebalancing involves buying and selling securities to maintain the portfolio's target asset allocation and risk profile.

- Incorrect Answers: A and C are not specific to the rebalancing process; D is not the primary goal of rebalancing.

Explanation for Q54:

- Correct Answer: A. Traditional IRA contributions are tax-deductible in the year they are made, while Roth IRA contributions are made with after-tax dollars.

- Incorrect Answers: B is incorrect because Roth IRA distributions are tax-free if conditions are met; C and D misrepresent the tax treatment of both IRAs.

Explanation for Q55:

- Correct Answer: C. Inflation-protected securities, such as Treasury Inflation-Protected Securities (TIPS), adjust their principal value with inflation, providing protection against inflation.

- Incorrect Answers: A and B do not offer protection against inflation; D refers to bonds that can be converted into stock but does not address inflation protection.Explanation for Q56:

- Correct Answer: C. A limit order is only executed at the specified price or better. If the stock never reaches $75, the order will remain unfilled.

- Incorrect Answers: A and B do not apply as the order is a limit order; D is incorrect as limit orders do not automatically convert to market orders.

Explanation for Q57:

- Correct Answer: B. Mutual funds offer professional management and diversification, which can help spread risk across various investments.

- Incorrect Answers: A is incorrect because mutual funds do not guarantee returns; C is incorrect because mutual funds do not guarantee tax-free returns; D is incorrect as mutual funds typically have lower fees than managing individual securities.

Explanation for Q58:

- Correct Answer: B. To restore the original allocation of 60% stocks and 40% bonds, the investor would sell some stocks and use the proceeds to buy more bonds.

- Incorrect Answers: A would worsen the imbalance; C and D do not specifically address the need to rebalance to the original allocation.

Explanation for Q59:

- Correct Answer: C. High-yield bonds (also known as junk bonds) are considered the most speculative due to their higher risk of default.

- Incorrect Answers: A, B, and D are generally considered lower-risk investments compared to high-yield bonds.

Explanation for Q60:

- Correct Answer: C. A stop-limit order triggers a limit order once the stop price is reached, and the trade will only be executed within the specified limit price.

- Incorrect Answers: A and B do not account for the limit price aspect; D does not accurately describe a stop-limit order.

Explanation for Q61:

- Correct Answer: C. Yield to maturity accounts for both the bond's coupon payments and any gain or loss if held to maturity. In this case: [(($1,000 - $950) / 15 years) + $50 annual coupon] / $950 = approximately 5.26%.

- Incorrect Answers: A, B, and D are incorrect as they do not account for the bond's current price and time to maturity accurately.

Explanation for Q62:

- Correct Answer: B. A sector fund invests primarily in a specific sector or industry.

- Incorrect Answers: A refers to funds that track a market index; C invests in a mix of asset classes; D invests in short-term, low-risk securities.

Explanation for Q63:

- Correct Answer: A. A margin call occurs when the value of the margin account falls below the required minimum, prompting the investor to add more collateral.

- Incorrect Answers: B, C, and D do not accurately describe the margin call concept.

Explanation for Q64:

- Correct Answer: B. A market order guarantees execution at the best available price, but not the price itself.

- Incorrect Answers: A and C involve price conditions; D involves executing the entire order or none at all.

Explanation for Q65:

- Correct Answer: C. The investor profits $5 from the stock appreciation ($55 - $50) and also earns the premium received for the call option, but if the option is exercised at $55, the total profit is $15 per share ($55 - $50 + premium).

- Incorrect Answers: A and B do not account for the total gain from the option exercise; D overestimates the profit, as it does not include the stock sale at the strike price.

Explanation for Q66:

- Correct Answer: B. When a bond is purchased at a premium, its yield to maturity will be lower than its coupon rate because the investor paid more than the face value.

- Incorrect Answers: A, C, and D are incorrect as they do not reflect the relationship between YTM and the bond's premium price.

Explanation for Q67:

- Correct Answer: C. A beta of 1.5 indicates that the stock is more volatile and therefore more risky than the market, which has a beta of 1.

- Incorrect Answers: A, B, and D do not accurately describe the stock's risk relative to the market.

Explanation for Q68:

- Correct Answer: C. U.S. Treasury bills are considered the safest and least volatile due to being backed by the U.S. government.

- Incorrect Answers: A, B, and D involve higher levels of risk and volatility compared to Treasury bills.

Explanation for Q69:

- Correct Answer: B. A debit spread involves buying one option and selling another option with a different strike price or expiration date, resulting in a net cost to the trader.

- Incorrect Answers: A does not describe a debit spread; C involves only selling options; D is incorrect as debit spreads involve a net cost.

Explanation for Q70:

- Correct Answer: B. A cover letter provides detailed information about the use of proceeds and the financial condition of the issuing authority, giving investors insight into the issue.

- Incorrect Answers: A, C, and D do not accurately describe the main purpose of a cover letter in a new issue.

Explanation for Q71:

- Correct Answer: B. An index fund aims to track the performance of a specific market index, such as the S&P 500 or NASDAQ.

- Incorrect Answers: A is not the primary purpose of index funds; C describes actively managed funds; D is not a specific goal of index funds.

Explanation for Q72:

- Correct Answer: B. A put option gives the investor the right to sell the stock at a specified price (strike price), so the investor profits if the stock price decreases.

- Incorrect Answers: A describes a call option scenario; C and D are not related to the objective of buying a put option.

Explanation for Q73:

- Correct Answer: C. The Income Statement shows a company's revenues, expenses, and net income over a specific period of time, such as a quarter or a year.

- Incorrect Answers: A shows assets, liabilities, and equity at a specific point in time; B shows cash inflows and outflows; D shows changes in shareholders' equity over time.

Explanation for Q74:

- Correct Answer: C. Investing in dividend-paying stocks allows investors to reinvest dividends, potentially increasing the total return through compounded growth.

- Incorrect Answers: A focuses on capital gains; B is incorrect as dividends are not guaranteed; D is not universally true for all dividend-paying stocks.

Explanation for Q75:

- Correct Answer: B. A lower debt-to-equity ratio indicates higher financial risk because it suggests the company relies more on debt financing than equity, which can increase financial leverage and risk.

- Incorrect Answers: A is incorrect as a higher D/E ratio typically indicates higher financial risk; C and D do not accurately describe the relationship between D/E ratio and financial risk.Explanation for Q76:

- Correct Answer: A. Liquidity refers to how quickly and easily an asset can be converted into cash without significantly impacting its market price.

- Incorrect Answers: B describes the federal funds rate; C refers to market activity levels; D is a component of liquidity but does not fully define it.

Explanation for Q77:

- Correct Answer: B. A stock exchange facilitates the buying and selling of securities, providing a platform for transactions.

- Incorrect Answers: A is not a primary function of a stock exchange; C is not guaranteed by any exchange; D is typically the role of financial advisors, not exchanges.

Explanation for Q78:

- Correct Answer: B. Long-term bonds are more negatively affected by rising interest rates because their prices are more sensitive to changes in rates.

- Incorrect Answers: A are less affected due to their shorter duration; C may be impacted but are not specifically sensitive to interest rate changes; D adjust with inflation and are less affected by interest rate changes.

Explanation for Q79:

- Correct Answer: B. The primary advantage of a Roth IRA is that distributions are tax-free if certain conditions are met, such as reaching age 59½ and holding the account for at least five years.

- Incorrect Answers: A applies to traditional IRAs; C is incorrect as both IRAs have similar contribution limits; D is not specific to Roth IRAs.

Explanation for Q80:

- Correct Answer: B. A bull market is characterized by rising prices and investor optimism.

- Incorrect Answers: A describes a bear market; C does not define a bull market; D does not relate to the definition of a bull market.

Explanation for Q81:

- Correct Answer: B. Value investing focuses on selecting stocks that are believed to be undervalued by the market.

- Incorrect Answers: A focuses on stocks with high growth potential; C involves selecting stocks with upward price momentum; D focuses on stocks that provide regular income through dividends.

Explanation for Q82:

- Correct Answer: D. Total return includes both capital gains and dividends: [($50 - $40 + $1) / $40] x 100% = 27.5%.

- Incorrect Answers: A only accounts for capital gains; B and C miscalculate the total return by not correctly combining capital gains and dividends.

Explanation for Q83:

- Correct Answer: B. Preferred stock typically has a fixed dividend and priority over common stock in the event of dividend payments and liquidation.

- Incorrect Answers: A generally applies to common stock; C is more characteristic of common stock; D is incorrect as preferred stock is not exempt from taxes.

Explanation for Q84:

- Correct Answer: C. General obligation bonds are backed by the full faith and credit of the issuing municipality, including its taxing power.

- Incorrect Answers: A is issued by corporations; B is backed by specific revenue sources; D can be converted into shares of the issuing company's stock.

Explanation for Q85:

- Correct Answer: B. The SIPC protects customers if a brokerage firm fails, covering the securities and cash in their accounts up to certain limits.

- Incorrect Answers: A is incorrect as SIPC does not insure against market losses; C is the role of regulatory bodies like the SEC; D is not the purpose of the SIPC.

Explanation for Q86:

- Correct Answer: C. Diversification aims to lower overall risk by spreading investments across different stocks, sectors, or asset classes.

- Incorrect Answers: A may be a benefit but is not the primary purpose of diversification; B is unrelated to diversification; D is not guaranteed in a diversified portfolio.

Explanation for Q87:

- Correct Answer: B. Short selling involves selling a security you do not own, expecting to buy it back at a lower price.

- Incorrect Answers: A describes going long; C and D describe long-term investment strategies, not short selling.

Explanation for Q88:

- Correct Answer: A. The ex-dividend date is the cutoff date to be eligible for the next dividend payment. If you purchase the stock on or after this date, you will not receive the dividend.

- Incorrect Answers: B is the declaration date; C is the payment date; D is the record date.

Explanation for Q89:

- Correct Answer: A. IRR is the discount rate that makes the NPV of all cash flows from an investment equal to zero.

- Incorrect Answers: B and D do not accurately describe IRR; C is a general description of expected return, not IRR.

Explanation for Q90:

- Correct Answer: A. Dollar-cost averaging involves investing a fixed amount of money at regular intervals, which can reduce the impact of market volatility.

- Incorrect Answers: B is a potential outcome but not the definition; C describes a sell strategy; D describes market timing, not dollar-cost averaging.Explanation for Q91:

- Correct Answer: B. Mutual funds provide diversification and professional management, which can help spread risk and provide expertise.

- Incorrect Answers: A is not necessarily true; C and D are not guaranteed benefits of mutual funds.

Explanation for Q92:

- Correct Answer: A. A call option gives the holder the right, but not the obligation, to buy a stock at a specific price before the expiration date.

- Incorrect Answers: B describes a put option; C and D incorrectly describe the nature of options as rights, not obligations.

Explanation for Q93:

- Correct Answer: A. Market capitalization is the total value of a company's outstanding shares of stock, calculated as share price times number of shares outstanding.

- Incorrect Answers: B and C are not definitions of market capitalization; D only refers to share price, not total value.

Explanation for Q94:

- Correct Answer: B. Bond ratings evaluate the creditworthiness of the bond issuer, indicating the likelihood that the issuer will be able to make timely interest and principal payments.

- Incorrect Answers: A, C, and D are not the primary purposes of bond ratings.

Explanation for Q95:

- Correct Answer: B. Convertible bonds can be converted into a predetermined number of shares of the issuing company's stock, usually at the discretion of the bondholder.

- Incorrect Answers: A describes zero-coupon bonds; C is not necessarily true; D describes mortgage-backed securities.

Explanation for Q96:

- Correct Answer: D. Alpha measures the excess return of a portfolio compared to its expected return given its level of risk.

- Incorrect Answers: A describes total return; B refers to consistency or stability of returns; C describes portfolio volatility.

Explanation for Q97:

- Correct Answer: C. A financial advisor's primary role is to assist clients in managing their finances and investments based on their goals and risk tolerance.

- Incorrect Answers: A does not accurately reflect the role of a financial advisor; B is typically the role of a lawyer; D may be part of the role but not the primary purpose.

Explanation for Q98:

- Correct Answer: C. Many 401(k) plans offer employer matching contributions, where the employer matches a portion of the employee's contributions.

- Incorrect Answers: A describes traditional IRAs; B describes the penalty for early withdrawals; D describes Roth IRAs.

Explanation for Q99:

- Correct Answer: B. Beta measures the risk of an investment relative to the market, indicating how sensitive the investment is to market movements.

- Incorrect Answers: A, C, and D do not accurately describe beta in financial terms.

Explanation for Q100:

- Correct Answer: C. Fiduciary duty refers to the obligation of financial professionals to act in the best interest of their clients, putting their clients' interests above their own.

- Incorrect Answers: A does not encompass all aspects of fiduciary duty; B describes disclosure obligations; D is the role of regulators, not fiduciaries.

GET YOUR BONUSES

Dear reader,

First and foremost, thank you for purchasing my book! Your support means the world to me, and I hope you find the information within valuable and helpful in your journey.

As a token of my appreciation, I have included some exclusive bonuses that will greatly benefit you.

To access these bonuses, scan the QR Code with your phone:

Once again, thank you for your support, and I wish you the best of luck in your Exam. I believe these bonuses will provide you with the tools and knowledge to excel.

Made in the USA
Las Vegas, NV
20 February 2025

18427707R00221